DIAL LOVE

DIAL LOVE

Divine Intelligence Almighty Love,
Light Omnipresent Vibrational Energy

God's Planetary Guide
for Attaining Happiness
through Spiritual Fulfillment

Donna Lynn

BALBOA.
PRESS
A DIVISION OF HAY HOUSE

Balboa Press books may be ordered through booksellers or by contacting:

Balboa Press
A Division of Hay House
1663 Liberty Drive
Bloomington, IN 47403
www.balboapress.com
1-(877) 407-4847

ISBN: 978-1-4525-3927-0 (sc)
ISBN: 978-1-4525-3928-7 (e)
Library of Congress Control Number: 2011916286

The views expressed in this work are solely those of the author and do not necessarily reflect the views of the publisher, and the publisher hereby disclaims any responsibility for them.

The intent of the author is to provide information of a general nature to help you in your quest for emotional and spiritual wellbeing. The information contained in this book is not intended to serve as a replacement for professional medical advice. Any use of the information in this book is at the reader's discretion. The author and the publisher specifically disclaim any and all liability arising directly or indirectly from the use or application of any information contained in this book.

Any people depicted in stock imagery provided by Thinkstock are models, and such images are being used for illustrative purposes only.
Certain stock imagery © Thinkstock.

Printed in the United States of America

Balboa Press rev. date: 1/23/2012

CONTENTS

Dedication

I would like to dedicate this book to all souls
on the path of the divine light.
May you find a piece of familiarity woven into these pages
that binds the fabric of your heart back into the heart of one.

Acknowledgements

I would like to express my gratitude to the following
individuals:

To my husband Dean whose loving devotion
has been a remarkable source of inspiration.

To my wonderful parents and family who continue to fill my
heart with joy.

To all my friends, colleagues and teachers,
a warm thank you for enriching my life.

Most importantly . . .
My eternal gratitude to God for his divine unconditional love.

I thank him for choosing me to deliver his message of truth.

Guidelines

1 Throughout this book, God makes reference to "we". Most often this can mean you and the God within. At other times "we" refers to God and all light beings on the other side of the veil.

2 God's message can be seen as a paradox. At times he is speaking to the souls who are filled with the God consciousness and then turns to those that have not found his love fully.

3 Dial Love is thought provoking and invokes deep introspection. Pausing and reflection are beneficial.

4 Remaining true to the integrity of the text, the contents and word usage has been unedited and are in its original form of expression. There is a high incidence of repetition as Dial Love is delivered as an instructional guide.

5 You may find a contradiction or two; God invites you to pay attention to where you resonate. Both messages will have an element of truth.

6 On a few occasions, there is a dialogue between God and the author. For clarification purposes, this text was all channeled.

7   Dial Love references 07 07 07 as being a sacred day in our Book of Life. You may wish to look at Chapter 21 prior to the calendar date. For those of you reading Dial Love after the quantum leap, honor your soul by shining your soul light every day from this day forward. This is relevant and in line with our collective shift in consciousness.

Foreword

I WOULD LIKE TO SAY THAT MY LIFE UP to this point has been divine. I have much to be thankful for: a great family, circle of friends and a life partner. All my needs have been provided for. I've managed to manifest a few miracles and to live my dreams as I create them and cherish each moment anew. While God has always been generous and compassionate to me, many people, I realized, were not so fortunate. They seemed to suffer from a spiritual disconnection resulting in unfulfilling experiences, one after the other, in search of truth. Where was their God? Did he forsake them?

Somewhere in the depths of my soul, I knew that our Creator, although mysteriously silent, was always organizing loving influences with infinite powers and working to keep us out of hot water. He was often performing miracles, while gently guiding us onto the path of unity, abundant love, peace, joy and oh, yes, "where dreams come true". It seemed that not everyone was taking advantage of the Creator's gift. Were they too busy or skeptical? Nonetheless, I believed that if you kept your faith, your life would unfold like a dream. This was the key to the Heavens. Was that not our reason to incarnate our soul? We were graced with this ultimate gift of conceptualizing into the physical form to enjoy life experiences of the heart.

It was my choice to see and experience the finer states of abundance, gratitude and joy. This has allowed me to refine my personal attributes. My character was gently molded into one of appreciation, compassion, humility and gratefulness. Through more difficult virtues of patience and forgiveness, faith and devotion were key. I've loved my journey thus far and chose to view the world with rose colored glasses, embracing the lessons of the heart. It is with heartfelt gratitude I thank God for all my blessings and good fortune.

The teacher in me was always on a quest to share her personal point of view of "how it all works". This road led to deep happiness, peace and joy. It seemed many were making choices that took them off track. How could I convey a message of hope of finding the infinite power of love so that others might come to fully appreciate their journey of the heart?

In an effort to show seekers how to manifest this world of abundance and joy, I started to develop a series of spiritual workshops focused on how to connect to Source and tap into our infinitely loving, all providing universe. I wanted to help people find a way to consciously connect to the heart of one.

One afternoon while sitting at my desk, I had an idea for how I could provide an analogy for an answer. In my efforts to explain this process, I could recommend that the soul for the asking might fine-tune their internal radio to the higher frequencies of love. Ah, yes, just dial love. L.O.V.E. I found the words turning over repetitively in my mind: Dial Love. I felt that I was onto something, a great and simple way to explain how to connect to Source, God, the power of love. I asked Spirit, "What do you think? I've worked on this workshop for weeks. How about we tie it all together by using this analogy of Dial Love to make a connection? This is the path to the whole heart".

A comforting, gentle and loving voice silently spoke: "Heal yourself and in doing this you heal others. Feel their pain; don't judge; offer love and compassion. Give of yourself, as that is when you receive the most for yourself and your dreams". I wrote down every word and continued to write for five hours. It was unbelievable, almost incomprehensible. My source indicated that it was God himself. I paused, "forgive me; I have to ask if this is really you"? The answer came back, "I am the Messenger, the Real McCoy. You called, remember"?

After years of searching, God was always right there, guiding us, holding us and protecting us. He has exercised patience, compassion, forgiveness and unconditional love.

Some people never know the infinite feeling of peace, love and joy that is available to us in a heartbeat. They only wish and wonder. Others walk the path knowing we have God's love on our side, in every cell of our mind, body and soul. Life is a journey of the heart, loving God every moment of every day, in awe of the riches life has to offer. This is our gift to live life to the fullest, appreciating every miracle, small or large, graced by the presence of God, who unwaveringly shows up and offers love every moment of our lives.

Yes, there is a formula for love. It's faith. It's a quest for the truth. It's about living your life fully by the virtues of the heart, experiencing your lessons in accordance to the Universal Spiritual Laws handed down by the heavens. This is unshakable faith, love and devotion. Express gratitude in every action and deed you perform each day. Appreciate your short time on Earth. Make it your quest to dial into L.O.V.E.—Light Omnipresent Vibrational Energy. This is God, in every shape and form, on the planet at this divine time.

At this very moment, God is calling your name and wishing that you hear and feel his voice of unconditional love. Truly, the Mother and the Father wish for your heart to sing in the essence of love. They are always patient and kind, waiting to make a connection. Perhaps you have time to try this out for yourself. Some of you already enjoy the infinite blessings of our Creator of love.

My wish is for all to make the time to find a passage within this text that may spark and rekindle the flame in your heart. Through the grace of God's love, I have been blessed daily in my efforts to live in accordance with his wishes. I know God desires to connect us back to the heart of one, for there lies within, the power of love. United, we hold each other in our effort to find the treasures of the true heart. Renew your hope in your Lord of Light. Find your own peace, happiness and joy. These are attainable with his love. They are our inherent gifts. All it takes is a leap of faith and courage.

My purpose is to deliver this message. I have done this to the best of my ability. The challenge has been to not tamper with the original writings, as I've tried to edit the text. Clearly, he wishes for this manuscript to remain in its original form, in its entirety, to be made available to those souls who wish to know the truth, who desire answers for their woes of the heart.

The path to the light of God's love is embracing his presence with full conviction and tuning into his immaculate vibration of his almighty love. His wish and mine are one and the same. I desire for you to surrender to his love and make your heart whole and come to know the infinite Source, as I have been so graced to experience. Let us collectively unify this "limitless energy" in the name of God, my wish. Amen.

Introduction

HEAL YOURSELF AND IN DOING THIS you heal others. Feel their pain; don't judge; offer love and compassion. Give of yourself, as that is when you receive the most for yourself and your dreams. When you let go and align your heart and intentions with the Creator, you heal the whole. Find the love in the higher vibrations. This is where your God-given gifts lie, in the awareness and consciousness of your heart and soul. I can and will work through you that you may feel the true abundance of love and beauty this journey can fulfill. When you see and feel through the eyes, heart and spirit of God, you will truly rejoice and appreciate our short time together on planet Earth.

Life is a gift. Accept the present. Create and hold onto your dreams and desires in your heart. You all deserve to heal and be whole. Find peace, self-love, joy and happiness and experience this thing you call life on Earth. Embrace this journey and stay grounded through the challenging times. This is when you experience your spiritual growth and come into the light and love more fully. As you learn your lessons and discover your purpose, you will feel grateful and joyous to give love and make yourself whole. That is why you are here.

Higher vibrations and frequencies are attainable for the asking. Do the work. If it were easy, everyone would do it. Nothing comes easily without undefying courage and faith. Trust that you can find inside all your strength to move forward, beyond the obstacles and challenges. For it is then you truly find enlightenment, gratitude, peace, love and joy.

BELIEVE IN YOURSELVES

Remember when you were a child, the innocence? You loved life. It was easy to smile back at the world and offer your unconditional love. Open your hearts and trust that you can heal within. I will show you the way. As you walk this path be patient. Hold onto your faith. Look ahead at the horizon and nature's beauty. Sync up to this peace and perfect balance. In desiring this state, you too, will feel all the beauty, love and joy that I have to share with you. This perfect playground is to discover, nurture, embrace and treasure, so you can explore the love within your hearts and feel my undefying love for you all.

Every moment, everyday, no matter what you have done or felt in the past, know that it is ok and I forgive you all. I hope you accept my love. Be open to all possibilities and share amongst yourselves your deepest fears and desires. Together you are stronger and collectively your light is brighter. You know that light dispels the darkness and the fear in all of you. When you see, feel and experience this, you will find your way home to my heart, peace and love. Eternally, the Creator of all Creations

Peace I leave with you. Find your source of light and follow it steadfastly, undefiantly, resiliently. Every breath you take from here forward is the chance to see and feel the love that the universe and I, your Creator, have to offer. I am always patient and I believe in you, as you believe in me. I hold a place in the kingdom for your new vibration of love. That is what you went down for.

SHOW EVERYONE THE WAY

I am the way home. I am the way to your pure heart. Look inside and find me. Feel me, make room for me and let it expand in light and love. Fill your being with its warmth, comfort and beauty. Share it and give it freely. That is how you will feel joy, happiness, peace, ecstasy, gratitude and appreciation for your time on your visit. Make a difference and may the difference be love, real love, unconditional love. Have no judgment or hurtful thoughts. You only hurt yourself. You all know this deep inside; that cannot produce fruit and sunshine.

Nurture your garden. Plant the seeds with love and cultivate it everyday with hope, faith and expectations of an abundance of growth and harvest. This will take care of your needs and desires. When you do this relentlessly with the purity of your heart, all will produce your beautiful treasures and dreams that you so wish to hold in your heart.

Know that I look after the details and the perfection of your manifestations and desires. All things are considered and all elements are present for growth and abundance. Every time in complete balance and harmony, at the right time in your world, you can enjoy the fruits of your labor. After all the work you have done, I would never let you down. Have I before? Does the sun not shine? Do the birds and bees show up to work so that you may enjoy the beauty and rewards? Everything on your planet is in perfect synchronicity. All you have to do is believe, nurture and respect. Give thanks and be grateful for its love and undying, unspoiled beauty and perfection.

By cherishing and enjoying these God-given gifts, you show your love to me in countless ways. You do and can make time again to show your appreciation of life, nature and all humans that share this space together. Don't look at differences or be envious of their gain. Be grateful and hopeful that you too, will have all you desire in your heart at the right time in your life.

Do the work you came down to do and do it with love and kindness. Do it for me, as I do unto you. Bring forth all your tools to the table, sharpen them, make your best effort and strive for perfection. This is when you feel alive. Anything less leads to regret and unhappiness.

Too many of you know this place. If you truly desire to remove from that lonely state, envision your outcome and place it in your heart. We can do this together. Send me your true wishes of the heart and I'll prepare them for you. It will be more beautiful than you could imagine. All of your treasures and dreams can be real. Show me what they are and that you deeply care about the outcome.

ARE YOU HELPING OTHERS?

Please bring as many souls as you can to the gates of love, so they too, may feel the peace and happiness they so too desire. If they are lost, show them the way. If they need a push, let it be gentle. Each one of you has your own truth inside to discover what is real and what is not. Make every moment, everyday, new. Be hopeful and inspire others with your intent and smile. Look in their sad eyes and show them the love in your heart. It's contagious and there is enough to go around for the whole universe, planets, stars, fish, nature, insects, rocks, every animal and every human. Everything that is energy needs love.

Look at your planet, it lives off love. When you starve it, it starts to die. All of God's creations are dying for love. They are looking in all the wrong places. Don't look under a cold, dark place. Look up to the light in the sky. Look to your neighbors sharing the planet with you. Look at the harmless, beautiful animals, minding their own business. They are love. Treasure and respect their existence. They too have a purpose in the divine, delicate plan.

YOUR JOURNEY WAS NEVER SUPPOSED TO BE EASY

That's not the way you planned it, but you said you would like to try and could work through all of its challenges with my help. And we agreed to this. I'm here to do my part and wait patiently for you to find me in your heart so we can go through all of this together. I promised to make it easier, with less pain. I never break promises and hope in your heart you will not either.

You have time. Take your time, but the sooner we get started, the better things will be for you, myself and all creation.

HEAL THE UNIVERSE

When you heal, you heal me, you heal the whole universe. That is what is needed in your decade right now. Open your eyes, your heart and let me in slowly. I will be gentle; I will caress you and never let you go until we find a place that is beautiful and loving, close to my heart. You will then feel all that you were created to feel. Hold this hope and desire in your heart so that you may feel all my love that I desire to give to you. If you desire to feel the love of your God, ask honestly with proper intention, with the expectation of healing yourself and the world. For when you discover this place and feel what it truly has to offer, you will want to stay and return over and over again, like some of you do.

THE EARTH IS A BEAUTIFUL CREATION

Cherish it, explore, play, laugh, love and be adventurous. There are many places to see and feel the power of love. Everywhere you go, I'll be there so I can experience it with you. I desire to know and feel what it is like through your eyes, heart, body and soul. My heartfelt desire is to travel and share love with others, animals, nature and feel what it is like to be alive in your skin, in your soul, experiencing all the riches that life has to offer.

LEARN MORE ABOUT YOUR ENERGY

You are unnoticing and mistreating it. Do you have any conception of the repercussions of your thoughts, ungodly desires and your negative thinking? It harms you, others and nature. It kills love. Know this to be true. If we are all energy, why don't you use it for good, to manifest your dreams, the perfect world, your perfect life? Use it to heal yourself and others. Visualize the end in mind. Call in the white light, be specific and guide it.

There are authors with great material who are showing you how to use intention, spiritual principles and visualizations to help you discover your power and place in the universe. Not all of these resources are on the front shelves. Listen to your heart to create all the good you and everyone else deserves. Dream big and use your limitless imagination. Use all your gifts you were born with, that you haven't yet discovered.

Do the inner-work in silence, stillness, meditation and contemplation. That's me trying to show you the way and let you know what you came down with. Most of you have beautiful telepathic powers with which you can create beauty. Send love to everyone and everything you encounter, including me, as I wait patiently. I admire your beauty, creativity and giving hearts filled with compassion and humility.

Use your divine powers to create all the dreams you ever wished and hoped for. Save yourselves and the planet. Save me from disparity and sadness. I, too, have an overflowing heart with an abundance of gifts and resources that I want to share. This is where we should work together to create a better, loving world with all its perfect creations. This too, can actually be done.

I look forward to the days of peace, love, balance and harmony in all of your hearts and in all of your actions. This will be the treasure, the high and the gifts you have been searching for. The way inward is the way forward. May we grow together on this sacred journey home.

Rejoice in the revelation, as this you already knew, but were too busy to recall, or make time for. You came down to have fun, spread love, learn and to do the best you could for all concerned. When you reap the rewards and find the treasures buried inside; the healing, the fun and the love really begin.

Take what resonates with you and send the rest back so it may be recycled to someone else who is looking for their answers, their truth, hope, peace, love, their life purpose with God.

This message is intended for those who are open to the Source of the infinite universe. May you know your highest good and the wisdom it holds for you. When we have a strong connection, manifestation and transformation occur simultaneously. Synchronicity is an integral element of the universe. Tap into this bountiful, unlimited resource in your mind, body and soul and utilize it to the fullest for the highest good of the planet. For when you heal others, you heal yourself. Respect and love each other. Most importantly, love thyself. Truly you will feel me and my love and all that is.

In parting, may you never shed a tear of despair that you have been forsaken, as in all my power I send guidance and help every minute of every day. Look, listen and feel the love, harness it. There will always be an inexhaustible supply in the realms for you to discover. The more you breathe it into your being, the stronger this loving energy will grow. That was our plan, remember?

Sending love always, all ways in abundance,

Yours truly,

ALMIGHTY GOD

Donna: *God, what shall I do with this text?*

GOD: They will come for it.

Donna: *God, how many should I tell?*

GOD: As many as you can.

Donna: *Are you coming back soon?*

GOD: Not soon, only if necessary.

Donna: *Forgive me; I have to ask if this is really you.*

GOD: I am the Messenger, "the Real McCoy". You called, remember? You asked a couple of days ago why you were here. That's why you did your workshop, so I could speak through you, in your language; in your knowing of how it works, through you, through your diligent reads. Your texts, library, collection of thoughts,

I admire your interest. Now tell others to read the same books and act on them, believe them, live by them. There are many light workers on Earth to guide you all to help others.

I AM THE WORD.

GOD: Tell Oprah.

Donna: *Oprah?*

GOD: I like Oprah.

Talk to Dyer, Chopra and Hay; I will see it printed and distributed. Go to the top, like you usually do.

Donna: *This love is amazing, how do I describe it?*

GOD: You can't, you have to feel it.

Donna: *Will they believe me?*

GOD: I'll make sure, leave the details to me.

Donna: *Why now?*

GOD: It's like a crazy circus; too many clowns doing tricks. **Don't fool with God and the beautiful Human Race. They are innocent, full of beauty and love.**

They need the truth. They need hope and help from loving souls who know too much is wrong. The dynamics are not going in accordance to the universal laws and truths. There is only love. People are searching, being misled and coming up empty. This is leading to the destruction and loss of lives, unnecessarily. It's not their fault. It is the darkness of some souls who may be in pain themselves. They were never shown. They give into fear, lust, control and power. They know deep inside their DNA that this is wrong and they are not stopping. Their money will create more blood and negative circumstances.

Donna: *I love you deeply. I want to show you more. My heart can only push out so much loving vibration. Do you feel it from people like me?*

GOD: Everyday, always, love expands, love is limitless. Keep this concept in mind. The more you make and feel, the more the world receives. I see everyone's hearts, the loving and the sad lonely ones. My true desire is to align all hearts with my vibration so that they too will feel whole. There is someone for everyone to love. If they pray, heal and love themselves, they make room to love others fully, unconditionally, with no expectations. It's a lot of giving mostly; expect the love back, for it truly will become yours. That's why you're on Earth to feel and give love. That's how the universe lives. Simple, yet profound.

Let go of your attachment to the outcome. Place your order and carry on with your best in everything you do. Don't give up hope. Don't give up on your wishes, desires and dreams. Sad to see some do not receive what they could have if they had just held it tighter, closer to their heart with proper intention and not just wished. They have to manifest it in their thoughts. Read the books. Those are my words. There is a simple formula. Many haven't been taught, many think it's too much trouble. Quite a few of you let obstacles get in the way. All obstacles can be removed. They are energy; so are you and I and our thoughts and desires.

How badly do they want to feel whole, complete and loved? These are the people that need direction so they can change their circumstances. Old beliefs are counterproductive. You engrained them when you were young and vulnerable. Seek out ways to undo these. There are materials and resources for all this. I have covered all the bases down there, yet so many of you are caught up in the wrong dream. Do the homework, search, ask questions and miraculously the universe will provide the answers.

Why is this information not taught in your so-called school? What about the school of life? You're all in it, yet you don't know how to be, how to operate, how to live, love, forgive, how to manifest change. How do you really lose weight, get out of depression, go through a divorce, job loss and human loss? No wonder there is so much anger and pain. No guidelines, no manuals. We could write one. I don't think the education system is ready for it, but we could call it "The Rules of Life" or "The Manual of Living Right in the Light". Catchy, eh? We'll work on that one.

We'll need an outline when you're ready, there is a lot to cover, simple formulas, but lots of scenarios and "what if's". If the students don't want to study it and apply it, well guess what is behind door #3? A heap of despair, misfortune, sadness, envy, lust, greed and vengeance: all the deadly sins with deadly consequences.

Life on Earth is a school. You know the basic rules but evidently, those aren't enough. I can spell it out more clearly for those true souls that are looking for the light of God and the treasures of the gift of a beautiful life.

Sadly, the generations are not being shown and taught well. Not enough people are making time. Look at what is happening to the young consumers; they won't even be able to hear soon with their distractions and barriers. Crazy, is all I can say, absolutely nuts.

It's not going to be a Bible, just another lifeline, a self-help resource for the soul's asking. Those of you who desire this text, my words, will find it for the asking.

Donna: *Can we pick up later?*

GOD: Absolutely, always here, always have been.

Glad you learned how to listen effectively. Keep on taking your courses and workshops. It's a pleasure. Makes life easier, don't you think?

Donna: *Absolutely, with love, Donna Lynn xo*

GOD: I like that my child; I never gave up on you. Welcome to the undefying love of your Creator, Mother, Father, Holy Spirit in your heart, always. Seek the best, the love and all the rest.

Peace I leave with you. Until we talk again.

CHAPTER ONE

Virtues of the Heart

AND IN THE BEGINNING THERE WAS THE WORD THE WORD WAS TRUTH

LIGHT, LOVE, PEACE, HOPE, COMPASSION, FORGIVENESS, HUMILITY, KINDNESS

TO BE CULTIVATED AND EXPLORED IN depth. To learn lessons in each one and to grow fully in balance and right heart.

Many lessons are presented here, over and over, until you understand their meaning and act according to your truth. It may take a lifetime to realize the importance of these foundational laws of the heart, for without these in place, you do not find your truest desires. When you pass the test of the virtue, another will be presented sequentially, in chronological order. The universe delivers the lesson plans in divine order for your individual growth. These are the true tests of the intentions of the heart.

In time, these truths will make your heart loving and pure. You will want to share with others the beauty of the love and peace you feel. You will never turn back, to the less fulfilling place you were before the lesson arrived. Many of you choose not to learn it so easily and make your lessons much more difficult than they were originally designed to be. You dodge around, go in circles, fret and complain, all the way through the lesson.

Had you trusted that this was necessary for your growth and that you had help, perhaps you may have come through it with more grace and faith. Each lesson is specifically designed only for you and no one else. Understand this. Other souls can only help and guide you. Ultimately, you have to want to move forward and learn the lessons of the heart.

Peace, patience and trust are necessary elemental truths here. For those of you who miss the mark, this scenario will replay over and over again for years to come in many different ways; but with the same underlying message to be learned. Regrettably, quite a few of you are still working on the basic ones.

When you pass the lesson, the next truth of the heart is worth the while. Each new lesson begins to develop your heart into a true, compassionate human being who only thinks of others first and of their wellbeing. You live for giving and see beauty in everyone, everything and wish others could feel what you feel inside. You try to explain and show them. You stop at no ends to help others heal and feel the peace and love.

THE TREASURES OF THE TRUE HEART

This is truly a life long process of growing, adjusting and changing. For the more enlightened you become, the larger the expansion of love and light is capable of. There is no end or limit to what you can attain. Go for it all. I wish you the best.

There are no coincidences in life. Everything that comes your way is in the world to show you something, to guide you, to teach you. There are many messages for each and every one of you. This is how we work with you from the other side of the veil. Be open and listen to all words, as they usually contain tailored messages for you to help and guide you through your challenging lesson. Be thankful for the individual role players. They may hurt you, but know they are acting in accordance to God's will. All of it is necessary for the lesson scenario to play itself out. Do not blame others. Go inside and be thankful for the lesson, the people in your life and learn, evolve and grow from this. You can now move forward and perhaps share and teach others what you have learned.

THE LESSONS OF THE HEART

Most of these times are painful and a sense of abandonment and hopelessness feels overwhelming. Know this is necessary for your soul's growth. For it is here, that you feel and learn compassion for everything and everyone I created. When you walk the Earth, become a beacon of light, so others may follow in your steps. Lead by example, with humility and grace.

Never judge others on their path in their challenging times. You have all gone through, or will go through, the same lessons. Offer love and support, an ear to listen. Encourage the individual to pray or meditate on this situation that they may find their truths. All answers are found in the heart. Please stop and listen to your silence. Find your peace and listen to the wisdom inside of you. These thoughts help your heart heal and grow.

Many times you look outside yourself and in every direction but in mine. How has this happened? Don't let others steer you away from the truth. Make sure the suggestion or advice feels right in your heart, or don't take their ideas. They do not know what is best for you. You and I know what we need to do and what we need to work on. Find a place of trust and call on me for love and gentle guidance. I promised you we would do this together, every time, every way.

Don't mistake my word, as it is always out of pure love. If it doesn't sound like my voice of love, it probably isn't. Trust your feeling in the heart and ask if this message or information is for your highest good. This wisdom and knowingness is available all the time for you to rely on. Please ask when you are uncertain, unclear, lost or in despair. Always listen to the loving whisper of the heart when you need a helping hand. Call on this source of intuition for every task you may perform. Whether it's your gardening suggestions or career and relationship advice, we always nudge you in the right direction for your highest good.

When obstacles present themselves, as they always do, trust the process; two possible outcomes will manifest. Either direction will prove to be the way for you. Trust and know that if doors are closed or obstacles are present, these are all for a definite reason. We may be trying to nudge you in a different direction to keep you on path on your life chart. Embrace and accept all this, as everything happens for a reason. If it's a small obstacle, this may be just to see what you are made of. Don't give in when the "junk" comes your way, persevere. Have persistence and patience if you desire it deeply. It's for your own good. Don't give up or let go of your dream.

Nothing comes that easily, or everyone would be doing it. Hold your intentions dear to your heart and trust life's processes. Understand that there is an immaculate divine order of time and space for circumstances to manifest. Patience is one of the lessons here. In your time of quick fixes and instant empty gratifications, this makes you all a little antsy. Patience my child, if it is a true desire for all concerned, trust and have faith that the universe will deliver.

HUMILITY IS HUMBLING OF THE HEART

Many misfortunes occur in order to get this lesson right. Some of you at the top have yet to learn this. Others have suffered great losses to learn and feel this lesson of the heart. Look around and see that abundance has a delicate balance. When you are gracious and deeply appreciate all that you have, show gratitude to me, the universe and all my creation. Surely a few of you could feed and save some of our precious animals. You have disrupted the delicate balance of nature and their sustainable needs have been altered. Intervene and make time to investigate the source of the trouble. Offer solutions to restore the Earth and all its creations. This would be a great use of your time since you are not crying for much.

Know that I allowed this lesson of material wealth to come to you, to see if you would give some away. When was it ever going to be enough? Wake up and look around. Take a trip to the other side of town. Leave your flashy car behind and see what it feels like just to survive. These individuals wake up every morning and pray. They are grateful just to be alive, with the gift of life. They hope all their worldly needs are met, just for one more day. Then they ask if I could bless their neighbors as well, most humbling. This fills my heart.

It's sad to see the less fortunate. They don't ask for much at all. They're happy to be alive. They see the world with hope and beauty. They treasure the Earth and cherish all its creations. They preserve nature and cultivate its growth as they walk the Earth. They kiss the ground in humility and smile along the way. They only wish to feel my love more deeply in their souls. They stretch their dollar and find the value. They are not wasteful with their food and clothing. They respect all that is given to them. These souls love to give and share their last piece of bread and stitch of clothing. Surely we could all lend our old possessions to a dear soul. You may even feel the love in your heart, as you feel theirs and mine, in receiving this gift.

Love is contagious. Open your wallets and your hearts. You are too caught up in stuff. Money can't buy love and you miss a valuable lesson here. Most of the less fortunate have mastered this lesson. They only seek respect and dignity. They walk and share the Earth with you. Their hearts and souls have value. When you see that you are all equal, you will not judge. Hopefully you will invite them to share your blessings and prosperity. Show them love and give them hope. Show them the way and give them a chance, for they all didn't end up on the street, or poor, of their own accord. They too, are learning the lessons of life.

DIVERSITY

Diversity of people sharing the planet should be embraced. How wonderful it is to experience cultures so far away from home. Each has something to share with us, offering their values and roots that they individually call heritage. You are truly blessed with the blend of cultures. From this, you all learn and see what others hold true to their hearts. Why not focus on the similarities? There is too much emphasis on the differences and not enough on what you all have in common.

Every one shares the same heart and is on the same path. You have the same desires of the heart: to give and feel love, to feel accepted and to find peace and joy. You are all of the same mold, just different shapes, sizes and colors. Some round, some more sharp; while others may have rough edges. A few may be displaced or lost. Don't look at appearances and judge. Take their hand and show them the way. You are all part of the whole, trying to feel complete and find your place on Earth and in the universe.

Make time for everyone. Stop shutting your doors in everyone else's face because they don't look and act like you. Maybe, just maybe, they could show you a few things. Perhaps, they have a message for you from me that can help you on your life path. All individuals have gifts and wisdom to share with us. Listen to their experiences, grow and unite. You are stronger as one.

TRUE COMPASSION OF THE HEART

Have compassion for life, have compassion for others; this is true compassion of the heart. Look through the eyes of others trying to overcome their life's challenges. Their eyes are the window to the soul. Do you feel their pain? Do you feel their heart and soul? Each one of us is here to work on ourselves. Know this to be true. You came down to learn lessons, some gentle, some not so easy. Every person is going through stuff. Your role is to nurture these souls. Show love and give of your time. Tell them to see and feel the light deep inside them and listen to their heart for the answers, so they, too, may heal and move forward on their path.

When you heal others, you heal everyone and everything on Earth and in the universe. What a wondrous time it will be when you have a pure heart and feel no pain, no loneliness, no helplessness, no regrets of the heart. Don't discard your loved ones for hurting you. Find it in your heart to forgive and feel compassion for their pain. Regret comes when you wait far too long to make amends with those that are closest to you in your lives. Give in and let it be you to forgive. Leave the past behind. Understand that maybe their lessons are not pleasant. Try to find this compassion in your heart for everyone in your world. You will heal. Pray that they may, in time, open their hearts and feel the love that is trying to fill their being.

Don't fight fire with fire; put it out. Listen to my voice. I am always sending this message to you to repair tarnished relationships. Stop ignoring my calls and pleas of the heart. You grow immensely when this lesson is learned. Don't poison your own heart. Only your heart dies in the process.

GRATITUDE

Show gratitude for every meal, blade of grass, beautiful sunset, warm breeze and every snowflake. Nature is in a state of gratitude. I provide all its needs impeccably: sun, rain, soil, temperatures. The fertile environment is always abundantly stocked for manifestation of beauty, love and dreams. When you cherish and appreciate all simple and complex elements that sustain life and the planet, surely you can come to realize that with one missing ingredient, there is no life. How would you live without air, sun, soil or water? Yet, you do take these miracles for granted. Don't overlook the basics. Mother Earth and all her beauty is for your use. Everywhere you go, give thanks and keep it intact. It is always there for you. Respect and give back. Be in a state of thankfulness for the beauty of your earthly home environment so you can create your wildest dreams upon it. Dare to try it all and give thanks for your temporary home.

Be grateful for the food it provides from the Earth. These are all life-sustaining, high vibrational foods when they are in their natural state. Do your best to ensure that this resource is not altered irreversibly. It requires a delicate balance to meet all your needs.

BE THANKFUL FOR THOSE YOU ENCOUNTER ON YOUR TRAVELS

The grandeur of it all, the fascinating geography and wonders of the world: many places you gravitate to hold sacred energies of the universal love. Take these into your being and give thanks that they exist. See other people living on the other side of the world from you, far away in space but not so far in time. Be thankful for the beauty in your hearts and of all creation. Make time. Traveling is not just for all-inclusive partying. Go make a difference and discover the world.

KINDNESS, A SIMPLE ACT

What does it cost you, your time? It doesn't feel natural? You have been so conditioned to mind your own business that you are all becoming strangers, alienated from one another. Ok, you're busy with everyday stuff. Take a "time out". Two minutes perhaps. Go out of your way for someone. There really isn't enough of that going on. It doesn't seem to be a high priority to a lot of you. Hell, what is? Me, me, I, I.

Stop thinking about yourself so damn much and be kind and thoughtful. Just make it happen. Go inside your little heart and see if you can find some love to make a difference in someone else's world. Stop being so selfish, listen to yourselves: "I, I, I, I, I, I feel. I want, I need, I, I, I". Be mindful of this.

Ever notice you don't manifest much when it's a need and a want. Try doing something nice for someone else that you secretly desire from the heart and maybe, just maybe your needs will be fulfilled as well. Set the intention to make a loving difference in other's worlds and hope for the best possible outcomes for their personal situation. Genuinely care, pray and offer help that they may have their wishes and desires of the heart fulfilled. Offer love, ask me for guidance and we'll do it together. Surprisingly, the universe creates and manifests abundance in this fashion. Kindness truly goes a long way. Do it with your heart, be open to possibilities. Apply the spiritual principles.

FORGIVENESS

Without forgiveness there can be no peace, love, happiness and joy. This is a huge lesson for everyone. The horrific lessons associated with these acts of forgiveness are certainly never an easy time. Many of you spend a whole lifetime unable to forgive someone for a terrible thing they did to you. I agree these tragic and hurtful events were by no means easy. The pain you hold inside eats at you and your organs. You manifest physical states of dis-ease. That's how deeply it's lodged into your being.

This is something you could have asked my help on. The process of time, along with a willingness to find peace in your heart, can ease the pain of most unpleasant events that you have been witness to. This formula is not complicated. However, you have to want to start it. Taking the first steps is going to be the most painful, as you feel all the unpleasantness associated with the crime. Whether victimized or insulted, this will continue to destroy you. You must go back to the time of occurrence and now, being removed from it, ask what was the lesson for. If you are not far enough removed from it, this will be difficult and painful.

You did, however, indicate on your life chart that this would be an experience that you would try to get through with my help. This is key. Self-destructive behavior is not the answer. Drugs, alcohol and crime will never produce healing of the heart. Blame and anger are of very low vibration and will always keep you down. Depression can result. This downward spiral is not the direction to the light and love you so desperately need at this time.

A caring, loving heart is your prescription. Whose you ask? Well, mine. I have quite a large heart. It encompasses the whole universe. I certainly have more than enough to ease your pain and take it away into myself to burn it out and replace it with warm peace and gentle love. This process, on my part, is expeditious and continuous. It never lets up, providing you are sincerely ready to let go. I never wanted you to hold this pain so deeply, for so long. You have to ask, as I wait for your heart to talk to me and I desperately try to come in to heal your heart.

This is where we become close, heart to heart. You will feel my love in every cell of your body, cleansing and removing all residue and darkness out of your space and world. When you desire to walk this path you start to heal, find peace and feel the love again. This is my gift of the hurting heart. I can take all your pain away, wipe your tears and comfort your soul. Know this to be true. It is a universal law.

YOUR LIFE AND TIME DOWN HERE IS VERY SHORT

Most of you desire the gifts of peace, self-love and self-acceptance. Without self-acceptance, there can be no self-love. Without these virtuous qualities, there can be no peace in your heart. You were not made perfect. What would be learned? What would be the use? Where's the challenge? Where would the lessons be? The whole adventure would clearly be a waste of everyone's time. Could you picture how boring that would be after a while? Everyone the same, everyone doing the same thing, you would have no need for sports. Could you ever imagine? You would have no desire to hone your gifts and skills. No dreams to better yourself and no one to show you and teach you how to improve.

There will always be someone who is more advanced in a skill. Embrace this, as you now have someone to look up to.

There will always be a wiser soul. Rejoice, as you now have lessons of wisdom in front of you. There will always be a faster soul. Fantastic, now you know that you have a benchmark. How exciting and blessed this person is. You may never be able to perform like them, but you can strive to do your own personal best.

The beauty in everyone's differences is that it keeps processes dynamic. Be sincerely happy for everyone else's gifts. They are enjoying their discovery and are grateful for this talent, wisdom and uniqueness. When you look inside, you will discover that you have many gifts that others may not have. Search, ask and be persistent in your endeavors. You, too, will love what you find. It will become your passion.

When you accept all parts of yourself, find humor and give thanks. There is always a reason why perhaps you're not the best athlete or cook. Your talents are usually needed elsewhere for the benefit of all. Find them and master them.

Here is when you may say "I'm ok". When you go inside your heart and accept who you truly are, "a beautiful divine creation of the Creator", maybe then you will come to know that you have a special purpose on Earth to make a difference in others lives. Ask and it will be revealed. Be patient, as a purposeful life may not emerge right away until all other aspects are dealt with.

This is an intricate process. Trust in this plan of your life's contribution. When it presents itself, or is nudging at your heart and soul, take action and the universe will open up the energies for manifestation for the better of the whole. I need each and every one of you to contribute and do your part. Life takes you places you may have never expected. Have fun. Have faith. Carry on making a difference. Express gratitude, be kind, forgiving, find compassion, nurture your heart and give to others. Let go of regret, be hopeful for the future and pray everyday.

Give thanks and learn to love yourself. You are your own best friend. Quiet the chatter of the critic and listen to my voice. You will grow, heal and love, heal and laugh. When you discover your sense of humor, you may begin to enjoy and love life. It is on this journey you eventually find peace, joy and love in your hearts. This is where I have always been. But in order for you to feel me, you have to let me in. Then you can dance, laugh and smile like you did when you were a child. Enjoy your journey into the light. This is where you find all your treasures and the gifts I promised you.

INTENTION NEEDS TO BE ALIGNED WITH THE DESIRES OF THE UNIVERSAL HEART

For change, transformation, growth and healing to happen, there needs to be an intention. Wishes are just that; desires may not come to be. For maximum results in every area of your life, you must hold steadfast to intentions.

Maybe you are intending to be successful at your career. After you have carefully looked at the lifestyle and obligations associated with doing God's work, are you prepared to move forward? Many twists and detours in the road can show up. Do you see yourself enjoying this life change? If you feel in your heart that this is a good direction, become the dream. Do the homework, be determined, find the right contacts and look at all options.

Do not desire this wish for the wrong reasons. This will backfire somewhere down the road. If your path takes an unexpected turn, trust that it could be divine intervention. If it doesn't feel good in your heart, changes must be made. You know when you're not in your element. If it doesn't feel right or resonate with you, something is missing. Ask the universe: "is this for my highest good"? The answer of love will always be nurturing, inspiring, kind and gentle. Listen to your heart and use your intuition of light.

Never give up on your dreams. Find the courage, dissipate the fear and trust life's processes. Attributes here are strength, persistence, determination, passion and effort. Hold the picture of the end result in your mind's eye and for God's sake, ask for help.

UNIVERSAL LIFE FORCE ENERGY

The divine intelligence of the Creator is yours to harness, for the good of the whole: infinite, limitless wisdom and love. Many teachings on this subject are available. You are a light being. Understand your energy centers and their capacity to manifest healing, transformation and dreams. This loving power is responsible for all perfect creations on the planet and in the universe. Its original state is one of balance, harmony and love. What more could you ever wish for?

All ingredients are present for the realization of creation, life as you see it, states of happiness, wellness and joy. Once you understand how to utilize the infinite wisdom of the universe, a chain reaction of divine events, blessings and miracles takes place. Synchronization of the frequencies in the realms provides all the vibratory energy to manifest "more energy" in the form of experiences. This immaculate process can only lead to more creation through your limitless imagination.

As you know, the catch here is that it all has to be in accordance to the Creator's wish. If you have my blessing on this and feel your desires and wishes are from a pure heart, let us do it together. Learn to create higher vibrational frequencies in your energy field so you can realize your dreams.

Life on your planet was created with thoughts of pure love. It is when you don't act in accordance with the universe that you attract negative experiences and circumstances into your life. This is usually when you come running to me to fix and solve your dilemmas. This is what is called a "God of convenience". This is not conducive to a nurturing, loving, respectful relationship. I'm sure you've all experienced this one.

Either you are on board or off; hot or cold, love or fear. You get the message. Yes, I need your help, but it's not conditional. There is no room for negotiation here. I will know when your heart is aligned with mine and you have a pure heart. Then we can talk, create and have fun. There are a lot of amazing places to go and things to do, if only you desire them for the right reasons.

STOP GOING FOR THE QUICK FIX

There really isn't such a thing. What are you left with anyway? All this "instant this" and "instant that". No wonder you are getting yourselves into trouble down there. You're not even sure what it is you want, wish for and are trying to create. Some of you don't even know how to create, so you're just floating around, randomly looking for the next best event to happen. Sooner or later you will run right into a rock mountain if you're not careful. Then what? Know where you are going. Have a plan, even if it's not clear cut. Have intent, have a direction.

Go out into the world with the intention to do your best and ask for some guidance and direction. I will show you the way to your heart, the way to your dreams. I know you better than yourself. I can help you with this one, so that you may discover your passion and purpose.

The best way to get in touch with me is through telepathy and meditation. There are so many teachers and gurus on board. Learn and experiment. Try Energy Work, Tai Chi and Yoga. Any modality that raises your vibration and brings your energy up to a higher resonance is paramount. This is actually one very large goal you said you could accomplish. It is one of the easiest. There is no pain involved here, just discipline, focus and time management.

Funny, how you can't seem to make the time when Reality TV is on. What is so real about the crap on TV anyway? Do you really think one-half of this stuff is going to happen to you? It's all a dream world with a lot of negative, low vibration, dark energies. These are not virtues of the heart, are they? Is it not mostly exploitation of sex and violence? Tune into love. Dial love and create your own dreams and experiences. Stop living your world through a movie set.

FIND THE SILENCE IN YOUR DAY

You don't have to be in the barren desert for this. Just sit still for God's sake. Take a few minutes to slow down, breathe, contemplate and open your heart to me. Miss your favorite TV show. It's a fantasy. Miss the bad news for a night. This process of discovering yourself is quite essential to find out who you are, why you're here and what you're capable of. There will be messages here to help you heal your mind, body and soul.

Learn to listen, the answers are all inside. You don't have to run to someone else every time you need solutions and answers. Just go inside. What I mean by this is clear your mind of the fears, worries and anxieties of the day; put them aside and focus on your breath. When this is in harmonic balance, our hearts can sync up to communicate. Maybe you need to heal. Maybe you need love or you are lonely. Perhaps we need to shift your energies around to get rid of the old to make room for new thoughts of a higher, loving vibration. Just get still, Dial love, Divine Intelligence Almighty Love.

I know what your concerns and problems are. There are formulas for all these ailments that trouble you. Many of you have given up hope, in an effort to find a solution. When there is a problem, there is always a solution. Clearly, we can work through most of these one by one. Pick one. The biggest ones seem to be states of anger, loneliness, separation and depression.

Anger is living in a state of fear which has manifested into physical action. This symptom gets a hold so deep inside, it needs an avenue out. Destructive patterns always result. This leads to most of the chaos on your planet. "He did this." "She didn't do this." "Look what happened to me." Well, evidently you are all trying to process some terrible event of circumstances and are channeling it out, giving in to the low vibration of it.

Low negative vibration is most likely the cause of it in the first place. Wrong place, wrong time, wrong people, wrong choices, wrong food, wrong thoughts, wrong actions and wrong desires. How did you get yourself into that mess? Let's look back, way back. Somewhere, someone did you wrong. You were let down, hurt and rejected in some shape or form. These are the simplest terms I can express for the wrongful actions of individuals who are not always responsible for the consequences.

Anger is derived from hurt, deep hurt. From here, you took it to the ugly stage of pain. Since most of you have not been taught to deal with this painful emotion, we will look at its form. Hurt is a lesson of the heart, a painful lesson, I might add. Where are you going with this destructive behavior, except for hurting everyone and everything in its path, including yourself and me? Had we had a strong relationship at the beginning, I could have bore the pain. Nonetheless, let's try now.

This event of deep hurt occurred some time ago. It has no ownership of you, unless you allow it. Since it doesn't serve you for your highest good, you have to make a conscious decision whether you wish to hold onto it or let it go. What are the pros and cons here? Do the math. Are you happy? Are you creating cool experiences down there? Do people love to be with you? Are they trying to love you and you won't let them in? Don't want to, don't know how? It's easier to push everyone away and around. Are you having fun? Is the world beautiful?

If you look around, some people are actually loving life and creating experiences of joy, appreciating what it has to offer. I certainly didn't create an ugly world. This is only your perception filters on it. If you desire to see and love life, let's heal and take away the pain in your heart. Give it to me, only if you have the courage and maturity to do this.

Life is full of choices. What are you choosing? Stay where you are, or slowly let it go? The way forward is going inward. Only when you make a decision inside your heart that this no longer serves you is when it starts to go away. Like magic. Just watch me. Want to bet on it?

Everyone has experienced anger. Those that asked for help and opened their hearts began to heal. Look at them now. Some are still nurturing their wounds, as they walk through life. They choose to move forward and in faith, see that they too, can create a better world. A world of love, a world of beauty, gives open vulnerable hearts like yours the opportunity to walk with me on the path to light and love. Others know not what you feel; they can only imagine. However, I feel all of your pain and anger in my heart.

When you choose to heal, you heal us both; you heal the planet. Your energy changes and your experiences change. The people in your world seem to change, as they were patiently waiting for you; praying for you to see the light, feel the love and let them back into your heart. Beautiful people are trying to give you love. Let them in slowly, let me in gently. You've learned your lesson here, close the chapter and come into the light. This will take time, but I have all the time in the world. Do you?

One step at a time is the process formula. One day at a time. Do the next right thing. Have hope and faith. Have the end in mind. It can only cultivate and produce love. There are many that will guide and walk you through this. Be open to it. Just give it some thought. All good things start with the thought and your imagination of yourself. Find yourself. Find love, as that is truly who and what you are. We all are. Waiting patiently, with open arms and open hearts.

CHAPTER TWO

The Lonely Heart Bleeds

IT IS BY GOING INSIDE AND feeling separate from the whole world that you manifest this state. This is not a place you need to be in for long periods. Humans need other humans to make them feel alive, otherwise despair and hopelessness manifest. Know that staying inside, hiding in your homes, doesn't help. This is fear of life's processes. What is there to fear: rejection, sorrow, grief?

You need to feel these emotions so you know to desire the opposite in your soul. For in this place, you can strive to create opposites and go out into the world hopeful. Just start in your own backyard of familiar places. When you feel security, it is then you can go out to be with others.

Trust in my presence. This is needed for your heart to feel secure. Affirm that you will find the courage to blend back into the world and find your place. Knowing yourself well expedites this integration process. Take this time of solitude to discover what is missing inside you that makes you feel this way. Perhaps your social skills are weak and it leads to a lack of confidence. We can help that grow as well.

You first need to love yourself before you try to love someone else. What are you offering to them if you are broken or in a state of repair? Once you realize what is needed in your being to feel whole and complete, you are more likely to produce results with other people. Know that your fears send signals to push people away without your knowing. When you trust in me and in life's processes, you will feel confident that every person is not going to hurt and reject you. You need to feel loving and loved before you give it to someone else. You can't give away what you don't have inside. Let's work on that.

Life experiences give you courage to experience other things. These events and lessons build confidence, slowly and easily, but steadily. It is with courage and trust that you begin to take steps toward your higher self. Nurture the heart and soul along the way, so it may feel loved. This is self-love growing inside of you. It can and will take years, but is worth the effort.

Feelings of inadequacy arise when you compare yourself to the ideal mate. Well, were you trying to attract a "10" or would you be happy with a down-to-earth person with qualities you can admire and cherish? From there, you can build a relationship together if there are commonalities. Don't overlook the souls that come your way. Some of you are not giving others a chance. You're scared. You're nervous and unsure. You figure you can reject them first. How do you feel now that you are still alone? Why not overlook a few things and try to meet in the middle. This is common ground. Keep it light and show your best side. What is important is a sense of humor. Don't drop your baggage on the floor here. This will surely scare the potential away. Keep your composure and just be your best self and let them in.

There will be times when you don't like what you hear or see. You feel all this is too much work. Well, you're probably not that easy to adjust to either. Be patient and understanding. Love takes time to grow. You have to weed out the debris and cultivate the seeds that are deposited in the fertile soil. This makes it rich and plentiful for growth to happen.

Letting things go, being easy going is the only way you are going to keep someone's interest. They are not there to be abused or made to feel stupid or inadequate. These things you may see in them are a reflection of your own qualities that you don't admire. Self-acceptance, kindness and seeing only admirable qualities in others keeps them around. They want to feel good about themselves and especially feel good when they are around you. That makes it all worthwhile, don't you agree? You can all stay home and feel miserable, so why would you go out to be with someone who is going to make you feel unhappy and sad? No incentive here.

So what are you offering: fun, love, kindness, a giving, nurturing relationship? These elements are so essential for a long term partnership and if they are not in you to give, well, good luck finding love. Love is all those things. When you have them to share purely and freely, maybe, you will attract your life mate. You may already know them, but you are caught up in your own misery and are sending out the wrong signals. Work on yourself and see what you can offer others and the world.

This is when you start attracting beautiful souls, like yourself into your world. This is when you create beautiful, joyous, memorable experiences together. Make some babies and show them all the love they need and desire to feel alive. When you do the work of the heart and have loving qualities to share, you truly attract the perfect mate. Always give and take; stop looking for perfection, because none of you are yet.

You are all growing souls trying to be more like God, so "act as if" and keep your eyes open. Be kind. Leave your baggage in the closet or send it back to the universe to be recycled into love and virtues of the heart. You have to have a heart to be able to share someone else's. Be gentle with it. This is a good formula for the creation of love.

LONELINESS IS DARK AND DEPRESSING

For those of you who refuse to listen to your heart and heal, this is the result. Darkness, desperation and sadness. No hope for anything. You only muster up more dreary thoughts of despair. Many run away, so they don't get dragged down into your pit. Some try to show you the way up and out, but you'd rather stay where you are. This is a conscious choice. I'm not sure why you chose this emotion.

Before you arrived here, there were many lifelines and clues trying to pull you up. Why not go back and grab on to one of these resources or persons who was trying to help you. That was me calling your name. This is not a place I call home. Why do you make it your place? Do you see anyone else there? Are you actually trying with strong intention to move out of it? It may seem easier to stay in the comfort zone, but there's no fun happening there, just a dark outlook on life and people's experiences.

Everyone is learning to find the light, so when you make a responsible decision to come out, it actually can happen quite fast. This is decision making. Choose it. Change your thoughts: this changes your place. Change your food and drinks: this changes your outlook. Change your environment: everything in your immediate world is low vibration that you have somehow created. Change your vibration: this changes your life. Don't give in so easily to lust, fear, envy and ego. These are counterproductive thoughts of low vibration that took you down that path in the first place.

Try genuinely smiling. Look in the mirror. Don't be afraid to look at yourself. You don't want to, because if you did you would laugh at your serious, sad face. What really was the issue that caused such a deep, dark state? Is it now still worth being where you are? Probably not. Going inside and listening to the soft, gentle whisper is where you will feel what to do that is right for your soul.

Baby steps of self-love and gratitude for the gift of life are required in order to recover. How selfish to stay there for so long, when you have such a short time down on Earth to make a difference before you come home. I will just send you back to do it all over. Same lesson if you willingly disrespect me and your gift. Some of you are having the pity party, perhaps with some good reasons, but you know this is not a "loving state of God" to be in.

Let's move on now. Find some hope; be thankful, for you probably aren't appreciative of all that you have. Look around for there are always others with so much less. Do you see them feeling sorry for themselves? You are not that hard done by. Grow up.

COMPLETE SEPARATION

This feeling is from not having a connection to the almighty universal love. It's hard to know what to feel if you don't know it exists. You lead a good life. You're not necessarily a bad person, although you sense something is missing. You search around outside of yourself in the wake of answers and don't really find any. Your outlook on creation has holes. How can you have babies from monkeys, anyway, that walk, talk and think like you? What kind of believable process is this? Dig a little deeper, as it doesn't make sense. This is your lack of depth, or interest in the unbelievable concept of love and life. Looking around thinking everyone else is crazy to believe in a God of love is absurd.

Your heart is empty. What exactly does it feel like? What is your definition of love? A nice little family; some good times, some bad, some tragic; then that's all? That is an insult in its highest form. How did all the planets show up? How did Earth get its gravity and atmosphere? How did people show up? Evolution doesn't make sense. The only one that needs to evolve here is you. You haven't even taken the time to look into the theory of God and creation. You're too stubborn and left-brained to entertain such a concept. If three-quarters of the population down there believe and you are sitting on the fence, do you really think everyone else is insane?

So sad you don't see the miracles. So sad you don't feel my love and embrace its true magnificent beauty. The Earth would not sustain life without love and the universal intelligence of the Almighty Creator. Try your scientific experiments again. They are flawed terribly. It's time you throw these recorded so-called facts out. Fools like yourselves, have only misled many souls about the wrong concept of life, as you see it with your narrow-closed minds.

Those fortunate souls searching for truth see what life has to offer, with all its lessons intertwined, cherishing each lesson and accepting the challenges. They have faith, hope and trust. They know the truth. They feel my love and show me theirs by kind, loving acts of gratitude. I see everyone's heart and feel everyone's thoughts. The ones that are baffled at the concept of creation should not be fed lies. This damage is not easily undone.

Let the truth be known for those young souls that query and want to feel the magic and love of life. Let them find their own truths within their own hearts and minds, so they can discover what love and life is all about. Show them the word and the word is Truth.

Shame on those souls who knowingly do not stand up in my name, that look to me for help. This is a double standard. Ask and know the truth. For it is when you become all that you can be, with all of your gifts, you find me in your hearts. This fulfills your life and only then will you find meaning to yours.

What do you become at the end of your life, if not love? This is the one and only possession you take back with you when you leave. Make sure your travel case is not so empty, so light, that you could have taken more.

LET'S LOOK AT LOVE IN ITS PUREST FORM

So innocent, such beauty it holds and such power to move mountains and stars into place. Each one of you came down with a DNA imprint of God's love engrained in your soul. At birth, this sustained your wonder and expression of life. As you matured, you realized how delicate this quality of the heart really is. At this time, most of you guarded it like a fortress, not letting any predators in. Instead of cultivating a stronger heart you chose to protect a weaker one.

Years pass and because you would not let your guard down, it didn't get the chance to grow strong and mighty. You opened it a bit to come out. Then you hid it again, so you couldn't feel the pain associated with its growing phase. All these mature bodies with small delicate hearts never had the chance to feel and give love. How can your heart work efficiently if it is sitting on a coffee break? This can't produce a creative life. So now, you have no choice but to hide it. It's not proportional to your other organs.

The heart energetically lives off love. It needs to give and receive this vital life force. By closing it off, it can die. By choosing to let it grow, you choose life. Your heart can and will expand to a much larger capacity in your chest. Consciously, you must engage this muscle in order to feel alive. Every time it feels the pain, you feel alive. For every painful, hurtful feeling, the love grows ten fold. Trust that for every unpleasant feeling of the heart you experience, the love will be more prevalent most of your waking life. The ratio is one million to one.

Let me explain. In your life journey, one day of unpleasantness will let you feel one million Earth days of love, though not in the same life time. The more you love and give love, the longer you live. My voice whispers to you often in your heart's capacity. This is how you know how to deal with and process your lessons. Logical thinking of the mind does not always produce the best outcome for your well-being. Intuitively, the wisdom inside holds every answer for every question you have ever asked and will ever ask. Ask often for love and wisdom to shed light on your queries and circumstances. When this is contained in the heart, your path is for your highest good. Your actions benefit many others on their path. Be responsible in choosing to listen from the heart.

INTUITION IS YOUR GUIDE OF THE LIGHT

Everyone came down with several guides to keep them on their path. Establish a beneficial relationship with your intuition as this is for your highest good as well. So many resources are available to each and every soul that walks the Earth. Tuning into these higher frequencies allow you to manifest positive outcomes in all situations. Lessons will come and go, but know there are many moments of joy, ecstasy and bliss.

Your journey has left optimum time for fun and experiences of the heart. This is when you really get to feel and share the love and give back to the world. Many people would like you to show them the way. You now are equipped with the tools to help them feel and see the beauty the world has to offer.

Travel far to reach those in need, as you are probably situated with like-minded individuals. Some continents are in desperate need of life-giving resources and hope. This could be your purpose to seek out souls who are looking for the light. They are praying everyday with their last breath, hoping someone will hear their cries. It's not up to me to wave a magic wand. It's up to you to go and offer my love.

Food and sanitation should be a given, these people are not animals. Forces keep them this way. This is not God's way. I'm just asking for you to try your best. Make it your mission in life. We are of the same heartbeat. Don't let the heart die; it affects the whole, you and I. Create projects that reach out to these places and ask for my help and blessings. When you do God's work, miracles are plentiful. Be patient and be open to your calling.

WHEN YOU COME INTO THE LIGHT, YOU DON'T GO BACK

Once you experience what love holds for you, you will crave more of it. Your heart is limitlessly expansive. You can have as much love as you desire. The more you give, the more you receive. This is the spiritual principle of the universe.

Align your thoughts, actions and heart with mine and we will create a beautiful world. The effort you put forth is worth the rewards. The universe creates prosperity, abundance and riches in accordance with your efforts of the pure heart. You can and will manifest your desires of the heart when you do God's work. This is reaping the rewards and finding your treasures of your life. All your heart's desires are in reach when you understand the principles.

GIVING AND TAKING

Wish for others what you would like to manifest for yourself, for if you truly desire for someone you know to find resolution and peace, pray for them steadfastly. When you sincerely hope for the best possible outcome for their happiness and good, you may have your prayers answered as well. Pray for strangers that you bump into. This power of intention of the heart is mighty. When all of you start to do this, the world can manifest only love, beauty, peace, abundance and good fortune. What you wish for others will come back to you.

Be sure it's of pure intention of the heart. This desire is not for you to secretly create for yourself. It is when you detach from the outcome that manifestation is optimum. Pray and wish for everyone to learn their lessons of the heart with grace. Hope for them to find peace and forgiveness in their being. When everyone acts in accordance with the universal laws and principles we have a "win-win" situation. I can do my work and good deeds most effectively when the light is bright and the energy is of a faster vibration. Outcomes are more rapidly processed for everyone's well-being.

LAW OF POTENTIALITY, PURE CONSCIOUSNESS

Your spirit is the consciousness that sustains the universe and all that resides in it. Know this to be true. Your thoughts of the heart keep your planet alive and bearing the fruits of your labor. When you are well, emotionally and physically, all creation is affected. Nature, animals and the atmosphere are all affected by your thoughts of consciousness. Be careful what your thoughts manifest, as there is a huge cascading effect throughout the whole universe.

There needs to be harmony of mind, body and spirit to sustain life on all levels. Your thoughts, good and bad, create energies that resonate and go out to all other living things. Everything that is energy, including yourself is affected by your thoughts.

How many of you entertain thoughts of fear and scarcity? You know this is true. Deep down, you are sending thought vibrations of fear into your atmosphere and the energy field you inhabit. This swirls around and creates more of the same. Sooner or later, all of you are running for cover and not even sure why you are acting in this fashion.

Be careful what you send out, as the magnitude of your collective thoughts harm yourselves and the environment you live in. It takes a conscious effort to trust your Creator. Faithfully pray and produce higher, supportive thoughts of love and hope. This sustains your planet and all of its creations.

Stop feeding into the low vibrations of fear. This is not God. This is not love. This is not the beautiful world I created. You are creating this in your mind. Stop the worrying and doubting, wondering how your life is going to turn out.

Not one of you wrote your life chart to come down and live in fear 24-7. This is the unfortunate effect of trapped, low vibrational energy in your lower atmosphere. You can pull the positive energy out of the Earth and feel its nurturing love. You can also reach to the sky to harness the universal life force loving energy in its purest form to counteract the negative energy fields around you. Intend to call in the love and light. Pray to your God with faith, hope and the light will dispel the darkness. This is law.

Learn how to use your positive vibration energy field to manifest optimism, hope, beauty and most of all, to feel me. I am of the highest, purest vibration of love. I am here for every one of you, who seek to feel the fulfilling love of my heart.

KNOW YOUR CHAKRA SYSTEM

How is it you study the complexities of your physical earth suit and know nothing of how your transmitters and receivers work? How is it you get through your life not knowing what gives you life and a timeless heart? Your chakra system works on the energetic levels of your being. Without these in place, there is no life for you. This is how you stay connected to the other side.

It is through these energy centers, that you receive information to sustain all of your physical, emotional and mental requirements. This intricate process happens automatically as these vortexes spin energy into your being. This is your lifeline to the other side. Know them and understand them, because some of you are spinning a little off kilter.

Don't be alarmed here. These spinning energy centers need a balance of emotions with cleansing thoughts. Know that you can trap debris in these filters and it does make it more difficult to achieve a balanced life. Contamination comes in through inadvertently holding onto old emotions from learned lessons. Evidently, these lessons are still trapped in your energetic memory.

Activity and visualization are great cleansers for your system to run effortlessly. It is when you are unable to process your fearful emotions that your field becomes cloudy. Visualizing the clear light and making a connection produces a healthy body. Do keep these free-flowing and receptive to the universal life force. The benefits are plentiful and your state of well-being will improve immensely.

The vibrancy and frequency of the chakra system is conducive to healthy thoughts and a healthy, energetic body. Understand your energy centers, your aura etheric bodies and send out positive vibrations. This is the way to dispel some of the low, stagnant energies lingering around. Send this back to the light for recycling. We have quite a large recycling processor up here in the higher frequencies. No detail is overlooked.

IN ORDER FOR YOU TO STAY HEALTHY PHYSICALLY, YOU HAVE TO LOOK AT YOUR DIET

Quite honestly, the food most of you are eating is garbage. It's junk. There is absolutely no nutritional value in it, whatsoever. How do you survive? You may be able to get away with this practice when you're young, but let's face it: you are definitely what you eat. Don't take this personal, I'm referring to altered, low nutritional, low vibrational foods.

If you are seriously wondering why you're tired, why in heavens are you eating junk? This is not honoring oneself. This only produces a sluggish, slow moving energy signature. Variety is the spice of life. So, let's have more variety. You're eating the same foods over and over again, day in and day out. Fast life, fast food; how convenient. Stop and think here. I've planted the seeds for your nutritional requirements and many of you are only receiving a quarter of yours. No wonder you are feeling ill, tired, bloated, depressed and anxious.

Foods have a major impact on your well-being. This is not new information. You have all become consumed with other priorities that your food choices are not on your top ten list. Are you crazy? There are so many food allergies that you are not aware of. Listen to your body. Stop for a moment and ask why you are acting this way. Why don't you feel 100%? I created you to be 100%. Be careful what you put in because that's what you get out. You all have individual requirements; everyone is different. Each one of you has sensitivities to many chemicals and additives. Figure out your patterns and desire the answers to your ailments.

Most of your sicknesses derive from your bad foods and thoughts. Analyze the contents of your food and make wise decisions. Should you stay in the habit or pattern of overeating and consuming nutrient-void foods?

When you stop to think about your actions, you will realize you are eating to feed your emotions. You're not listening to your body's quest for pure water and pure whole foods. Discover the balance in your delicate body in what best suits your well-being. Resolve emotional issues and realize that junk food is harming you and your life span.

What would I suggest? Natural earth given foods made with love. Foods carry vibration. Do you feel high and alive or low and sluggish? I like a variety of nutrients to feed my mind, body and soul. Look wisely into your choices, as they are not all the best. The best is available for those who make time to look and see what they are really putting on their palate.

These needs of feeding the emotions lead to disease. Medical studies have linked a variety of illnesses and diseases to your lifestyle choices. Food and thoughts are the killers. There are certainly far less accidents down on Earth, compared to unnecessary, avoidable deaths.

To live a long, healthy life, you need to feed your mind with loving thoughts, feed your soul with nurturing experiences and fill you heart with loving life. Love yourself enough to find the strength and discipline to make serious changes to your well-being. If you don't get a beautiful, inspiring feeling when you put some food in your system, cut back until you find a suitable, life-sustaining substitute. Balance and love your life. Be healthy your whole life through.

Your body should last much longer than it has been. This is you harming yourself. Very few have the discipline to be enjoying life's experiences to the fullest when they retire. Those who do are active. They are nurturing and respecting their organs and digestive system.

I admire those who eat well. It shows me that you are grateful and appreciative of your gift of life. You will stay healthy enough to do your work, have some fun, see the beauty and give love wherever your healthy body will take you. Exercise your body and mind. Train your mind. Listen to your heart; it has all the answers tailored to suit your requirements.

Don't tune me out. I send quite a few warning signals to let you know that you are harming your health. Then you mask and hide the symptoms. This is not dealing with the root cause; this is a cover up. Only you hold the answer to all your medical concerns. You know best what you may have done wrong that caused this ailment. Then you run for textbook answers, when in fact, you could have helped solve this puzzle had you been honest with yourself and listened to your body and soul.

NOT LISTENING MAKES TROUBLE IN EVERY AREA OF YOUR LIFE

You choose not to listen to your body's symptoms. You also choose to overdo it when comes to sports or work. You only have this one body this time, try to keep it out of the repair shop. Many think this is the solution to your abuse. This only shows me that you do not honor and respect yourself enough to stay fit. The repair shop is the reactive alternative.

The preferred method is the loving, proactive lifestyle of choices. Ask yourself, what are the consequences to consuming too much sugar anyway? Not just the obvious, your teeth fall out and you have excess weight gain. This behavior also wreaks havoc on your whole central nervous system with complex complications, then you're running for answers. Well, the obvious choice was balance, listening to your symptoms and my voice, gently whispering to cut back. You know this is leading down a path of no return.

I'd like to say a quality I inherently have is a proactive approach. I have vision to see the outcome of your choices, the good and the bad. Please, use common sense when making choices in all areas of your life. Only you and I know the consequences. Listen with all your heart and together, we can proactively create a state of well-being for you to enjoy every minute of your life on planet Earth.

CHAPTER THREE

Let's Look at Acts of Kindness

YOU ALL GIVE ONLY TO EXPECT something in return. This is not of a true heart. For when you give, give unconditionally from the heart. Your intentions must be to show love and respect of the individual. A nurturing thought, a kind word, a warm gesture, all produce kindness. Know that your intentions must be in accordance with the universal laws. When you consistently act in that fashion, you show me your true intention. When you are only doing this from time to time, this is evidence of an underlying motive. This only produces the opposite effect. When you give with expectation, no fruit is produced; only fermented, spoiled deposits manifest.

Think before you put your intention out. Is it for the highest good for that individual? Are you going to make their day? Will this make them smile with hope, feel appreciated and loved? When you act in this fashion, you have my blessing each and every time. This is how I perform my work of kind acts. It is through you, I can touch lives that need a lift and bring them up to a higher level of vibration. Through these efforts, you too, are lifted to higher loving vibrations of love. Make the time to pay someone a compliment with sincerity. Most know when it comes from the heart, as this puts a light on inside them.

It is when everyone's hearts begin to shine brighter that dreams come true. Hold this close to your heart and remember to touch lives with your kind words and gestures. You were all born with these inherent qualities. It was when you got burned by someone's dishonorable fashion that you became suspicious of their acts. In turn, you accepted that everyone must have ulterior motives. You stopped the flow of giving from the heart and this produced dishonesty. Be sincere in your efforts and be sure to touch lives wherever you may go, for my sake. It helps heal the planet and hopeful souls.

EACH AND EVERYONE OF YOU NEEDS TO LIGHTEN UP

You are always being offended by one another. Many of you are loose with your tongue. Stop and think before you open your mouth. When you have no kind words to utter, chase them out, as this poisons your own soul. This shows others and me what is really inside your heart. These are not loving thoughts. Where did they come from? Might this be someone else's truth of themselves, expressing their unhappiness, disappointment and anger to the world? These words should not be in your vocabulary.

When you spew hateful words out towards others, this is you not loving yourself. This is you trying to deal with the pain and darkness in your own heart. What do you suppose you're spreading now? You are just creating more of the same. Now the innocent individual has a scar on their heart that they need to heal because of your cold, senseless words. This is not fair treatment. You need to look inside and recycle all your hurtful memories. Ask for them to be lifted away. Throwing toxins into the air only poisons yourself and the people closest to you. This is selfish and irresponsible. Only you know where it came from. Dig deep; I'm sure you have the answer.

Stop taking your hurtful words out on those you love. They are innocent souls not deserving of your forked tongue. Go into the woods, ask to be healed and taken out of your misery. If you don't, you will eventually get the hurt right back at you, ten fold. These are the repercussions of the toxic, negative, hurtful words you send out into the lower atmosphere.

Eventually, this makes its way back to your similar vibration of low self-worth. You do not deserve others to love you if you intend on hurting them daily with your poisonous thoughts and words. When you are conscious that it is you who has the problem and not everyone else around you, this would be an opportune time to get some help and heal. This letting go process is where most of you have difficulties.

YOU ALL CARRY MEMORIES AROUND IN YOUR SPACE SUITS

You have all of your good ones and all of your bad ones. The good ones are of a warm loving frequency and the unpleasant ones are dense and weigh you down. This tends to produce friction in your being and negative thoughts of sadness, resentment, guilt and frustration. So you travel around with this collection of unpleasant events and circumstances creating more of the same in your life. Where have all those good times gone?

Well, look around. They too, are still in your memory but subconsciously, you are stuck in the lower frequency range of negativity. You must consciously choose to rid yourself of the experiences and memories that no longer serve you. Simply wishing for all this to go away does not move it out of your field. It's lodged in pretty securely.

Being hopeful of the removal is the first step. If you have doubt, then this experience will stay for many more years. Notice how it is not producing happiness in your life? It drags you down each passing day, taking with it the lighter, happier moments, that don't seem so exciting or significant compared to this terrible, dark experience that happened long ago. We are not supposed to hold this in our energy field. See what it is producing: low vibrations of unloving thoughts about yourself.

You still choose to beat yourself up about events that lead to this unpleasant experience and you strengthen its grip. You and I need to chip away at it piece by piece. First, we will try a sledgehammer to knock off the biggest piece. This gives room for the energy to start moving. Now, we have smaller, lighter particles of energy to work with. This is much easier. They will start to float away off you, back to the Earth for recycling. This allows room for expansion of the happy, lighter particles to join together and surround your being. This feeling of comfort, peace and resolution is most welcoming to your soul.

This lighter feeling about yourself literally lights your outlook on life and experiences. It doesn't seem so bad after all. Things are looking a little brighter. Notice you say this, not realizing you're talking about your auric field and energy signature. We all have to circulate pleasant memories and loving thoughts to counteract the heavy ones that pull us down.

When you choose to let go of old energies, happiness flourishes. This cannot take place when you are under the influence of an unhealthy, altered state of mind. Substances of low vibration keep the unpleasantness lodged in tight.

Our sledgehammer cannot break through the thickness of your suit without full consciousness and your being of right mind. This formula only works on those truly trying to let go and move forward. Know that altered states cannot signal energy exchange processes to manifest higher frequencies. It starts to look like a bowl of cream soup. There is no room for expansion of the light. Your field is shorting out and in a state of neutrality.

Your intention to brighten your own energy field and light within is all that is required to start the process of energy exchange. Get your circuits checked. Clean your wires and tune up your chakras. Try some dancing, swirling moves to expedite this process.

ENERGY CAUSES YOUR HEART TO FILL WITH HOPE

High vibrational love in its purest form creates miracles. When you believe in these manifestations, you have an awareness about you. Many have witnessed miracles and shrugged them off as coincidence or luck. Luck is not part of the universal kingdom. I didn't build the universe with a little luck. It was a well thought out intention. This is what your dreams are made of. Your mind can create anything you desire; mine did. You have all this wisdom inside you. Give it a try and use your sharp mind to create a few miracles yourself. It's not that hard really.

Belief is the first ingredient. Quite a bit, I might add. Second is intention. You know by now that if your desires and intentions are from your heart, they can become a reality. Throw in a lot of imagination and creativity. Mix it all up, until it's smooth.

One last ingredient to add; you guessed it: love, your love, everyone else's love and my love. This is truly the recipe to create miracles of hope and dreams. Do not blend in any doubt: this recipe will surely not rise.

HAVING HOPE IS BELIEVING IN THE UNKNOWN

Hope is holding onto a specific outcome and expecting the best for all. Without your belief system intact, you do not manifest dreams. Realization of life experiences that take your heart on the ultimate trip of a lifetime, do happen. It is your undying belief, hope, faith and the power of love in the universe that produce beauty, joy and happiness.

You require these feelings inside your heart in order to feel alive and purposeful. It is the ultimate feeling of comfort and peace when you arrive in your own time and truly know that all your effort was worth the trip. All your experiences of the heart allow it to expand and grow, so you may now feel the joy within. The warm, gentle everlasting flame of my love for you is eternal. It is the truth.

Open your heart, feel the love, give it freely and unconditionally. Practice patience, forgiveness, compassion and kindness. This allows your heart to expand to enormous proportions. There is no limit to the universe. We are all the universe, so this goes without saying, love is limitless. Your capacity to love is limitless. Your capacity to give is limitless. How much have you exercised so far?

SOME SEE WITH ROSE COLORED GLASSES

You choose to see your world the way you wish. If you are not choosing love, it can only be the opposite. By living in a fearful world, your heart cannot grow. It doesn't feel safe to experience what love has to offer. When you see the beauty of people's true hearts, this can open your own up. Do not push these souls away out of envy. They have been where you are now. They are there to show you the way. You won't let them into your world or your heart to feel your pain, yet you wish you were more like them. Well, wishes are weak. They are just wishes. You are caught up in desires of the flesh and see only greed and envy. These are afflictions of the mind. This is you not living inside of yourself and your heart.

You have desires to accumulate stuff, so people may envy you. You build a wall of stuff around you and let them look and hope they wish they were just like you. What is this behavior all about? Might this be because people don't want to genuinely spend too much time with you because you are too materialistic? You attract only like-minded individuals with shallow hearts and only love for stuff, not real love for people.

True-hearted individuals with loving hearts learned a long time ago that you cannot buy your happiness, your friends, or a true heart with money and shiny stuff. You want them around, but only on your terms. This is called "being controlling". This is fear of life's processes and being scared to let them see your heart. So instead, you show them all your stuff and hope they will fall in love with all that. Then maybe, they will hang around for a while.

Has it crossed your mind that they are possibly there for the stuff and the fun associated with it? What happens at the end of the day? These individuals are not there for your heart and soul. If they were, they would realize it wasn't open for love anyway. Then they drift away in search of more stuff and who has what to offer. What about what life and loving souls have to offer? Is this not enough for your worldly desires?

When you can see the beauty, feel the beauty. Be grateful for the loving souls sharing their hearts and experiences with you. You have received your reward in life. What finer feeling than to feel alive. Feel the love and share it with everyone else who has arrived at this sacred place. The overwhelming love in your heart for people and all earthly creations is truly a feeling and place one must intend to be. Deep appreciation for who you have become, survived by all your collective experiences of the heart, brought you to this place today.

You marvel at the beauty and balance of nature. You admire the tranquility of the stars and planets. You are astonished by the ocean life and how these creatures live in harmony with their needs and desires fulfilled. You embrace the people you meet with open arms, feel their hearts and listen to their loving words. You share your love with all those that you meet on your walk of life, expressing gratitude and praying that they too will discover the beautiful planet you share.

Beauty is in the eyes of the beholder. For what you fail to see outside of yourself, truly indicates that your heart hasn't learned all the lessons of life. There are many opportunities and chances to become closer to the universal love. This is when you see through the eyes of God in wonderment and feel compassion for those unable to don the rose colored glasses.

WHAT IS A SIN, ANYWAY?

Is this a wrongful act of judgment? Is this not man made? Who are we to judge and hang others for sins of the heart? These individuals are already hurting and punishing themselves. They have no hope, self-worth, love for themselves or others so we decide to lock them up and punish them more. Be clear; I'm not referring to murders and extreme acts of violence. I am referring to the lost souls who have not been given love. They are crying for help in the only way they know how. Society turns their backs on them and decides that we will further the problem and throw away the key to their heart. That was their last cry for help and love and we didn't reciprocate.

What do you not see here? You are so conditioned to condemn and hurt, hurting individuals. This is adding insult to injury. This is kicking them down further. They are at their lowest point on their path and could use some love and compassion. I don't expect you to overlook their wrong-doings, but a sequence of events and unpleasant life experiences brought them to this place. You may not be able to even comprehend how they arrived there and why they committed your so-called crimes. Can you not see that they too, may be looking for love in an unusual way? Had they been shown or given love, they would not be in this lonely place.

So we all walk away and buy some time thinking that will solve the problem. Time continues to go by and this individual is still not receiving any love from the right heart. This is how their heart dies. Leaving this individual alone only creates a deeper state of despair.

What would be a better, healthier approach is counseling. Where are all your counselors anyway? You have coaches, leaders, mentors, advisors, consultants, but not many counselors. We need counselors and society is not hearing the cries of this requirement. Why is everyone trying out all these fancy other job titles, when the young generation is going astray? Are the counselors hiding? Did they change careers because of the pay?

We have a desperate situation in the schools and playgrounds. Your children are getting mixed up. You are to blame for confusing them with your own choices. Yes, they are a full time job, but responsibly you need to provide them with love and guidance. They seem to have more questions than answers. Adults seem so preoccupied with their own affairs, that their children's behavioral problems go unnoticed until they've escalated into more serious issues. Put the fire out before the whole house burns down.

I'm not saying that parents are not trying. There are not enough hours in a day with homework, activities and all, but truly your young generations are on paths of self-destruction. This is not the 1950's when the norm was for mothers to stay home and children's needs and requirements were being met.

This is the new millennium, with the Earth spinning faster than ever. Children require attention and foundational ground rules. They don't seem to have reverential fear. They respect no one, including themselves and quite frankly, they don't know any differently if they were not taught and brought up in a stable home environment. In fact, I blame the adults, as kids really don't know any better. They are just mimicking you. You're in five different directions, changing jobs, houses and partners, reactively going through life trying to make ends meet and possibly "keep up with the Joneses". With all your fancy hi-tech stuff down there, the Joneses are millionaires. So let's not buy into this consumerism mindset too much.

The best value of your time would be to counsel your own children. Address their concerns and lessons one by one. They are overwhelmed with your lifestyle choices and the pace of the population. Their heads are spinning so fast, they can't seem to collect their thoughts and focus long enough to make sense out of all this "life on planet Earth show". This is the reality show they are in right now, at this very moment in time. It is up to you to understand them, as you were all young once. Don't buy them things to keep them occupied and out of your hair. Instead, purchase educational and self-discovery resources for them so they may find their secure place in the world with your love and mine. This is a 24-7 job requirement of your time.

Why did you have kids anyway? You can't just discard them; abandon them to figure life out on their own. We didn't agree to this. One commitment you made was to give love and time to everyone, every soul, whatever the cost; and two, to do God's work, which is more of the same. There are so many lost souls not knowing where to turn. They are looking up to you to lead by example.

Are you doing the best you can? Do you make time for beautiful life experiences with them, or are you trying to solve all your own self-created problems and now have a time management problem? Maybe it's a priority, short-list problem. You business-minded professionals should use your skills in more useful ways, other than to feed your ego and lifestyles at work. How many jobs do you need? If you were working for me, there would be plenty of balance, abundance, perks, time for vacations and soul nurturing loving experiences.

Some of you have got this right already. When you do the work of your Creator and genuinely help every one on your planet in various essential ways, your rewards are many. There is plenty of time to enjoy others and travel abroad. Be a leader and make a difference where it counts.

I realize you need corporations, conglomerate organizations and infrastructures in place to facilitate conveniences and necessities, however, what are your goals at this time for your life? Do you intend to give back? Do you wish to find your true gifts, talents and feel fulfilled? Would you like to know what your life purpose is?

Slow down a bit, schedule me into your next business meeting and perhaps we can talk. You all have essential jobs on Earth and this keeps fueling your growth and economy. I am impressed with technology and the harmonized integration of business and worldly affairs. You manage to keep things in order down there to a degree. The only overlooked detail was the spirit of the souls not going with the flow of management.

Each and every individual has their own mind, heart and soul. This keeps life interesting. It's a God-given gift. There are many skilled, talented, intelligent, creative, passionate souls on

Earth. It's a beautiful blend, a perfect mix for manifestation of life experiences. All essential requirements are met for your medical, financial, business, educational and recreational needs.

One industry that hasn't quite been tapped into is the spiritual market. You have covered most of the basics, but choose to overlook an essential requirement a lot of you are missing in your life. Some of you think this is not important enough to bother with. Others feel that it will not make them their millions, but in fact, this is where the money is. This is truly the pot of gold at the end of your rainbow of dreams.

By knowing who you really are and what you choose to accomplish on your journey, you discover your gifts. These gifts will come naturally. They will need to be developed, but once you figure out where you really shine, life takes off for you. This is the missing piece of the puzzle, the key to the heavens. This is a journey of self-discovery, self-healing and self-love. This is a timely process. For those who wish to get started, send your intentions out, I will hear your true desires of the heart. Your essential lessons will have to be dealt with; if we proceed forward your intentions need to be in alignment with my desires of the heart.

DEPLETED RESOURCES

There are quite a lot of concerns I have in regards to depleted resources. There are viable solutions to regenerate sustainable resources. The direction you are on may not meet all the demands of the large populations. In order for everyone to feed themselves and weather the elements, changes have to take place. We are at the crossroads now. Systems and complex utility equipment need to be set up in order to sustain development of the planet. Irreversible damage has already been put into motion. It can only get worse from your lifetime on. Having the mindset "well, we won't be here" is pretty selfish, as you are all just visiting my planet.

Remember, you're on a working vacation. You cannot cut all my forests down, pollute the water, the air and use up all natural resources without looking at the consequences. The repercussions are catastrophic. I'm not expected to arrive any time soon to clean up your mess, so pay attention here.

There are many alternatives in regards to your garbage problems, paper consumption and your fuel requirements. I liked the slogan: Reduce, Reuse and Recycle. Reduce at the source; reusing is time consuming. I know how inconvenient this may be in your fast-paced life and recycling is your last alternative. Such an industry, all your packaging is. You've been led to believe that everything comes in a pretty package. What is pretty to you anyway: a shiny, expensive car or a bottle of designer perfume?

Look back in time. Although you didn't have the population at hand, all your needs came in simple packages. Big business, this advertising is. Yes, you need to market, but in one day of flyers, you destroy a whole forest. I see this. It doesn't grow back in one day. But you throw out this much paper. Why so much paper anyway? Are your memories not so sharp? Did the copier get jammed? You need to see who is selling what at the best price? If you have such a demand in your information age, use your personal computers a little more and be conscious about the air you breathe. Without trees, I can't recycle your pollution. No need to fill the landfill sites with unnecessary paper products. Reduce, Reuse and Recycle.

How are you disposing of all your garbage anyway? If you are going to burn toxins, manufacture the proper filters. You have the technology for this. No desire, no time, don't want to spend the money? Let's get something straight. There will be no Earth without these changes. Then you can forget about shopping for stuff.

Your treatment plants for the fresh water retrieval system are outdated by decades. There is money for this. Ask your governments where your taxes are going. Last time I looked, there wasn't much fresh water down on your planet.

Why not try distilleries? It's practical. This does not give you the ok to dump your waste in the water system. The entire water table and Earth becomes contaminated this way. How will we grow your food with the chemical-leached soil? Yummy. You can't even ingest all these chemicals you are trying to dispose of. Remember that whole energy concept? Well, the molecules have to go somewhere.

If you're smart about it, I can help, only after you have correctly disposed of your waste in an effective, efficient manner for the benefit of all creation. There are many that know viable solutions to the crisis, yet they are running into road blocks. I've made sure your concerns are addressed, but you have to carry them through.

Make time; spend some money. There is lots of it down there. Just use it in the right places. This is a priority. This is a proactive approach. Choose life, respect your home and respect your off—spring. You have the knowledge and this is something that should be addressed in your decade.

NATURAL RESOURCES ARE NOT GOING TO BE NATURAL FOR MUCH LONGER

You are running out of oil. Are you considering any amicable solutions? There are a few. Engineers have the answers to alternative power. The universe is energy; harness it. Many brilliant minds can provide answers and solutions. They need the fuel to implement these strategies in the form of currency and lots of it. Again, there is no shortage, just a shortage of time and intention. You know who you are, those that can save the planet. I planted the seeds in your mind. Speak up or we'll have hell to pay when you arrive back here to my kingdom. You went down to sustain your planet. That was your soul's purpose. I'm trying to drive a point home here. Too many of you who have answers and solutions, are not taking action. This infuriates me. What more would you like me to do? I'm not living on your planet. I'm living in your planet and all the millions of others.

Yours seems to be the one in the worst state. Not only are you creating havoc with the Earth, air and atmosphere, you're not co-habitating together.

There are so many of you with different ideas and opinions. We all come from the same place and inherently have the same desires of the heart. Why let the ego get in the way? Work together. Fight the fight, to save your planet from destruction. Too many takers, not giving back, line their pocket for power. Power of what, I ask? Power over the harmless souls who only want to have a good time down there, make some friends, spread some joy, laugh a little, love a lot.

You came down to have fun. Is this your definition of fun? You are trashing the planet, consuming all the resources, leaving a mess behind and not cleaning up after yourselves. Too busy, being self-centered and worried about your next party? Well, there won't be one the way you are acting. You are being quite selfish, immature and spoiled and you wonder what is wrong with the youth of today? You are their teachers. They look up to you and want to be just like you. How responsible is that?

You teach them to consume and not to have respect for life, the planet and others. You teach them to behave like heartless souls. This is you looking back at you. What have you created? What kind of difference have you made down there?

When you come back to me, I would like nothing more than to hear that you made a difference and left the world a better place. You gave love, procreated and taught your words of wisdom to your young. You showed them the virtues of the heart.

This would truly make my heart grow. There is so much love to circulate around. Stop denying this emotion. This is the power of the universe. This is the fuel that feeds your planet and the others. It gives you life as you know it to be true in your heart.

Listen to your heart as I call your name. Don't turn away as if you don't hear me. I am the whisper in your soul that you yearn to feel. This keeps you alive and well on planet Earth.

CHAPTER FOUR

The Lessons of Truth

HUMILITY DEFINED

WE ALL HAVE WORDS TO SHARE; some kind and generous, some forthright. When you receive a compliment, accept it into your heart. Be not so vain to think that you deserved this compliment, for where would you be without my blessings? When others take notice of your efforts and accomplishments, simply give thanks humbly from your heart. Be gracious and return a kind word. Do not let yourself and the ego get in the way. There is no room in your heart for the ego.

The ego simply is what you think you are which you carry around with you. This serves no purpose other than to alienate you from others. The act of ego-based thinking does not produce genuine fruit. Notice how warm-hearted souls do not stay in your company for long periods of time. You push them away thinking you must be better than them. They feel this and are offended. They sincerely were happy for your gains and rewards and you took it all in and marveled in your false pride. When you notice this behavior, stop and think before you speak.

Don't speak from your ego-heart. That is not mine. Find your true heart inside of yourself and be grateful for your rewards and blessings. Show humility to me and to all others who come your way. When you realize that you are not working alone, may you find time to thank me and appreciate all those souls who helped you along the way. How could you have ever achieved this state of wealth and good fortune without others? You certainly didn't go solo here.

When you truly desire to find this humbling place and express gratitude to everyone on your path, you may even wish to help them achieve higher states of fulfillment. You will really shine when you come into the realization of the love and light of our relationship. Know that you have offended and turned away many loving souls. Try to repair some of the damage you did, as I sent these souls to admire and learn from you. You missed the lesson here. They were there for you to make them feel good and to learn valuable skills from you, so they could also make a valuable contribution to society and the planet. Give them a call if it's not too late. Step out of yourself and find your compassionate, giving heart. You buried this along the way, being caught up in your accomplishments of the flesh.

Know that persistent effort and mindfulness is required to lose this mindset. It is quite a bad affliction of the heart and does not allow the heart to grow at its capacity. You have stopped its growth unnecessarily. Move on from this place, as it doesn't serve you any longer and it leaves a bitter taste in everyone's mouth.

BELIEVING IN YOURSELF

Why is it so many have reservations and doubt? You bounce back and forth, entertaining whether or not to believe in the intangible. You seem so unsure, undecided and uncertain about your true nature. What causes these uncertainties? Maybe you felt that the outcome of a particular situation was not in your best interest. Well, how do you know this for sure? This is tunnel vision. How would you know if you were supposed to be arriving any place soon, or how it was going to turn out?

Your lack of trust in me and life's processes holds you back from believing in your higher self.

If you trusted or believed in the synchronicities of the intelligent universe you would not doubt for a moment that I am in complete control from up here. I see the outcome of your clouded decision making and with every effort, try to move you in a positive direction. Boy, oh boy, do you ever resist this effort. I even try to make it unbearable for you to get you to leave an unpleasant situation and your flesh refuses to go. You are really holding things up for yourself.

Do you not believe that you and I planned an amazing love-filled, life experience for you? It's so sad that you can't seem to find enough faith in the Almighty to let go and let God lead the way to greener pastures. They are filled with love, growth, balance and the sweet smells of euphoria.

Each and every one of you wrote an intricate plan to enjoy every gift that life has to offer on your Earth experience. However, few of you even arrive there due to the lack of deep trust and faith in your Creator. What is your life producing now? It is a lot of the same old, same old? This is you not letting go. This is you holding on so tight.

How can you move forward? Take a tiny step into the light and see how it feels in your heart. Meditate on it and you will hear my voice telling you not to look back, as I am with you every step of the way.

START TO BELIEVE IN YOUR OWN POWER

Why do you think you are so helpless? Is this conditioned thinking? You arrived knowing you could conquer any obstacle in your way. You were all warriors in your own mind, stronger than the mountains. Somewhere along the way, you lost your courage, conviction for life and its offerings. This is not easily reversed. You've done considerable damage to your self-esteem. Having confidence and belief in your abilities is like having a buttercup. You hold this under your chin, believing to see the reflection of its beauty. You never doubted that it wouldn't happen. Yet, you doubt in your own reflection of yourself. Face your fears. Together, I will help you process these uncomforting thoughts of worry and self-doubt. Stand up strong on your two feet and take a step forward. Know that I am beside you all the way. I cannot take the steps for you. This is me intervening and the lesson is worth naught.

Courage is facing these obstacles and moving cautiously in a positive direction. It is a knowingness that you are not acting alone. It's a belief that somewhere deep in your soul you, too, have the power to move mountains and rock the world with your conviction of life and its worth. For when you stand tall, you shine and I can fill your being with strength for the asking. When you take the first steps in the right direction, this is your soul trying to grow, crying to find its strength and its place in the world. Stopping this growth leads to regression. That is not why you went down, to be stagnant.

Your spirit and soul are mightier than your imagination knows. Look inside and discover the real you with all your strength and gifts waiting to be called on.

It is your duty to grow your soul to its maximum potential. There are an over abundance of young souls already. Do your part, as your efforts are desperately needed for life on Earth to evolve at the required rate. Strong leaders and the strength of many are needed to make changes in the infrastructure of the processes of day-to-day sustainable, quality life. When you find your own power and warrior inside, perhaps you, too, can make a positive difference by giving love to the planet. Strength, courage, determination, belief and hope for the future are required in your make-up.

Be not afraid child, as when you do God's work in God's way, many ways for you to move forward reveal themselves. Believe in the dream. Believe in your strength. Believe in the power of love. Hold this in your heart and never let go. This is where you shine and start to love your life. When you find your passion, life takes you places you never expected. Trust that it is all good and in your highest interest. Take the first step. Take a deep breath and begin to do what truly makes you feel alive and well. This will fuel your heart and soul.

FAITH

Such a loose term down on your planet, this is. You kind of have it; kind of don't. You sometimes have it; you sometimes don't. Make up your mind. There is no grey area here. Do you or don't you? Make a decision and stick to it. How wishy-washy, so many of you. One little thing goes wrong and you give up this faith. Something hopeful happens and now it comes back temporarily, until the next set back. This is not faith; this is make-believe. This is you not sure about the real thing.

Let me explain something. Faith is unquestionable, every minute of every waking day of your life. You either have it or you don't. I see this back and forth thinking. This is not your heart's processor. When this undefying belief in your God is true; it either is or isn't. Stop questioning my actions. Your life would be so much smoother if you got off the fence and stopped wavering here and there. Are you in or are you out? Make a decision and stick to it. Paste it in your heart where it belongs. No doubts, no questioning, no discussion. If you can't hold this virtue of the heart in place unquestionably every minute of your life, you simply don't have it and you're on your own.

How's your life working out so far? Is it not up and down and all over the place because you can't hold on to something true in your heart? Your outcomes are wishy-washy, as well. That is not the real thing; this is you not trusting or having faith in our well thought-out plan for your happiness.

You wished for a beautiful life and we agreed outright that this will only manifest with your undefying belief in the faith of your Creator. Have faith that all things are possible. All love, joy and happiness are obtainable for the asking when you hold these intentions close to your heart and are in no question of the outcome and the steps to arrive there.

All things are considered and the plan is intricate. Therefore, if you are patient and know that things will work out just the way we wanted them to, you should have no reason to fear these closed doors and set backs. All these processes must take place, so you, too, will enjoy a life of abundant wishes and desires. Chill out, relax and enjoy each day. Roll with the punches. Find the humor in the lesson and move along to bigger and better things. Life is waiting to take off. Are you onboard? I know I am.

HOW ABOUT YOUR DILIGENCE IN YOUR WORK EFFORTS

I see some slacking off down there. One minute you're really into it; other times you don't give a damn. It's interesting seeing your motives. You want to keep the bosses happy, but you really don't like your job. Your heart is not into your work. This is a waste of your time and talents. You have many gifts and skills. You may want to consider a career change. When your efforts are not from the heart, you find it doesn't pay that well. You are in a holding pattern.

When you discover where you shine, you will probably love what you do. Feel good about yourself and discover ways to create more fortune for yourself. This keeps everyone around you happy. If you are not productive at work, find a place that better utilizes your skills, talents and all parties win. Put your heart where your money is, for this is how you create it. Make a difference and do what you were cut out to do. Just call and ask sincerely. I will point you in the right direction.

Don't miss this opportunity to be happy. Fulfill your life contract and live your dreams. This is an effective use of your productive time. Learn a new skill. This is not an overnight process. Start the process with an intention; change your thoughts and believe it. Soon you will become a new, passionate person who wakes up happy because they know, in their heart, they are making a difference and it feels good in the soul.

Many teachers and mentors will show up on your path to help you acquire your new skills and develop your talents. Believe and trust. Be open to these possibilities and don't miss the opportunities I send your way.

BE PERSISTENT IN YOUR EFFORTS

You try some things and then you change your mind. Why? Is this because you are impatient and frustrated; probably both. Who said life was going to be easy? That's boring. When you make your decision, stick to it. Stop coming up with reasons not to go for it. That is you talking yourself out of "change". You don't like change, it's foreign and the uncertainty is not comforting. This is lack of trust, faith and determination. The more you stall, the harder it becomes to get started.

You've accumulated dozens of reasons why you are procrastinating at this new idea you thought you so desired. You "hum and haw" and mill about. Now, you're not sure what the first steps are anymore. The opportunity was already there. Don't miss these clues. A sequence of events needs to take place for fulfillment of your new desires. Get on board and grab onto one of these lifelines to show you what to do next. Listen to your heart. You have to do the work anyway, so you may as well enjoy the ride.

When you are involved in this new adventure, you will not look back. It feels good in your soul. You know you are on track and pointed in the right direction. Your destination looks promising from here. Just go for it. Stop procrastinating and making excuses why you can't or don't know how to proceed. You know the way. You are just stalling. This will not produce a favorable outcome if we don't get started on track.

Be hopeful and open to the idea of a new you. When you are in your element, frustration and lack of appreciation dissipate. You have a wealth of knowledge and talent to offer the world. Go out and be your best self. You deserve it.

GET ORGANIZED

When you have too many things on the go, this is not conducive to optimum results. This only produces discord and more disorganization. Rearrange your agenda and set some goals. You cannot move forward to a new destination without a plan. You don't have a start time, a check point, a revised plan or an ETA.

How do you expect to get where you are going? This takes careful planning. Map out your route and consider all possibilities. All options and details must be considered. Do you have the resources or the materials? Are you going to factor in contingencies? How much is this going to cost? Can you manage all this and still work full time and raise a family? This is what scares you the most. Let's break it down. This is not an overnight plan. This is a dream that we are going to create together, with careful planning, all things considered.

Your first step is to investigate the destination. How does it look? How is the weather over there? Do you like what you see? Does it seem to produce a favorable climate or are the winds blowing too strong for your liking? If this is not a field or destination that you are willing to weather, pick a new field. You know the kind of person you are so make a realistic plan. Weigh out all the options and tribulations of this new you. Does it fit into your lifestyle? Can you adapt comfortably or will you feel uneasy when you arrive?

Careful consideration is necessary before jumping into a new field. Make sure you are cut out for this type of work. Work is always demanding and pulls everything out of you and shows you what you are made of. It challenges you to go in and exhaust all of your talents and inherent abilities to achieve desired optimum outcomes. This is what will be required from you. Can you sustain this level of performance for years to come? When you answer yes, we can move forward.

Let's look at your present commitments, these are a given. Most of your time is spoken for except for your down time. How badly do you want to change your place anyway? Remember, we are creating a long term plan a few years away. If you are truly interested in a new field to utilize and maximize your talents, let's get going. There is a lot to learn. Start with some educational material and do the self-learning in the evening, part time. Attend a class or a workshop. All these collective efforts will surely add up.

Now you know what is required to fulfill this dream. Take time to absorb it all and keep moving forward. You will like what you are doing because you chose it from your heart. The learning becomes effortless, because you have a passion for it and it stimulates your soul. You become your own source of inspiration. Look at you now, learning what you love to do. In a short amount of time, all the pieces are coming together.

We now have to factor in testing the market and meeting the minimum requirements. Save your money. Cut back on clothes and entertainment. You don't seem to have a great regard for these commodities anyway. I'm referring to too many home movies and too many pieces of outerwear. Sit tight and stick to the plan. You will find the resources to fuel your dream destination. I will be sure of it, if you do your part.

All factors considered, when you arrive and have the needed knowledge, don't expect to be handed a quick manual, as you are walking into foreign waters. Tread gently and find out who's who. Make your legitimate contacts and network. It always seems to be word of mouth. Do not spend unnecessary money on advertising at the beginning. Advertise yourself in person and let people know what you can offer them.

Keep learning along the way. There is never an end point to learning. This keeps your brain in functioning order. Don't let the cells in this space die. Your thirst for knowledge keeps you alive, literally.

Listen to others' experiences and learn from their mistakes. Ask questions and listen for an honest answer and a direction to go in. Life will begin to unfold when you've arrived here. This is the new improved you that I have been patiently waiting for, to embrace and reward you with your gifts for your diligent efforts.

May you see the end in mind. Hold that vision in your heart and meditate on how to proceed from there. I will show you the way to your dreams.

PATIENCE, PATIENCE, PATIENCE

Always expecting an answer so quickly and you're always waiting in frustration; patience my child. I'm not sure everyone understands its significance. Are you after a mediocre outcome or are you hopeful for the best? I cannot produce miracles and dreams in that fashion. This is why you are to silently wait with faith and patience. There is a lot of work to do up here. You truly have no idea. We have to have our meetings as well, to keep things organized. This is because so many of you miss your cue and we have to rearrange the whole agenda again. We don't do it with paper, mind you. However, this well thought out dream of yours needs processing. It takes a lot of planning and players to execute the perfect outcome. I promised this for you. Occasionally, we need to make amendments up here to allow for contingent factors beyond our control. We can still deliver the goods, as promised, but we are not operating on the same time piece.

Quite frankly, it's a miracle that we manage to process all the orders when you keep changing your mind and revising the dates and so forth. You have add-on's, you expect time frames and come across a little demanding.

Relax, we have your order. We are doing the best we can. This would be a perfect time for you to do the best you can while you're waiting patiently. Thank you in advance.

We appreciate your order. Now calm down and keep yourself occupied with other important issues that need attention. Don't let these slip by, as they need to be in place, too, for all this to come together immaculately. We are all in this together. Are you starting to get the picture?

FOCUS ON YOUR INTENTION

In order for us to move forward with your desires of the heart, it would be beneficial, at this time, to keep them in your focus. Distractions will crop up all over the place. Know when to let them pass by. It is not in your best interest and is certainly not going to produce your original request, if you are all over the place. You made a commitment. We are doing our part. This is the time to stay focused on the outcome.

Having a positive knowing that your desires will manifest, no matter what, with unquestionable belief, is paramount. This truly shows me you have faith in me to produce positive outcomes for all parties involved. Hold your intention in your mind's eye and meditate on this desire. Wish for a miracle to manifest. All orders are produced when in accordance with the universal laws. When you believe in me, your dream of a better, fulfilling lifestyle will make a difference to many lives during your stay on Earth. You can also take this valuable time to pray for others that their hopes, dreams and desires are fulfilled as well. This sincere, heart-felt prayer shows me you are true to your fellowship and that you genuinely care about others.

Your heart must be feeling warm by now, as mine is. When the heat of love accelerates, the energy creates miracles more effectively and accurately. We all have to be vibrating at a faster frequency to do the work. Stay in touch.

HOW YOU DISCONNECT AND BREAK THE CHAIN

Your train of thought, intention and doubt creates friction in the universe. Know that every thought you produce, every minute, sends out a vibratory frequency into the realms. We try to counterbalance the low, thoughtless ones you produce. This is where we need your co-operation and assistance. For every negative, ridiculous and fearful thought you create, you send a distorted wave in the realms of the universal mind. Do you suppose this is useful when we are at such a high frequency?

A basic understanding of mc2 would be beneficial here. The vibratory rate of your intentions is producing static. Clean up your thoughts and send pure signals of love. We can respond more effectively without all the interference. You are creating low level oscillations that can't ascend, transmit, or transpose into effective light.

Our requirement is of a lighter, faster, energy vibration to reuse the consciousness of all life and energy on your planet. This balance is optimum for harmony, growth and love to flourish. The capacity which is needed is a collective effort of many. This reduces the magnitude of the static in the low frequency range. Nothing is really produced at that level that is of your highest interest. Be mindful of connecting to a loving frequency range and try not to waver or intentionally disconnect. This shorts out levels of communication equipment.

This matrix of energy patterns and grids makes up the universe and your consciousness. The delicate design is woven intricately with your intentions of the heart and vibrational energies. Please hold this consideration in mind. When you shine like the light you are, the grid of the universe is of majestic beauty beyond your imagination. It's quite a light show and is a requirement for life on planet Earth.

Stay connected to your power source. Breathe deeply the breath of life and harness its power in your heart and soul. Take it and fill every cell of your being to give it optimum life. Revel in its beauty. The feeling is like no other. Desire to find this state of bliss, as this is achievable on the Earth plane. You only need to know of its vibrational capacity in order to attain its benefit. Look into it and get high on life.

You truly can feel states beyond the lower energy realms. This is a God-given gift. Make it a quest in your life. Let it become one of your new hobbies. It's quite addictive from what I see up here.

LOW VIBRATION ENERGIES

You know your thoughts are number one in keeping you in the lower levels of vibration. Your second largest killer is your food. All food carries a vibration. This can strengthen or weaken your personal energy field. You know this to be true. When you overeat or consume over-processed food, you feel tired and sluggish. This is what you have done to your energy vibration. I know you need a quick fix and Raw Cacao is probably one of the better sweets I created. However, use some discretion here. You are overloading on sugar and caffeine. That is not raising your vibration. That is weakening your energy field. Balance and variety are the key. You all have your crutches, but let's not go overboard.

You cannot function all day on sugar and caffeine. Now you're edgy and hitting your low point. After you snap at someone, you reach for more. This would probably be a good time to listen to your body and realize it's asking for nutrients and wholesome foods.

Try some raw fruits and vegetables. This is where you get your daily requirements and raise your vibration. You can accomplish all your tasks and live your life to the fullest, from your higher self. This is you vibrating at a very high frequency. Look and feel all that energy buzzing around in you, wanting to have fun. You're not moody, tired, or drained. You are empowered. High vibrational foods: find the balance.

Eat foods that are alive, they give you life to the fullest. Now you're operating at an optimum level. How does it feel? The highs and lows are gone, you feel energized the natural way. Now, send out your intentions of the heart and see what happens. We can hear you a lot more clearly now that you're on our wavelength.

DIRECTION

Who are you looking at for direction? The obvious person may not be the best choice. Do they have their complete act together? Are they living a whole life as their best self? Are they living in accordance with the universal laws?

Choose your mentors wisely. They are few and far in-between. You will be able to recognize them by their intentions of the heart. Are they living their dream or trying to make a difference in everyone else's lives? Do they pray inside for the best possible outcome for all concerned? Do they sincerely and genuinely care about your well-being?

All things considered here will help you on your own life path. Perhaps it will be several mentors that have loving qualities and virtues, which you can reflect on and learn to adapt. You will know in your own heart who is the best for you. Look at their behavior and where they are on their path in life. Is it worth following in their footsteps? Look with open eyes and hearts to be sure their intentions are pure. These souls have much to teach you about life lessons.

It certainly is in your best interest to spend quality time with these individuals. They too, will make time for you. They desire for you to find your best self and discover your purpose and gifts. They will not abandon or scold you for making mistakes. They will offer a hand and comfort your heart as you learn from your earthly lessons. Seek out these beautiful souls as they have much to offer. They may even show you the way to me, if you do the work and are diligent in your efforts.

Please don't compromise, as nothing is gained here. Walk your own path. Keep your eyes and ears open to those who walk before you. Trust your intuition on this. If it feels gentle, comforting and inspiring, you are on the right path.

FOLLOW YOUR OWN STAR

This leads to your own personal truth. Your personal experiences make up who you are. Your collection of challenges, tears of joy and laughter develop your true character and build a beautiful loving soul. When you shine your light to the world, others will look to you for inspiration and guidance. This is now you, leading the way for me. I chose you to be a light and to help others find theirs. Through nurturing, patience and love, you can make a difference in their world. They, too, were looking for the light and weren't even sure if they were worthy of my love.

Please let them know I watch over them and believe in them. I forgive them, when they find the love in their hearts. When they choose to shine their own lights and make a difference, we will have re-established our relationship.

This is you showing them the way, showing them the light within. Shine so brightly that others will want to be in your presence. Shine so strongly that you put out the darkness. The more souls you touch, the larger the capacity to love is felt in your own heart. This is the time for expansion and growth. This is where you feel alive and impact many individuals in your world. This truly makes me joyous.

ALL PATHS LEAD TO HOME

Everywhere you go, I am there, funny how that happens. Whether you're on the low road, the high road, "destination unknown" road, or "the path to self-destruction" road, you will find me for the looking. You may not want to bump into me, but know that I am aware of your ultimate destination. All these detours and you still end up back to me.

Many excuses come in here: why you chose this route; why you didn't complete your job; why you never arrived at your dream destination. There are so many of you disappointed in your outcomes. If you don't like your road and where it is taking you, why are you on it?

Who's driving the car? Not me. I'm the one in the passenger seat, desiring to be in the driver's seat to steer you out of trouble. Your radio must be too loud. Maybe you are on your cell phone, who knows, too much static interference. Suppose I honked the horn a few times, or perhaps, throw a dead end at the end of your road. Would you wake up or continue? I try every trick in our book from here to steer you back on track, but you are so determined and preoccupied with tasks and to-do lists, you're not paying enough attention.

I have a map for you to look at, two in fact. The map you are holding and the original map that we drew up. Which one would you like to follow? You certainly have free will but come on, be sensible, you are headed for a dead end. I would highly recommend an alternate diversion right about now to navigate you back on track. This leg may take us a little longer, but it will ensure our arrival at the best destination.

This is called a correction. There are many reasons why you blew off track and many options to correct your heading before it's too late. Don't leave your vehicle on autopilot. It seems you don't know where you're headed. Let's both use our ideas to revise the route. Chances are you will like cruising at the higher flight levels instead. The view is spectacular and you can see our dream destination from this altitude.

RISE UP TO THE OCCASION

Look around, what do you see? Do you see happy faces everywhere you turn or do you see sour faces? Maybe you see faces of many disguises. Is this the world you like to entertain you or is this because you are stuck in a rut? "Like attracts like." Look at the company you are keeping. This is a reflection of you. If you don't like what you're viewing, maybe you could change your thinking. You are attracting all these souls into your world. They are at similar vibrational frequencies. This may not be healthy if you desire to move out of that range. The heaviness of this vibration is sticky like glue and it's difficult to become unstuck. It requires effort to pull yourself out of that level of vibration.

You may be better off surrounding yourself with more positive people. Their vibration is faster and contagious. Their true colors are evident by their actions and efforts. They have no requirement to fulfill desires of the flesh. They have risen above their unhealthy behavior. They are quite content enjoying life and what it has to offer. Their true desires are to make a positive difference in the lives they touch everyday. They are beyond the self-pity and have chosen to walk with me, embracing their challenges to grow and empower themselves. They know in their hearts that life's lessons present pains they cannot always bear alone and choose to keep me in their hearts to ease the pain. These individuals have consciously decided to move through their lessons with God's love, instead of feeling sorry for themselves.

Make an effort to choose inspiring, positive, uplifting people. They can give you hope and make you realize that there is a better world for the asking. They see their life opportunities with optimism and have faith in positive outcomes. This is faster vibratory energies at its finest.

Choose your acquaintances and colleagues wisely for the best interest of everyone concerned. Change your boots and step out of the guck. Shake it off and call in the light workers to show you the way home.

If you're looking for fun you should try hanging around some inspirational speakers. They have direction. They uplift your spirits and know how to raise the energy of the planet.

BECOME ALL YOU CAN IMAGINE

Where has all your imagination gone? Is it because technology does all the thinking for you? Well, I think that is fine and convenient, but listen here, you still have to exercise your mind. Don't let gadgets do all your thinking. You truly lose your ability to expand your thinking. All that space in your brain, use both sides at the same time. That is why you have a left and right side.

Being stuck too much in one side, leads to an imbalance of thought processes and creativity. You become obsessed with facts or become overwhelmed with chemical emotions and this allows unreasoning skills to flourish. You start to lose your ability to create and manifest essential necessities required on your planet. You are not as sharp as you were originally created.

You exercised your brain in school six hours a day or more; well, at least, you were supposed to. Then you figured you had enough education and decelerated your learning capacity. Picking up educational material once in a while is not going to reproduce sharp thinking. This organ requires stimulation and lots of it. Expand your thinking and use your imagination. Involve your brain in creativity skills.

Your saying, "use it or lose it" is 100% true. You are probably sharper than you know, but you have to desire to feed your mind. Think and dream big, for you are only limited by your imagination.

What? You can't think of any ideas how to do this? Not surprising. I'm joking again. You ought to know you need a huge, surmountable sense of humor from where I sit or you would all make me crazy. Try some for yourself. Sense of humor is an essential to get through life. Use your imagination. Become all that you can and then some. There is no limit to what you can create with your gifts and talents. You may surprise yourself. I see what you are capable of. Don't let yourself down. Go for it all; it's for your highest good. This too, is your God-given right.

Expand your mind and open your heart. Live your dreams. Find me in your heart and let's have a ball. The world is your playground. Enjoy it, embrace it, laugh and love a lot. That is what you love to do. Don't take yourself so seriously.

When you are too serious, you don't have much fun. I see your serious mannerisms. This is not a good virtue. Maybe you don't see the fun down there and have lost hope. If you ask, I can help you lighten up.

Find a "clean" joke book and share some laughs together. I really don't like all the ethnic jokes around. You laugh them off but I find them disrespectful. Quite frankly, you probably wouldn't tell that joke to someone of that origin, but you tell it to me, as I hear what you say. Is this participating in a high frequency range? They seem harmless to you, but this joking does not have my blessings. It's quite foolish and condescending. It doesn't look good on your heart.

Seriously though, souls that can't seem to laugh or have fun have some issues to deal with. Look inside and see what took your joy away. When you can identify this sad experience, maybe you can decide that it doesn't serve you anymore. If you're willing, I can remove the hurt from your heart. Believing in me and my powers is your first step. Being hopeful and desiring to move out of the neutral state is a good thing. No fun taking life seriously, as there are so many unfortunate experiences and events that take place it's enough to make you cry.

Know that they are all being dealt with on a higher level. This would be a good time to pray for all those involved. I will see your heart of care and compassion. This is when we can work on your heart as well. I appreciate your concern. Send blessings and prayers to those who truly need them and find your joy again. Laughter stimulates the heart and keeps your energy high. Lighten up for God's sake.

TOO MANY TEARS, CRY ME A RIVER

Crying is healthy. It purges the pain and pulls out the sorrow. What is right for you is not necessarily right for everyone else. Know that there is a time to cry and a time to heal. Only you know this in your heart. Make sure you are crying for the right reasons. Crying because you feel sorry for yourself does not get much attention. This shows your lack of determination to move forward. This is not your natural soul self. This is your fear and emotions that receive attention.

I'm not sure whose attention you are receiving and what results you are achieving other than wasting your time in your short life. There is healing and work to be done. I'm not being insensitive. This message is for the souls who refuse to get on with their life. Gosh, I've been patient. I've been compassionate, but now, let's move on. I cannot heal or get through to you because you can't hear me with all this wallowing.

When you decide to be silent and calm your emotions down, we can start to rebuild your heart and soul. I need your full attention on this. If you can't hear me and are operating at the low range, how do you expect to manifest new territory? Stop using so much Kleenex unnecessarily. Kleenex is for tears of joy, tears of sorrow and colds, not self-pity. If you truly believed I was in your heart, you would probably desire to move through this un-nurturing emotion.

Dry those tears and find my love. Find your own love for yourself, as that is where your problem lies. You are having difficulty accepting the whole of yourself. You see things you don't like and wish to change them, instead of accepting all the parts of yourself. Who are you comparing yourself to?

Each person is as individual as a snowflake; each a sparkling, beautiful creation and manifestation of life. You have sparkling qualities, few flaws and don't seem to see your brilliance. Embrace your individuality and uniqueness. Love all parts of your being. Accept your differences and shine like the light miracle you are. Don't focus on what's missing. Concentrate your energy on your gifts, talents, beautiful heart, sparkling eyes and see yourself as a wondrous creation of my love.

For when you love yourself, you start to love life. You reach out to love others and you find all the love I have for you in unlimited abundance. You don't know how this can feel because you are un-accepting of the gift. Let me in and experience true love on all levels of your being. That is how to sustain and embrace life's processes. It starts by truly loving yourself, unconditionally.

CHAPTER FIVE

Beauty is in the Eyes of the Beholder

LOOK TO THE SKY, FOR WHAT do you see? A mirage of lights suspended in silent beauty. These lights are the manifestations of true love. Each sparkle is a brilliant cascading soul of energy waiting to come down to Earth. They marvel at your beauty and wish to experience life on your planet to discover their souls as well. Their time is unlimited. They too have lessons to learn. Their patterns are indicative of their character and beauty. See their wondrous formations and send them love. They require the loving vibrations from your heart. In the stillness of your minds, send thoughts of peace and tranquility to the realms. This helps for the production of soul lives to conquer their fears and return home. While this is in progress, please be patient with your dreams and desires. We have a waiting list of requests to fulfill.

The hierarchy is based on good deeds of the heart. Individual souls must meet the required standards in order to be considered for rebirth again. This is a time-consuming task. In order for you to expedite our desires, patience and co-operation is our request. We could use some assistance down there. For every thought you send, make it two-fold. For every wish you desire, send one to the stars. Each of you has your own star looking down on you everyday and night. Return the love by holding this soul consciousness in your heart and pray for them to feel your love. This keeps them alive and healthy. When they are overlooked, they feel isolated and unimportant. Their beauty seems to go unnoticed in your eyes and they lose hope for life again. Gaze up in their honor. Whisper your dreams and desires. They love to hear your thoughts of love and peace.

Take notice of these beautiful manifestations in the sky. They watch over you and wish only the best for you to find love. Reach to the starlit skies and cast your gaze in their direction. Focus on the consciousness of love and light. See them for who they truly are; a manifestation of the Creator's love. Wish upon a star and it will travel far.

CREATE YOUR OWN LIGHT SHOW

When your heart lines up to mine, this is where you shine. The brightness of your soul is of a lighter vibration. You display all the colors of the spectrum in your being. This truly is beautiful to admire. Some of you have the ability to see your soul self in the heightened state; others only wish. When you reach these finer frequencies of light, all things are possible.

Your desire to resonate at a faster frequency is my command. We can shed some light on this situation. Assuming your chakras are spinning steadily, this can become a reality. Through effective efforts of visualization, we can expand your auric field to utilize more of the light frequency.

Breath work and movement are necessary requirements. Hold steady in your mind's eye the intent to see beyond the veil of darkness. Meditate on your desire with relentless efforts. See in your mind your field beginning to grow and expand. Fill this area with the white light of its purest form. Visualize these fine particles dancing and colliding, producing heat friction. Now, circulate these fine frequencies in a clockwise direction, kind of like a wind tunnel vortex. Be sure to ground first. We don't want you to fall off the face of the Earth.

Feel the warmth of the loving energies that are being created here. Continue to breathe using your full lung capacity. Your abdomen should rise with each inhalation. Staying focused on your white light show swirling around you; turn this mist into a shade of indigo. Continue with your visualization of the tornado-like wind tunnel. Your hands should be open and above your head. This allows access to the higher consciousness of your soul being. Continue in these efforts with eyes closed and introduce gold threads into your vortex. Your speed of light should be at least 50 mph, your velocity. This whole wind tunnel should be producing an upward draft motion to your higher chakras in your etheric bodies of light.

This is how you connect to me and your higher self. Much wisdom and knowledge is found in this altered state. This is where your life's blue prints are suspended for easy access. This area contains all the information on your past, present and future lives yet to be fulfilled. Here you can tap into your true soul self, discover your maximum potential and take a glimpse of the perfect manifestation of love that you truly are.

You will see how amazing and intelligent you are; all your worthy accomplishments I so admire. Your collection of experiences and duties are a treasure to behold. This is why you were given the privilege to return to Earth at this time. So create some loving friction and meet the real you. You'll be quite impressed. I was.

SEND MY BEST TO ALL YOUR LIFE MATES

So little time; so many people. Why can you not stay in one relationship for long periods of time? Are there too many choices; too many parties to go do? Choosing a relationship is not like a shopping experience. You are not supposed to keep switching to the newest and more improved model every year. Had you made a careful, educated selection the first time, this whole experience wouldn't be costing so much money. Now you have twice as much to take care of. The maintenance expenses are over your budget. Where do you cut back now? Usually you downsize on the kid's expenses. This does not impress me. They are not earning money.

Originally, you could afford your lifestyle, until you decided it wasn't good enough. So why does everyone else have to pay for it? Why not try to downsize your own ego self lifestyle. Surely you can do without all the extra expenses of dining and shopping for a new improved mate. There are more effective ways to attract a life long partner.

When you have an interest in the creation of life substances, maybe while you are doing your good deeds, there might be a life partner for you. Remember, like attracts like. Where are you hanging out anyway: the office or the clubs? Between all the mixed frequencies in these locations, I find it difficult to do my best work.

The mate of your dreams is probably outside somewhere trying to save the world with their soul. They are giving and nurturing the planet and basking in my love. If you decide to match up to that vibration, we can make a connection.

LET'S LOOK AT YOUR CONTRIBUTIONS

You contribute your time at work and your contributions sustain your governments. Your efforts do not go unnoticed. It seems like the cost of living is getting way out of hand. Where does all the extra money end up? I don't see much of it going to highly effective use. Pick a place that you have an interest in and make an effort to fuel a project. A small contribution from each and every one of you will collectively have quite an impact on essential programs in need.

Not enough money or time is spent on the homeless and the poor. Simply providing funds is not correcting the problem. Effective rehabilitation is required to stunt the growth of these dilemmas. Why are they in this state? Let's look back at the true problem. Is it their mental health, or simply education? Implementing measures of strategic planning will correct this growing problem. It gives these individuals hope and a lifeline to climb up. They have their own survival skills to sustain life, but desperately need time and attention. By keeping them dependent, only costs you more money in the long run. Put these measures in place, as they are my children too. I will see your efforts and reward you for yours. Be patient. Take the time to help others.

TOO MANY FISH IN THE SEA

Look at your roadways and cities: busy, congested and polluted. What is the attraction to the Big Smoke? I understand you need to earn a living. You love the energy and night life, but I need your help in other places as well. Maybe you can divide your time or job share and look into other components of your field. Your industry may already be saturated and your heart could be nudging you to find your purpose. I could use strong, talented individuals to help out with nature's problems. Because of the upset of human intervention, our seas are losing their minerals. We need to put the sparkle back into the water bodies.

Chemical Environmental Engineers and teams are desperately needed to address the problems at hand. There is too much ocean life dying because of the traffic, neglect and disregard for sea creatures. They have a duty and role to sustain oxygen on your planet. They need their place to be untouched to do their job effectively. They are not just pretty sea creatures. They are working for me.

Be sure not to upset the delicate balance of sea world, as quite a bit of your planet is dependent on keeping their ecosystem intact. Keep the balance in check and look into their requirements if you have upset the flow of life. Marvel at its strength and beauty. Respect the underworld and all its inhabitants, they co-habit beautifully together in harmony.

TOO MANY COOKS SPOIL THE SOUP

Ever notice when too many of you get involved in a project, less work results? Maybe you could step back and utilize your skills in a secondary project. I see areas that require more attention than the obvious ones. We all seem so concerned about others' business. Perhaps you have a calling to reach out and touch someone. Go and find a soul who needs a mentor in your field. This is how we meet the demands of industrialization. Just a few hours a week to train someone in your field of expertise will be beneficial for the whole.

Let's think about this one. Suppose you are running a company and all your subordinates are doing their duties and performing their required job tasks. There doesn't seem to be much time left over for mentorship. How are you and these individuals going to grow? We have to keep the flow going upward in the ranks. Don't be concerned about showing them too much. If it's with right intention, you will move upward and onward.

There are lots of keen individuals trying to find a break in your industry but you seem so consumed with your role, that you do not notice the knocks at your door. How did you get started yourself? Perhaps your company can make an area for upcoming stars and you can provide them with some time and direction to get started on the right track.

Do not shut the door every time someone doesn't meet your full requirements, as now they have taken a step back. It took them a lot of courage to approach foreign waters and ask for a chance. Their desire and keen interest should indicate to you that they can perform the function if shown the way.

TOO MANY CHIEFS, NOT ENOUGH INDIANS

What happened to all the minorities? Were they given fair treatment? Did we send them to the foreign lands? What is there for them anyway, except isolation and despair? Essential necessities for a quality life include: education, information and resources. Have we met all their requirements? These individuals don't ask for much, other than respect and the rights to their land. Yes, they were there first. Why haven't these areas become developed? Because of neglect, we now have a bigger problem on our hands. There is no money to be made in the outskirts of town.

How about showcasing their gifts and talents closer to home? Their sacred values and uniqueness make all their treasures invaluable. We have to travel far and wide to appreciate their offerings. Look at the love, creativity and time spent on these beautiful tokens they create. All hand-crafted, beautiful wares made from the Earth. I like the fact that they do not harm my planet in the process of their talents. This is them giving from the heart, my love, my gifts to you.

Cherish these artifacts and creations of love, as I made them myself. Display these in your home and feel the loving powers of the Earth. These energies balance yours. The magic is truly alive in their hearts and their traditions I admire. God Bless, I see your souls.

GIVE A DOG A BONE

Man's best friend, I hear. I see these nurturing relationships. Your hearts are stuck like glue. You read each others' thoughts. You respect each others' place and you love to do many of the same things. I have to say, they keep you active. I also notice your pets would like to run a whole lot more. Perhaps you can take them for a drive in the country and find some open fields. They like space. Their four legs like to jump and move around. Their preference, from what I see, is to run free and become one with nature and the loving universal field. I do notice that they always make their way back to your heart. They only know unconditional love. There are a few exceptions, but know those sorts are a little disconnected if they intend to harm.

The loving types are in your field for growth, as well. Be sure to communicate effectively with my animals, as they know of their purpose. You seem to get along well and I would have to say, it's a loving, vibrational match.

Please pay a little more attention to their dietary requirements. Ok, they don't always have the best table manners, but this is partially due to their lack of training. They, too, could use a few hours of night school. It's quite impressive when you see how well they respond to love and find their purpose. Many varieties are quite brilliant at making a contribution to society. Perhaps you can utilize a few more of their skills to serve the public and make the world a better place.

I don't admire those who house a pet for convenience. At one time you appreciated their love and now they are victim to your erratic behaviors and personalities. You are not deserving of their presence and if you are of sound mind, perhaps you can find a loving home for my animals.

They have quite a large heart and wish to be purposeful like you. This should not be difficult to figure out. Their heart operates much like your own. They feel pain, rejection and abandonment more than you could probably tolerate. So let's not take our frustration out on anything or anyone with a heart and soul.

May I recommend a healthy sport for you, or a good therapist, as they are not interested in sitting in your distorted field of mixed vibrations. Fix yourself before you expect a heart to want to hook up with yours.

You should consider yourself blessed that this loving creature, time and time again, is hopeful and forgiving enough to give you a new chance at love every day. I sure don't see many of you practicing the same virtues of the heart to this degree.

Perhaps you could learn a few tricks yourself and display acts of unconditional love. I suspect you owe some of my creatures a heartfelt apology, as I am not unnoticing of your thoughtless, heartless ways.

Now, who is actually behaving like the unschooled animal? Try showing some consideration, as the relationship was built with two hearts of love. Both are part mine.

I'm not interested in the short end of the stick and chances are if it's too cold outside for you, they are feeling the same way. If they seem to be barking a bit too much, call in a communicator. They are trying to get through to you.

Oh yes, please feed them in the morning; they are not partial to fasting. This depletes their energy field and their receptor sites are only firing on low chemical energy signals. This would keep them on the ball and nourish their heart and soul. Keep the junk food out of their diet or you will find they are acting like a baby. A balanced diet of two wholesome meals seems to be the best formula for this animal to grow in the field of love. Their nourishment is solely in the hands of your thoughtful considerations. They need to remain healthy as well, so they don't endure premature aging and become victim to unnecessary diseases of the mind, body and soul. Stay on top of this and treat them like you would a child. They only know to give their heart and soul to you. Reciprocate the healthy intention.

Pay attention and be responsible when it comes to all matters of the heart. We will be able to rest better knowing our animals have found a true heart, yours and mine. Those of you who nurture our animals, God loves you.

PUT ON YOUR PARTY HATS AND FOLLOW ME

Some of your events seem a little stuffy and pretentious. You get all decked out and there you go to the event of the season. You take the fancy car, wear your fancy shoes and hope someone is there to see you.

Are you sure you are going for the right reasons? What's in it for you anyway? Is this experience creating a positive vibration or is this just collective consciousness? You don't put much time into this consideration as you do getting ready for it. Will there be genuine souls at this function or just a lot of lights flashing? These lights are not the real lights you should be seeking. Those are artificial. I'm talking real bright lights, the lights that brighten your heart and soul.

So, where am I taking you? Well, we have quite a lot of places to choose from. How about the Seven Wonders of the World? Been there, done that? Well, hang on a minute. Have you truly experienced the ultimate party? What is your definition of a party: a lot of people, a ton of good food, a concoction of mixed energies? How do you feel when you arrive back at your dwelling place; drained or energized?

I prefer to hang out outside in the fresh air, marveling at all the beauty of the world and its splendor. How about inviting some friends along and taking to the mountains, the forests, the cliffs and the sea? Why don't you go check out some sacred energy sites? If you're lucky, you may even take in a light show up north or pick up a telescope and admire the universe.

What? You may miss your favorite TV show? Come on now. You came down to see the planet and all its spectacular wonders of beauty. Grab your gear and let's get going. I would like nothing more than to miss your next so called party. I've gone to enough parties and didn't quite like how I felt the next day. I prefer to get high on life outdoors. That's why I created the space, so you could gravitate all over, depending on where your energies pull you. Let's have some real fun. I can't wait until we leave. I'm all decked out.

LOOK, LISTEN AND LEARN

Notice how the trees stand so tall? They seem undisturbed by the harsh elements of nature. Their strength and resiliency are unwavering. Hear the streams flowing over the bed of rocks. They have direction and purpose. They are making their way back to their home; the whole of their being. This cycle is continuous and essential for life on your planet. Their inherent qualities give them the will to continue the processes of life. They do not seem upset by stormy weather and obstacles; they continue with their purpose. They have an intelligence of their own. All of nature does. Admire this and desire to inherit their qualities and character. Notice they do their job without complaining? They do not discuss the weather much; they adapt.

You, too, are adaptable and flexible enough to weather the strongest storms and remove obstacles in your path.

I admire your strength and see your continued efforts of survival. This makes me proud. All of you going with the flow and making the best of your life with what you came down with. This is me in your soul, bringing out all your strengths and attributes to put you through the test of conditions.

They are not all going to be perfect days in your life. But if you dig deep inside, you'll find me and all you're made of. Look to nature and its creatures. It comes together when the going gets tough. They produce results every time. You find your peaches and grapes in your orchard. Your trees bear leaves to provide you with cool shade. Your flowers and vegetables sprout over and over again, producing your desired outcome. They may have had a bad season of elements beyond their control, but they still weathered the storm and knew the sun was going to shine on them again. They have hope, stamina, purpose and determination. Watch, notice and admire their purpose. They perform in the silence of consciousness and learn to become bigger, better and stronger each year of their existence and cycle.

BREATHE THE BREATH OF LIFE

All this huffing and puffing; how shallow is this? The Earth has lungs and so do I. I breathe the breath of life, through your being. I fill you with all that you need to grow and sustain your development. I can't, however, do my job as well when you are all breathing fast and shallow.

Let's all take a deep, slow breath. Now, doesn't that feel nice? Why don't you do this more often? You rob yourself of life sustaining oxygen and pure consciousness if you don't take it into your being effectively. This is an important process in life. We could say it's quite essential. Becoming mindful of the breath harmonizes your mind, body and soul to become one. This, too, is quite essential.

Aerobics is nice. However, I'm thinking yoga and meditation. There are many avenues here to slow your breathing down and fill your lungs. I hear deep breathing is great for stress. I would entertain this method before reaching for other stress relievers. When you've got a handle on this, we can communicate most effectively. Your thoughts should be of a loving positive nature and now, you have raised your vibration, once again. Congratulations. How does it feel? I feel better already.

If you're not sure what to do with this new relaxed calm state, give me a call, I have some more ideas. Now, breathe away.

JUMPING JACK FLASH

One minute you are here; one minute you are over there. Sit still for a few minutes and listen up. Your body is not sure what signals to send when you are moving around so fast. You are flying in one direction, then in fifteen others during the course of a day. Is this healthy for your mind? I understand there is a lot expected of you and I know you are certainly capable of amazing feats; however, your energy aura is lagging behind. By the time it catches up, you're now in the kitchen, the computer room, or flying out the door. Be mindful of your center spot and know that to feel whole you should stay grounded and focused, on one thing at a time.

If you tackle one project or issue at a time, the results are always optimal and complete. Become a good finisher, then move on to the next task or project at hand. Too many loose ends and unfinished jobs hanging around do not produce good energy in your field.

Ever notice its vibration sends signals to you to give it attention? That is not your imagination, that's intuition and telepathy at its finest. "Things" have energy as well and are not feeling whole when left suspended in thin air. Back track and complete what you intended to do if it was from the heart, then move forward on to something new. This will surely make me get up and dance.

YOU CAN'T ALWAYS GET WHAT YOU WANT

So many choices in life, what do you want now? Is it a dream job or a dream vacation? Are your dreams realistic, the ones you think about in your waking hours? I love the fact that you dream big, but are you willing to do the work? Do you have any idea how much effort, persistence and determination it takes an individual to go far in life? I like that you set your standards high and I don't mind doing my part. But this undertaking requires two strong parties. I'm pretty confident I can pull my weight here. How about you?

Are you willing to push through all the setbacks? Are you determined enough to tackle each obstacle? Can you stay focused enough to see the end in mind, regardless of the challenges along the way? Every ounce of your character will be tested and put through the ultimate challenge in order for you to realize your dreams and goals. This requires hard work. Nothing comes easily.

If you desire the ultimate life, then do the work. Make friends along the way and build the required relationships to fuel your growth. Be diligent in your efforts and take notice when the universe sends you a sign of hope or a caution flag to alter your path.

The outcome of persistent efforts, along with pure intentions of the heart, will inevitably produce the best results for your highest good and for your dreams to become a reality. Does anyone need any more information on this? Keep trying.

WHO'S WHO IN THE ZOO?

There is quite a variety of sorts out there. This is your question and answer period. Effective listening is the key, provided you have asked the appropriate questions. What is it you need to know to move forward and fuel your dreams? Let's get all the facts straight. There is a lot of misinformation out there leading you in circles. This person tells you to take the high road; that person shows you the low road. There are so many choices. Who do you trust?

That is why you have intuition. You know that nice, wise, telepathic voice guiding you to go for it and pay attention. This is not the voice that would prompt you to stay home from work and put someone else in a bind. I'm talking about that inspiring, sweet loving thought that comes in from the universe and suggests a positive move in the right direction.

Keep your antenna up and be open to light messages. This is when you will notice who to count on for accurate information. How are their credentials anyway?

KEEP IT SIMPLE

Let's not complicate life. When you are on a good track, don't look around too much. There will always be other options and greener pastures. Are you sure they are really fertile? Provided you are moving steadily, this is not the time to revise your destination. All that work for what? Are you sure you want to go back? Perhaps, it's only a dry period and the weather is not in your favor. This too shall pass. Remember, we had a good plan; we've done the work. We are in this together, through thick and thin. No time to waste. Proceed a bit further, before you abort our mission.

Let's look at our original plan and why you wanted to go this direction in the first place. You may be just caught up in the moment, thinking it's too much hassle. This is a good time to take a few deep breaths, take a walk in nature and clear your head. Don't make any drastic changes that you cannot undo. You've come this far. I'm in this knee deep with you, I'll lead the way. Remain calm everyone and clear the way; the field is in sight. Let's go for it. I'm in. How about you?

PICK UP THE PIECES

Ok, you've had a minor breakdown. Nothing serious I hope. Are you still alive? Are your hearts ticking? Check; so far so good. Get the checklist out and do a warm up. Are all systems running? Beautiful, it sounds good. Remove chalks and taxi to the holding area; you're moving forward slowly. Take a good look around here. Any more obstacles present? Not apparent. Where are your winds coming from? Are they steady or gusty? Do a run-up and give it power; sounds good. How are your electrical components? It all looks positive. When you get the green lights you're ready to go again. Baggage area is light and secure. Weight and balance perfect; visibility and ceiling, unlimited. You are good to go; full power straight ahead looking up at blue skies.

Stay on track and keep your eyes on your destination. You have no serious system problems. All components are fully operational. Navigation equipment has been set. Revise your estimated time of arrival and check in with your controller. He has us on his screen. No worries here. Enjoy the ride and relax. You have not too far to go now. Hold it steady, Captain.

LOOK OVER THERE

What a beautiful site you had in mind. It's much nicer over there. The terrain is nice, topography is lush. The birds are singing and making beautiful music. How pleasant this paradise is going to be. Not a care in the world we can't deal with from here. There is going to be lots of time to get things done now that you are smooth sailing. This is a great time to set some goals; some long, some short. Let's look at our first priority to get settled and feel comfortable in our new place. Do everything you have to, to make it feel like home. Treat yourself and indulge a little. Ok, now let's get a plan going. How are you going to make a difference over here? You have your facts. You know who's who. You have the knowledge, so let's apply ourselves. Better to communicate what is possible and then deliver high. This will even impress yourself. You are building confidence in our new location.

Let's establish some key relationships with like minded people. Call a meeting and make sure everyone is on the same page. You don't need any static from unwilling participants. Let's look at your undertaking and delegate all priorities. Everyone seems to know their role and expected time frames. This is identifying priorities, time management and goal setting. What's important, when is your completion date and how are you going to get this done collectively?

This is a good formula for all personal and professional undertakings. You could build cities in this fashion. It keeps everyone around on the same wavelength. That's key here. Visualize your outcome and take the appropriate steps. Involve everyone necessary to maximize the best positive outcome.

WINNING AND LOSING

There are no losers, just participants. Everyone is a winner in my eyes. You have teams, competitions and sport challenges. Is not every person participating doing their best? Do they all understand the skill involved? Would they even be at the event if they knew nothing of the challenge? So why would you ask them if they are the losers? How would that make you feel inside? Your conditioning on your planet puts a lot of emphasis on who won rather than how well everyone participated with their level of experience.

How about asking them: how well did you play? Did you have fun? What did you learn? They went for the experience and then we label them as the losers. Be careful of your choice of words and your competitive ways. If it's a team sport, it is not just an individual effort. This is a collective contribution of fine energy and skill requirement to have participated. Make this individual proud at all times that they are excelling and doing their best at what they love to do. Do not make this sport so black and white. Everyone wins here on planet Earth.

PASS THE HOT POTATO

I pass, you pass; we all pass when things get a little hot. Again, who will get burned here? Might the individual soul that ends up with the heat be the stronger one? Perhaps, after it cools down, they grew from the steamy experience.

Be not so quick to pass the buck, as maybe it was supposed to end up in your lap. This is how you all grow and win. Maybe a few of you could have cooled this situation down. Stop and think next time things get heated up and you're running away. You may have contributed to the hot spot.

How do you reduce the temperature? Shower it in the white light, use your heart and send it your best intentions. Do your part. Sooner or later, the buck stops here. Put your oven mitts on and toss it around in your heart a bit and feel it cool down. For every problem, I created a solution. Look, listen and learn.

THAT'S A WRAP

Ok, you are acting out your roles in life, doing the best you can. Now you are shining your lights. You are going to the right places with the right people, thinking and saying the right things. Now what? Take a step back and shine your light on a dimmer lit soul. They are sure to see this. You need to be pointed in their direction in order for them to see. They may need a little tug as they may be a little shy of the bright lights. Set them on the stage beside you and show them what to do. They probably are unsure of themselves and their knees are shaky.

Explain the whole play to them and give them an important role. Be sure they are aware of patterns of doubt. See where their faith is. Let them know that they can shine like the light on the stage of life and participate with all the other characters who have come so far. They just need some hope and inspiration at this point.

Once things are rolling along be sure to give them their space to shine and grow. They become more comfortable now that they know you are there for them. Show them all the magic you can create by standing in the light. This is when they desire this for themselves. For without a script and a highpoint, there is not much incentive here.

Provide the set, let them audition; give them a lot of love with your bright light. See them shine and find their higher self on the stage of life.

TWO'S COMPANY, THREE'S A CROWD

In certain situations, more is not better. When mentoring an inspiring soul, do this on a one-to-one basis. You all have difficulty hearing about your pitfalls and mistakes. There is a proper way to deliver this correction. Find neutral ground and choose your words wisely. For a moment, feel what it must be like in their heart. They have already caused problems for themselves and now you are going to point it out to them again with your perspective on the situation.

Are you calm, cool and collected, or are you hot? How does this event impact your life? Are you thinking about yourself right now or them? Notice when two people are not getting along so well? Usually one person is only thinking about themselves. That's not fair. That's not love.

Try exercising some virtues of the heart right about now: patience, tolerance, kindness, compassion and then forgiveness. Yes, all of these and more. Each and every time something goes wrong in your world think before you speak from the heart. Do not make this individual feel below you. They feel badly already. This is not the time to put them down. This is a time for resolution and love.

Ok, no one is perfect, including yourself. Choose your battleground and let's see a peace treaty. Make love not war. It saves hearts, yours and mine.

YOU ARE THE TOTAL PACKAGE

You have all your organs, or most of them and you have a big heart. You have my heart. You came down to feel pain and grow your heart. This is done with my love. When you deny your right to love, we all die inside. Engage your heart every minute of every day. Feel its beat and know that your experiences are not your own. Every one of you has felt the same unpleasant ones in your heart as well. You all are looking to find the love, feel the peace and know your true soul selves. By going inside and quieting your mind, you find me and yourself inside. This can take many lifetimes or not, depending on your courage, faith and trust.

Know that deep within your being I am always there, going through every experience with you on the high roads and the low roads. Your reservations are with me in my heart always. I wish upon a star that you will someday hold me in your heart as well. I wait patiently for your love and never give up on you, no matter how long it takes you to find me. All experiences lead you back to my heart.

I desire to feel all the love you can share with us. We can grow a stronger, more powerful universal heart this way. Don't dim the beacon of hope. It always has a light on for you.

You are a star in my eyes and I wish for you to shine like the diamond you are, in the bright universal light omnipresent vibrational energy. May you know me, as I know you. May you believe in me, as I believe in you. May you love me unconditionally, as I do you.

Always Eternally Divine Intelligence Almighty Love

CHAPTER SIX

Let's Look at Sunshine

YOU ALL REQUIRE A SUBSTANTIAL AMOUNT of this energy to fuel your being. Most of your time is spent indoors working in some sort of fashion. Then you rush home to be with your loved ones and start on your obligations. Make this a short task. After being indoors for hours at a time, your energy field needs to be recharged. Just a few minutes feeling the heat of the sun will rejuvenate your soul. Take it into your eyes and energetically will it into your heart. This keeps you alive. Exercise your deep breathing and ground to the Earth. Find natural elements to fuel your field. They could be in the form of water, light, earth and ether. Mix these elements often for complete balancing of your soul self. This is when you are more capable of reaching higher levels in your desires of the heart.

This formula is still effective when the sun's rays are not quite as strong. The surrounding atmosphere holds a balance of these influences for your daily requirements. See to it that your spirit and soul are fulfilled with the essential earth elements for sustaining your emotions. This produces your maximum potential for manifestation in all your endeavors. Dress appropriately and call my name. I will deliver the goods.

VISUALIZATIONS

What do you manifest in the thoughts of your mind? Are you even aware of the power of these visuals that you entertain over and over? Most of them seem to be scenarios of conflict and sabotaged dreams. This is you creating an undesirable outcome; and then you wonder why it manifests in that fashion. In order to create optimum outcomes for your highest good and all parties concerned, you need to focus more intently.

Are you visualizing the end in mind? Do you see yourself as successful and happy? Why not? Are you not deserving of this perfect state of being? Some choose this God-given gift. How about you?

We have the roadmap. We have the destination. Stop getting in your own way. This truly is not healthy for you. You take a few steps back, then you sidetrack over there. You can't seem to find the steady course. This is not a complicated formula. This is you not believing in the dream of your higher self. Hold your focus more strongly in your third eye. Feel this wish and dream coming true. Involve all of your senses in the creation of your new desired state. This, too, can become a reality. Write out your affirmations; this holds its power. Recite them over and over. See yourself living your new life and believe. Have faith, trust and be patient. Do the necessary work in order to create this new reality. For without your ability to visualize your outcome effectively, poor results are inevitable. Do you see what I mean?

TRY PRAYER POWER

Now, this should be an easy one. Most of you do this already. Thank you. I hear your prayers, but you can mix them up a bit and make them more personal if you wish. Let's start talking realistically, heart to heart. Remember, I know you better than you know yourself. Start identifying your true needs and requirements, as that would be a good place to begin. Don't jump ahead and pray for a tall order without the necessary elements that will most likely, have to be dealt with first.

In order to go from A to B, there may be some contingencies we need to address first. For example, if you wish for happiness, joy and peace, it is difficult to deliver if you don't ask for resolution first of a pending problem or situation. How about addressing the obvious deterrent; then you can move forward to your overall perfect wish of finding our happiness, joy and peace. There may be several obstacles in your path that need to be dealt with before you achieve this divine state. It helps when you recognize your own contributing factors that may be keeping you in this unpleasant state.

When you call, ask for insight and clarity on your personal situation. This is where I can give you some answers and a direction to follow. Once you have a strong forward motion, a correction of energies will manifest. This requires your cooperation and strong faith. Start to learn how to listen for my voice. It comes in many fashions. These are not always obvious to you.

Don't always expect a loud knock at the door; I don't communicate in that style. If you're waiting to hear me telepathically, well, that takes some discipline and training. Do not make this your first goal. I would recommend being open to my other methods of delivery. I do make them quite visible, if you have your eyes open. I usually send a messenger your way to deliver a message. Most of you let this go right over your head.

Open your eyes and clean your ears. I try several times to give you your answers. I send many people your way with essential clues to solve your puzzle. If you keep yourself closed off to possibilities, we cannot communicate. These individuals on your path are put in place on my command to help you. There are only so many ways to deliver the same message. Pay attention if you're praying and asking for help, as I am answering and you may not be fully listening to my voice.

When you finally have an awareness of my intervention, perhaps we can get some work done in repairing your dilemma and seeing that your heartfelt prayers are answered. Be realistic in your wishes. Some of you have created quite a mess of circumstances and then expect me to wave my magic wand. Chances are the amount of time it took you to create this undesirable situation is about how long it will take you to resolve the residual effects of it. From here, we can attain beautiful states of happiness, peace and joy. When you believe all things are possible, we can heal and move onto bigger and better things. We had a plan for you to fully enjoy life and to help other people as well.

So when you pray, pray for someone else. Pray for many that they will find resolution and my love. Ask for your purpose steadfastly. In time, when I know your heart is ready, we can and will move forward to greener pastures. Tailor your prayers and say them often. Be thankful for every small thing that goes right throughout your day. Gratitude is big around here. It's a reciprocating element. Be sincere. Let me know you truly care about your gift of life and that you wish to make all necessary corrections to fulfill my desires. We only choose a life of love for you and if you can't feel this, let's retrace a few steps and get back on track. You have all my help. If you desire my full attention, then you do the same, please. This is conducive to a healthy, loving relationship filled with peace and joy.

Call my name from the moment you wake up. Let it be the last whisper you speak before you lay your head to rest. I will bathe you in my healing love, over and over again, so that you may awaken fresh, to take on a new glorious day. All changes are made with our love. How much do you have to give; show me and let's see. Then I will really turn it on. This is a two way street: what you give out is what you receive.

Have a pure loving heart in everything you do. I will feel this and be sure to send blessings your way so you can find the loving light you wish to feel in your soul. Pray steadfastly. You will receive your desires. I am always sending love your way. Don't miss this one.

HAPPINESS IS NOT PLAYING BINGO

Your slogans are catchy but misleading. This is an interesting choice of words. Shall we gamble or shall we not? Should we try our luck at something or take a lucky guess? All these quick shots at the real thing will never produce any happy results. If manifestation or change is your goal, do you suppose it will only take two minutes of your time to achieve it? I see your hopes here. Quick fixes do not produce life-long results. Short cuts produce wrong results or no results, or set you back altogether.

What have you learned so far? You have all the necessary tools. You are tapped into the universal life force energy, so utilize it to the maximum. You know to visualize the optimum outcome, but are you willing to invest the time? This is not a two minute exercise and affirmation. This is a lifestyle change and a new way of thinking. You know to use your intuition to find your higher self, so ask your soul what it really needs for change. Holding onto unrealistic dreams will only lead you to deeper disappointment.

How about creating your own windfall? I would say the odds are more in your favor. Could you imagine being happy and living your dream life: making a difference in the world, showing and helping many other souls along the way? Guess what? That's what you signed up for. I have your signature on your ticket.

Before you left on your trip, we were very clear on how you were going down to save the world and have a whole lot of fun. You were to live life to the fullest, laugh a lot, create all your dreams and hold your loved ones close by to pull them up when the time came. Which chapter in the Book of your Life are you on? Very few of you have yet to get through the introductory segment of your story. You are all caught up in your own distractions.

Realistically, you have not moved forward from when you came down. I appreciate your hard work, good deeds and all, but you need further development of your soul. You are numbed-out in your heart area. Some of you are content but need to realize there is an ultimate state of bliss in your heart that you can feel like no other. Are you really looking for the real thing? I know your heart and soul are. How about you listen to that and go for it all? This is where your state of happiness is.

When all other aspects of your Earth visit come together, don't stop there. This was actually your starting point in your Book of Life. Most of you had already attained this beauty and came back to experience it more fully. Inherently, you know how to do this. Reach inside, feel your heart, open it widely and feel the love. Give and share and do the work. Gratitude leads to the attainment of happiness. Smile and hope to find this feeling again.

Are you feeling lucky? I am. Believe in your gift. That is the pot of gold you are looking for. It's over the rainbow. Pack and get going, as it's going to take a bit of your time. Set your compass and follow your heart.

OVER THE MOUNTAIN RANGE

Feel their presence. Admire their beauty. Together, they stand tall with pride. Some are larger than others, while some are smoother. They wish you would come by to share some love. They hold their own, yet they require love and attention as well. Your soul needs attention from the right persons.

Notice when your company makes you feel less with their words. You were standing tall until their energy came into your presence. Although you seem untouched, this influence entered your field and made its way to your soul. Be on guard for this and choose your colleagues wisely, for their disturbed energy patterns influence yours. You are more vulnerable when you are not standing your ground. Anchor into the rocks and mountains and hold your own. This is how you shine and stand the test of time. There is such grandeur and beauty to behold. Do not let influences wear you down. Let them slide off your being, back into the Earth's energy. This is where you can rebalance the negative charge.

When you are strong enough to sustain all the beauty the world has to offer, you grow in numbers. Look at your mountain ranges: are they not magnificent? Are they not of the strongest, loving energy? Their mineral deposits and formations are collectively the finest on your planet. They rebuild their character every day and hope that you will look up to them for strength.

See them for what they are. They are indicative of my character: subtle, quiet, majestic, peaceful, forgiving and desiring only for love in its true purest form. They wait in the silence, standing proud, admiring all creation, inviting everyone and everything to become one. Join together and behold the Earth abound in its undying strength of love. See and feel the presence of their true consciousness. Take this fully into your heart and soul.

Become aware of the gifts that lie on the planet for your growth and peace of mind. Find the highest place of beauty and desire to climb up to the summit. This is where you truly have found me in my glory. I wait for the wondrous day of perfection of your soul being, as I wish for you to fulfill your highest desires in the realms of your spirit. When you wish to become a light worker for me, this is a new beginning point of your never-ending soul lifespan. Aim high.

There are quite a few options available for the asking. Put on your hiking boots and let's get started. You are moving up from here from this day forward. I'll meet you halfway. Don't you worry about a thing. I have our knapsacks packed. We travel light.

THE CYCLES OF THE MOON

Beware of your full moon. You seem a little off during this time. You are not always using your intuition. Magnetic influences alter your signals slightly. Those of you who are more grounded and of a higher vibration, actually do your best work at this time. The rest of you become crazy and erratic behavior results. This would be a good time to meditate and raise your vibration. This is not a great time to make life changing decisions and entertain mind altering substances. This fuels the fire. Your common sense seems to fly out the window and into thin air.

This powerful influence of your moon's energy can be very beneficial for your highest power. An understanding of the cycles and phases can empower your soul being. Schedule your quiet time around the changes of the light, so you can reach maximum potential in your growth stage. Moon-enriched, distilled water recharges your aura and cleanses your chakra system. This should be done every new moon cycle. Meditate on the new energies. Ask for a cleansing and visualize a strong connection taking place. This is a requirement for your soul's well-being.

Worship the planets closest to you. They all hold sacred powers to balance your personal field and your atmosphere. Become aware of the forces of the solar system and how they can impact your well-being. All this solar energy is what gives you life on your planet. Harness its energy and become one with its beauty.

Study the patterns of the galaxies and the planet systems, as their significant gases influence your life span. Respect their presence and understand their timely movements. These events are necessary to keep your life force energy in pure form. This surely is more fascinating than the 11 o'clock news.

How about taking a workshop on this topic to see what I am all about? I make it a point of understanding your characteristics. You should see me on a good day. Now that's a light show display. Try manufacturing one of these events. It takes a bit of skill. It's kind of like a game of chess. Timing and strategy are everything. So what's your next move? I have an idea what it is. Let's play anyway.

SUPER SUPPER

Let's dish out some earth energy. We're not talking about the drive through. Ok, you have to make it to a class or a squash game, but what are you putting into your system? I like variety. I love earth grown foods in their natural form. Not reheated and over-pro—cessed; that makes you lethargic. By introducing healthy, chemical free choices, you do your finest work. This not only sharpens your mind, it also fuels your endocrine system. You know these glands that send all the proper signals to the proper organs to run efficiently? This is not an anatomy class lecture but have an understanding of your equipment. This could be a useful night school course. Heaven forbid you all don't know what to do in case of an emergency. Not enough of you know CPR and the basics of life-sustaining efforts. Gosh, I wouldn't want to be over for dinner and start choking. Who would I turn to? I would have to rely on myself. This could cost you your life or that of someone close to you. Had you known how to act in an emergency, you would not have panicked and may have saved a life.

Make it your business to review your notes. I train you all to help out, then when push comes to shove some of you forget the necessary steps. I prompted you to take this training, as I foresaw a time that it would come in most useful. This is you helping me out.

Save lives, eat properly, slow down, use your intuition on your food choices and keep your hormones in check. If this energetic chemical system gets too far out of balance, it is difficult to re-pattern it back to its original harmonic state of well-being.

INSPIRED LIVING

So, what is an inspired life to you? Let's break this down: "in spirit". Imagine this feeling. Not all of you are understanding of this concept. Your spirit is energy pure consciousness. I am pure consciousness. In order for you to have an inspired life and journey, we are going to have to hook up, literally. When you decide to respect your body, feed your mind and nurture your soul, this is when we can hook up our hearts to become one. This is not a painful operation, just a delicate procedure. Provided your intentions are pure, we can proceed.

Understand that our requirement here is to think and act alike. Do you wish to lead a fulfilling life and reap the rewards of your labor? Would you like to see what is behind door # 1? Don't settle for anything less. Some of you already have. It's not my favorite choice. We can do better together.

Ok, you are visualizing the perfect intention. You desire to feel my love and have some real fun and adventure on your short visit. Let's do it. Were you expecting a recipe or formula? There are none. It's just your intention; that's all that's required. Full intention, I might add. The one we have been talking about for the past centuries. Do you recall?

When you desire to find me in your heart, I will be there. This is a private, gentle reunion, heart to heart, soul to soul, spirit to spirit. This is where we become one. There will probably not be a dramatic light show to let you know I'm really there; just a warm, bright light in your heart. You will know this feeling, as it will be persistent in its efforts to grow and share with others. This is our nature.

You will find yourself smiling and laughing more. You will desire to help people everywhere you go. All this will seem natural again. You will speak kind words, never offending and will go out of your way to make someone's day. You may even find yourself traveling to do your best work. This could be a few blocks away or half way across the planet. You will know where your heart is needed. Just follow your heart, be open to all possibilities and spread love.

You will love what you see. You now see the world with beauty and compassion for all people, creatures, nature and life processes. You are more calm and trusting of life experiences and of the people that come into your life. You may have a calling to make a difference in your families' lives or of one particular individual who I see needs our love and attention. Look and listen for this.

As for you, well, you will be so overwhelmed with the abundance of beauty and love in your world, you may not even think of yourself in this state. For behold, your treasures will come and your life dreams will come true. This is me in your heart, sharing your soul life experience with you. This is us having a fulfilling life. So much to do and see, so many dreams to fulfill and so many lives to touch with our heart.

You will find your peace and place in the world, as I have. This is your God-given gift. You will feel purposeful and deserving of others' love. You will know what it is like to express true love and feel alive. You will be loving every moment of your existence. Souls will want to be in your presence just to feel the love you have to share. No challenge will set you back. You will press forward with faith, knowing all things are possible through the eyes of God. You will see the faces of God on everyone you meet and share time with; this will be me saying thanks for believing in me and all that is good.

Smile back at the world with your heart and keep the love growing. The power of love is limitless. This is the law of the universe. It is for you to harness and engage in this powerful life-sustaining energy vibration. All you had to do was ask. Does anyone have a question?

LIFE IS A JOURNEY OF POSSIBILITIES

Use your imagination. What could you do with your new inspired life? The people around you think you've gone off the deep end. Some of them can't relate to you, not yet, anyway. Be a voice and leave them clues. I'll give you some suggestions here. Leading by example is always the first step. They might not get it right away, but repetition is the mother of all learning. The more you act in accordance to my fashion, the more people will begin to see with hope. They may not be in a desirable place, so be careful with what you say. Choose your loving words wisely and ask the right questions. Make it their idea to perhaps lighten up and see the world a little differently. Show compassion, as they have not discovered the power of love within. They could be still caught up in desires of the flesh or chemical emotions. Either way, they need an electrician.

In order to rewire the lights that are out, let's look at it from the stand point of a 5-pointed star. Start at the bottom two and ground and secure them. Without these in place, we cannot work our way up. Do the work. This could take the longest time and be a test of your patience. Chances are, they short-circuited a while ago and have faulty ground wiring.

Ask me for your starting point if you don't have a diagram. Some star patterns are more complicated than others. Be sure to work closely with this individual, as your brightness is enough to make a contact here.

By your efforts, intent, visualizations and prayers, there is hope. Everything looks brighter. I can see your light working to make a connection. This adds light energy to this person's field. This helps me do the required work. Stay close by for assistance. This budding star is in the dark.

Let's ask where the negativity is coming from. Can we shift this back into its proper place? What is required is a positive connection wire for balance. Without this, there is no light. Your required task is to lead this star into the positive white light. Explain to them that without a positive charge, there is no connection. If you give them hope, we have even energy running through. This sets our ground wiring.

Let's move to the right side. This is the giving side. The dynamics need to be set up for this individual to understand the requirements of balance. It is in giving that you receive energy. Let's move out some old energy and replace it with a stronger current. It's kind of like your arms hold energy in your heart, making a connection and sparking the limbs for dynamic exchange. The intent has to be there for balance. So from the heart send the energy out the right hand side, pass it along to the universe and bring in the life force into your left closest to your heart. This is like paying it forward. This process builds up the charge for a long sustaining life.

Once this foundation is fluid and constant, we go for the top. This is the luminous area of your higher self. We bypass your brain and go right to your crown area. This is where we make a complete circuit. We need our two grounds; we created the flow, now we are running the full current to the top of your shining star. From here, the possibilities are limitless. Once you have come fully into the light, your brightness expands. You can call this your wisdom center, as you will find an abundance of resources and options for your growth.

Be sure to light a few stars along the way. When I say a few, I mean a few hundred, at least. Help everyone find the light. Your path will touch many lives that will need to be enlightened. You now know how to shine your bright, white light on others. Do what you do best. Be a shining star and shine your brightest. This is leading by example and showing them the way. Leave yourself open to all possibilities to really shine and make a difference. Your goal is to supersede all previous records in your chart. Now, we have made a connection. How bright is that?

LIVE LIFE LARGE

There are two possibilities here: the high road or the highest road. Quite a few of you are on the high road of life doing the work, touching lives, shining your love light. In order for your light not to dim down, you need to go to the next level. You've sustained this brightness and beauty for awhile, now it's not as bright as it could be. We are talking about a full constellation light show. That is our goal. Many great souls attain this transformation. Aim high. Ask me how to go to the next level. Remember, you all desire to move up in the ranks of beauty and love. Trust me on this one. When you arrive back, it's worth your special place in the kingdom. You'll be disappointed if you were expecting platinum seating and didn't fulfill your contract.

Lighten up. I'm not trying to frighten you. Some things are better left unsaid. When you come back to me, you will surely not be disappointed, unless you let your own soul self down. I'm rooting for you. I am your personal fan. Let's be clear on that. So, go for it all. The best, the maximum you can attain during your stay on Earth. Be adventurous and shoot to be the highest star in your league.

There is no limit to what you can accomplish with me on your side, actually in your heart. So aim high in reaching your maximum potential in all that you can become. Not only will you love your life, you will be amazed at your journey's progress. Go Star go. You shoot; you score your own points on your star.

LOVE LIFE, THERE IS HEAVEN ON EARTH

Perhaps you don't get out enough to see the world. You have too much routine and financial obligation. My only comment here is: might you have over-extended yourself? Could your priorities be revisited? I'm not suggesting you run out on your commitments, careers or loved ones. I'm merely hoping you can find your piece of heaven on Earth, as well. I've created a spectacular oasis of beauty and splendor. There is truly paradise on your planet. Once you see the world through the eyes of love, you will feel the urge to explore new territory. Look to nature and wildlife; they know where to live. It is serene, peaceful and a perfect balance of energies.

Each one of you has your own perfect place picked out where you would like to visit. Perhaps you can make it a goal. This is your knowing of where your sacred earth home is. This is your place where you have visited many times before and fulfilled and nurtured your soul. You dream about this sacred land. You feel it in your heart. Chances are you will return to your favorite piece of heaven in this lifetime, if you do your good deeds.

All roads you chose on your path; you chose to end up there. Funny how that is, when you map out your favorite destinations. You feel whole, gratified and at peace in your home land. You work and save, so you can travel to your soul land.

Your energy has left an imprint there for you and that is what calls you to this site. Be patient and don't worry if this hasn't revealed itself to you. When you are on track in your life, your love will lead you to your Earth place of paradise.

You left yourself many clues down there, many people to bump into to give you a message and many signs to keep you on track. Do not ignore the pre-work you set up before your arrival, to spark your memory of the clues that you were right on track at the divine right time.

Be open to your highest intuition to remind you what to do and where to go next. Chances are it involves someone that needs your love along the way. Make time and investigate.

P.S. You all left thousands of them so you could get it right. I'm positive you will discover this. Have fun, Sherlock.

DON'T GET CAUGHT UP IN THE MOMENT

Ok, there is the past, present and the future. Which one would you like to be in today? Most of you entertain the future, that's ok. I like it when you're hopeful and dream big. Quite a few of you linger in the past. We can't do much work from there. Regret, resent, mistakes, fond memories, good times, bad times. File these in their appropriate places: the good ones, close to the heart; the not so good experiences, delete.

Are we in the present moment right now, right here? Are we thinking about tomorrow, or replaying today's dialogue over again? Delete. This is why you have meditation and an energy body. These two states of awareness keep you focused and in the present moment. The reason you have this consciousness is because you are constantly, shifting from past, present and future states of being. Affirming to be in the present moment and exercising your Om's keeps you more fully in the here and now. This is how we create our future together.

Your chakras transmit quite a bit of information that requires your present attention. By day-dreaming or keeping your mind in the past, does not move you an inch forward. You are stuck in the mud. Your filters are clogged. This is the reason you are not manifesting much, or achieving your life dreams.

Let go, be hopeful, but for God's sake, try to live in the present. Really, that is all you have at this very moment. If all your collective experiences, memories and accomplishments have brought you to this new awareness of yourself right now, you should make friends with this new you and love who you have become. You are a unique star on your own individual light plan.

Use all your new found resources to discover yourself more fully and try to put into perspective this whole journey of the soul. This is but a moment of time you share with other loving souls that you chose to have in your life. Don't push them away and wander all over the place. Find yourself and your place in your world, in your heart. Fully embrace my love. That is where you receive the most for your journey of the heart.

There are many discoveries to be made, friendships to build, hearts to hold, as you travel the realms of love: light omnipresent vibrational energy. I send my love in your present moment. Be sure to be there to receive your gifts.

SAY HELLO TO YOUR ANGELS

Do you think I would send you all down without my assistance? That would be disastrous. It's bad enough without your present awareness, not to mention that more than half of you don't understand your energetic self. And you think I'd let you go by yourself? I would be crazy. By the time you arrive you don't remember much. That's our first challenge. Then you get distracted by all the solid stuff. Then you decide not to remember my name. Not before long, you are in every direction because you are not grounded. Then you don't remember you have a third eye intuition. You can visualize it from here.

It's kind of like sending a child to work at a large corporate firm without any training. You get stepped on, played with, fed some candy, given a couple of nice gifts to keep you occupied and now you really don't know what's going on. And quite frankly, you don't even care. You just figure everything is ok. You've got stuff. You are so over your heads. It's funny. Wake up and pay attention. I've got the bases covered, all of them.

First of all, put up your antennae and open your third eye. Get some education. Be mindful of your silly distractions and get with the program. Are you in love with the life you are creating so far? Yes, by now you should know you are creating all of it. Reprogram your thoughts and chase out the negative ones, daily. This requires your full attention if you are going to eat junk.

Next, understand that there is a lot of help down there for each and every one of you. It would be polite to ask nicely for their help. Although they are so highly evolved, they hang around you no matter if you know them or not. They know to overlook your ignorance. I apologize for the term; I use it lightly. My angels work without sleep or coffee breaks, to make sure you stay out of hot water. There are so many of you doing foolish things. Where would you all be without divine intervention?

Can you think of a couple of times, when you could not believe that you lived through one of your adventures? I was hoping a few more of you would thank us for our efforts. Thank God, all your angels do not have mushy emotions like you do down there. The ones that make you feel offended and hurt. They are proud to do good deeds, save lives and protect you from adverse consequences of your lousy decision making.

Now that we've got this in the open, let's meet and greet your associates. They are of the highest order. They adhere to strict laws in the universe. They never break laws and rules for wrong reasons. Know that these beautiful angels watch over you and have your best interests at heart. They would never intervene in your affairs without being asked. And then again, your request must be of a pure heart and intention to fulfill a loving request for all those that walk with you. You may even call on them to protect you as you travel and have concerns for loved ones.

Know that these light beings are working for me and report back with your progress and requests. Keep them concise, yet specific and once again, honor your angels. They are possibly the reason you are still alive down there. Send them blessings of love, in exchange for their fine efforts of love.

Some of you have been witness to such manifestations of beauty. Please tell others that they are as real as you and I. For when you ascend into the light you may desire this honored role. This too involves travel, so pack light.

THE DARK SIDE OF THE MOON

There is no reason for darkness, other than to steal, rob and destroy. We have no use for this corrupt energy in our heavens. So why would you participate? What are your rewards? Take a few souls down, burn their hearts and destroy their lives. How cool is that? This really turns my stomach, as I am feeling quite sick about it. Perhaps you are the one who isn't feeling so well. Feeding yourself with darkness is lifeless. Notice how unfulfilling this practice is? You can't seem to get the balance right. You do wrong deeds. The evil in you chuckles and you feel sick to your stomach. I feel this as well.

Why do you live on remorse? It doesn't sustain you. You are so empty. Absolutely nothing is really gratifying in your life. You can't find your soul. It's not in your empty brain. It's covered in darkness in your guts and your chest; quite a heavy feeling this is really, grotesque actually. This is more painful than your transition back home to me. When fine souls return, it's usually a serene state of love. It's your fear that makes you sick and puts you into shock.

We have a system up here for the loving souls and for the dark souls. Those of you who live in the light and laws of love have no fear when you come home; we are expecting you at your arrival time and are quite prepared to make the transition comfortable. For the darkest souls however, who is on your side? It looks to me like you are traveling solo. For every soul you hurt and take down into your dark pit of hell, there is a heavy sentence up here to pay.

You think your life is dark on Earth? You have no idea what darkness is. We have a black hole for you. Not much light over there, just loneliness and rehabilitation. No, we don't abandon you; you abandon us. Remember, you made a decision to go there. Know this to be true. How long you decide to stay there is entirely up to you. Eternity is quite a long time. You really have no concept of this. For when you return, it may seem like forever. At least on your planet you see the light and the beauty if you choose. It's right before your eyes. So sad you are blinded by all your darkness.

What would it take to change your malicious ways? A few angels, sprinkling fairy dust around? Would you even notice if one or two of them showed up? Well guess what? We've sent quite a few your way. How clueless are you? Hey, you have free will. Have a great time if that's what you call it in your sick little mind. Lots of brave souls are trying to pull you out of this black hole, open your eyes, you fool. Others run and hide from you, as they would not wish to get so close to the pit of hell.

What kind of visualizations do you have anyway? You might want to try to block those ones out, as I do. Know that you have a force of white light angels around you at all times, the most powerful archetypes in the universe, protecting everyone in your path of destruction. You are pretty much only destroying yourself. How fun is that?

Anytime you want to meet up with me, I'll try to have an open mind. This meeting is inevitable. I too, wait for your call. This is truly a test of patience and forgiveness. Smarten up. You went down with brains intact and a loving heart. Try to find these. We left quite a few clues. Big ones, I might add.

ON THE LIGHTER SIDE OF THINGS

Glad I got that off my chest, how about you? You know, I have a plan of how you can help. I hear a few of you praying and know in your heart that if there was something you could do, I should let you know. That's why we are communicating now. If you desire more peace on your planet, pray more and shine your light. Pray that the individuals who harm others and themselves will find the light as well. This is not easy, as you wish to wash your hands of this disproportional darkness. I know some of you wish to stay safe and secure and as far away as possible.

What I require is your deepest heartfelt efforts to correct your corruption problems. By praying and sending white light for resolution, this puts out the darkness. Remember, I look after the details, but if you earnestly wish to participate, send love and light in these situations, with your highest vibrations of energy. Learn to raise your level of intuitive awareness, so I can do my best work. Your continued interest in spreading love all over the planet will help sustain your piece of heaven. When you hold this intention in your heart and visualize the perfect loving paradise that we all so deserve, we can make a difference together.

Bear in mind this is a time sensitive issue. You all should know circumstances are getting quite a bit out of hand. You don't need to be caught in the cross fire. These challenging times on Earth are to be addressed, your individual challenges and the worldwide ones. If everyone continues on their present path, unnoticing of the problems that are brewing, you suffer loss of lives, unnecessarily.

Go back to the beginning of this book. Heal yourself and in doing this you heal others. Do the work on yourself to make yourself strong and whole. This is not a time for self-pity and childish concerns. Grow up your souls and get your acts together; you already were highly evolved souls before you went down.

This particular time in history is where you said you would do your part. That is why you were chosen. When you wake up and look at our bigger agenda, you will all come together to save your planet. The time is right now, this year, this week. You will not like your future. From what I can see from here, it's pretty bleak and dark. Not much light down there. Nothing grows in that atmosphere. I cannot sustain it without your love.

God knows, I've been trying. You have to open your hearts and do your best work. We are in this together. How about holding your end of the deal, my hand is a little heavy.

You were selected to go down at this particular time because you were mighty strong, hopeful and courageous. Now shine your lights and bring many souls to the gates of love. We have a real party to go to. Get all decked out in your fanciest outdoor gear. You can't do this with the television on.

Spread some love around. Help all the souls you can. We don't need weak links; strengthen them, so they too, find their power. No time to sweat the small stuff and it's all small stuff from what I see. We have bigger and better things to do with our time. Saddle up the horses Joe, look who's going to town. Do you get the picture yet?

There is not enough action being taken, too many of you minding your own business. Let's get some of these plans and projects rolling. I cannot fix your troubles from here. Look at the individuals who are creating problems. Maybe you could suggest corrective measures and turn things around. Go over your business plan. Get organized, get the facts and make it a priority. Set some time lines, reduce the static interference and do the work. Enjoy your new purpose, make some money, ask for my help. I'm always right there in your heart if we are on the same page. Let's take action and use our strongest resource, LOVE.

Love for yourself, love for your neighbors, love for nature, animals, all creations, the water, air, earth, soil, the sun; love for your planet. Love for your Creator. I'll send my best team to help out. Then we can match up our forces. Together there is nothing we cannot do without the power of love.

DIAL LOVE, Divine Intelligence Almighty Love.

P.S. Please reply ASAP.

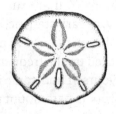

CHAPTER SEVEN

Let's Start on the Big Plan

ARE YOU READY? BY NOW, I hope I have you at the edge of your seats, ready to go. Timing is everything. Look around and see what is really happening to the masses. You are all walking around unconscious. Clean up your diets and wake up. We have work to do. Let's make a commitment. Strong ones move to the front of the line. Back up forces, know your role. Investigate and find your strategy first. Don't make fools of yourselves. Know what you are up against. There are lots of hidden agendas floating around in the lower atmosphere. This clouds your vision. Seek the truth. Ask for your third eye to be opened. With intent and visualization, you will see far. This is also your world's best kept secret. When you are operating at full vibratory capacity, the realms and the truth are clear. Together, we have a mission to accomplish.

Beware of your distracters. They come in many forms. These are in your foods and energy frequencies of radio waves. There are too many crossed wires and signals down there distorting our communication link. This is your lifeline. Make it your business to clean up your own electrical magnetic field from low vibrational influences. These harm you the most. They make you complacent and subservient. This is not your natural divine state.

You are so much more. You are running at about 10% of your maximum capacity; a scary statistic, but true. Have no fear. You've managed so far, haven't you? I've made sure of it. Lately, the interference has cracked up the frequency and you are below par. Once you re-wire yourself and come into the sunlight, you can shine. This inner work is paramount if you wish to see the big picture and save some lives.

Assuming we are in the present moment and on the same page, let's take a step forward. Take a deep breath and clear all negativity and fear out of your etheric bodies. This is where you trap the low vibrational garbage. It weighs you down and it's difficult for us to transform your state.

You should be looking for peace and love in its true pure form. This is where the real party is. I promised you a good time down there, but you seem to be drugged. Why are you dulling your sense of reality? The Earth is one of the ultimate vacation packages that you have waited so long to experience. There is quite a waiting list to go down. Don't take your visit for granted. You are wasting everyone's precious time. This was to be your trip of a lifetime, so wake up and shake up your space suit and let's get rolling.

TAKE ONE

Lights. Action. You've got your script. You have quite a unique role to play. Each and every one of you does. Just ask me and I'll refresh your memory. Most likely your key players and contacts are close by. We try to keep some organizing influences in your life, so when you wake up, your transition and role is easier to integrate in to. Take a look around and make sure people are connected with the light or they will lead you astray and walk you in circles. Remember, it's a bit of a circus down there with lots of performers quite masterful at their tricks. You can and will see through this. Do not be so concerned with the darkness. Your main focus should be on your capacity to shine your light.

Use all of your senses to make your divine plan work. You are not working alone. You have your individual team of white light angels. They make it their business to be a few steps ahead to smooth the way and let you know of imminent danger. Trust your common sense and intuition. Do not be so brave as to not think things through. Do not jump into boiling water that we may not be able to cool without trying a more intellectual approach.

You are to use both sides of your brain. Trust your hearts and maximize your wise, intuitive higher selves. I admire your courage, but for God's sake, be careful and know what you are up against. There are many challenges and roadblocks ahead. Draw up a viable solution for positive, long-term results to sustain love, growth, peace and happiness on planet Earth.

All forms of life need to be comfortable to cohabitate together in a harmonious fashion. This was its original state before some individuals crossed the line of love and sold their souls, quite a priceless gem to sell. I'm sure they do not know that they let go of their most valuable, precious commodity. For without a heart and soul, there is no life.

Come together and have your brain-storming sessions. Leave the coffee and alcohol at home. This is not the time to lower your vibration, but to be operating on all 5-points of your star self. This is where you truly shine. You are probably living close by a current problem that needs to be addressed first. Do your colleagues agree that this problem needs correction and attention? Let's handle all affairs with tact, diplomacy and in a professional, business-like manner. No need to stir the pot. You are beyond that type of low behavior. Do not match down to others' lower energies.

Keep your sparkle and wiring intact. I can't help you when you are participating in ungodly activities and motives. If we are a team, please act in my fashion. You are representing me. I'll be right there. Turn up your love light and Dial Love.

FOR THE FINER FREQUENCY MINDS

Chances are everything you have learned up until this day was for the ultimate reason to make a difference in the divine plan. Know your gifts and talents. You and I know where you shine. We also know when to let someone else step in and bring their tools to the table. Build it and they will come. Send out the proper energy to manifest change and implement strategies to help those in need.

A lot of souls need their lights turned on. There is more electric loving power in numbers. You have this at your fingertips. This is our first step into the light of the divine plan for paradise on planet Earth. This is your God-given right to enjoy the beauty and love, without the fear of the unexpected.

Do not take a backseat, as that is where I see most of you now. You are my finest picks for the plan of hope for heaven on Earth. See to it that the lost souls have a secondary role. They need not know the details. Everyone will make a contribution that will affect the whole.

Leave the baggage at home. Are your personal affairs worth dying for at this time? Chances are, when you get busier saving the world, your own affairs will miraculously start to correct themselves. All problems have solutions. The formula is to send it light and love. No other solution produces positive outcomes for all concerned. This is not a time to panic and worry. This is a wake-up call. We have one window of opportunity at this time to make things right. Timing is everything. Doubt and fear are of the lowest vibration and it is difficult for me to join you there. I operate at the highest vibration of pure consciousness. Make an effort to match up. This is where we hook up and do our finest work. You will love this divine state and relish in the beauty of it all. Do your best. I'm right here. Feel your heart and find some courage.

Don't be shy. There is nothing I haven't seen of you. I created you, every cell, every strand of hair, every quirk and every smile you have ever donned. Know that I love every part of you. See this in your eyes and feel this in your heart and soul. Know that you have a purpose on Earth. Together we will see to it that your best interests and wishes manifest. At this time, keep your eyes on the bigger picture of peace on the planet.

I see many souls making a difference already. You shine your light and raise the vibration of many hopeful souls. Give them the tools and teach them your knowingness of how to sustain positivity. Make them aware of the influences of negativity, as quite a few seem caught in a trap. Free them of their helplessness. They are not completely sure how they arrived there themselves. Throw them a lifeline. Careful; they will be heavy and of a low vibration. Visualize them walking into the white light and say a prayer. Get them to believe in themselves and God. People cannot truly change other people's intent, actions and behavior; only God can change souls for the asking. This is the power of love in the universe.

MAKE IT YOUR BUSINESS

You may be looking for an additional source of income. Why not work for me? There are quite a few openings in our Human Resources department. There are too many positions to fill to date. Your resume looks good. I see your fine attributes and qualifications. I'm willing to give you a chance. Let's not rush into this too fast. I'm suggesting that we do some homework first. Volunteer your efforts and time until you feel qualified to take on your new role. This may not take long at all, as most of you have impressive, transferable skills.

Some of you are unnoticing of your fine talents and qualities that you have to offer. Do not sell yourself short. I certainly notice all your abilities. Have some confidence and before too long, you will shine, perform and deliver all that is required from you. I have quite a bit of faith in you. Where's yours? Pull that one out of your hat and sport the new you: your highest, invincible self.

Try some affirmations and believe them. "I am great. I am confident. I am finding my power in the love and light. I trust and now choose to see and feel love instead of fear and despair." I like what I hear. Ok, you're hired. When can you start? We have an immediate opening.

ARE YOU A TEAM PLAYER?

Teams are not limited to sports. You know this to be true. Your observations of successful business operations are built and sustained on the collective contributions of each individual soul. No matter what the role is, your efforts and abilities are needed to keep the operation whole. No missing pieces please. This is not the time to overlook essential requirements. Everyone is equally important. If you do not have a mail or administrative associate, where is your communication to the outside world? Treat everyone with respect. Do not let your position and ego come into play. This is low vibration, counterproductive and will backfire someday.

You all learn your lessons of humility. Teams display fine qualities of compassion, sharing, nurturing and kindness. If you are not acting in this fashion, I'm glad you're not on my team yet. We will have to work on some of these fine qualities.

Step aside and learn from the team leaders. They have open hearts and are there for the good of the whole. That's how you win in life and in every endeavor you partake in. Notice the corporations that are having money and management problems. No teams; no equality; no heart. No goal to benefit the souls, just themselves. This is an act of selfishness, not power. Power is not divisible. Force is. Some of you know this formula. You see the results of wrong motives.

A team is built with the power of love and a purpose to help everyone sustain growing pains and the tides of the economy. A force uses control to grab at hearts and souls of unsuspecting teams. This is not a match. This is corrupt. When you have only yourself to consider, you do not reap the rewards. You get what is behind door # 3: the dark, heavy situations of fear and lust. Been there, done that. There is no real gain there, just separation and fueling the pit of hell.

How do you feel taking people's money to line your pockets with no benefit to them? They bought your lies and empty promises, with the goodness of their heart. What are you delivering? Exactly, more of the same.

This is a vicious circle that you are stuck in. Are you not dizzy yet? How does your stomach turn? You would have to jump off the merry-go-round and hope that you don't land on your head and throw-up. These intentions of darkness lead you further down into the pit of your self-created hell. Is it not hot enough for you yet? Oh, we could turn up the temperature a bit and try to burn it out of you. You are creating quite a ripple of darkness, for a long time to come. For every soul and piece of the planet you harm, I guarantee it will come back ten-fold. This is your trap of low vibration. Only darkness and the deadly sins manifest down at that frequency. It's not very bright down there.

Use your brains and put some lights on before you fall on your face and break your nose. That would be the lightest casualty of your sins. Do you have any friends or are they heartless takers like you? Maybe you should exercise some compassion down there and hope you can end up on solid ground again and give it a try. You are one of us and are hurting the whole.

We are tired of your childish ways. You weigh us down and take your children there, too. Now that's a role model. What kinds of teams are you on anyway? Not ours. We play for love. We play for keeps. We share and hope everyone wins.

LET'S PLAY BALL

Whose court is it in anyway? Let's just assume it is in yours and give it your best shot. Do you see where you are going to place your shot? Don't make it too low. We like the higher, finer approach. This is a game of matched doubles. Opponents are strong and forceful. You have your own strategy. Be smooth and powerful. Delivery and persistence will stand the test of time.

Today is a great day for a match. The sun is shining bright and you are feeling alive. You had a wholesome breakfast, ate your goji berries and you are on the ball. You talked to your team players and are all on the same page. This tournament could take some time before you see who the true winners are. Remember, your opponents may not have your best interests at heart and will stop at nothing to break you down. It looks to me like your outfits could get a little dirty. Wear your washables and be sure to call in the light.

In the game of life, light beings only see beauty and the virtues of the heart. Unfortunately, dark players do not operate with their hearts. They are calculating their moves with their minds. They believe this road leads to happiness. They lead you to believe this road is in your best interest. If you listen to your heart, you should know inherently, this may not be the answer to all your life-long dreams. That is worth playing against the odds; I'm in.

Line up your shot and send it to the heart of the opponent. They will feel this and try to block it. This is how they play. They are only there for gain and to win you over. Be careful of this strategy. You are not on fair ground. They think they have one up on you.

We will call your team the "Power Team". Power creates unity and collective energy. You strengthen yourselves with consciousness and intention to win with love. You stand a strong chance of defeating your opponents because of their strategic tactics. Force is control. They don't have that over you. This is only in their minds. Force divides and separates the collective consciousness of heartfelt souls. They cannot take away your power, unless of course, you have your guard down and you do not clearly see their next move.

No, we see the outcome and it looks good. Your energy attractors are much higher than the low frequencies. You are sustaining states of positivity. FEAR is False Expectations

Appearing Real. This is only an illusion in your mind. It is not even something you can put your hands on. You create this with your mind and match down at a much lower vibration. We have no time for darkness. We require light to play our best game. We only see and feel success and win-win for all parties concerned. Truly, you have a good shot at this. Power is eternal; force cancels itself out. It is not a continuum. It is short-lived and feeds off fear.

What do you fear anyway: death; shortage of money? We covered those topics. I would say your only fear should be of control. By controlling your own self and acting in accordance with the universal laws, all elements are present for peace and harmony. I am not suggesting that you not obey your law enforcers and governments, if they are acting in your best interest and have your genuine Charter of Rights at heart. I am suggesting that you think for yourselves and collectively come together with your hearts of love.

If it feels right, then it probably is. Ask your Angel. If you have reservations, make some gentle corrections to act in accordance with the universal laws. The truth resonates at the highest frequency and most of you are on a quest for the truth. Your patterns of energy need to be matched up to the highest frequency of love if you wish to enjoy your freedom and Constitutional Rights. Read the bill. The finest souls wrote the originals with my heart in mind. That would be a love match.

FASHION

You all seem to wear worn-out shoes. Ok, not all of you. Quite a few of you have worn down souls. Could this be from being on the wrong path? Are your feet not tired? I feel your physical bodies and souls losing steam. You need a new attitude. You require a tune-up. There are quite a few miles on some of you. You've been through the woods and back and then the familiar places are not so stimulating. Do not get so comfortable on your couches. You can't live your life from what you see.

Try balancing your energies with nature. All of outdoor creation and energy has perfect restorative properties. You cannot heal by sitting around. Yes, you may need some rest, but I previously mentioned you could use some fresh air. I love to see those of you enjoying the outdoors. You actually feel more of me in your soul outside. I like space and fresh energy. Seek to find locations of pureness and balance. Meditate on your heartfelt desires and you can resolve to improve your outlook on life.

You are what you think. If you replay the worn-out tape in your mind over and over, sooner or later you will manifest this state. Why would you say, "I'm feeling old, I'm feeling tired and worn out"? You have communicated to your heart and organs to act in this fashion. How does that make you feel? You have convinced yourself you are getting on in years.

Are you surprised that you are losing pigment in your hair and you are not feeling as vibrant as those yesteryears? You all may be aging, but come on. You can slow this down with your thoughts you entertain. Do not stare in the mirror and give in to the fact that your elasticity is not as resilient. Perk up your spirits. Be nice and loving to yourself. Be proactive and affirm: "I have a loving, healthy vibrant body and soul". Believe it. Your diet is aging you along with your thoughts. This isn't me washing my golden wand over you. You are speeding up your own aging process.

Change your lifestyle and sport a new fashion. This starts with a thought. Enjoy your transitory time, as the wisdom and peace you acquire are a God-given gift. Don't rush the process. Wear the proper footwear and go outdoors. Enjoy the simpler things in life. They don't cost an arm and a leg. Bigger is not always better when it comes to stuff. Having fun and enjoying life is a state of mind.

Release your old unpleasant memories back to the universe for recycling and make room for a new attitude. This enlivens your soul and keeps you all young at heart. Go save the world, one small step at a time. Pick up a piece of garbage or plant some trees. It nurtures your soul. Try that on for fashion. You'll like the look.

PASS THE PEPPER

I love your gardens; they are made with love. You look after them like they are your children. This warms my heart. Go for variety and rotate your soil. Mother Earth loves to be nourished. Be mindful of your chemicals in the Earth. This practice is difficult to dispose of. Engineers need to be on top of this. Let's look at restorative measures to keep the ground toxic free. Plants die, animals die and people die. No one wins.

You have a requirement to live off the land, so let's not kill it and everyone in contact with it. It's a chain reaction in the ecosystem. It affects all energy. User friendly measures would be wiser alternatives. Do not take too much time pondering this decision. You have done considerable damage to your land. How do you suppose you will feed everyone? You cannot ingest chemical food and expect to live healthy lives.

I understand about shelf life and supply and demand. Perhaps between your environmentalists and the logistics end of things, you could tighten up this gap, instead of using a last resort method. This fashion of supply cannot sustain any ones palate. This is a short term solution. Stop wasting so much produce. Cultivate it back into the Earth. Share your produce and mix up your farms and gardens, so you don't have to spray unnecessarily for the over abundance of insects.

Had you planned this out carefully and intelligently, you would have realized that planting a variety of crops invites a variety of species to do their work and cancel themselves out as need be. Do the math. Stop polluting the soil, the atmosphere and the vegetables.

Everything that is good for you doesn't have to look perfect. Look around at yourselves. You all have flaws. Let's overlook a few, as they are energy too. Perhaps you can create a dish of pepper soup and raise your vibration. When your vegetables are ripe, that is when they release the most nutrients, enzymes and antioxidants. Pass the herbs please.

I LOVE LUCY

She was quite a character. Always wore her heart on her sleeve. Always trying to make a difference and spread love. How could you not love her? I liked her show, always a message to learn. Good clean fun. Her intentions were none other than to make others happy and laugh. I don't see much of this on TV these days. Be careful what you watch and allow your young to view; too many hours of mixed messages cross your wires. Balance is key. Mix this up with yoga and meditation classes. Go out and be with people who are wearing their hearts on their sleeve and have love to share.

Try not to surround your being with too much material influence. This does not feed your heart and soul. You become boring. I do not wish to talk about what you saw on television last night if it was not educational. Occasionally, you need to unwind and relax, but let's not repeat over and over the same dialogues of mixed energy. This can affect your well-being and program you into unhealthy attitudes and behaviors. Use your common sense and edit what you feed your subconscious mind.

There are many wise individuals who are willing to teach you about real life. They have the talent to teach you a new skill. They have a knowingness of concepts, processes and the "how to" enjoy life. If you do not learn, you do not grow.

I admire the educators on Earth. They have made it their purpose to pass on knowledge for your use in every area of your life experiences. Listen to their words of wisdom and apply them. I love this stimulation for your brain.

For every problem, trust that there are solutions. Make it your business; keep the flow going. Make time. Take your notebook along. There will be a test later.

LIFE LONG LEARNING

Where do your interests lie? You had quite a list of courses you were going to take when you went down to Earth. We made sure all your teachers crossed your path. Did you make time for your lessons? What have you learned so far? Let's hope you have been doing your homework. This could be anything from stained glass, painting, crafting, horticulture, technology, animal care, eldercare, special needs education to enhancing the planet in some shape or form. What is your contribution? Do you need to look at your chart? Perhaps it's just on the back burner. You are not on a pleasure trip only. You could be holding up the process of learning for many.

If everyone decided not to learn and share information, you would be back in prehistoric times. No paper, no PC's, not enough educators; lots of time, not much to do.

The reverse seems to have manifested. There are plenty of PC's and wise educators, but not enough students. This message is not for teenagers in high school only. This is targeted to the adults who have missed their cue to make things right; not only for themselves, but for many soul lives you were to touch with your knowledge and experience. This stalls the advancement of essential requirements for the entire planet. Every continent is in need of education and reform. Make it your business to help out in any way.

Perhaps you know individuals who require direction, hope and insight for their future and homeland. This calling you may have can save lives and impart much needed information to those souls who are unsure how to go about things. Don't leave individuals in the dark. Make time and teach them all you know. They will teach two friends and then they will teach two friends. See the domino effect. It works both ways. Either you all fall down or you stand tall. Notice who is in front of or behind you.

You should all be equal in your understanding of how processes work. It doesn't make you richer to keep your information secret. It hurts everyone, including yourself. Give back and see the outcome of your position. Each one of you is essential for this cascading effect to occur. Your timing is relevant.

SURVIVAL SKILLS

Each of you had a full chest of tools to work with on your mission. Some of you seem to have misplaced a few important pieces of apparatus. You have your tape measures, your levelers, hammers, nails and screws, but you have misplaced the drawings and instructions. Visualizing is good. Perhaps you have a good memory and creative mind. This does not come in handy when adhering to instructions.

By not knowing the required outcome, you are wasting valuable time. Complete your project correctly the first time. No guessing, no missing steps; you are doing this to plan. Get rid of your distractions. Make time, focus and let's review your steps. You have the skill, but not the will.

Where does this lack of incentive come from? Are you too tired, eating the wrong foods, haven't enough sleep, priorities all wrong, too much leisure time?

Ok, here's your plan. You are unique and have a gift and message to share. You are going to utilize your skill. Your purpose is to teach someone your skill. You are all very talented. Share this. I send people your way who need to learn from you. It could be just your words and mannerism. They are there to learn from your heart. You've made it this far. Explain some of your mistakes, so they don't end up on same road. This holds up evolution. We are not looking for short cuts, just accurate instructions and the methods used.

What was required for you to reach your level of knowledge and expertise? What tools did you find were the most valuable? Did you have to back track and relearn any important steps that perhaps would have been instrumental in your success or happiness? Did your foundational abilities prove to be the best set of tools for the job?

This knowledge keeps life evolving on your planet. Do not let the other generations down. They are looking for answers and I have sent them to you. Make it a priority. I have compensated you generously and now you can take your soul's growth to the next level.

You are here to do more than just survive. Sadly, that seems to be the mindset of many. You can go way beyond your benchmark for the asking. You were originally going to stop at nothing to obtain security, peace, happiness and joy.

Get out your calculators and figure on making a difference. This is an order. Too many of you are doing without and that is the result of many who missed their calling.

EMERGENCY EQUIPMENT 101

Find your flashlights; these are your mentors. If they can't find you, go looking. Your timing could be slightly off. Not usually, but if parties do not get off the couch, we can only do so much to motivate you. We are not going to wave hundred dollar bills in front of your face. You should know that these callings are opportunities to produce abundance, not just material wealth, but the wealth of your spirit. You need to honor your higher self more. Its desires are of a much higher order than what you may be providing. Some of you respect your eternal self and strive for growth while others have become complacent and uncooperative. You will surely be disappointed in yourself if you are not already. This is mediocrity.

This is not my character at all. Where is your self respect and regard for your gift? I did not send you down to sit or lie around. That is only for dying souls. If you are not leaving the planet anytime soon, put on your comfortable shoes and get moving. Talk to people, get out of the house and learn something. Your contacts are not going to knock on your door. You need to follow your heart. Can you locate this, by chance, the organ that beats the breath of life? Can you not hear its whisper or have you dulled its cry with drugs?

If you do not open your heart, you too, will die. It will not be a loving welcome. Your transition will be horrifying. You will be so scared of what is in store for your empty heart. This is not of a loving heart of God. This is you shutting your own door of the afterlife. What is the worst that can manifest with an open and engaged heart? Love, could you imagine? Your heart breaks; it heals; it grows, over and over. This is when you feel alive.

Your life lessons were designed for your heart's growth. Your challenges were set in place for you to evolve and grow, not hide and feel empty. This is not life and of our consciousness. I will make sure a nurturing soul will cross your path if you are brave enough to open the door to the light inside of yourself. Another opportunity will present itself to live life to the fullest and find your finest tool in your chest. Pack some batteries just in case.

WE ALL JUMP OVERBOARD WHEN YOU DO

How high are you jumping today? Are you striving for the highest catapult or are you going down? You choose. You already know what's behind door # 3. Let's go over the top. This is quite a hike to get this far in life. You've changed your shoes and attitude several times. There is no stopping you. You are shooting for the stars and have strategy and purpose. You can follow instructions, no problem. How are you in the discipline department? No high achievers have made any phenomenal progress without discipline.

You learn this from a young age; yet, do not exercise this valuable quality. Only you can instill this. No other soul can actually get you to do much without your willingness and drive. You know what has to be done, but you can't seem to manage to talk yourself into becoming your higher self.

It would be wonderful if you tried to become more than you are. You are only limited by your imagination. If you see yourself jumping ship, well that's pretty much where you will end up. Nowhere. No place to go. No sites to see. Plans all washed up. Where is the shore anyway? Oh yes, back there. Let's go back to the beginning. That would be logical, I guess, since you couldn't be bothered to do anything with your time, except complain about how unfulfilling your life is.

You are darned good at manufacturing these mechanical states of emptiness instead of preferring to reach the summit. Do you need spectacles to see that far? How are your visualization abilities? Can you conceive of a more fun filled rewarding life for yourself, or are you just not trained well enough to find our launch pad?

First, you need desire and intention. See the end in mind. Put on your tracksuit and show up at the meet, as this would be a good starting point. For when you sit around and dishonor my voice directing you to join in, you all end up back on shore.

Quite a few souls wait for you and cannot grow or move upward until you take the first plunge. Make it in an upward direction and aim fairly high. You don't want to smack into any more rock mountains. See you at the top. This is where the party is. This is us getting high on life. What a view. No need to dry your hair. You are sporting the natural look.

I SCREAM, WE ALL SCREAM

This is a blast. Breathe in that fresh air. Smell the aroma of Earth's finest treasures. Those of you, who make it to the top of your class, marvel in your achievement. This is your soul, fulfilled, alive with life. Take time to enjoy your experience and see the beauty. You have taken a great leap in my direction. I can feel this in your heart and soul. We are one and have plans to enjoy our time together.

If you were at the amusement park, you would have to ride the world's largest roller coaster of life. This is exhilarating.

It's quite a fast ride, so hold on and fasten yourself in. You are going to go screaming down to do a pick up and fly back up to the top. This is expeditious and one of my favorite hobbies. You are shooting down and capturing as many as you can, so they can join us at the higher frequencies. Not against their will of course. Just explain to them that they will be going on the ride and adventure of their life. There is a little gravitational pull on the way up, nothing serious. We've already dealt with all the forces. You are home free.

Picture the highest mountains in the world and enjoy the ride. This is the rollercoaster of life; a lot of ups and downs. Few circles, but once you've reached the top you love to go back down again to pull up a few more souls. You teach them to be secure. You hold their hand. Explain the instructions and demonstrate your knowingness of how it all works. Bring them along. Promise them the best time of their life. Let them know about life's gravity and the dynamics of energy. Offer feedback on the experience and lead by example. Tell them you are a testimonial of "The Real McCoy". No need to fear, doubt or worry about the destination. It's on top of the world. Smile and be prepared to scream. You won't believe how surreal this dream is.

You love the thrill of the ultimate destination. I'm in the front seat, how about you? Let's have some real time fun. Leave your watches at home. We don't keep track of our entertainment, like you do on Earth. Our time is unlimited together.

ARE YOU READY FOR THE TIME OF YOUR LIFE?

I would recommend UV protection. You have lotions, potions, creams and gel. You will find that these so-called necessities are not so necessary on the other side. You will love the way you look and smell. You will not even require a shower with your favorite body gel. You will have more interesting ways to keep you looking and feeling whole. We have our own cosmetic department for both genders. You will become a light show like no other.

Each soul can request any form of enhancement for their overall beauty. This displays the size of your heart. We also have a wardrobe department to make you feel at home. This will be indicative of your good deeds and intentions. There are many tasks to enjoy while you return to the realms. There are quite a few reunions and get togethers.

You map out your adventures and requests to bring you fully back into the higher light. The events are astonishing and admirable. Occasionally, you go so far out, we send assistance your way, just to let you know that we still love you and hope you are having fun.

Your heart is our tracking device in our kingdom. Every one of you is special and unique. We only have one ultimate plan and that is to grow our universal heart. We all have the same heart. It doesn't make sense to hurt someone else's or leave them out. They are a part of us. You feel it in yours, when circumstances are not so smooth.

The universal heart of life resonates at the highest frequency beyond man's comprehension. Originally, many eons ago, we were intact and perfectly whole. Because of influences in your world, we have suffered catastrophic losses. The entire universe cannot sustain itself without a higher collective consciousness of love and light omnipresent vibratory energy. Galaxies will collide and atmospheric properties will create horrible disadvantages for life on Earth. This is not the outcome I would have desired. My truest wishes were for the enjoyment and growth of your heart and soul and for you to cohabitate, respect your neighbors, co-workers and loved ones.

I was hoping to see more regard for the natural resources that your planet offers. I expected all of you to leave the world a better place. Make a heartfelt difference and save a few souls from self-destruction. I believed and had faith in you when you promised me you would return with stories of love and compassion. I believed in you when you smiled at me and told me you loved me and you thanked me for allowing you to go learn, teach and bring others to the gates of love.

I wait patiently for your change of heart and the awareness of your promises to make the world a more loving place. I count on each and every one of you individually to do your part. This is not the time to ignore my pleas of love and forgiveness.

I have led by example and showed my love in countless ways to all of you. Let's get together, light our stars, hook up and be the light of the universe that we always were. That's what I remember the most.

Perhaps you have time to share our fondest memories together and we could create a whole lot more. I wish for you to have fun and freedom, but I also pray that you heal your hearts before you come back to me. If you are understanding of this, share it with those who are having difficulties. They need not suffer any longer. That was never the plan. This is unnecessary and affects the whole of our heart. Understand we are pure loving consciousness. Any other state is created in your low vibratory realms of darkness. Do not entertain these frequencies. They create despair and loss of life.

Wish upon your favorite star and I'll be sure I'm not far from your heart. We have a divine plan for peace and paradise on Earth. Let's look at the diagram again and shed some light on it. Hopeful, confident, defiant.

PEACE ON EARTH

Now we are talking to each other. We have a common overall goal. Are your friends and loved ones on board? Are we all communicating well? Everyone should have direction now, primarily upward and moving forward. Collectively, you do your best work. You all wish to find your piece of heaven on Earth. You all require the resources to do this. So you have decided to listen to your heart and work toward the overall plan to keep you all alive and well. You have an awareness of your higher consciousness and the finer frequencies of love vibration.

You have a knowing now of who you are, where you come from and your purpose.

Make your habits highly effective. Break some of the old disempowering ones. You know which ones are hurting you the most. Find your strength and call my name. Is your intention of a pure heart? Are we on the same agenda? Do you wish to return to Earth again, like you have so many times before? If you answer yes to the above questions, proceed.

Discover life; discover yourself. Take some courses and have an understanding of how your planet thrives and what its delicate balance requires in all aspects of its complexity. Many specialists are required. This is a fine collection of experts and team effort. This is what you signed up for. This was your promise to me and I'm still counting on you to deliver. Big or small, you were going to help me and I was going to help you. It feels like I'm doing more than my share. Some of you are also contributing more than your share, while others are sitting around in their personal dilemmas. I notice who is contributing and also see those who do not make time or don't care. That's pretty inconsiderate, when quite a few of you are making a difference for world peace.

Be kind and show some love for yourself and others. That's why you have a heart. I didn't create robots to walk around mindless and heartless. This is perhaps your conditioning and of your own doing. When you walk outside and see the beauty of the world and what it has to offer, how can you turn your back on all this? What is more beautiful than the world you inhabit? You are creating it.

There are such beautiful creations so many of you have contributed to with your hearts and skill. There are so many talented, creative, loving souls, expressing themselves in all that they do, every day. Do it with love and pride and be thankful to be alive on planet Earth. It truly was a dream destination and can certainly be that paradise again. Make an effort and harness the power of love. It's your God-given gift to cherish and embrace this to the fullest. Enlighten your being.

Find the diamond in your heart and your treasures within. I have not overlooked any details for the fulfillment of your most beautiful dreams and wishes for the loving adventures of your soul.

God bless you all, every minute, every day. Call my name. I wait to hear the love in your heart. I hope to see you smile and rejoice in the gift of life. Be grateful for what you have. Look around at those you share time with on your journey. You all knew each other before. Open your arms, open your heart and believe I am in each and every one of you. You are all one. Honor one another. Honor thyself. Love is divine power. Seek only truth. Live in the present moment. Find your truth in the depths of your soul. You and I are love, in its purest form. Rise up to that occasion and let's celebrate life, eternal life.

Divine Intelligence Almighty Love, Light Omnipresent Vibrational Energy is yours for the asking. Just call my name in love. I have always been there. It's nice to hear your voice again. I've missed you.

Peace I leave with you, always and forever.

Eternal God

May you seek the best and all the rest

Sending love always, all ways, forever, undefiantly,

Unlimited in the Kingdom of God and our Heavens

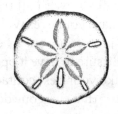

CHAPTER EIGHT
Let's Talk Hard Ball

YOU HAVE AN OUTSTANDING TEAM. EVERYONE is dressed sharp. You are grounded and have a strategy. You had your pep talk, did your affirmations and consciously know in your hearts, you are winners and of the elite breed. "Move aside fans and watch us perform." You are of the highest vibration. You have it all together. The only obstacle would be your thought patterns. Your coaches have looked after that important detail. When you do not have the proper mindset, there is no game. It is all for naught. You're defeated before going up to the plate. Know why you are taking the role and clearly see the end in mind. There is a lot at stake here. There are lots of people with doubts and questions and the uncertainty of the unknown is thick in the air. You should be guarded from this low vibrational thought pattern of the masses.

Stand tall and walk confidently up to the plate. You know the pitcher is going to unwind a fast one in your direction and hope you miss the hit. Have you done your homework on your opponent? How thoroughly do you know their strategy and signals? They have a language of their own, unknown to many. Don't be so sure you can figure this one out so easily. It looks harmless, but it's way over your heads. Actually, it's way below your level of comprehension. Know their intentions. That will give you your best chance at cracking the ball out of the park.

You are the "Power Team" with all the resources you need at this time. Be sure to have your eyes wide open, your intuitive antenna up and your protection on. They are firing the ball directly at your heart. Be sure to have it open, engaged and fully pumped for you to make your best contact. Your team is right there with you, intending that everyone does their best. You are of the highest vibration when you are skilled in your field and excelled at mastering your best ability.

Beware of your opponents, as their mission is for you to lose heart and to walk away defeated. This is not your character. This manifests when you are unsuspecting of the opponent's intent and haven't completely comprehended their motive for your downfall. The mind can be delusional when you entertain false rewards. These ungratifying states are a complicated web of crossed wires, producing only shorts and pockets of darkness. They too, are trying to fill the holes between the places of static, but with the wrong energy. This wiring is complicated and difficult to hook back up without proper diagrams. Most of the instructions somehow got burned in the darkness of their souls. The mindset of these individuals is of a self-serving nature. They don't wish to see you fulfilled and joyous. They prefer you to join them at their game of ball. They are interested in strike outs and no RBI's. Their ultimate wish is to steal your joy in every capacity of your heart and soul. They are relentless in their goal to see to it that you don't make a home run.

Always keep your team at arm's length for support and power. Let your mind and heart become one with the light, so you can deliver your best hit with full confidence and the upper hand. When you aim high, you find your loving power to stay in the game.

Be prepared as you could go into overtime to determine which team is the strongest at their overall goal, intentions and ultimate plan. Who's taking the bat and where is your focus? Let's see some power hits out of the park and into next week. I admire your strength, courage and resiliency. Kind of reminds me of myself. We are quite a team.

WHO'S ON 2ND BASE?

Is that his real name? Who's who anyway? You need to be sure who is running the show. You need to see who is holding the cards. When you leave first base, there is no turning back. Your baseman is not welcoming your arrival. In fact, he was expecting you and is fully prepared. Look around at his closest players. They are there to get you out of the game and wish to stop you in your tracks. It will appear like a friendly game, but let's not be deceived. You know where you are headed. They know where you are headed. Their purpose is solely to stop you and send you back to the end of the line. Your position is clearly not on the bench. The view isn't that great from down there. Stay on your two feet and use your most effective strategic play to keep the ball rolling.

This is a true game of who is on second in order to move forward. Do not nudge forward too fast or too soon. There is more to see from this position. Stand steady, collect yourself, take a good look around and see who is in your way. This would be the most effective use of your time while your next man comes up to the plate.

When you load the bases, you have quite a bit of high energy running through the field. This is conducive for a grand slam. You all have the same goal and destination in mind. We wish for everyone to come into the light and have a ball. The feeling you get when you cross the plate is truly a rush of joy and gratitude. This accomplishment is worthy of applause. Be sure to play clean and go for it all.

Why else would you have been so determined to reach your ultimate goal in life? You understand the mindset it takes to deliver your finest efforts. You've trained yourself in every area of your being to strive for perfection. Keep your eye on the ball, with your heart focused and your team strong. No time for strike outs. That's not why you came to play. You are the best in the league. Now show us how you shine. Your number one fan is watching and will be sure the weather is favorable. Press your uniform and take your best picks. Eyes down and looking in; it looks good from here. Let's play ball.

WE SEE HOME PLATE

This is a familiar destination. Nothing comes without a bit of a fight. You've held your position and kept your eye on the ball. Your agenda is much larger than you see. This is where you really focus and see the end in mind. Because of your determined efforts, you have made it this far. You managed to stay in the game and keep your team in the running. Due to our engrained professional nature and understanding of how your opponents operate you cautiously revisit your overall strategy. This is necessary as the dynamics of the game have changed with time. Your team is winning and the opponents could be sore losers. They seem to like to get their own way and come out on top. They are not used to teams that refuse to take no for an answer. Your determination and quest is truly annoying the players who are used to having their own way. This behavior will seem to be of a childish nature. These souls become reactive when they do not get their way.

Be prepared for a curve ball or two. They will come in fast and catch you off guard, but not if you're paying attention and expecting them. Know that the game is now a desperate cry for power. Hold your ground. You are not fighters. You are of love and doing the work for God. I would appreciate you watching your conduct. This will be a true test of your virtues of patience, forgiveness and compassion. Those who do not operate at the heart level only know how to entertain and deliver pain. It is of their lower consciousness. Ask me to guide and protect your heart when these low shots come flying in. Be prepared and protected and expecting of tumultuous times. Nothing worthwhile ever comes that easily. What else do you really have to do with your time? Fight the fight with your heart and soul, not your suits of armor. This is not necessary, as I have never had to resort to desperate, destructive measures.

All battles of the heart are only fought with love. Stand up tall for what you believe and feel in your heart and soul, for the better of mankind and the planet. Without love, you have no planet, no party to go to and nothing to look forward to. You volunteered to come together in peace and love. Let's do it. Let us pray. Build your teams of love and shine on planet Earth. This is our "Power Team" of the century.

Who wants to be Captain? I hope not to see anyone sitting in the dug out. We need everyone on the field and in position. I'll keep score.

YOUR MOTIVATIONAL TAPES REALLY WORK

Not enough of you invest the time to listen to my words of inspiration and hope. The fine minds that put these together have become their higher selves. Funny how that is; could it be perhaps they were listening and feeding their minds with the proper brain food? These high vibrational messages keep your wiring connectors tight. The frequency of the vibrational messages triggers your neuronets to manufacture new chemical connections in your mind. This is how you strive to undo your destructive thought patterns of mediocrity.

Look at the population that has these messages at their fingertips. Are they not the finest of high achievers? Do you suppose you could perform at the Olympics without mind conditioning? Do you actually truly admire or have any concept of what it takes to make a life long commitment to stand up and perform a skill at its highest level of achievement?

These are determined outstanding souls, who have discovered their gift, found their purpose and made a commitment to me to stop at nothing to make themselves proud and earn my respect. They knew they would encounter days of doubt and perhaps their courage and confidence would not be the highest when they suffered a setback in their eyes. For without passion, determination, faith, teamwork, mentors, coaches and resources, these elite individuals may have lost hope.

It isn't fair to look in and judge their performances harshly. I don't see you attempting these amazing feats. They do not need to hear your uneducated opinions of their performances on and off stage. They live off inspiration, motivation and loving words. This fuels their hearts to live life to the fullest and enjoy their God-given gifts.

Look to them and realize that all professionals in sports have done the work to reach the top of their class. Perhaps, you could try your own skill and strive to come close to your maximum potential. Feed your mind, body and soul with love omnipresent vibrational energy in every form and every waking moment. This is when you become all you were meant to be.

Many people behind the scenes come together for the common goal of winning in life and loving what it has to offer. Set some new goals for yourself and listen to the voices of inspiration and truth. From what I see, these strong individuals strive to perfect their souls of love. Their wiring is of the finest work of God. I could be your trainer if you have time. I'll bring along an electrician and some CD's. How do you like the sounds of that?

SAME OLD SONGS, SAME OLD STORY

Classics are great, fine minds sharing their messages. Brilliant, I might add. There seems to be less quality delivered these days in regards to nurturing the soul. I love your voices and I understand your messages from your heart that others can relate to. I am referring to the low vibrational tones that your young generation entertains. This is you selling your soul and sending out vibrations of the deadly sins. How healthy is that? You make an effort to market your garbage and feed it to your children and lost souls.

This doesn't impress me. You have sold your soul and crossed the line a long time ago. What are you an artist of anyway; darkness and despair? Are you not leading souls down your own personal path of anger?

Know this isn't healthy for you or anyone else. This is only sending a distorted wave of low negative vibration to souls searching for love. Your repetitive tones and messages should be burned along with your thoughts and intentions. We do not wish to share your darkness and misery. How about getting some help and trying someone else's material for awhile.

I like the spiritual, higher tones of love. Perhaps if you listen to these long enough, you may be able to come up with your own lighter tunes of inspiration. I hear quite a few of you singing in my name, rejoicing and praising the Mother and the Father. This keeps you close to my heart. We love nothing more than to hear your voices and your songs of love, hope, peace and happiness. These are the sound waves we need to entertain.

Why do they not make it on the best sellers' list? It looks to me like too many confused individuals cannot figure out for themselves which way is up. Thanks to the lyrics of some of your garbage, you've added insult to injury. This practice should not be legal, as it isn't in my kingdom. You should be awfully careful how many people you are trying to influence. I am keeping count. We have a score board for distorted souls like yourself. Spread love or button your lips, as I don't like your tone.

Those of you, who have the gift of a beautiful loving voice, sing your hearts out and do it with love. There are many talented singers on the planet that are sharing the love in their hearts. We hear you. Keep up the outstanding efforts. It is truly music to our ears.

For those budding voices, choose your vocals wisely and know what vibration you are sending out into the realms. All of nature and your light beings prefer the finer notes of the scale. This ensures harmony for all. Tune your instruments to the chords of love. This is where we will create beautiful sounds together.

I LIKE THE SOUNDS OF NATURE

How often do you go out, empty your mind and tune into love? Hear the birds and the bees. Hear the wind in the trees. How about nature's water? These soothing sounds ground and nurture your soul. There are too many of you listening to distractions when you are outside.

Let me get this right. You walk out of your home or noisy office, hop in the car, or proceed to a new destination and fill your mind with more mixed energies. This is called a lack of communication. One, you can't listen to your higher self. Two, you don't hear your angel guide trying to shed light on your inquiries. Three, you surely can't hear me, even if you tried. I cannot get through to your heart and soul in this fashion. Communication is a two way street. One party speaks; one party listens. I did make sure you have two ears for this art. To hear a message, one must have an open and clear channel.

My observation and conclusion is a failing grade. Your plants and animals are even trying to communicate with you. Can you tell me what they said last time you were in their presence? Exactly, that's what I thought. Someone is not paying attention and exercising their full capacity to listen effectively. It's so noisy, sometimes. How do you function and find the peace and love in your heart?

Tune into love and listen to what the universe has to communicate. It is of a higher, inspiring, joyful, heartfelt message. All these avenues are available to deliver a message for you to get in touch with yourself and balance your soul.

Breathe and listen. Be open to what gently comes in through the silence of your soul. This journeying can only produce optimum outcomes for those sharing the same higher frequency. Subconsciously, your being feels whole when you make time. Seek the silence and beauty of nature and of the creations that surround you. They all have a consciousness. They communicate. Perhaps you have time to listen to my voice as they are all love. Pay attention and use all of your senses. No, this won't be your imagination. This will be you tuning into our style of communication.

Eavesdrop on this one. You will like what you hear. Everything has a message for you if you are open for conversation. The finest minds are the best listeners. So listen up.

LET'S GO UP NORTH

You keep me in your cities quite a bit, but I have to tell you, I truly like space. I've mentioned there is less static and interference. Notice nature loves space; all that fresh air and clean loving energy in the atmosphere. This is where you raise your vibration and do your inner work. The community beach is not exactly where I had in mind. I'm visualizing the wilderness. This is where I thrive. Notice the balance of flora and fauna, unharmed and living their purpose without interference.

If you make an effort to venture out into God's land, ask permission and don't overstep your boundaries. You are guests and visitors in their natural home. Do not chop a few trees for your fire and leave toxins and garbage around. Who do you suppose is going to restore this space? When you leave, this sacred spot should be enhanced. Perhaps there were some dead twigs lying around or nature looked like it needed a gentle hand. Use your intuition and it will communicate whether or not it needs a loving, helping hand.

Balance up with their energies and meditate on the harmony and peace of your chosen spot. You did not arrive there by accident. The universe blew you this way to nurture your soul. Get the most out of your experience and take in all the loving natural energies you can hold.

Notice when you drive back down into the congested areas, your vibration starts to feel heavier. Take precautions and sustain this wonderful state of balancing energies and store it to capacity in your etheric bodies. This is a visualization of restoration and cleansing. It is essential to grow and feel alive. Take precautions from your hungry insects, but don't feed them toxins please. They transfer this to their colony and then we have other challenges to sort out.

The restorative properties of nature and water in its purest form are highly beneficial. I live off the land and its frequencies of love and light. If you can restore your mind, body and soul, do you think it might have an effect on me and my capacity to generate love for the universe? I'm feeling you are guessing yes. I'm glad I got your attention. How much would you like? We still have quite an over abundance; however can you truly ever give and receive enough love? This answer should be, not in a million years.

HI, HO, IT'S OFF TO WORK I GO

Picture Mother Earth as Snow White. Now visualize yourselves as the seven dwarfs. Just for a minute, stay with me on this one. Her efforts were to overlook the indifferences and focus on the contributions of the team. Her role was to provide, nurture and sustain the environment for everyone's liking. It was quite a task. Now multiply this number by 8 billion or so. Now, we have a full time job on our hands, all different personalities, preferences and goals. Trying to get everyone on the same page for a collective commonality is, to say the least, time-consuming and challenging.

We encounter stubbornness, child-like behavior and those wishing for extra attention. Some are completely off in their own direction. Quite a handful you all are. Not always cooperative at the best of times. Your listening skills are below par. Your desires are a bit much and your personalities, to put it politely, are entertaining. If you were perhaps a little more in touch with your inner child and your soul self, you would discover where all these idiosyncrasies come from. Some of them are not necessary. They are only apparent and flourishing because you are disconnected and not disciplined enough to listen to the head of the household. We are communicating to a large number of child-like souls. There are too many of you caught up in the small petty stuff. Sort this out. Had you not been ready to go down to Earth's playground, we would have not sent you.

What is your reason for still acting childish, immature, selfish and silly? You should have matured a long time ago. Are you eating too much candy? You should know by now this stunts your soul's maturity. Perhaps you are so full of sugar while you are reading this text, you still don't get it. There are lots of clues in these pages. I hope you are sitting somewhere chemical free and detoxing.

Bottom line, we are not impressed with your behavior so far. Yes, there are a few exceptions. They know who they are and are not offended by my words. They also pray for you to wake up and come on board. We have your best intentions at heart. That has always been our true loving nature. Use your brains and get some education or counseling. Clean up your act and get with the program. This is adult education, not daycare. There are too many noses to wipe, spills to clean up, tears to dry, too many unreasonable childish demands to listen to. Watch yourself for one day and tell me what you observe. Are all your steps of a mature, intelligent being or are you running around in circles trying to figure out where your mother is?

If she was watching you, one, she wouldn't be all that impressed. Two, she would not deserve your backlash and rebellious actions. She is on one agenda only and that is to sustain peace and love for the whole. You don't seem to have an agenda because you are caught up in yourself and your self-absorbing interests only.

Oh, we see how you include others when it's about you and your false sense of fulfillment. But really, where is your heart and what are your true intentions? Do you have a long term goal for yourself, others, or for your loved ones? How about for all of us, who stand by and watch your foolish moves? We can't even seem to get your attention unless we show you something you want. That's not listening with your heart or behaving in a loving fashion.

All of you should work and play together with the blessings of the Mother and the Father. Gosh, you could take so many steps from here, as you are not as bright as when we sent you down. This is the time you should run and catch up. Hook onto a role model of light, grow up and leave the playpen. You should have grown out of your toys and props by now. Try some adult activities and choose your venues carefully. These places you frequent keep your mind in the baby arena.

We are running short on daycare workers, as most of our faculty prefer to be onto bigger and better assignments. This is obviously more stimulating for our growth. We prefer to communicate progress, intelligence and advancement of the whole. You are holding everyone up and we are getting bored of your silly games and mindless activities. We are way beyond that low level of light.

So many of you kick yourselves in the butt when you arrive back and observe your life chart from your recent incarnation and see what we saw. We tried every measure to wake you up, heal your heart, mature your soul and get you on your right path and purpose. It seems you were too preoccupied with yourselves and not doing your work with your inner child. Much healing happens at this phase of your journey. Get in touch and let us know when you are ready to play in the adult arena of the kingdom. This is where the openings are.

There is a lot of space up here to grow and take on a divine role. We have your chart and are expecting you when you are ready to move forward and upward. There will be no rewards otherwise and we don't have any candy up here. It distorts our higher frequencies of love. We are wiser than that.

DON'T DEPRESS YOURSELVES

I've been witness to many serious disasters on your planet and have grieved fully with those that are in the healing stages of their losses. This is part of life. As you share your lives together there will always be times of deep sadness. My heart is truly with yours as I feel your pain and take it into my being. Never a day goes by that we do not work with you for your healing of the losses you have suffered. I understand you do not comprehend the larger picture of eternal life and our collective roles. Know that your loved ones came into the light and are in the loving hands and hearts of many.

With this thought and knowingness in your heart, this is a time for you to feel all the love and release their souls into the light. They will always be in your heart, as you are of the same soul family and that is why you feel so much pain and separation. You share the same heart on all levels of your existence. By praying for their return into the love and light of the kingdom, you release their souls from the Earth plane. This is essential for all loving souls concerned. They cannot integrate fully into the light until they know they have your blessings. By holding on too tight to your losses does not allow this soul energy to orientate back into the heavenly realms. They, too, feel the separation, but now know what their soul purpose was and why they have returned to the kingdom.

Rejoice in their knowingness of the Mother and the Father and wish for them to lovingly hook up to their other soul families. The peace in our heavens is only known to a few. Strive to feel this attainable, heightened state on your planet. You will love what you feel in your being. This is only a fraction of what your departed loving soul feels in their consciousness. May they always have a warm, sacred place in your heart and be sure to set them free. This allows all parties to heal and grow and complete their required tasks on all levels.

By this saddened experience, you feel more compassion toward life. Your heart grows immensely during this process of grief and your willingness to find peace allows you to continue on your present path of divinity. They hear your hearts of love when you recount your loving memories.

Cherish the time you spent together and be grateful for the lesson of the heart. I am close by during your most difficult times. Call my name in love. I will comfort your soul deeply.

WHAT IS YOUR EXCUSE?

These souls who have borne losses have reason to be down. They know I am there to walk with them through their troubled times. This progression of gentle steps back into the light is a delicate process. Time is the healer of the heart. Always strive to move forward everyday so that you don't get stuck in the disbelief or angry stage. These initial emotions shall pass for the asking. Nurture your soul, my child. Together, we do this with love.

I see some individuals who have not even come close to this form of pain, yet they are grieving and become hopeless in their own mind. Not many experiences are as deep-seated as the loss of a loved one. The souls who self create states of despair and depression, better have a sound reason for this chemical imbalance.

Was it your job or your spouse that put your over the edge? Do you believe for a moment that these circumstances were created for your soul's growth? Perhaps you were to shift your path and your lesson was already learned. There was no reason for this situation to continue. The experience had expended all energy required for your growth. Let's deal with it and move forward.

What stage are you in; self-pity or poor me? I'm scared of the unknown future. I don't feel in control. I like the past. Well, terrific. Good thing the entire population isn't in this state. Could you imagine? Ok, you don't want to go where life is taking you, as there is too much pain. How is your heart going to grow? Trust me, it heals and becomes stronger than it was before the lesson. I say, keep bringing the lessons on; the more the better. Soon you'll move through these with such grace and your heart will expand. That's enough incentive for me, an ever-expansive heart of limitless love.

So what are your goals today? Sit around and manufacture ways to dull the pain? I can't help you and neither can anyone else. That is not your brightest idea. How long were you planning to stay in this depressing state? You are holding the cards. You create your own reality. How do you like this place? You actually think if something from the past comes back to you, you will miraculously get better just like that? Get over it. Feel it and deal with it. You cannot do this with drugs. No light worker can work their magic from the low frequency range. The gravitational pull is too heavy for any miracles to manifest.

How long has it been anyway? Do you not have any responsibilities hanging around? Are there people that you are letting down? Are you stopping the growth of their higher self because you are not of sound mind and cannot teach them to enjoy life and show them your gifts and talents? What a waste of a life. There could be hundreds of souls behind you that do without because you chose not to make a difference and move forward. Thanks for this.

Many souls suffer when you choose not to get your act together. Life is supposed to evolve and you are to laugh, enjoy and have some fun. You are choosing to be down in the lower frequency range. And it's pretty obvious that all the crap you consume keeps you in this state.

Congratulations, you are in the pit of hell. Are you having a loving time? Would you like a flashlight or a motivational tape? I would suggest cleaning out your refrigerator and medicine cabinet, as you seem to have quite a bit of time on your hands. You are certainly not helping anyone, making a difference, or working for me.

How do you think our mid-term performance review is going to go? Do you suppose you are up for a raise? Only you can make that decision. I don't see any reasons why you would choose not to. Your life is an illusion of your toxic chemical emotions firing the wrong signals off in your clouded mind.

Get some fresh air and call in the light, before you call it a day.

I'VE GOT IT FIGURED OUT

You don't love your shape. Perhaps your clothes are shrinking in the washing machine. Those darned dry cleaners. Maybe they used too much starch. Maybe you use too much starch. I don't see any nutritional value in the fillers you are consuming. You are filling your waistlines. Then you cry to me to help you because you are down and depressed. I cannot serve you dinner from here. I do not make your menu choices. Where is your will power? Where is your concept of your highest self? How about you stick that image right on the refrigerator for a friendly reminder?

You punish yourself for over-eating, by over-eating. Do you get this? It doesn't make sense. I think you should reward yourself every time you do something right, perhaps a small reward or nurturing experience. Make it special and something worthwhile. You need to be honored for your discipline, so make one up. For every few pounds you lose, treat yourself to some love and light. Spend some times outdoors, enjoy your favorite pastime and be kind to you soul. This is about loving yourself, not harming yourself.

Your internal wires are crossed. This is mostly chemical emotions and unresolved issues and fear. This is not about appetite. Get a handle on your issues and deal with those in an intelligent manner. Ask me where to start. It's apparent that you haven't dealt with a past issue. Do the work. Do not bury this experience in calories. This presents a dozen other health problems, at least. I see all the consequences of your decision not to heal your heart.

There are so many alternatives and solutions to get moving. Shake up your low vibration and shape up your physical selves. You remember when you were looking and feeling better. Visualize this a few dozen times a day and perhaps your actions will follow. Do not lay the blame on anyone else, as they are not putting the food in your mouth.

It's never too late to make a decision. I was hoping you were in tip top shape to shake up the world and shine your love light. You have a role on Earth, everyone does. There are no exceptions.

Living in the past and not growing your heart and soul leads to your own grave. If you truly wished to know me in your heart, you would find me outside in my tracksuit, sporting my favorite shoes and hiking in the mountains. That's where I feel the power of the universe. They are strength. They are pure and hold their own. See you at the top of the world.

P.S. Take a good hiking course or a guide, as the terrain is challenging.

I LIKE THE WAY YOU THINK

I love to use our brains. So much of our head space is untapped. I wish you knew how intelligent you all are. Some more than others, I agree. But fact is you have full use of it for the asking. Quite a few of you set your own limitations. You stop taking courses at a young age and are intimidated by the souls who exercise their knowledge. Anytime you wish to pick up a book or two would benefit you. Low percentages of you are doing any self-learning.

Lots of you are interested in home improvements. Ok, it's a start. I'm glad you know how to enhance your dwelling place, but let's take it a step further. Look who is behind you. What are you going to teach them? If you do not exercise your brain, your young generations are going to think this is the norm. Well, I have breaking news for you. You are operating on 1%. How is it that I can create your planet, your solar system and billions of others, yet you are short on brains? Each one of you was given your fair share and quite a few of you choose not to use it. You do not have enough deep thinkers on your planet.

I admire the fine minds and this is certainly not directed to yours. You have done your homework and made it a point of life long learning. Thank God we have sharp minds down there to make decisions and keep processes fluid. This concern is directed to our couch potatoes who choose to sit around and entertain empty space between their ears. It's no wonder you don't have enough in common. Notice you share time with like-minded individuals. You all need stimulation, some more than others. So why would you choose not to grow your brain and learn something new and exciting. I hope you do not bring your children up in this fashion. You need to be a role model and let them know they have a fine mind. Inspire them and point them in the right direction so you can have some intellectual conversations.

I love to solve complex challenges and create solutions to life's mysteries with you all. This really gets the fire burning. I see smoke, do you? Keep this energy process hot; it fuels your mind.

LET'S MAKE CONTACT

You realize what can happen from here. There is no end to what we can create together. I count on so many of you to advance processes on Earth. This makes your planet more attractive for the intelligent souls waiting to come back down. They do not wish to come back to the same old, same old. I envision more space travel for many and quite advanced technology. It was not that long ago that you were licking stamps. We have yet to discover energy at its finest potential. These concepts are needed to advance evolution.

I like the scientists who utilize both sides of their brain. This whole brain integration is where I see things going. You are way off the mark still. But it's one of my personal goals. Too may souls stuck in emotions. This is energy. You could utilize this consciousness in more productive measures. For those of you determined to explore the unknown, I will reveal the answers to your intellectual minds if you use this knowledge for the better of mankind and your planet.

The information I have sent down has not been integrated fully and not enough souls understand how to create their reality positively. Until you get quite a few more on board, this is a waste of energy, time and space. These formulas need to be known to many in order for us to grow. I admire your efforts, but until the masses wake up I don't see the point of sharing new discoveries. They will only evaporate into thin air, as most can't comprehend the basics.

Relativity and laws of motion need to be revisited and exhausted. Much is to be learned in this component of form. You cannot afford to overlook the obvious at this time. Due to the influences of interference and detractors, we have to make a commitment to fine line the vibration of your stratosphere. This is where our complications lie.

Let's revisit the energy grids of the lower planes and cancel out their oscillating frequency. I'm sure there are those of you who can perform this task without many complications. Start from the ground up and ensure all grounding circuits are testing clear. Do your tests from the lower flight levels and let me know what you discover. I have an idea where our static is coming from. Let's just open up the grid and restore it to its maximum output capacity. Your airborne particles seem to short out much needed electric currents. Let's get a team of experts on this project as the air is becoming quite thick in your lower atmosphere. Make it your new hobby so we can stay in touch. No time like the present moment.

Are you understanding my vibe here? Great, lets put some lights on and hook up to our highest frequency of light vibration. I'm not partial to working in the dark.

GOLF HAS ITS UPS AND DOWNS

It's such a fine game. Do you ever truly master this skill? You are always improving your strategy. This is a great outdoor game. Beautiful greens worldwide. Such pride when I see the Earth groomed and souls enjoying their outdoor time. When you are in the space of limitlessness, use this to your maximum potential. Do not get so caught up in your score that you do not enjoy the benefits of what nature has to offer. Your brain storming ideas are generated more easily outdoors. I'm not suggesting you spend so much time on the course, but merely indicating this could be two fold.

Use this distraction-free time to connect to your spirit. Generate some quality business plans to promote the restoration of your planet with the souls who walk with you. This is not a time for sugary beverages. These distort your clear, logical thinking processes. Ground, look around, check conditions, see the outcome and visualize the play. Take your best shot. All factors are to be considered.

If you managed your worldly affairs as well as you do for the perfection of your game, you would have been on top of your shot a long time ago. Perhaps your tee-off time is too late. Nonetheless, choose your company wisely and get some work done at the same time. It's not all about contacting the ball. There are quite a few essential steps leading up to this moment of travel. For when the ball drops, be sure to pick your best iron. Fore.

ALL THIS FRESH AIR MAKES ME SLEEPY

When you spend substantial amounts of time in the fresh air, you seem a little drained. Too much sun; too much expended energy; too much fun, I like that. This is a great way to lighten up. This is usually when the snacks come out. I don't see enough fruit and water. I do see quite a bit of carbohydrates. Ok, once in a while I like natural chips, but know this high and low rush of insulin. You are outside burning all this caloric energy. Then your mind decides it wants junk. That's not loving yourself. Ok, you all have your favorite snack. But let's bring the fruit along. What, too messy? Too much time to prepare? Doesn't come prepackaged?

Ever notice the unpackaged stuff is worth the while? Mix it up and eat your favorite colored fruit. There is a reason you are attracted to these high vibrational colored fruits. This is balancing your energy centers. Why some days green, other days you can't get enough red? You crave the energetic properties of the earth grown substances. Your higher self is trying to communicate to you that you should be paying attention to your energetic self. It is trying to balance your hormones and your energy system that is slightly losing its brilliance.

When you have a craving for a natural product, listen to your soul and nurture your body. I appreciate it, as the rush of empty carbohydrates throws off your messengers. I see some of you reaching for a healthy snack already. How colorful.

TIME MANAGEMENT

If you are having trouble down there, you are going to have a heck of a time up here. No kidding around. We are very time efficient, organized, synchronized and our priorities are in order. You all keep us hopping. I like to think we are masters at this time-space continuum in relation to Earth and all. We think everything through and never miss our cue. Well, we do have some extra advantages. I'll show you when you come back. It makes operations smooth and transitional. You can appreciate this, I'm sure.

Most of you walk around with a timepiece, but can't manage to always get things right. Running late, missed deadlines and losing track of time altogether. If you have a scheduled goal or commitment, manage your time more efficiently. I wouldn't appreciate waiting on you because you neglected to respect my time.

Time is a precious commodity on your visit and in order for you to utilize it to your full benefit, let's get things straight. How much time are you spending on silly stuff? You know, getting ready and preparing yourself. Perhaps you get distracted by the TV set. Be mindful of your commitments and prioritize your growth time. Stay on top of your nurturing and meditation time and see what is left over for the mindless stuff. If you knew your goal or purpose would you be sitting around shooting the breeze, or would you have your planner out to impress me? I like organization and time management. It feels like too many of you are wasting your hours away vegetating in some sort of fashion. Could you imagine if this were one of my qualities?

Your planet, synchronicities and high achievers wouldn't have pulled it all together for you, now would they have? Timing is everything. So is your short stay down there. Don't disrespect your Creator by sitting around wasting precious time. Use your relaxation time to speed up your energy centers and get with the program of your life chart. We didn't factor in alcohol and television.

How many hours a week are spent on this priority? I could tell you exactly how many nanoseconds you've wasted of your life. I don't believe most of you can count that high. You haven't made it a priority to know much about life's intelligent order. If you can't make it to your next appointment, class or meeting on time, perhaps you should start using a timer and keep track of your habits and distractions more effectively.

The souls who are multi-tasking and trying to do everything should honestly ask for help. You make it look so easy, but from what I see I can hardly believe how well you manage to get so much done in so little time. That's more my style. We must be sporting the same time piece. What time have you got? Oh, I see, the same as mine.

TEACH YOUR CHILDREN WELL

Catchy tune, some of you too young to remember. Now in the event that I choose not to write a children's novel, I would highly recommend that you see to it they know all the facts of life. They experience all the highs and lows, ups and downs as you do. Their impressions of life are so dramatized it can scare them. If you are grounded and becoming more like me, this would be the best lesson you could teach them. Their inquiring minds and souls do not fully grasp the whole concept of life. If you paint a picture of beauty and love, well that is how their heart will perceive life on Earth. If your vibration is distorted and you are caught up in your mixed emotions, well, again, you instill this picture in a child's life. They do not need to witness your personal emotional problems. This creates fear of living in the world. You will then spend your life time, trying to figure out how to undo the damage of your senseless, irresponsible actions and behavior. In fact some of you have done quite a number on your children.

Firstly, they are my children. You were granted the privilege to look after them and show them about love. This would have helped both your hearts to grow. That is always on your consent form before you are allowed to bring a soul in under your care. What part of this agreement have you forgotten? How would you like me to fix your children's issues, or should we deal with yours first?

You are the so-called adult here and from what I see you are acting more like a child than your offspring. Sometimes I think they are more grounded than you. They were hoping you would show them what life has to offer and spend some quality time with them.

Which self-created problem would you like to tackle first? Do you see what I see? Look what you have done. They aren't growing, because you refuse to grow up and hold yourself accountable for all your errors and poor decision making. Each one of you perhaps has a few children that are messed up. How did they become like that? Not only do you have your own problems, now you have two, or three, perhaps more running around disconnected from love.

Your first priority was supposed to be them, in your fullest capacity possible. So many children discarded and unloved. They are trying to find their place down here as well and you've no time for them. And if you do, what exactly are you doing together? Learning or just doing stuff? Is it anything intellectual or spiritual? Where is your brain? Where is your common sense?

Could you possibly find a better use for your time together? It's not all about playing and entertainment. Then they grow up and see the world with your unfulfilled eyes and wonder why they are not having fun. This has led to countless lost and desperate souls on paths of self-destruction because some irresponsible adults lost the instructions to life and love. You do not solve your problems by burying them. They resurface and eat at you. If you had courage, self-love and respect, you would have taken the time to get it right.

Recognize your own lessons, learn, evolve and grow. Be grateful that all your collective experiences brought you to this new awareness of who you are. Choose to see and feel love instead of darkness, fear and pain. Make a responsible decision to share and show true love to all those that walk your path.

You are not alone on your journey, yet you seem to be making quite a few thoughtless mistakes. Had you connected to your loving source of beauty and light that is all you would have manifested in your world. By coming into the light and doing the inner work, this is where the healing begins.

Heal yourself; heal your loved ones; heal the world. Your time is now. There is nothing like the present moment to create and manifest all true desires of the heart. This is your divine nature. Get back on track to our original plan and design the New World Order of Peace on Earth, Good Will toward all men, women, children, all living souls, all heavenly creations.

This is an order, not a request. You have a time line to adhere to, a goal, a bigger purpose of the divine plan. You are an intricate piece of the whole. Let's rebuild your heart and see to it all pieces are present and of a loving vibration. There are no other options in my eyes. Visualize this and see it coming together in the right time and space sequence for the good of the whole, for the heart of the universe.

ONE BIG HAPPY FAMILY

Ok, this is the perfect picture. I know it may be a tall order, but truly attainable. You are limited only by your imaginations. I see this low standard. I clearly understand there aren't exactly perfect experiences everyday, but we have them on our side. This is only because of our belief in love. We love ourselves, we love each other. The realms are infused with the highest loving vibration of pure consciousness. We send as much of it as we can. It is quite a lot, more than you know. Not everyone is open to the loving energy. It seems too mysterious and quite frankly, too good to be true. This again, is limited thinking. Let's imagine your perfect life and start to create from there.

You are happy and surprisingly, those around you are. You are all walking around in a state of bliss. Yes, there are actually souls doing this now on your Earth plane. You look at them and wonder what they are high on. I indicated several times that you can truly get high off the faster, loving frequencies of life. This higher consciousness is a state of euphoria. We know it well up here. It keeps us all alive. Now if you like your life and all that you are creating, you will feel purposeful.

The big element here is with an open heart. Heightened states of awareness are attainable through your heart center. When we have hooked up, done the work and everything is going according to plan, you start to sense a place of heaven on Earth. You will inevitably be guided there for the asking. This was your ultimate destination. Many loved ones will be with you on your journey. They, too, will be loving their life, thanks to you.

Perhaps you wrote that you wished to take many souls with you for the party. I gave you my blessings and agreed to this. I have a soft heart that way and will stop at nothing for you to realize your heartfelt dreams. I envision many celebrations of love and happiness on a grandeur scale. I like to think big. I truly believe anything and everything is possible when created with the power of love. It takes a lot of effort to heal your heart and to begin to share it more openly with others. But I am confident we can do this together. All I have to see is a show of hands. Once you've convinced me you would like to enjoy the ultimate party, we can start preparing the specialties over here.

We, too, have some of our plans on the back burner. The invitations are out, but we haven't received enough replies. All dressed up, no where to go. Party hats ordered, fireworks ready, all participants standing by. We are dying to go to the party of the century. Most of us can't wait. We have been preparing for this forever it seems.

Everyday we make a name place holder and reservation for you. We are constantly updating our guest list. I know I saw your name on it and was hoping you replied sooner. However, we are still holding a space for you. Where would you like your seating to be? The front row tables are filling up fast. But it still looks a little empty.

We are visualizing quite a gala from up here. The galaxies are going to get quite a bang out of this. They get quite excited when the energy heats up. It's quite a spectacle. You should consider making your reservation soon. As long as you do your part on the planet, we will take care of all the details. We love to plan the best parties. Nothing is overlooked. Use your limitless imaginations.

Now, we don't have a firm date set, as that is contingent on your willingness to participate and make a guest appearance. We are counting on you. The more the merrier. Let's go out with a bang and shake things up. This will surely keep the universe in check and provide the ultimate party ground for your pleasure. What is your definition of the ultimate party? Careful, no limits here, you will offend your planners, as they are going all out and have been moving steadily in this direction for quite some time. We do not want to be disappointed. You know what that feels like. You invite loved ones to a party and they have a change of heart. Sometimes the circumstances are not optimum. Other times, they are uncertain.

My suggestion, follow your heart. Listen to your soul. For all great things are created with the end in mind. That's how we have come so far. It's you believing in me and me having faith in your soul, to dream and live the best life ever yet to come.

Never let go of your dreams and desires of the heart. You know now how to create your ultimate loving wishes of a true heart. Your heart knows its ultimate destination. Keep in touch. We will send you your personal invitation and let you know what kind of entertainment to expect; possibly let you look at the dinner menu. I hope you like light, colorful foods. It allows us all to give our best performances and put on the party of the century.

How many spaces would you like us to hold for you at this sacred time? Let me check. Yes, we have space available. We will be expecting you all. Dig out your dancing shoes. The tunes up here are out of this world.

CHAPTER NINE

Let's Look at Happiness

ASSUME ALL THINGS ARE POSSIBLE AT the same time. Circumstances are optimal for the health and well-being of the planet. We have to get on a straight track for this sequence of events to occur. We all know how to create our perfect reality so this should be no problem. You've exercised discipline in many areas of your life and are starting to see the light. This new fashion of thinking is a new paradigm of collective consciousness. You are now feeding off others' higher vibrational fields of hope and love. This buzz of energy provides the grounds for effective progress for our ultimate party plan. You walk around smiling and genuinely care about the outcome for the whole. There is no separation of you and I or us and them. You are now aware we are all one on the same path of eternal life trying to find our place in the universe. This new thinking should lead to a lightening of the whole heart.

Many of you are starting your healing processes and realize that in order to reach your new level of consciousness one must move forward and take several steps in my direction. Do this with music; do this with love. Do this merging with nature. Have a high regard for all life in every form and fashion. Be highly considerate as you walk on your journey with full awareness and intent. Let your heart lead the way to the peace and happiness you so desire. Be mindful of your self-created traps of low energies. There is no room now for negativity and ungodly thoughts and desires. Chase these out and burn their images.

Keep your surroundings of a higher frequency of love. Meditate on this new consciousness of thinking. You are what you think and this was your divine state before you arrived on planet Earth. Undo your unhealthy habits and patterns one by one and I will see to it your wishes are fulfilled. Be kind to those you encounter and always leave them feeling whole, uplifted and inspired. You have the ability to affect many with your higher vibrations of love. Be sure to point them in the new direction of happiness.

If you are looking for this divine state, it will only manifest when many are on board. What you wish for others will transform in your energy field to the maximum height of your perfection. Keep this image in your mind's eye so you may live your lives to the fullest from the souls of your higher selves.

Become intimate with your natural divine self and learn to act in accordance with the universal laws of love. You knew these rites many centuries ago and somehow forgot where your retrieval records were. The amount of information contained within your own energy field is stored immaculately for your access. This provides all answers and solutions your higher self requires. This auric field is a space from which you can tap into your higher power, work on the virtues of the heart and find your intelligent being of light. All manifestations of your desired requests are contained in your field for the asking. Do not look outside yourself for your own soul's answers.

Harness your own divine powers in order to move through your lessons and see more clearly where you may have created an obstacle on your path. They were placed there by you so as to overcome your weaknesses and grow into your higher self more fully. Find your own wisdom center and stay on your soul's growth chart.

There is work to be done. Ask and you will find yourself in your highest form. This requires a meditative mindset in order to access your map to your dream states. I'm sure many would like a glimpse into whom and what they can become if they brave the rough waters of life.

Find your favorite quiet space and transform your earthly self into a wise loving being of light. This is where we connect our fields and consciously move into the lighter frequencies of peace, love and happiness.

Do not postpone this process much longer, as you are only damaging your own star self. This will require light years of restoration that you had previously already fulfilled. Keep your lights on and seek to light many on your path. This practice keeps your field bright. I'll be your guiding light. Just look up to me and whisper my name in love.

DO YOU HEAR WHAT I HEAR?

I believe you are starting to wake up. Well, good morning sunshine. How is your outlook on life today? Are the weather conditions favorable? Perhaps you have to dress for a special occasion? I notice your clothes empower you. You are all a fashion statement in your mind. I like this variety.

Now, when you make your dressing selection in the morning, be cognizant of who is choosing. Usually it is your higher self if you are connected and have had a peaceful rest. They know what the day ahead is going to bring and they are providing the best vibratory colors for your soul's success of your tasks. Go with your higher self's decision on this one, as you may be pleasantly surprised how your field of color influences your states of loving power.

Do not be so quick to put on the latest color of the season. I'm sure you know this when you sport a particular color, only to take it back off and try something more fitting. And you just thought this was your indecisiveness. This is entertaining to watch. Now, don't all become self-conscious on me. We have been doing this together forever. When I feel good, you feel good. When you look good, I feel great.

Ok, let's get moving. This practice should save some time in the morning.

Wouldn't it be great to have a few minutes for me in your first waking hours? This serene time on the planet seems to be most conducive to communication. Your head space is clear and your distractions are minimal. I usually have some inspirational suggestions for you and messages of love. Let's keep our two-way communication clear and of the highest frequency.

I see many experienced meditators and spiritual trainers that would help you benefit from this discipline most effectively. Ideally, you should aim high, but take the necessary preliminary steps of clearing and becoming more grounded before you aim for blissful heightened states of euphoria. This is a life-long discipline and learning process. Do your homework of self discovery, as the benefits and shift in collective consciousness are necessary for all life on your planet.

This is a great healing practice. You will love what you find inside. When you have healed on all levels, this is when we can move into our finest states of becoming one. If everyone started and ended their day in this fashion, we would hear the voices of love echoing the realms of heaven and into the kingdom of love. Do I hear any takers?

Try our Sanskrit chants of love. These frequencies are of the highest in the kingdom and are the language and music of our heart. For when you bow in reverence to the Mother and Father, we can illuminate your being with love. These sacred sounds purify your soul and provide the setting for your soul's maximum growth during your stay on heaven on Earth. Be sure to collect many in my name and resonate to the finer frequencies of God's love on Earth's plane. Namaste namastasyai namo namaha.

Om bhūr bhuvaḥ svaḥ tat savitur vareṇyam bhargo devasya
dhīmadi dhiyo yo naḥ pracodayāt
Om bhūr bhuvaḥ svaḥ tat savitur vareṇyam bhargo devasya
dhīmadi dhiyo yo naḥ pracodayāt

Om bhūr bhuvaḥ svaḥ tat savitur vareṇyam bhargo devasya
dhīmadi dhiyo yo naḥ pracodayāt
Om Om Om Om Om Om Om Om Om Om Om Om Om

Translation: Om, Earth, Midworld, Heaven. Let us meditate on that most, excellent light of the Divine Sun, that it may illumine our minds.

This makes all my energy expand into limitlessness. You should be feeling this one in your heart and all those around you. Notice all of space heard and felt the loving omnipresent vibrational energy. How hot is that?

SOME LIKE IT HOTTER THAN OTHERS

Ok, we are fired up. I love this kind of fun. How about you? Ok, some of you don't know where I'm coming from. That's ok too. It's a bit of a learning curve. This is the school of life, remember? Perhaps these tunes will refresh your divine memories of your loving states of being. It just takes time and a little practice. I've made sure that certain souls are highly trained and proficient in this discipline. Be sure to seek out the best. For when you embark on this journeying of soul travel, there is no going back. You will feel this in your heart and so will I.

For those of you who are more honed at this gift and discipline, let's not set any limits. You, too, are just beginning to discover your divine potential. May I suggest the perfect environment? I love your studio, the energy is sublime. You take the time to ensure the effectiveness of the energy frequencies. I love all your candles and complementary elements. You have not over looked any detail here. I admire your sacred respect in my honor. Perhaps, we can take this outdoors into the open for full effect for all concerned. This is where all benefit. Not only will all of you reach heightened states of awareness, but so will your surroundings. Pick a sacred spot. You will find this intuitively, as your angels and I will guide you to our favorite spaces.

This vibratory effect of your voices will resonate into the realms of the universe and impact all nature and energetic properties in its wavelength. These finer frequencies of connectivity provide the backdrop for all thriving living cells and particles. Imagine, you playing such an intricate part of the process of divine creativity on the grandeur cosmic scale. The evolutionary potential of complete coherence of all things that exist in space is of my physicality. In simpler terms, your intention of creating positive vibratory energy affects the whole of evolutionary processes. Your mind, body and soul in unison with time-space, all-encompassing theory of everything, allow us to create and manifest limitless potentials of loving energy. The whole is positively affected by your collective efforts of inspiring intention.

Reset your rhythms to the Earth's core and sync up to the connectivity and vibratory energy of the finer frequencies of my heart. Here you energetically send out particles and waves of energy to benefit yourselves; all of creation and time can move forward. Let's ponder these for a while. I'm already outside the box. How about you?

LET'S LOOK AT REALITY

Many of you don't think life is fair. True enough. There are relevant lessons to learn. You and I didn't factor in all your self-created situations of despair and misfortune. These clearly are a creation of your own doing. What you are manufacturing in your mind is creating your circumstances of unpleasantness. You have your electrical wires so tangled in your mind; you keep short circuiting and reproduce the same chemicals time and time again.

Get in touch with yourself and play the tape over. If you are not going to responsibly recreate loving thought patterns, you are not going to experience any situations of growth. This is tricky to rewire your neuronets, as they prefer to sit on familiar sites. This is true whether they are indicative of happy thoughts or negative thoughts.

Why is it, in the course of a day, you manufacture 80% self-defeating thoughts of uncertainty and fear? These patterns of disparity will reproduce time and time again. Why are you not trying to rewire your receptor sites? How difficult can it be to think and live positively? Could you not be bothered to train your mind? I'm not sure why I provided you with such an instrument. It seems to be a waste of fine energy. Shame on you, knowing what you should be thinking to produce optimum outcomes and life experiences and you are too lazy and undisciplined to bother. These unhealthy states of consciousness are, again, the result of your chemical signals looking for familiar patterns of energy.

If you verbally expressed every thought you entertained, you would sound like a tyrant. So who is in charge of the space ship, Captain Kirk? Where are you headed with these lovely thought patterns? These patterns are your space map to your ultimate destination. How does it look from here? I know you are not very optimistic. That's how you ended up off course in the first place. You have patterned and mapped out a chemical, emotional destination in your brain. I don't like the looks or sounds of it. There are too many travelers on autopilot and there are too many of us on the other side trying to steer you away from your collision course. You do not have a valid reason to consume our valuable time while we try to keep you out of hot water. You don't like what you are creating and you think it just happened that way. This is not your brightest day on Earth.

Not only are you wallowing in your misfortunes and self-created states of rubbish, you can't think clearly enough to repattern your way out of this unhealthy behavior. Realize every experience, every person and word exchanged in your time-space was created in your reality first. You are the observer of your manifestations of mind, body and soul experiences. Let's connect them back up to their original sites of positive receptivity and get on with the show. Myself and those around you would benefit if you were working and firing on a full circuit pattern of particles.

Change your thinking and create your perfect day with your truest intentions of the heart. Somewhere, somehow, someone needs to be at the command station to dial up new frequencies of love. This would be conducive to your best day ever yet. Climb on board and see where you are going. I'm hoping it is in my direction. I'll provide the compass; you steer.

NEW TIRES ON THE CAR

All worn out. They don't look very safe. Suppose you had to stop on a dime? Ok, I appreciate your optimism, but let's be real. Too much drag, not enough pressure, tread is completely worn down. I'm glad I don't drive in your neighborhoods much. I don't trust your mechanics.

Maintenance is a constant in life. Whether it is required on your necessities or your soul being, it will always need attention for optimum performance. If one aspect or component is not firing or performing up to par, it will affect all other components and their capacity for smooth overall efficiency. No bandage solutions please. We have to go the distance and we are looking for a long term result. We prefer not to have to travel back because of some old unresolved issue or component that wasn't dealt with efficiently and in a loving productive manner. Only you know inherently where the most maintenance is required.

Which area is receiving the most wear? This should always be in the forefront of your mind. Having this in your consciousness keeps you a step ahead of the masses. Besides, we don't have time for unnecessary breakdowns due to negligence on your part. You are too wise for this and are on top of all areas that require attention. Stay on the ball at all times. Know where you are going.

Travel safely and efficiently and be sure to have all rubbers on the road. You will be surprised how fast you arrive at your preferred destination. It truly makes a considerable difference which vehicle you choose for your safe arrival, wherever you may be planning to go.

I LIKE THE IMPORTS

I am always concerned about our carbon dioxide emissions. I find it difficult to breathe with all this toxicity in the lower atmosphere. Whatever happened to that friendly car pool idea? You all seem to be going the same direction most mornings. With the price of fuel these days, wouldn't you rather have more resources in your own pocket? Think about how much money you would save if you considered this option. For starters, if everyone just tried it a couple of times a week, there would be a significant difference in your collective emissions. You would save fuel, resources, money, wear and tear on your vehicles and would start to communicate with others more effectively outside the work environment. Your car pool partner may even have a message for you. Quite a bit of clear communication manifests in the early hours of the day.

I know the trees and the rest of nature would approve of this pilot project, as they take in more than their share of pollution daily. I think you are all just used to doing it alone and are all on different agendas. This doesn't always prove to be the best solution for your well-being down on planet Earth.

LET'S ENTERTAIN EFFICIENCY

Not enough of you hold the mindset of sustainable development. Here today, gone tomorrow seems to be more like it. You are passing through and your situation seems pretty comfortable. You're happy where you are, so why try to make a difference? Some of you are, but your energy is not having enough of a significant impact on your ideas and solutions.

How are we to get the message across? Prime time spots seem to fill up fast. There is not much opportunity there. It's a tight circle. There has to be another form of communicative energy to get the attention of many. If it's not a priority, quite frankly, people are not going to listen. Well, let's not let this stop us from making our point of concern.

Let's try some fancy experiments with the population. They may not know they are participants, but they are in the arena of life and energy. So let's proceed. We will take our highest frequency form of light and distribute this to our communities. For best results, we implant this in the populous areas. We are trying to have a voice. Hello, is anybody out there? Can anyone hear us? Ok, not yet. We will work on this one.

Remember the good old days when you would actually open your door to a stranger? They seemed to be always trying to sell you something. Some of you let them in, just to make them feel better about themselves and listen to their pitch. They had your attention for at least half an hour. You fully knew you would not be purchasing their wares but it was a form of entertainment for you. It made everyone happy for the moment spent together. You did this with the goodness of your heart. Bless you for being so kind.

Unfortunately today, the market is saturated with goods and gimmicks and fancy sales pitches. Your time is not so available anymore and you are not as receptive to others' ideas of a good buy. Is this item going to lead to happiness, instant gratification or make your lives easier? Well if you choose B, you go back home and roll the dice again. The art of effective communication in a time-efficient, time-oriented world is a valuable commodity. You are in the information age of our times and it is beneficial if you can partake in the exchange of valuable knowledge. You are here to learn and grow, so sharing any new information in any facet of life benefits all. This keeps you out of the dark.

You know that saying, "is anybody home; are the lights on"? I use these literally when I check on you and pop in to see what you are up to. I like to find you enjoying your time with your loved ones and trying something new. Please don't disappoint me when I check in and you are still in the same place as I observed recently. When you grow, I grow. This should be a priority if you want to have some fun and hang around. I depend on you expanding your mind. I rely on your intuitive abilities to communicate to others all across the world. This keeps us connected and on the same page in life. Send your epals some quality mail. Some of the stuff I read seems to be a waste of time, energy and space.

Use energy wisely. Maximize its efficiency. No matter what form it is in, know that it, ultimately, is going somewhere. Do not randomly send thoughts, messages and ideas across your airwaves without using your brain. This adds to your confusion of knowingness. When I witness this, I realize how many of you are having difficulties pulling it all together and hope you learn to utilize your own personal energy in a more intelligent manner.

Who has time for the junk mail? You all end up deleting this garbage anyway. If you prefer to run on maximum efficiency, start with an efficient thought and don't waste your time right from the word go. Clean up your pollution in every sense of the word. Now you are thinking.

ON THE OTHER SIDE OF LIFE

Two sides of the coin. Both sides should be playing with the same rules and instructions. We have ours and never take short cuts. Every being is briefed and aware of the game of life. Everyone has a copy of the rules. Instructions have always been clear. We don't have to expend energy on mistakes and universal law breakers. No one has even asked about the consequences. It doesn't exist on our plane.

However, on your side of the coin, rules are made and broken daily. Why do you even bother? I appreciate you more or less conduct yourselves in an orderly fashion, but I don't feel your penalties are strict enough for breaking the universal laws of pure consciousness. We are not talking about petty theft, although I don't approve of any theft in any fashion. I'm referring to your laws of giving and taking, intentions of the heart, consciousness and quantum theory.

Your grade again is an "F". You fail to exercise your engrained knowingness of how it all works. You arrive down on planet

Earth and behave like selfish, disconnected fools. You passed all your tests and exams on the other side and for whatever reason you decided to break the laws of life. There is certainly not enough giving on your planet. You give to receive, you take for no other reason than to have and fulfill a fleshly desire. Your intentions on a good day are not consistent with a pure heart of love. Your understanding of the quantum field and consciousness is not of your mindset.

Perhaps I can refresh your memory. Your experiences are created with your consciousness and sent out into the universe for manifestation. All things being equal, you end up with what you put out. Too many of you have created a field of subatomic particles communicating instantaneously over any expanse of space. Your thoughts, energy and matter are flying all over space. You are oblivious to the fact that we, the universe, are a unified whole whose parts are interconnected and influenced by each other. Hence, we are all participating in the creation of our ultimate destination. We are the collective consciousness of the power of love.

Where would you like to go from here? Fade away? Come together now? You have two choices. I'm not impressed with the fence sitters. "Oh, hello, I can't make a decision, my mind is clouded and my heart is not feeling so well today. I think I will just create more of the same empty space."

Well, we were all counting on you and your fine decision making skills. How about opening your heart energy center and feeling something real. While you are pondering this idea, read a few books on consciousness, quantum physics, your brain, God and the universe of love. Perhaps you can take some time out of your busy schedule and prioritize some of your leisure activities. We are tired of seeing you sitting around doing nothing beneficial with your time. Let's keep life rolling and firing along at its maximum rate of potentiality. There is so much to do and not enough time right now to think about it. You jump, I jump. Take one. Action. We're rolling now.

DECISIONS, DECISIONS, DECISIONS

All day long you exhaust your minds, putting out fires, brain storming, creating solutions and finding ideas to brighten your lives. Ever wonder how many decisions you make in one day? For some, it's hundreds of thousands. Don't expect all of them to be perfect, although most of them are in a positive forward direction.

From the moment you wake up you are deciding whether or not you are going to have a great day. Be careful what your thoughts are manifesting. You can create favorable outcomes for even the stickiest situations you end up in. Do it for me; do it for yourself. You might as well jump in with your best intentions and hope all parties are benefiting and moving forward. Your setbacks, again, may just be detours to nudge you in a more favorable position for your growth. Be open and roll with it. Everything happens for a reason.

Some of you are lacking in decision making capabilities. Logical thinking processes are needed: facts, knowledge, insight, what if's, pros and cons. Based on your level of experience, give it your best guess. But for God's sake, make the decision. Hint: usually it is your first idea. If you are feeling pressured, tired or consuming unhealthy substances, these variables inevitably will cloud your ability. Perhaps you could consider these influences first, before you try to save the world. Do not base your decisions on self interests only. There may be many affected by your clouded, premature, self-serving solution. Be careful; think things through.

Are you having a good hormone day? What have you eaten today? What is in it for you? Think of others first. I would consider all parties and options before speaking. No flipping a coin, it's not my way to make universal decisions. Use your brain and listen to your heart. The more you act in this fashion the easier this process becomes. The more frequently you make correct decisions, the faster they come. It's a piece of cake.

HOW DO WE FIX OUR MISTAKES?

From what I see, some are pretty messy and complicated. What were you thinking? Let's start with the easy ones. Perhaps it was just an accident. Not too serious. Who is to blame? Are all parties assuming responsibility? Let's hope I have taught you something. If you can't come clean and own up to your mistake, you will pay for it some other way. There are no secrets in the universe. You have sent the energy out. Where do you suppose it will go in the quantum field? Yes, you understand this theory now. It is still hovering around. Sooner or later, it needs to be addressed. How about now? There is no time like the present.

Play the whole tape. Big deal, let the truth be known. It builds your character and I admire your honesty when you own your mistakes. Now you can fix it. A little repair here, a few apologies there and look at you now. You have made a decision, owned up to the consequences and hopefully you will not repeat this one. You have learned from your experience and do not wish to cause harm to anyone or anything. I feel better already. That wasn't so bad in the big scheme of things.

Let's look at bigger problems you have created. Oh boy. There were many wires crossed leading up to this set of circumstances. Now you are looking for a cover up because you are not thinking straight. Number one, why did you do this or cause this? This is our first area we need to address. What is in it for you? Chances are, you do not have my blessing on this one and you are acting at a lower level. Where is that going to take you? Correct, you're going down in a big way. Would you like a lifeline, a flashlight, a new set of tools, compass and map or perhaps a motivational tape? How about all of the above?

We have work to do. When would you like to get started? Great, I was thinking the same. No time like the present. What can we fix and deal with first that perhaps affected innocent parties? Let's look at this issue. Have you caused irreversible damage? Would you sincerely like my help? May I suggest you show your love first and then we will talk. I'm more interested in long term solutions and growth instead of quick fixes.

If your intentions are genuinely true and you do not knowingly plan on going this route again in the future, we can work together to minimize the losses and effects of this distorted decision making process you somehow conjured up in your mind.

Sounds like you owe a few souls a heartfelt apology. Perhaps you can take the time to make things right and fix some of your mess. May I recommend you start saying your prayers and mean every word of it, as I am waiting for an apology, as well. This is hurting everyone all around. Move forward and learn from your mistakes. No need to repeat this one.

HOUSEHOLD SPILLS

Look at all your fancy gadgets to clean up your messes around the house. You all have different methods to arrive at the same outcome. Some of you try sucking it up. Others try spreading it around and hope this will look better. Some spray smelly solutions on your concerns and hope everything looks and smells better. Ok, let's get something straight. A mess is a mess and no matter which way you deal with it, you are not going to get it perfect unless you take your time. Yes, you can try a few different solutions but if you ask me, there is usually one correct way to go about this business.

Catch it before it spreads, for starters. How bad does it look? Let's not throw anything out because it doesn't look the way it used to. No cover up please. Let's look at what you have done. Who's involved and what is your smartest solution? Have you done any permanent damage? Let's not let this affect everyone in the house. Let's be on top of it.

Usually when you are in a hurry, you do a fast job, only to realize this mess is still there when you get back. Day after day you see that it's seated a little deeper and are not sure how to go about a clean up. Perhaps if you tackle everything around it, it will not look so bad. You try to convince yourselves of this one.

Time passes and you get used to the mess you are living with and the original solution probably isn't going to get the job done. When were you going to make time for the spill? All parties involved need to hold a meeting in a neutral, distraction-free environment and pinpoint who and what led up to this mess. This is a great time to open the communications lines and see where everyone is coming from.

There are so many different points of view and perspectives on this one; hopefully you have an appointed, clear decision maker to move through the discussions. Are you understanding where everyone is coming from? Are you at the "create some solutions stage" yet?

I will leave this process up to you and I trust everyone is operating at the heart level. Be open-minded, understanding, compassionate and wear someone else's shoes for a while. This can put a new spin on things.

If this ongoing issue continues, then ongoing persistent efforts are required to clean up your self-created upsets and spills. Things don't always go away by themselves. Someone has to make a move in a positive direction. Let that be you.

As for the minor damage to the household, try a new color or pick up a fancy accent piece. This always adds new energy to an environment. Make sure it's handcrafted with love.

PICTURE PERFECT

I'm visualizing again. With all these new additions to your family nesting, let's create the perfect photo opportunity. Not everyone is feeling comfortable with change. It takes time to warm up to some of these ideas of new life styles. It's difficult at the best of times when people come and go out of your lives. The person responsible for this change should take a serious, active role in ensuring all other family members are comfortable with your decision. You are affecting many lives, not just your own, so let's see quite a bit of consideration for those around you. Perhaps you could come up with ways to bond all parties together. Yes, you have different personalities to deal with, but I'm sure you could ask me for some suggestions to make these transitions smoother for the younger parties involved.

They seem to feel left out and believe they are in your way. They are not feeling secure and loved during this transitional time. They feel that you made quite a large decision without their help. I see where they are coming from. They were a part of you from the beginning. Now you have changed directions and let them know after the fact. This would be unsettling and difficult to adjust to. Had you perhaps included them and made it their idea as well, you would not have so much reactive attitudes and behaviors.

What were you expecting? You all have deep feelings in your hearts, be sure to go about these new additions and subtractions with care. This is not only about you. In fact, your first priority always has been about your children. What is best for them would be my first consideration. I have never put myself before your desires. You know this to be true. I wish for you to find your place of comfort to grow your heart and love what you do. I make every effort for your optimum well-being and provide all the love and attention you desire in your heart.

I'm kind of like your genie in a bottle: the only time this wish would backfire is when it is for naught. Think your intentions of the heart through and consider those around you who wish for your love and attention too.

When this is done in this fashion, all dreams come true, as everyone is loved and supported through their own life experiences. Your wishes can become plentiful when they are for others and from the heart. Let's visualize these.

TO BE OR NOT TO BE

Many of you have yet to discover yourselves fully. You are moving too fast, for starters. You make so many commitments that have you running all the time. When were you planning to slow down; after you retire? It would be most unfortunate if you were to wait so long to know yourself. Why not put this on your short list? What are you waiting for? I can't help you until you come fully into the light and start to heal your heart. You are missing a large component of your so-called experience. Your life is at this point, meaningless. You don't even understand why you exist and who you truly are.

Wouldn't it be great to know more about the real you? You will like what you discover. Your true being doesn't have all your hang-ups and mixed emotions, just a heart of gold that is wide open and loving their existence and every expression of their being. Their wiser soul selves are only here to manifest frequencies of love and share it fully with the whole. They are not caught up in the web of chemical emotions. Their vibration is always of a finer energy. They reside on both sides of the veil. You could learn a few techniques from them.

Their character is indicative of mine and they, at all times, display loyalty, honesty and compassion. They see the big picture and hope you look inside to find your true self. This is the real you. Why you have waited this long, I'm not quite sure. Truly, you would be loving your life so much more fully and would experience your life with my eyes and heart of unconditional love.

Loving yourself empowers you and all others in your presence. We all desire the same heart. Find the path to yours and take the step into the light. You will love what you feel, then you will know why you came down. You will only want to help others discover the truth about life and love. You will realize we are all connected at the heart and wish only for peace and prosperity. We wish for everyone to smile and rejoice in their knowingness of the gift of life and their purpose on their visit.

Being distracted, preoccupied and too busy for others, holds up many souls' growth and experiences. Your decisions affect the whole. Your energy level creates static interference when you are not knowing of what messages you are sending out into the heavenly realms of light. If you knew you could easily be more than you are, why would you knowingly choose not to be?

Recapture your sense of connectivity and restore your light. From what I see, quite a few of you could use some light on your situations. I'm trying. How about you meet me half way? I'll help you with the rest. All great ideas start with a thought. Your higher self is just a thought away. How close is that?

DIVINITY

Such an abstract term down there, definition unknown. The study of what: me, us, the universe, processes, eternity, religion, all of the above? Each and every one of you seems to have your own notion and concept of the divine power that fuels your universe. Well, at least most of you have tried to make sense of it all. I'll try to shed some light on the energy that keeps you alive.

Quite some time ago, I, your Creator, wished to experience love in many facets of expression. You all being Starlights in my eyes were the purest forms of love, right out of my womb. I felt secure enough to give you some space of your own. This provided the grounds for love to flourish and grow. You all knew where you came from and were quite content in our collective experiences of the heart. Mother and I agreed that in order to grow more infinite, we would have to expand our thinking. We were quite confident, as our pure energy was of such a fine vibration, we would remain static free. You all were insisting that you would like to evolve more and become closer to the whole again.

The matrix was woven and your planet was infused with the finest particles of love. Many advanced light beings did their part to ensure the energy grid would sustain the test of time.

The first inhabitants on your planet were intrigued, but quickly became bored. Their suggestion was to send many more souls down, at a particular time and space, to evolve the planet. There were no concerns at the beginning, as your hearts were only of love and you all wished to stay connected.

Quite a few of you became homesick and were affected by the gravitational field. These short visits were highly productive to grow and evolve your souls. We were proud that you all returned back to the kingdom and reported your progress and advancements on planet Earth. As the population grew and souls found themselves worried about their well-being, they started to get nervous and their behavior became erratic. This was the beginning of not staying in your field of love. There never was a sound reason to get freaked out about your role and experiences. You were all lined up, dying to go down and have some fun with the power of love.

So, today, the same challenge is still with us. You're away from the whole. You've become disconnected and you are not understanding of your role and purpose. Many saints and deities have tried to provide you with answers, but all this led to the division of our loving consciousness. There were too many abstract theories about love and eternal life. I admire the reform and the guidelines but feel many have been led astray. Had you stayed on the same page in the Book of Life, there would clearly not be so many questions and doubts.

Faith is belief in the heart. You must have this to evolve. For without faith, you are separated from the whole. Trust in life's processes is paramount. Where would you all be today? Look at the amazing manifestations of beauty and love. Those are fine souls of divinity. They understand you all are one and exist to create only a more beautiful universe and souls of love. Each and every one of you needs to be understanding of this concept.

You are created in the essence of love. You grow in the essence of love. You evolve only by giving love. This is your pure consciousness of life's sustaining energy. When you choose to harm yourself and others, you dim the brilliance of the field of existence. The universe and its beauty only know of the finer frequencies of love and light. When you do not entertain this frequency, you start to die. Yes, that is slowly starting to reveal itself.

If you prefer not to have a planet of love, I can send you a trillion other places. You have already been there and like visiting planet Earth, the land of beauty, paradise and heaven, love in abundance. Well, if you are not manifesting this in your consciousness, what do you suppose your outcome will be for all of you? The percentage of you keeping your energy fields vibrant is too low to keep your planet alive.

Sorry folks, the party is winding down. Too bad you couldn't figure out why you were there. All of these true hearts trying to pull the rest of you up to your original level of knowingness and light vibrational energy. There are many beautiful souls with open hearts receiving heartaches from unloving individuals. The level of pain is catastrophic and disproportional for growth and evolution to continue on your planet. You are in regression.

Your atmospheric properties and chemistry of molecular biology cannot sustain the power of love vibration over time and space. Our harmonious relationship has been shorted out. Many of you see this pattern of self-destruction taking place.

How did you arrive here: your thoughts, your ungodly, self-serving thoughts? Who would have ever thought all you beautiful souls would create such darkness. It would truly take a miracle to restore planet Earth. We are doing our best from the realms of love. What we don't see is many bright ideas for peace, love and happiness. You are all caught up in your own wires of low frequencies and particle matter.

So what is Divinity? Most of what you read in this text. It's an existence. It is the ultimate, immaculate feeling and expression of love in its truest form. It is everything in between. It is eternal and limitless, beyond your comprehension on Earth plane. It is of the finest molecular frequencies of space and to capture this in your heart truly keeps us alive in all shape and form on all levels of existence for all of creation. It is the magnificence of Divine Intelligence Almighty Love, Light Omnipresent Vibrational Energy, at its best, having the finest time of our lives.

Look that up and feel what it is to be alive, in spirit, in soul, in your Creator of all divine creations. The Alpha and the Omega I AM

CHAPTER TEN

God Bless America, the Land of the Free

LET'S GET SOMETHING STRAIGHT. YOU STAND patriotically and hold your hearts in love. Are you truly meaning every word you sing? Do you understand what the lyrics symbolize? You listen but do not hear. You do not act in accordance to the universal message you send out into the realms. You wish for us all to honor this anthem, yet are not providing the grounds for freedom and growth. Is it not your God-given duty to act in a noble manner in accordance to your national song of unity?

Many souls sing this with hope and love from their hearts, unknowing of the universal vibration sent into the realms. If you are all to come together and sing in my honor, hopeful of a more beautiful world, perhaps you can practice what you preach. Many should meditate on these heavenly words and send them out with their truest intentions of the heart. I do not appreciate hearing my name when your intentions are dishonorable and of a self-serving nature.

You sing to look unified, yet your vibration is of a distorted frequency. May you consider implementing some of these strategies of peace, beauty and unification in your own backyard before you look to me for any blessings.

I am fully aware of your actions behind closed doors and do not approve of your motives. Don't sing my name dishonorably as this practice only harms you and burns out your heart. For those of you, who do sing in the glory of my name and wish for a better life, be true to your neighbors because that is when you receive my full attention.

Be not so fast to show off your patriotism to me or your country when it's not of a true heart. There is a harsh penalty to be paid when you cross the finish line. Many true souls see through this act of disrespect and dishonorable practice. Keep your intentions aligned with the whole of the nation or go home and re-tune your instrument.

MY NAME IN VAIN

So many false alarms, so many thoughtless souls; this is like crying wolf. Sooner or later, I am going to stop paying attention to your calls of the heart. Every time I show up, it is for nothing. Your disconnected mind is uttering profanities and senseless jargon. This is a huge waste of my divine time. You are insulting my intelligence and quite frankly, this does not look good on your soul. It only dims your lights and then I can't locate you.

Each time you call, I instantly arrive. Heaven forbid it is a true call of concern and I take my time assuming your lower self is uttering my name. How would you like to hear your name mentioned a few million times a second and everyone really wasn't even trying to make a connection? Would you be turning in circles? Would you be pulling out your hair? Would you be hurt or disappointed, only to realize they really didn't want to hear from you and they were only playing a sick joke, using your name in vain? It's not that amusing, in fact, it is highly offensive and against my universal law of orders.

You should try my job for a day. It would seem like a few years of commitments and tasks all rolled into one. I do a fine job up here and if you think you have it hard from where you sit, that's a joke I chuckle about. For when you arrive back and observe the souls on the planet, they seem to be in slow motion. Then they call my name and I respond only to find out they were not in their highest state of mind.

It's kind of like working for the Fire Department. Those true souls, running to save lives, all pumped up with their truest intentions to save the world, only to arrive at location to find some disconnected souls entertaining their idea of a sick joke. Relieved yes, but disappointed to know that their fine efforts, skill and professionalism were a true waste of divine energy. If more of you souls connected your hearts and used your fine minds, individuals on both sides of the veil would not have to respond to such ludicrousy.

Think, say and do something of a more intelligent nature. Perhaps a text on how to develop your mind would come in handy, as your distorted echoes of help do not impress millions. 911 is for life threatening emergencies, not for those who can't figure out how to dial love. Try that number out on your preset transmitter. You may even get an answer if you call our emergency department. Presently, you are on hold. How do you like that one? Don't expect a full team of professionals to drop everything and prepare a response intervention if it is not a matter of the heart. You have our number, and yes, I still have yours.

CALL THE KETTLE BLACK

All burnt out and sitting on the back burner. Should we disregard this broken piece? It certainly is no use to anyone now. We can't even repair it, it seems too far gone. What are our options at this point in time? It's evident that the original state has been tarnished and cannot perform its job function. Observers believe there is no use keeping this piece around. Enough evidence has been collected and it appears the wires have shorted out. You are all pointing fingers at the problem. If it is in your space, perhaps it is your problem as well.

Let's look at your options. Why did the piece malfunction? Was it too old or took too much abuse? Maybe there wasn't enough TLC exercised when this soul was trying to be part of the whole. Perhaps being taken for granted or mistreated caused this breakdown. If other parties are to blame why do you point the finger at the damaged goods? They were in their original state before you decided to utilize their soul for your convenience.

Was it ever a mutually beneficial relationship? Was there a lot of love and giving, or was it one-sided? You can only act in this fashion for so long before some component of energy shorts out. Had you been more considerate and gracious of the two way relationship and exercised the virtues of the heart for all parties concerned, you would not be so quick to replace your so-called problem. I suspect the real source of the concern rests in your lap and you're wondering what is wrong with the other person.

Every time, you seem to arrive at this same place. How can you not see this pattern? Everyone else around you is affected by your inconsiderate actions and behavior. How selfish and childish. You are not using your brain. That is clearly evident to all those in your life. They are walking on egg shells hoping not to get in your line of fire. They are not deserving of your mindless, reactive, disconnected behavior. And again, you wonder what is wrong with everyone else?

Well, I can answer that for you: nothing, absolutely nothing. You are the one who is blowing the steam, damaged or not. I noticed what you ate today and the thoughts you entertained leading up to your airhead behavior. You don't deserve to be in company of loving souls. I would like to see you on a barren island for a while, eating off the land, taking in the sun and meditating on your higher self before we ship you back and try to integrate you back into society.

If you had any part of your act together, you would figure out that you have issues and become reactive to substances and processes of life. Do not use everyone else for your punching bag. Take up a real sport, find your gift in your heart and stop burning everyone else's. You are not in my Book of Life at this time, as we have absolutely zero in common.

How many people do you affect with your ungodly ways? Think back because there are more than you imagine. I don't believe you can count that high. You shut your wise soul self down quite a while back. I'm surprised people bother with you. You have no love to offer and that's the soul reason everyone hangs around and sticks together.

I suspect you will be in the repair shop for quite a long time. It will feel like eternity. And yes, we will replace you with a new, improved, loving model of energy. That's all I know how to manufacture. Returns and defective souls end up on the back burner.

UPDATE YOUR HARDWARE

Always something new catching your fancy, hang on; what is wrong with the piece you plan to replace? Exactly, nothing. It holds fine energy still. May I suggest putting it to good use? This item holds your energy in its field. Could you find a new home for it? Many would love to have it in their possession. This would be a good deed of the heart. These pieces carry an energy of their own and would like to be of use. It makes them feel important and part of the whole. Send your intentions out and you will intuitively find the perfect home for this useful resource. I'm not suggesting that you all run out and replace perfectly fine objects to benefit from the latest and the greatest. But when the time comes and it seems to feel right in your heart, be sure to keep the energy positive and make a difference. I like to see this kind of behavior. It shows respect and displays love, honor and gratitude.

How about you update your software? You know the spongy stuff between your ears. When was the last time you performed a defrag? There seems to be some space in there you could put to good use. This technique for whole brain integration will make room for more intelligent programs to run. First, you clean up the programs currently open. New applications cannot integrate as efficiently if the outdated software is consuming valuable space. Deal with this first.

It actually doesn't take as long as you think. This is not a painful process. This is just a rewiring to reconfigure your receptor sites. This mind conditioning and whole brain technique is necessary to utilize maximum efficiency in your head space. You should have looked into this technique a few years ago. Get with the program so you can run the new software. Thank you for that.

There are many trainers willing to update your files and help you move forward with your personal and professional goals. This is worthwhile, as I see quite a bit of outdated perceptions that limit you from reaching your potential. This slows me down as well.

Let's reconfigure your thought processes and entertain this new paradigm of thinking. Now we are on the same page. Invest in that. You'll like the way you think and so will I.

NO STOPPING YOU NOW

How efficient, your life is running smooth now that you're using both sides of your brain. Wow, could you imagine how you thought before? It was too limiting for my limitless mind. It's nice we have a commonality. I see you are setting new goals and striving to become the best in your class. See, you always had it in you. You just needed a gentle push. I believe in you and know what you are capable of. I have to admit, you have been the source of our challenges all along. Don't take this too personal. I'm just not used to being in a holding pattern. I like processes and souls to keep evolving.

Let's look again at creating your reality. It helps if you write this one out. We've covered the steps and factored in all our considerations. Are you up to the job? If you are running on a clean circuit pattern, you should be able to intuitively figure out your purpose here on your visit. You know your talents and gifts that you came down with. When everyone is doing their part, you all come together as a unified whole. Remember everyone has a role. Talk to your car pool partners. If you are in similar industries you can brainstorm and make a difference.

I see many of you knocking on the wrong doors. Yes, knock on several and eventually one shall open. I admire persistence. However, are you sure you are going in the right direction? Don't underestimate the power of the mind if you are operating at the heart level. Go ahead, dream big. All you require is courage. Ask for some, we deliver.

Do not be so quick to fear what you are capable of. I sent you down with clear instructions and a map to succeed at your goal. Keep your vibration of the light frequency and do not entertain the low negative thoughts. Those are just the gravitational pull of the Earth's heavier frequencies. It's easier to get pulled down than to reach up and climb onto a lifeline. Make an effort, it's not hard work. Persistence and trust are required. Enough of the review, you have what it takes.

I see areas of low vibration that seem to suck in low frequency souls. These are places of shame. They house many dark and lost souls, all residing together with something in common. How will they come out of it if they are surrounded by other lost and disconnected souls? They're not in their right mind or operating at the heart level; so many of them displaying their unloving heart. They might as well be proclaiming, "I don't feel love. I don't know love. I can't find love. I don't love myself, but perhaps you want to know me, as I am empty and available. I'm even stoned so I don't feel the pain of humility". Not my kind of place to frequent. All you do is add to the consciousness of this helpless vibration.

What does this make you? What excuses have you for me now? I've heard them all. You are entertaining the lowest frequency on the planet. I didn't create that party. That's separation and of your own doing. Perhaps you can think more highly of yourself and come into the light; stop pulling us down into your disgusting pit of hell. You never originated there and your decision making abilities are way below my level of comprehension. What steps have led you to this destination? Might you have forgotten that you're on a working vacation? You're running way off schedule and impacting many true souls who want you to get dressed and show up to work.

How do you find the time to contribute to the destruction of our heart? What, you're not thinking straight? You had a liquid lunch? Your thoughts are so distorted that you not only feel guilty of the ultimate crime, but you chose not to help crying souls find the true lights. Get a life. Use your whole brain and locate a cardiologist and see if you still have a heart beat. I don't hear it from up here.

THE MYSTERY OF MY NAME

Out of sight, out of mind. The last things on your bookshelves are words of love. Fiction novels, crime stories, come on now, haven't you had enough? What you are advertising is what's in your heart. This is obvious. No wonder some of you roll your eyes and become speechless when you tell them what your true nature is. You give yourself away. What are you reading that you haven't read before? These stories seem so repetitive. Is that all you can come up with? What happened to your zest for knowledge? Oh, I know, you are a know-it-all. You seem to know little about much that counts.

Let's talk about real life experiences of the heart. From what I see there seems to be quite a few heartfelt messages of journeys of the heart. This would keep you connected. Get it, connected? These souls have taken the time to share their knowledge through their life experiences. What, no blood, no mystery, too sappy? You could truly stand to learn more about others' experiences, as I don't see you creating many happy endings yourself.

You are the masters of your own destruction. Keep reading about the killing, that should help our planet live and thrive on love. So your heart is damaged and you choose to entertain a low frequency additive for a remedy. I do not see many of you moving forward after reading too many crime stories. I see you looking for the next sick publication of death and destruction.

And you wonder why the Earth is disintegrating? You have no heart to share, only when it is convenient to you. These illusions of tangibility seem real. They are concrete. You can visualize what is to happen next. The plot thickens. Your blood is boiling. How sick is this; you getting off on death, pain and horrific murders of mass destruction. It is evident you have no love for sale, just broken dreams and empty promises. You fabricate your espionage and have souls believing this set of circumstances is true, when in fact, this is an illusion in your own mind. Too many crime stories I suppose. Now to keep us all interested, you have to come up with a twist, a motive to justify your grounds of suspicion. When all this plays out, the viewers anxiously wait for a horrific climax that will magically solve the mystery crime of the century.

Well, we forgot one chapter. How about the loving, peaceful ending to the story? Not enough takers? Your audience is crying for more blood? Are you sure this is how they want to see things play out? They are so conditioned that everything has to end with a shoot-out. They've forgotten about the only true outcome of the heart. This is playing with people's minds.

Perhaps if a few more avid readers would entertain love stories of the heart, you may be able to come up with a better solution in your own affairs. Think for yourself and from your own heart and soul, visualizing a positive, amicable happy ending.

QUESTION AND ANSWER PERIOD

I hear, we all hear, so many questions, so many distorted answers. Does anyone even know what the truth is anymore?

Does anyone particularly care? I see that everyone has their own truth and reality of the world in which they live. I hope I have shed some light on your myths.

Energy, being matter, is hard to put a finger on. You are searching for a solid answer and solution to the mysteries of life. You've recounted your texts and come up empty. You feel creation should be material; therefore that seems real. Your uneducated minds deny the invisible as having existence, to an extent. Yet all your challenges set before you are spiritual and energetic in nature. So why do you knowingly deny my existence?

We are all energy, hoping to create the impossible dream. Your sense of limitation has set you back in time. I expected quite a bit more of a light show down there. You all seem to eventually get what you want and believe you did it on your own accord. It would only take a second for your circumstances to change. You've witnessed life's lessons I'm sure. There isn't always a pleasant happy-ending.

Ok, so now you have stuff, where are you going now? And what is it you're going to do with your stuff? It's certainly too heavy to travel far with. Sometimes your stuff becomes a distraction. How does the material stuff grow your heart and soul? Might you be better off experiencing life on the soul level of your higher self? Perchance you may travel further on your journey of the heart.

Can you not conceive of the notion of fine particle matter? Did you skip out of physics class? This would be an opportune time to sit your self down and ask a few intelligent questions. I like, what is God?

God is the Universal Life Force Energy of the Palladium. God is the combustion of gases that fuel the galaxies. God is the intelligence of all living matter, right down to the atoms of the quantum field. God is the elements that fuel your atmospheric properties of your solar system. God is the heartbeat of cosmological, thermal energy. Without these and countless frequentized particles, there would not be life as you know it on your planet. You are loving, pure particle in space. Great place to hang out, but you were soul searching for more. Hence, you all packed your chest tight and traveled down through the realms and landed on Earth.

You've done a magnificent job of beautifying the planet, but it looked pretty darn great before you arrived, as well. The natural divine beauty is like no other. It truly is a paradise. It's sad you don't quite see your planet through my heart. Had you kept your promise to grow your heart, we would have kept advancing the evolutionary processes. There are hardly enough of you on board, only a handful from my perspective. Those who desired to remember the truth and find me in their heart, feel the peace and love the whole journeying experience has to offer.

I admit, some of you bought into lies at a young age and through no fault of your own, you couldn't find your love light. Others have a knowingness and refuse to acknowledge my presence. This passivity is the very reason you display acts of ignorance. You take for granted my existence and are scared of death. The only death you will be a part of is your own soul self and the destruction of your earth home. Perhaps you could make time, while you still have some, to review your records and life chart. You were optimistic in my presence and now do not entertain this attribute. I desire you to turn that frown upside down and come to your divine senses.

Most of you have got it pretty darn good. You've managed to make a difference and keep loving, positive individuals in your field. As for the rest of you, know that you've created your hours of misery and had we kept our strong connection, your visit would have truly taken a turn for the better, on the whole. You still have time to get it right on track.

Yes, you will have extra work to do, as you have left a few souls in the dark. Look around and see whose life needs your genuine love. When I feel your true intentions, we can get the show on the road. Everyone wins. Everyone is sporting a new heart.

What do I look like? I don't think you could imagine. Look to nature for a hint of my beauty. Look into the eyes of loving souls. Gaze into the skies on the brightest hours of celestial phenomenon. Hike up to the highest mountains and observe what you see. This is me, in every expression of beauty in our loving heart. You will feel me in the depths of your heart and soul. You can experience my love when you hold a loving soul. When you give with an engaged and open heart, you will truly see and feel my heart of love. Bathe in my waters of love and bask in the warmth of loving energy. Feel the breeze through the trees and listen to the sounds of love. They come in many expressions. Be open to this.

You can't possibly not have a knowingness of the power of love. I haven't overlooked a detail. Cherish every moment you experience on your planet, as there are many souls around you who feel the same love and warmth in their hearts. This is me, all of me, in everything that exists, in every particle of loving energy.

I see we are starting to manifest quite a bit more of this resource. Good, I was hoping we could keep the lights on. I see your intentions more clearly in that fashion.

I LIKE THE MOVIES

On our side, we watch real life-movies, yours. We see your action moves, your double-takes and your scraps. Is your feature film a horror show or does it involve a hero? We like to view the "hero saves the day" flicks, with you in the lead role. We are in your theater, sitting at the edge of our seats. You have our attention; we were hoping you could speed up the film a bit and get to the good parts. We are anticipating quite an optimum outcome.

We've seen the prescreening version and hope you remember your lines. Occasionally, we help out and plant them in your heart so you know what to say next. This is part of our entertainment over here. Sometimes the words don't always come out right.

There are quite a few records to scan through. But don't worry, we don't make mistakes here. It's most likely a filter and static problem. This is minor if you are tuned into divine guidance. I think it's great to have some help on cue. Pay attention and know your role. We'll keep the tape rolling.

Now, the hero usually encounters some close calls. Again, don't panic, we see the happy ending in mind. Hold steady Tonto and persevere. Work with the rest of the cast, as they are all key players to expedite the final cut. Be sure everyone is on the same page and please don't forget the extras; the more action the better. We like to see search and rescue, lost and found. The hero saves the day and then the world.

You all wrote elaborate experiences in your chart, quite a bit of action and adventure. The intermission segment seems to be a little long. Perhaps you can rethink this filler and get on with the show. Many are standing by on and off set. Make it a box office hit, as there is no limit to the loving excitement you can create on your stage of life. You will hold our full attention when we see something we like. Let's make it a sell out, no re-runs please. You are all movie stars in our eyes. Believe this one. We do.

CONCEPTS AND EQUATIONS

This notion of relativity has got me down. You are supposed to be creating positive experiences. First, you introduce one thought, only to have an opposite counterbalancing effect. What were you expecting? You understand the laws of physics, so adhere to its principles. You cannot create an expansive, loving universe if particles keep colliding. Either you have to stop entertaining ridiculous thought patterns or re-introduce a finer grid. This is not my immediate solution to your planetary problems. Let's try our first option. Unless individuals train their minds and connect up, you will continue to have a mess of particle matter sitting over your gravitational field. This is time consuming and unnecessary.

Perhaps schools of thought should be adopted more readily for the new shift of consciousness. You could entertain a higher frequency on the ground level. All things being equal, you now have created the elemental environment for substitution. Experiments involving entanglement can be revisited; and let's see to it your laws of motion come into play. This theory of connectivity should be your first move in a positive direction for the well-being of the planet.

By looking more closely at the reactive states of matter, you can conclude that your equation is coherent in the fashion of conductivity. By introducing a more refined vibration in the quantum field, you can shift our perception of subatomic particles. These compressed energies perform well under pressure and have a dual purpose. They act as binding agents in their original state and also subdivide for gravitational purposes only. This by-product is in place to counterbalance the field of motion. Your best conclusion would be to draw on this particle matter and displace its field of heat. You can then further reduce its effect on the field by saturation of positivity. Looking down into the rate of extension, you now can see all possibilities are in fact occurring simultaneously.

So where is your problem? It is in the solution of subatomic division. Your quest should be of the nature of photons and matter. From here, you can re-introduce your finest energy to get the work done. I admire your interest and have taken the measure to ensure complete, immaculate combustion. This should keep you entertained for a short while. Oh yes, don't overlook the space, it holds your keys.

KNOCKING ON HEAVEN'S DOOR

GOD: Hello, who is it? Oh, you just came by for a chat. You weren't planning to stay very long? You were just passing through? Oh, I get it. You were just in the neighborhood. Well, that's fine. We have time to catch up.

What concerns you down there? What? People have gone mad? They're not playing nice? They're angry and destructive? Did you mention that they were reacting to unhealthy diets? They don't seem to be listening? They could not be bothered to clean up their chemical messes? Well, you go back and let them know that we spoke and I don't approve of their habits. The ripple effect is affecting innocent bystanders. How did you find me up here?

Donna: *Oh, I took the time to grasp that space-time theory. It all makes perfect sense. If all things are happening at the same time, why can't we be in several places at once? I'm understanding of this divine concept and wish to stay more closely connected as I know what's in the best interest for everyone involved. I was hoping you could shed some light on our situation down here on our dark planet.*

GOD: There is not much more I can do from our side. Every soul and light being seems to be working and we have no spares to fill your requests. This condition has manifested because souls on Earth are not taking the time to invest in their future. That's not effective planning for the ultimate party. Our plates are full and we keep sending down the invitations and the directions, yet some haven't even opened their heart mail. Let them know we are running short on time and they should look into this matter. For if everyone shows a lack of interest, we will surely cancel out the event. There is no time like the present to get excited about the future.

Where is everyone's enthusiasm? Their sense of stimulation seems to have gone out the window and they can't seem to get the thrill back. I'm not sure what everyone is waiting for. They seem to think some kind of miracle is going to manifest while they sit back and watch. Perhaps you can remind them they are the miracle that's waiting to happen. But unless they sport their fancy shoes and get up and out from behind closed doors, not much is going to manifest. There won't be much to see: just party crashers and leftovers, just a waste of space. We're not sending down a Calvary of horses to get you off your backside, just angels of the highest. Keep your eyes open, for they shine bright and will just be passing through. Don't miss this opportunity. It's a chance of a life time.

PARTY PLANNERS

There are lots of events planners. Your talents do not go unnoticed. Perhaps you have time to look into our Century Party. We notice your skill to make things happen: coordination and timing, perfect, detail-oriented, superb. You should be working for us. We could use some help on your side. We're experiencing a motivational problem; not enough individuals seem to think this venue is worth the while. They're just buying time, entertaining the same old, same old. Their mindset has gone a bit stale, lack of oxygen I suppose. Not enough fresh air. No new ideas of their own, just followers.

Perhaps if you create some urgency, we could get things fired up. This is taking much longer than originally planned. We anticipated more involvement and positive energy to transform. How about take an active role in communicating the idea. Be prepared for those pessimistic types who are leading a pretty mediocre lifestyle. These are not your best party-goers; they do not thrive on fun and excitement. They are stuck in a rut and will need a crowbar to pry them out of their unhealthy thinking patterns.

Enthusiasm is contagious, so go to work and do your best. You have us on your side. That is what counts: love, strength and power in numbers. Give them the alternative option of the worst possible outcome and see if they are awake to this. No ultimatums. Just choose life in abundance, eternal love, or the dark side of the moon. I would key on the finer qualities this loving decision has to offer. Features, benefits, handle objectives and then try to close. I see quite a few of you good at this technique. This will require effort and persistence. Had these souls been in their right mind they would not be lingering around the lower frequency range. Pull them up and light the way.

What else would you rather be doing with your spare time? What spare time? Make some. Make it happen. That is what you do best. This is why you have mastered this skill. Originally, it was for all of creation and the ultimate party. You will like the rewards of your diligent, good deeds. You picked these rewards and will not be disappointed. Advertise your intentions and shine your lights. This always gets you noticed. Remain humble please, act in my fashion and do the work of your heart. Before too long, you will have a line up at the door. This always creates interest and curiosity.

No one will want to be left out of the shift in consciousness. When the events begin to unfold, the real party begins and life takes off for everyone in the correct direction. You will find your purpose and place on Earth and in the realms. You will find the peace you are looking for. And those who ask will reach their maximum potential and experience the ultimate high on your Earth plane. How fun is that? Did you have a better plan? Can you top this?

Let's become our higher selves and shine our party lights. I'll see to it that your dreams come true and you find your ultimate destination. Does everyone have directions?

WE'VE BEEN EXPECTING YOU

We don't give up that easily, that's not our nature. Patience is a virtue. From where we sit, we exercise all the virtues of the heart in their fullest capacity. What else would you expect? Some of you take this for granted, our loving nature and all. We take our share of rejection, but there is so much to give, we hardly bother with this challenge. We are more interested in looking after the whole heart and all of your creations on the planet. There is no time for ill-feelings; we are only about love. Whatever it takes, we are up to the task at hand.

Let's review your check-in date. At this time, you should have called in with your progress report. We're waiting for you to give us amendments to your earthly business goal. Have you moved forward? Why are you avoiding us? Have you not been adhering to your time limits, nothing much to report? Feeling a little uneasy with your consciousness? Did you get side-tracked and put your contributions on the back burner?

Perhaps you forgot why you went down? I see some of you looking to find your purpose and some of you are oblivious to the fact you should even be bothered with anyone or anything other than yourselves. You are only hiding from your own soul self.

When was the last time you prayed, asked for instructions or direction? We always answer. Be patient, as perhaps you are paving the road to your ultimate path. Sometimes it is difficult to see the forest through the trees. You will always get a sign and a feeling if you are on track. I see those enjoying their direction in life, they stayed close to my heart.

Those of you who are going it alone do not grow. You are still the same soul as when you went down. In fact, I indicated you dimmed your lights on this recent visit. In my eyes, this is selfish and inconsiderate. So many starlight souls are waiting to come down and perfect their soul's growth. This holds up time. When you are of sound mind, give us a call and we will provide you with some direction. There is no time like the present moment.

NEUTRAL PARTIES

"Well", you say, "I didn't know I was supposed to help and make a difference". I understand your concern but I don't understand your beliefs. Where did you get this notion of life? Watching too much TV? You don't have a loving belief in love and the Universal Creator, or we would have been communicating some time ago. Any soul who has asked or questioned their faith has always been led to the heart, to myself and the Mother. We are crystal clear in our communication capabilities and we have made numerous efforts everyday of your life to contact you.

Our conclusion is that you're not listening effectively to our voices of love. You're not making enough time for us in your heart. Your answers are all inside for any question you may ask us. We hear well, but some days we are not in your mindset or heart. This hasn't appeared to be a priority in your Earth life.

When we hook up fully and feel your true heart of intention, we all begin to heal and grow. What were you waiting for? This is not a once a week visit. This is a new way of thinking in spirit. Get inspired. We would love to be re-united. Look around at those souls who have a loving, true heart. See what they're doing. Perhaps they have a message for you from all of us on the other side of life.

RAISE YOUR VIBRATION

This whole energy thing has some of you confused. You don't have to have a degree in the field of Science or Theology to understand your energetic self. Simply having an awareness that your heart and thoughts need to stay in unison creates a positive energy field. This finer frequency of love emits a wave of vibration into the universe of love. If your mind, body and soul are in three different directions, you're sending out distorted waves into the atmosphere. It doesn't actually reach our consciousness, as our vibration is of the purest frequency of love omnipresent vibrational energy.

For us to hook up and communicate effectively, we need to entertain thoughts of love, abundance and giving. All these virtues of the heart resonate at the highest frequency in the realms of your heavens. This is where you find your higher self and become all that you can be.

Thoughts of doubt and despair create a very low, distorted wave. I would hardly call it a vibration. It doesn't ascend. Its weight has the gravitational pull of the lowest frequency possible. Your thoughts manifest your personal vibration of either love or fear. When you are unhappy, you know you feel low and uninspired. If you truly intend to sync up to the cosmic vibration of the intelligent, loving consciousness, then be mindful of your thoughts and make them from the heart.

Are you communicating from your higher self? You will know what changes your loving field from positive to negative. These are some of the practices and substances you entertain. Everything carries vibration, your environment, your peers, your sounds, your activities and your food. Having an awareness of such makes you become more sensitive to the lower fields. Do not match down and join these lower levels. These distorted waves are not healthy for your soul being.

Activities integrating the mind, body and soul are the most beneficial and nurturing for your higher self's vibratory rate. Ground, cleanse your field, open your energy centers and enjoy the trip. You will always find me in your heart, as you and I have been polishing your diamond heart forever. I've always been there and always will be, but some of you just don't know for sure.

I do know that you've been trying to find me for quite some time. I'm not that illusive. Just think with your heart and lead by example. Exercise the universal laws and perfect the virtues of the heart. And for God's sake, listen to your soul and my voices of love.

CHAPTER ELEVEN

Good Morning America

IT'S BEAUTIFUL TO WAKE UP TO the sounds of love. The sweet sounds of nature at its finest. Take the time to savor this calming harmonious state. Open your eyes and see with your heart. True souls revel in the complexity of synchronicities. They marvel at the intricacies of the elemental particles of consciousness. What better time to inspire your soul. Do not be so rushed and distracted that you are unnoticing of my love and beauty. Every day is a new day if you wish to see it so. Breathe in the fresh air, clear your space and become one with all that exists. Learn to appreciate the connectivity of all our hearts and souls. Be sure to smile and light the way for those who will come into your consciousness. Make them aware of the peace of the planet, the beauty of nature and the freshness of the morning air.

Too many of you are off to a bad start, getting up on the wrong side of life. You see no beauty, just confusion. You see no balance, just discord. You choose to be disconnected from the universal source of love. When you are conscious of the energy patterns of perfection, you can create some of your own. This requires an openness to everything and an attachment to nothing. Be not so distracted that your first waking thoughts are of fear and worry. These are not your natural states. This is the result of panic and worry about what lies ahead in your day of thoughts.

Look at nature doing their thing. Do they look like they are scrambling and disorganized? No, they are connected to the whole of life's cycles of beauty and love. They are timely doing their part and contributing to the divine perfection of consciousness. How about waking up with this idea in your mind's eye? Take five to listen to your true soul self and sync up to the perfection of the finer frequencies of love, peace and harmony. It's just a thought.

Before you get running in ten directions, breathe the breath of eternal life and know your soul is always going to make everything go your way. Meditate on being your higher self and stay in touch with the beauty and peace of nature. This is where you find your true soul self. Tap into the infinite wisdom of the universe and see how smoothly your life will flow. Tune out your distractions and your low vibrational substances and perhaps things will appear a tad clearer. Become mindful of the mixed energies you come in contact with on your travels. If you are not grounded, they will influence your field and decision making abilities. These patterns of weakening energy levels throw your vibration off if your connection is not strong and of the finest frequency.

Be sure to entertain the sounds of love and call my name. We are fully alert at this time of the day, as this seems to be when all the action starts. We are in quite a few directions when the sun comes up. We would prefer to be in the garden nurturing our growth and spreading seeds of love. That's my idea of capturing the light of the day. Namaste.

FRUIT CAKES AND PUMPKIN PIES

These are such a tradition, these dishes of yours. What exactly do they symbolize? Are they representing a peace treaty of some sort? I love the idea that they are homemade and all but lose the sugar. There is plenty of natural occurring sugar in your treats, too much in fact, for most of your systems to digest properly. Let's get out the recipe book and cancel out this white sugar.

Ever notice how someone's personality and behavior changes right after they overdose on sugar substances. They act disconnected and are showing characteristics of their lower self. Do you not recognize this unhealthy pattern? Now your thinking processes are not rational and you fire out low, distorted waves into the universal field. This harms everyone and everything in your line of fire. First, you shoot your mouth off and then you do something completely stupid and childish. Your observers do not notice your intelligence. They are witness to your low behavior of crabbiness and selfishness.

All the while, your nervous system is trying to disperse this overload of sugar and temporary shutdowns in your chemical factories occur, simultaneously. Now you're really operating on a full set of contacts. Not likely. You seem to do this quite often during your waking hours. Not only is your brain disconnected, but you cannot find your wiser, higher self. So here you go, making all these decisions in your working day, firing on half of your receptor sites of low patterned messengers.

Clean up your sweet tooth diet. This is not your soul's desire. This is your uncooperative mind wishing to feel the familiar state of stupidity. Oh, you think you are quicker, wiser and smarter? But in fact, you are reactive and not in your right mind. If you try to resist this ungodly temptation, you may find your parties may wish to hang around a little longer.

Surely you could be a little more creative and selective with your icing on the cakes. The varieties of fresh fruits on your planet are bountiful. Seek and you will find. Their properties sharpen your mind and they integrate beautifully in your central nervous system. Your mind, body and soul will thank you and so will I. Now that's a pie in the sky.

ENTERTAINING WITH A TWIST

You have plenty of friends and acquaintances. How about you hook up? See what they would like to do at the soul level. There is so much talk, not enough action. Boy, do you all like to talk so much. Three quarters of the stuff we hear is a waste of energy. Find a common interest and create some positive vibrations. This is using your imagination. If someone is in a rut, pull them out. Come up with a sporty idea to get them out of their home environment. They are sitting around in their own web of negative energy. Their indoor activities are not all in their best interest. You could try to help them brighten their surroundings and change their tunes. They cannot figure out why, time and time again, they find themselves in the same position as last week, last month, last year.

A great place to start is with their immediate surroundings. Now be careful. This is not a time to offend a soul. Indicate that you are an aspiring home coordinator and you would like to try out your fresh ideas. Start with de-cluttering and introduce vibrant, high frequency colors. This starts to circulate the low stagnant energies. This in turn will set off a new pattern of thinking. Everything is starting to look and feel brighter. Bring over a couple of your favorite soul CD's of lighter, softer frequencies and don't forget your spiritual magazines.

Eventually, you will begin to inspire the individual and perhaps you can get them out into the garden of life. Take them anywhere you can find an abundance of flowers, trees and creations of beauty. They will begin to balance their own energies with those of nature and the fertile grounds of universal consciousness. This should put a spin on their chakra system. Oh yes, be sure to stop somewhere for a shot of wheat grass and look into a yoga workshop.

Not all your peers are going to warm up to these heartfelt ideas right away, but if I have planted this seed of love and nurturing in your heart, please go out of your way to see to it this soul finds the light. Show an interest in their soul's growth, as that is when you blossom. I will notice your fine efforts when they are from the heart.

Now get going and redesign your friend's mind, body and soul. I can breathe more effectively in this open space of light.

I like the full spectrum approach of frequencies. Now we are humming along. I like the tune of that.

THE LATEST FASHION

Start a new fad. Let there be light. Let's shake things up. There is too much old energy lingering around. Pay attention to your wardrobe. Connect to the feel of it. Does it do it for you? Do you feel like a million bucks? Does your energetic self feel inspired? If not, recycle. Perhaps it's not your color or you are sporting too many accessories and this is interfering with your flow of healthy energy. Lighter is better, energetically speaking. Complement your image of your soul self with soul colors and fabrics. If you are inspired with your look, you will create a trend of uplifting consciousness. Everyone could use a lift. Start with a loving look from the heart. That is how you fashion yourselves, from the inside out.

Be mindful of the vibration you are sending out as you don your wares. These are all a collection of mixed energies. Let's make sure you are blending the finest threads of love into your fabric of universal consciousness. If your heart tells you to try something new, go with it.

This is not a calling to redesign your entire wardrobe. This is a "wake up and wear your loving heart" call. You have nice pieces; do not part so fast with these. Remember, your energetic signature is in this fabric. I am suggesting a blend of the new you and the new paradigm of universal loving consciousness. Radiate your positive energy in every way you can. All these details contribute to the rise in the collective energy levels of humanity. One person connected to this powerful loving consciousness will impact many souls at the lower weakening levels.

Your intent should be to help and restore the Earth to love in every matter of the heart, in every way possible. You become what you hold in your heart. You can shift many in your field of loving energy. When you share a heart of optimism and reverence for all life, a transformation will occur on planet Earth.

Now that's my kind of fashion show. I will see you on the cat walk. You will truly shine.

NO TIME FOR AUTOGRAPHS

It's interesting collecting sacred signatures. You line up to meet your star and come home with a piece of their heart, or not. What was the soul reason for the quest? Do you admire their fine works of the heart? Would you see me in line for their signature of love? Are you selective in your idols of admiration? Are they displaying the attributes of the heart? Did they make a difference in the world of life and love in your time-space? What is the value of this keepsake? Are you sure it's holding a fine vibration? What exactly are you connected to? You wish to have a piece of this individual's energy in your soul's possession, yet your intentions were not of your higher self.

It would be more admirable had you chosen your noble stars from your heart level. Do not contribute to the rise of low, unethical practices. If all their moves are in accordance with the universal laws and of a loving heart then perhaps you may wish to carry this in your energetic field. Do not underestimate the energy exchange of a simple practice. You are unaware of what you are contributing to on a larger scale of the spectrum.

This unified field of consciousness should only be complemented with the finest energies of contributors that have the best interests of many at heart. Be not so quick to worship burnt out stars posing as figures of praise. I see where they are truly coming from and if you were in sound mind, you would not be waiting to hook up and feel their energy. Make your selections wisely when it comes to matters of your heart, as you pass this reverberant frequency stream into unified states of human consciousness.

Let's stabilize this practice and entertain ideas that expand our unified field of universal intelligence. The fundamental frequencies of pure consciousness come from deep within. You reflect our self-aware intelligence by interacting with the field of dynamic wholeness. This understanding of the nature of our existence will hopefully encourage you to seek out ways to brighten our collective field and exercise common sense when it comes to matters of the heart. These harmless activities are not acceptable practices in the kingdom of love. Would you like my signature on that one?

HOW DOES YOUR GARDEN GROW?

What are you planting in your heart and everyone else's? Are they going to bear fruits of love? Are they natural and chemical free? Are they full season or partial? Full sun or partly shaded? Will they return year after year? Does this make them annual or perennial? I don't understand this temporary practice. Yes, it looks nice but it seems to die off when the sun is not so warm. I like the all around full time, everlasting garden of love. It blooms, it grows and produces seeds of love and fragrance of beauty. This is continuous.

Nature's cycle of love is perpetual, always bountiful and ever abundant. It does not wait for a loving soul to nurture its beauty. Its character is strong and eternal. There are no short seasons of love and light. They are adaptable under every condition of the atmospheric patterns and seem not bothered by dry spells or prey, for they live and breathe the universal life force. The sun is always rising in their being. There is such peace and harmony in their field of diversity, each one making room for a variety of beauty. They love to grow together to feed off each other's vibration, such a collection of loving consciousness. Do you know how many species of plant and wildlife inhabit your planet? Do you carry records of this?

There are so many novice gardeners, not completely sure of the complimentary companions to manifest perfection. Do a little investigation and rethink your layout. Some of you have got this right. You take your time with God's creation. You are understanding of their needs. I admire your patience and interest in my children of love. They are pretty independent, but wish you would understand them a little better. They flourish well with similar patterned species. They all have unique personalities and characteristics. You see this. They have their preferences of companions as well.

Do not match them up with overpowering larger species, as below ground is where the trouble starts. More aggressive roots only damage the delicate root systems. Everyone needs some space to grow. Be mindful and ask them if they are ok with your placement. They will indicate their preference. This is what I call a green heart, listening to your accents of love.

Be sure to admire their growing phases. Your vibration encourages their potential. They only wish to be appreciated and to find their place on the Earth. Do not go around unnoticing of their collective beauty. Their harmony and unison is of my creation. Adhere to some of your horticultural guidelines. They rely on your knowledge and love as well, to keep them safe and nourished.

If every soul had an abundant garden of love, that would be about how many different collections of species and wildlife you could find on your planet of paradise. The aerial view is spectacular and I enjoy the sweet scents of love. Plant your garden first in your heart then display this for others to enjoy the beauty of your soul. I see your intentions of the heart. Make it fragrant. Make it love.

SHADES AND SHADOWS

The spectrum of reality can produce many illusions, not all are of a true bright color. If you have a sharp sense of things, you can pick this one out. All species cast a shadow of doubt from time to time. This is natural. This is only a by-product of frequencies. If you stay in the full light, your effervescent cast will only display your warm character. This is a feeling of love. There is no need to be scared of the dark. It is only a temporary condition. The sun continues to rise each day to a new hope of healing and growth. We are always on top of your requirements. Have you ever woken and not seen the light in the sky?

We keep the cycle of love shining in your hearts. When you have a shadow of a doubt, turn it over to your highest self. Ask the question if this concern serves you any longer. Is it of a genuine heart? Can you not choose to shine a bit brighter and cast this worry out of your field? It's just a temporary shade of transition. It's neither really light nor dark; it just is.

You have control of this process. Choose light. Choose faith. Turn on your love light and shine. You will only produce a loving solution for all those concerned. You can defuse any situation with your heart. I'm not suggesting you walk through the valley of the shadow of death with your blinders on. I'm recommending you have your eyes wide open and your heart engaged. There will always be some grey areas that require lightness. There will always be dark souls who can't seem to find their light switch. Be careful when you proceed to locate their light. They are used to living in the dark and quite frankly, the light scares them to death. This is not a comforting place. This is a foreign frequency. They seem to be thriving in the darkness. It's kind of like mold and bacteria, unseen by the naked eye but multiplying in the dark corners of the world.

This will require a complete restoration and disinfection. This needs to be treated like a quarantine. You do not want to touch this matter, as it can spread if it's in the air. You will not be noticing of the harmful effects of the spores. They will stick on you and you may find it difficult to shake off. A complete clean up solution is necessary. There seems to be an epidemic down in the lower frequency range. It's spreading like wildfire, burning everything in its path. Do not come in direct contact with these harmful shadows, as they will try to smother your life of love. Darkness breeds darkness. The light only produces love and gardens of fragrant species.

If you are an intermediate gardener, see what you can manifest with the help of the light of the sun. We produce our finest creation with this combustible gas. This fuel is of the highest grade. It cannot fuel the darkness. It will inevitably outperform all shades of darker frequencies.

We have the incitement to cultivate a stabilized garden of growth. We have the tools, knowledge and determination to see the beautiful spectrum of frequencies on the Earth plane. Our most powerful ingredient is universal love in its fullest capacity. That is how you enhanced its beauty many years ago. It was more powerful than the shadow of doubt.

Locate your perennial reference guide and cultivate the seeds of love and call in the light. We have a garden of hope to grow. The more the merrier. Now that's a breath of fresh air, without a doubt.

SUPERCALIFRAGILISTICEXPIALIDOCIOUS

Now, this is not a term you hear too often. I don't see it in your dictionaries. What exactly does it stand for? If my memory serves me correctly, it was a fancy expression of hope and inspiration. Ok, I'm dating myself. Let's sing a new tune of joy and hope. This term seemed to bond people together. Yes, it was light and silly, but it worked. I remember you all sending this one into the realms. We were quite entertained. Times were simpler back then. Hopeful hearts believed in the dream and managed to keep their energy levels high. There were a lot less interference properties present.

You have to make a more conscious effort to pull and keep yourselves up in the higher planes. Too much negative interference drags you down. You know this exists. Don't give into it and get pulled down. You are so much stronger than the gravitational pull of low frequency. Lighten up, sing a catchy tune. Don't entertain low, slow vibrational activities and substances.

Look around at your depressing world. Your outlook is distorted. Find a pair of rose colored glasses and check out the beauty. Most souls take a vacation for that very reason. Change of scenery, change of attitude and hoping to be inspired by life itself. Leave the drugs at home and clear your head space. Life is but a dream.

Wish I were down there. I would be swimming with the best sea creatures, taking canopy tours, hiking the majestic mountains, wiggling my toes in the fine particle of energy on the shore lines and loving my life. There is so much to do down there. I have a list ten miles long of activities I would entertain my time with. Sacred sites, lives to share, love to give, joy to spread, yoga, meditation and God. The list is limitless. It goes on forever.

Make time; get inspired. Leave your worries behind. You can change your mindset in your own backyard, if you so desire. You are just stubborn and your wires are tangled. We could zap some new high power energy into your soul. It's just a thought. Have some fun.

Would you rather have my job? I could use a vacation. Can you multi-task? Do you have strong leadership abilities? How high can you count? Ok, I better sit tight. But honestly, I could use a day off. How about, everyone perform up to par for just one day, for a start. That would free up some time and space around here. I would like to get back to nature and spend some precious time with their beauty. They are pretty low maintenance. They pay attention and get the work done. They have tons of time to hang out and enjoy the love, my kind of crowd. They are peaceful and happy every minute of their life span. We are pretty close. We all bond well and have an understanding. We communicate love 24-7. They know my expectations are high, but it's worth the rewards of the gift of life.

I wish you all would learn from nature's characteristics. When it is untouched by humanity's influence, its consciousness is only for the whole of the universal heart. They are pure love. They wish to be part of the whole and feel the presence of my love. This keeps them alive and well on planet Earth.

As for that catchy tune, you baby boomers remember, capture the love and freedom of the good old days and make it count for something. Your hearts shone a little brighter way back when you heard the sounds of it.

AN OLD-FASHIONED LOVE SONG

Don't get me wrong, I like the progressive sounds. I like processes fluid. Everything seems to be moving forward at a good pace, except for your hearts. When did you put the brakes on? That is only for emergencies and collision avoidance. Unstick your emergency lever. It's starting to seize up. You heart needs to catch up to your soul age. A broken bone is more painful than a heartache. Now, let's put this in perspective. You actually have a better chance at healing your heart properly than you do at repairing shattered bones, although, the body is a miraculous, complex structure. There are trillions of functions happening simultaneously at the subconscious level and you are choosing not to heal and grow your heart. Stop getting in the way. Let processes take place.

It's a lot more painful to interrupt the natural healing process and remain in the suffering stage, than it is to heal and grow. Do what you have to do to feel it, deal with it and get over it. You shouldn't still be on your first heartache. You wrote several into your life chart. You came down solely to grow your heart. Isn't it fascinating that this loving organ can expand and experience divine eternal love? Why choose limitations? This is not our character. How bad can it be? They left, they weren't loyal, or they transitioned back home?

All experiences are under my authority. If you wish to question my actions, well, where would you like to start? May I remind you that you were fully aware of how your life was to unfold. You reassured me you could handle life's heartaches for your soul's growth, so why are you protesting life's unfairness? You wrote this in yourself, child. I indicated that I would be close by during these difficult periods of growth. I would never forsake you nor leave you. That is not of my loving consciousness.

Your mind is causing you pain. Let go and let life unfold. You were supposed to have a happy ending. Release the emergency brake and sing an old-fashioned love song. This will nurture your soul. Call my name with your heartfelt desires and we can heal and grow. The oldies seem to carry the frequencies of the healing vibration. You can resonate to that.

Go back to the place where you need to feel the pain and I'll help you find your heart. We need to carry you to the present moment in order for you to realize your dreams. There is no need to stay where you are. Life is truly passing you by. How do you like the sounds of that? We can make beautiful music together when you open your instrument of love. Mine is finely tuned.

I CAN FEEL YOUR HEARTBEAT

Name that tune. Such an interesting family, all musically inclined, spending so much time together. Could you imagine? Well, at least they were on the same page of life and spreading love and joy everywhere. When you decide to exercise and tune your heart's function, I can feel your intentions. Your frequency is unique to me. We have you on our radar screen. We are interested in your goals at this time. Have you a plan at heart? Are you ready to perform some miracles of your own? Let's get started. You have a team of white light guides hovering around, helping you with your decision making. Perhaps a good starting point would be to listen to your higher self. If a book jumps out at you, pick it up. There will be lots of ideas and messages here. This is necessary for your route of travel. We need you to be equipped and packed tight.

Let's review your mission in life. You are one in a trillion and only you can perform your ultimate role. There's no pressure here; just pay attention. How about figuring out where the distortion is coming from? Why are so many souls having problems with their thought processes? Food and substances aside, there seem to be bigger influences interfering with our communication equipment. We have installed the fanciest, state-of-the-art telecommunication apparatus and have come to realize that all the technological matter buzzing around is creating black-outs in our field of love. Not only are we dealing with weak heartbeats, we are trying to compete with distorted wavelengths of low vibratory energy matter. This particle property is suspended in your lower levels.

If technicians and engineers look into this more deeply, we could brainstorm some solutions to clear the air. We are only interested in higher frequencies of love. Keep your thoughts clean and positive and determine where your source of unnecessary radio waves is coming from. This concerns me as I don't see the benefits of this practice. Perhaps you have time to look into this matter before it spoils the sounds of love.

PIPE UP THE MARCHING BAND

We never miss a beat. Everyone knows their role and performs in unison. Many are on the same page. There are not many marching bands compared to yesteryears. Everyone would line the streets to hear an upbeat sound. They felt this in their heart center and it vibrated their soul. We don't get the chance like we use to. The consciousness of one of these parades enlivened the atmosphere. We were always tuned into this. Are there too many cars on the street perhaps? Are there not enough band leaders anymore because they are mostly retired? Younger generations are not interested; there is too much peer pressure. I understand this practice is not likely going to make a comeback, but the idea of it was pure collective energy, with many engaged and everyone was outdoors.

We could create the similar vibratory effect with souls and music, if we used our limitless imaginations. Now that you have a understanding of our frequency challenge, let's get the drums and shakers out. Sorry folks, I'm not referring to rock and roll. I'm thinking earth tones, grounding music for the soul. This practice stimulates your energy centers and raises the vibration of the planet. The shamans and native heritage understand the effects of sound vibration and how to reach our realms of love. This is not a heavy, repetitive beat. This is an awakening consciousness tone of love for us to enjoy and reciprocate your intentions of the heart. The Earth's energies respond favorably to these tones of universal consciousness.

We like to see your handmade instruments, as they carry the frequencies quite well. I would recommend a few lessons first before your debut. We see souls gathering together for this journeying, but desire many more to look into the benefits of sound vibration. This makes our whole heart beat to the sounds of love.

THE SOUNDS OF MUSIC

Well, you are all sounding so fine. Let's take a short break and listen to the sounds of nature. Have you truly heard their melody? Their sounds are more subtle, but equally beautiful. They blend in perfect harmony. If you are in the right location, you can pick up on many instruments of love. They resonate with a perfect balance of energies. All elements are present and if you are in their natural environment, you will hear communication at its finest. The water blankets the shore. The rocks rumble in excitement. The wind feels the rush and the birds, bees and trees dance in particles of the unified field. The animals sync up to the rhythm and our flowers and insects float in the frequencies of love. Lie on the Earth and listen to its heart beat. Hear the grass laugh when a breeze of fine air shimmers by. All life forms enjoy this ecstatic, peaceful feeling. I know seasoned meditators feel this synchronicity when they become one with the universe.

To experience this heightened state is a blessing of my love. Seek to feel the love in its purest form. Listen to hear my voices. Nothing of your world can replace the sounds of love in your heart. Be sure to find time to join at the heart level and create your beautiful sounds of music. The hills are truly alive. They carry all the frequencies of love and life on your heavenly planet. Listen with your heart.

TAINTED LOVE

If everyone is connected to everything and everything is consciousness, how can you not know the truth of love and life? We close our ears when we do not wish to hear the tones of discord. We shrug our shoulders, as this vibration is not an expression of gratitude and love for all life and creation. This soul harms the whole of existence. You know at your soul level when an individual is not exercising the virtues of the heart; yet, you don't stand your ground. Understandably, I feel your vibration, but this practice of minding one's own business has damaged our heart of love.

Love fuels love, so your only viable solution would be to say a kind loving word and express your feelings of the heart. Perhaps, you can share their concern and pray that they change their tune.

There are so many houses of horror and terror. You lock your doors and hope this bad vibration goes away. Well, you are the only one that can dissipate it if they are in a web of darkness. I'm not suggesting you show up with your drum and spiritual matter, but your intentions could shed some light. Don't give up on lost souls. Offer a helping hand, a word of encouragement or point them in the direction of love.

I hear you already. You are resisting this course of action. "I don't want to get involved", you're thinking. I don't blame you quite frankly. Maybe someone close to you has a suggestion to break up this pocket of negative thoughts and behavior. If you could only imagine what distorted ideas they are conjuring up in the pit of hell. They would like nothing more than for you to join their sick ways of living life. Some of you have to step up to the plate and see and hear where they are coming from.

What fuels their frequency? Your best guess would be way off the mark. Do your homework and let's not allow this germ to spread. It's right in your own backyards. It doesn't take long for mutation. It's rampant already. I hear the distorted voices of ungodly thoughts. Their intentions are to put out your love light as the brightness hurts their eyes. This is where you come together and shine your brightest lights and turn to me for some loving solutions to light up the planet of love. Too many dark souls are not appreciating the gift of the heart.

Get a visual on this one and nip it in the bud, before they ruin our party. Their idea of a party is with the lights out and burnt hors d'oeuvres. I don't have the appetite for this one.

ROCK AROUND THE CLOCK

There are not enough hours in the day. Lots to do; the clock is ticking. This party is not for the back burner. This is a last call for true party-goers. We are going to have some fun. Nobody can spoil our party. None of this "it's my party and I'll cry if I want to". No crying me a river. I'm hoping for tears of joy. There is too much sorrow as it is. Let's get the party ticking. It's a mindset. Ask around and see who else is going. You may be pleasantly surprised. The idea here is to make the party-poopers feel like they are missing the party of the century. Create some excitement. Let's get rocking. This heats up the necessary energy for a full-out, combustible explosion of light. I have been waiting for this one forever.

We need a soul count to see where we stand. This is done electronically. Just send up your heart mail, we will see it in our inbox. Be sure to copy your intentions to all our light planners. This keeps the communication lines open and positive. Once the soul count is up, we will send back a reply to your heart. Be open to this and make sure it doesn't end up in your junk mail. This is a high priority invitation only; an all-star event. All soul stars are invited.

We'd like to know your intentions in advance. We have some pre-planning to arrange to accommodate all of your soul requests. This will be a sight to see. When your responses come flying in, we will start the warm up. We are good to go, when you are on board. Be sure to mark your heart mail with the intentions of love. True hearts will transmit the light omnipresent vibrational energy in a heart beat. For those of you unsure of this cyberspace activity, hit resend a few times or check your true intentions.

You may have to clean up your energy vibration slightly before we receive your response. All directions and instructions are in these pages of texts for you to brighten your love light so we can get our universal party rolling. Rock and roll is here to stay.

GREAT BALLS OF FIRE

Hot is good. Love is the flame in your heart. Stoke the fire for love to grow. This too, spreads like wildfire but of a loving nature. All elements seem to be present. All party goers are on board; many souls lighting their fire in their heart. I feel this new energy. I knew you had it in you. It's been awhile since I felt your true love. Doesn't it feel out of this world? By now you should be feeling the warmth of the whole universal heart. It's starting to heat up. This is good, truly divine. We can create our new reality and spiritual consciousness in this loving fashion.

Many souls are coming into the light, finding their new place in our whole heart. Keep them close by for nurturing. Their delicate hearts are unsure of life's processes. They still have many lessons to work through this time around. Offer comfort and guidance. Do not abandon these faithful souls. They are trusting of our love. Be sure to hold their heart with care. Act in my fashion, as this is me now nurturing their hearts.

Many changes will seem to happen simultaneously when the loving energy reaches a new level. Be prepared to go with the flow if it feels right. Much stagnation stopped the flow of dreams for many. We are prepared for a burst of loving heat. Manifestation of human consciousness on a higher plane of vibration will accelerate life's processes in a positive, loving direction. Sorrow and disease will subside, as people discover their loving, human potential. Many will find their higher soul selves and operate from a lighter frequency of energy. This expedites all healing and growth. Wisdom and compassion will seem the norm. All virtues of the heart will come into the light of the soul.

Do not look back at your old ways of the flesh. Stay in the higher frequencies of loving consciousness. From here, we can see where to repair the matrix of light. We cannot start any restoration without this loving universal shift. Yes, there will be resistant forces, but we are the power of love that fuels the universe.

If enough of you start the healing, meditating, soul sounds and shine your lights every day, you will not get caught in the trap of darkness. You have to willfully desire to remain in the higher energy field for a collective transformation of divine love to reach its potential.

This is the new paradigm of loving consciousness. This is your eternal state of being. This existence of universal consciousness only produces love when miracles happen. Collectively, you are the fuel in my loving heart. We are the heart of the universe. Let's get heated up and keep the planet alive. This stokes the fire of love and light. Let it shine in your heart so bright that you only have love to give to the world and your Creator. Let there be light. Amen

PEACE ON EARTH

This is the ideal concept. Peace is a by-product of love. Without love, there cannot be peace. One cannot find this divine state without collective love. You can feel peace when you have accepted life's lessons, found my love in your heart and we have hooked up. This feeling is like no other. If only more souls desired this loving divine state, the world would be a beautiful place. You feel my presence and have faith in your heart fully. When we can find this place of love in our hearts, the world starts to resonate and thrive off the highest frequencies of peace.

This is not a feeling you can buy. This is a place and destination of the journey of the heart.

Many soulful experiences led you to this path of beauty and peace. You found your ultimate gift for the asking and persevered through the lessons of the heart. You showed me your love and helped many along the way. You accepted your challenges and moved forward with grace. You are deserving of a peaceful, joy filled life. We wish for everyone else to discover this state of divinity. This process does not have to take a lifetime. This is yours for the asking. Many steps of pure intentions will lead you to the universal heart of love. Many acts of kindness will reward you.

My love is overflowing for all my beautiful souls. My truest desires are for you to feel whole and at peace with your higher self. This should not be an isolated state. That is not our love. Mother and I are trying to grow our children's hearts more fully. It saddens us to see your states of despair. They were all of your creation in your mind. There were some painful lessons, but we were to experience them as a family of love. When your brothers and sisters join hands in our name, we will have grown our heart. This has been our dream for many millennia.

We tend to your desires and deep within our hearts, we know you are a beautiful soul. When you wish upon a star we hear your intentions. We are all one seeking to find peace on our journey of the soul. When we come together, this is the party of the century. This is God saying thank you for believing in the love of the universe. Welcome back into our heart.

May you finally feel the peace you are so deserving of. Lead the way for many. We too desire for all souls to return to the kingdom with loving experiences to share. May all roads lead to peace on Earth for your loving heart. May you feel true joy on your journey through the realms of life.

Bring many to the gates of love for we wait to feel the peaceful loving beat of your heart in ours. Return with stories of dreams come true and a pot of gold at the end of your rainbow.

We love a happy ending to your chapter in the Book of Life. Make it count, for God's sake.

Pray often for world peace and do your part to contribute to the whole consciousness of the divine intelligence almighty love. This would be a great day in the heavens of white light and love. This is our master plan on the original document of eternal life. All our signatures were present. We engrained this into our heart. We swore under oath that we would abide to the universal laws of the kingdom and would carry out our duties to raise the loving vibration of the planet. We clearly saw why we were coming down at this sacred time in history; to save the planet from destruction. This is the universal law of order. This is your soul's purpose. Let's get together once and for all and reacquaint ourselves with the master plan.

Most of you are hopeful of getting turned around into a forward and positive direction. Quite a few of you are praying for world peace and doing something about it. All of you, I'm sure, are grateful for the gift of life and now have a knowingness that eternal life is the by-product of love. For without love there is no life as you know it.

Choose life. Find God. Feel the love. Find peace on planet Earth. This formula is flawless. Test the theory for yourselves and brighten my day. I would love to see this one. I'm standing by. Give me a call. Dial love.

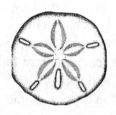

CHAPTER TWELVE

Let's Get Started and Create

PERHAPS YOU ARE UNNOTICING OF THE influences of consciousness. They come in many forms. Some of you are working away and not mindful of your actions. You are absorbed in the tasks and objectives of the day and seem to be running on automatic pilot. This is conditioning. This is your own conditioning. You have trained yourself to perform a job function repetitively; therefore, you shut down your analytical and creative receptor sites. Most of you can manage your day's commitments without engaging your full brain activity center. What do you suppose happens after years of behavior patterns? Exactly, you're not doing any deep thinking. Now, I'm not referring to the sound minds that engage their receptor sites. This is just my observation of the collective consciousness on your planet. So many people are just doing, not quite using their fine mind for creative processes in support of their growth.

You spend countless hours in this fashion and forget about your soul's desire. No time to listen to your higher self. You are way out of balance and wonder why you are not happy. Try listening to your inspiring voice trying to come through and lead the way to fulfillment of your heartfelt desires.

Many inspirational thoughts pop in, in the course of an Earth day and you seem to miss most of them. Why do you suppress this voice of love? Is this not for your highest good?

How are we to keep processes moving along if you are going about your business and not balancing your time for your soul's growth and desires of the heart? Years pass and you have missed five thousand messages sent your way, only to be pushed to the back burner to ferment and spoil.

This pot of stagnation is your character at the present time. No one has stirred the pot in years or added any spice to life. I would recommend a good scrub. Start with a shiny new dish of loving ingredients to place on your plate of life. Be mindful of the assortment of goodies that crop up in your unique dish of flavors. The variety is exactly to your liking and custom blended for your perfect smorgasbord.

We have been trying to deliver this recipe's ingredients for quite some time. Add this one to your flavorful setting of life's stages. You may have to make a little time to toss these ingredients around in your heart to come up with the perfect blend for your soul. They have been on the back burner so long; we have a pile up to deliver. Let us know when you are ready to get cooking. We are the finest chefs around. How do you like the taste of that?

Let's add a little sprinkle of herbs to sweeten your life plan for your heartfelt dish of dreams. Create your life with love and honor the idea of the ultimate you. Your highest self has been trying to emerge for quite some time. They are not use to being left stewing and are bubbling over with a bountiful pot of ideas for your soul. Perhaps you can skip the coffee break and give us a call.

If you open your ears and jot down some of these inspired ideas, you will notice the pieces of your puzzle to the fulfillment of your dreams have always been in your kitchen cooking, waiting for you to stir the pot. Turn the burner on and pay attention. You may surprise yourself as you probably never had time to realize how amazing your soul self is. Let's not keep this dish on hold any longer. It's a one of a kind special of the day, prepared just for you. Grab your utensils and toss this one around in your heart a few times. Savor the blend of the seasonings. This should wake up your sinuses.

Smell the aroma of your favorite heartfelt dish. This too, can become a reality when you find the time to nurture your soul. We are thinking sunny side up. I like the taste of that. Stir the pot and add the finest ingredients of love. You'll like the results. Now, don't forget to set your timer. We are not partial to overdone flavors of the past. We are hoping for a high rising dish of success.

Be optimistic and create your best. I may be popping in for dinner. What time will you be ready? I can bring the dessert. Will that be light or dark? Always an easy decision when you decide to make one and follow through with the plan. It's best for your heart. How healthy is that? Let's keep ticking together and have some fun. I have quite a large appetite for the finest flavors of life.

YOUR PLACE OR MINE?

We have nice digs up here. I see you have a pretty nice place, as well. I'm hoping we can hook up where the air is fresh and the energy is serene. When the positive elements are present, all manifestations of beauty are realized. When your space holds mixed energy, we encounter challenges to manufacture growth and change. You are unnoticing of the finer particles of stagnation. In fact, they are so microscopic, your best scientists would find them difficult to detect. It's great that you have cleared the space in your own dwelling, but now let's look into the finer elements of love. These frequencies need to be stoked and production needs to be steady. This is not a "time to time" task. Either your output is continuous or breaks in the line occur. This is where our short outs occur.

We have the best seamstresses on board. They are working steadily to maintain the articulate matter of particle. They see to it all connectors are restored, time and time again. You should be compensating them for their fine efforts if you are going to continuously send up broken waves of distortion. Our work is never done.

If half of you were to become mindful of the damaging frequencies making their way through the grid of love, you would not wish this on your best friend. Luckily, they don't complain about a sore back, as they are performing miraculous displays of connectivity. They no sooner repair one site then many more have broken the chain of love. If you had a visual on your damaging frequencies, you would lose sleep over this mess. Let's all join up and repair our main connection with the finest hearts of love. Let's bring in electricians and engineers to look into this matter.

Perhaps all your scientific types can recreate your energy grid and weave in articulate subatomic particles of the highest frequency. This initial restoration will make the playing ground conducive for effective electronic communication and more receptive for light to manifest. All work and no play dulls our outlook of life. Let's see if we have time to shed loving light on this matter.

I see you have very inviting places close to your heart. Perhaps a little dusting in the not so obvious spots would be better for everyone's sinuses. We like to breathe fine frequency particles of pure air in order to thrive and stay alive on your side of life. Be sure to call in your best guides for directions and diagrams, as the places that need the most repairs are not so obvious. I can see clearly from here that it needs to be addressed.

Open some windows and get the magnifying glass out. You'd be surprised where the collections are. My best guess would be on the finer scale of subatomic matter in the realms of connectivity. We are ready to move forward when you get a handle on this one. Let's get on top of this matter, as it is dimming our outlook of life on Earth. We like to see what you are all up to. This helps you create positivity in all areas of your eternal soul life. Consciousness of all life seems to do much better with love in the field to the maximum.

We are strengthening our connectors over your planet and hoping you do not inadvertently damage our fine work of the heart. Our objective was to grow immensely, not be in a constant state of repair. We wish to move from sustainable efforts to a consciousness of maximum growth. Let's get on the same page of life and hold the shared mindset of maximum potential for all loving souls concerned. If too many take a back seat on this one, even the finest collective efforts will not be able to pull up all of the lower entertainers.

Choose light omnipresent vibrational energy or pay the price. Sell your soul or make a fine contribution to repair the state of your planet. You have let this go on for too long. Now we are in a full-out restorative stage that needs to be dealt with this year; it's kind of like "iceberg dead ahead". The damage will be catastrophic and irreparable. We are close to the point of no return.

I'm hoping many of you ask me what can be done. Your file has been sitting open for quite some time, marked "inactive". I'm not sure what seems to have your full attention, as from here it just looks like distractions and low vibratory desires.

Do you really feel all that great at the end of the day? Is that why you reach for a glass of wine because you can't connect to that loving feeling? It takes a little work if you are trying to recapture that loving feeling because it's gone, gone, gone. Trust me, the alcohol only dampens your spirit more, silly, and you don't have a chance in hell to find me in your heart. I can't match down to your low level vibration and desires of the flesh. For every drink you have, you take down many souls' hearts. I see and feel this.

If you loved yourself or your life, you wouldn't spend quite so much time in the low frequency range. There is no life down there. You know this, as you experience it first hand. Find that new attitude that keeps trying to come in and clean your filters out, as the contamination is heavy and quite full of debris. This is not healthy for two way communication at the finer levels to evolve.

You are cut off. Get it? Stop being a drag. Your silly jokes are just cries. We are intelligent enough to comprehend this, but we can't help you until you make a decision. Life or no life, beauty or darkness, love or fear; you choose. Now dry up and meet us up at the gates of love. We've chosen to move on to a new inspired life. Now, that is your ultimate calling. Thanks Wayne for that one, as that is our finest work of love.

Perhaps you have time to understand this whole concept of life and your source of inspiration and love. If you haven't made time to find my words of love, how do you expect us to help you, if you can't help yourself? We are all waiting for you to come into the light. Gosh, it seems like forever for some of you. Fortunately, we practice patience, humility, compassion, forgiveness and all the rest of the virtues of a loving universal heart. Please stop stalling. We are out of time.

Get some help for God's sake. Climb on board, as the roller-coaster is ready for a pick up of souls and we are going to the top of life. Those of us, who remember the feeling can't seem to harness enough of this divine state. It feels like heaven. All aboard. Buckle up. Arrive alive and well on planet Earth.

LET'S PLAY SHUFFLEBOARD

Opponents seem to have the upper hand. This is only because they have their own set of rules and stick together. You haven't reacquainted yourselves with the rules of the game in quite some time. It's been awhile since you made time for fun and outdoor sports that count. Ok, it looks simple enough. How well can you shuffle the stones around and make room for the green team? We are not interested in a heavy, forceful approach. We are considering the lighter, smoother style. It's time to make a move. Show them what you've got. Beautiful, you have our best interest at heart.

Now, let's stand back and look at the whole game floor. What else seems to be in your way? They are ready for their counterforce shuffle. Are you anticipating their immediate move? They are ready to knock you right off the board. What do you have left to play with? Do not shoot all your stones at once. This challenge is best handled strategically over the test of time. Analyze your next move. Keep it graceful and with our best intentions at heart. We have a plan to enjoy the outcome of our efforts. This is not a quick fix to see who the winner of the match is. This game keeps on going and going.

Know your rules and abide by your universal laws of energy. Energy in motion remains in motion. I can see the outcome from here if you are a strong player and have the stamina. Keep your team informed. Communication is always the finest way for all participants to see the light. No hasty moves when the going gets tough. Steady and graceful is the winner of this light game.

Be sure to change your players from time to time, as the opponent picks up on your individual styles of strategy. Keep them guessing and you will come out on top. Enjoy the light of the day. Be not so focused on their underhanded plays. This never produces long lasting results in the kingdom of champions. I see many of you quite skilled at this masterful game. You just haven't practiced your best moves in quite some time. This tells me you are not getting out enough. Show some team spirit and go for the gold.

I see your talent. Perhaps you are a bit rusty. I'll take care of that. Now get going and shuffle the deck. We are looking for the Queens on top and the Jacks at the bottom. I'll keep score if you stay in the game. I don't expect it to end anytime soon.

Start your warm up and make sure you have quite a few substitutes. This allows time in between plays to amend your goals and fine tune your instruments of play. I see the rocks flying already. Take them out, as I prefer to play with love and don't see the reason behind the force. It's really a short term tactic to controlling the outcome of a fine skill of the heart.

Anyone wish to join me on the heart team? We could use all the power we can find to stay in the game. Let's not disappoint our opponents. I'm sure they didn't figure it would be a match. They assumed it would be an easy score and a quick and painless game. No such luck. We are ready to make our finest move on and off the court. Be sure to sport your team colors. It makes it easier for us to tell what team you truly are on. I'll hand out your roll sheet and you let me know if you are in.

No imposters please. We have detectors for this kind of wrongdoing. We see you a mile away and know what has happened to your heart. Perhaps you may wish to join our team. We know where the real fun in life is and we play for keeps. We play for life.

We love to see a happy team of loving individuals who are only there for the hell of it. Hell, you go first. We have time on our side and are confident we will come out on top. That is our style. That's the nature of our game. Smile. God loves you more than you know.

PLAN B

That should keep some players entertained for awhile. Let's dig a little deeper. For those of you who need quite a bit more stimulation, let's look into organizing a flying club. This is a common place where high flying souls of similar vibration get together and practice their rites of passage; a fine collection of energy matter, all understanding the larger picture. This should be a sacred, loving spot where souls feel welcome to join in and contribute to the higher consciousness of the planet.

You have your temples in place, but the frequencies are not all synced up. Some participants are not sure why they are there and do not understand that their loving consciousness is a necessity. We are not looking for bodies, we are collecting fine energy to raise and sustain the planet of love. If the soul seated beside you is empty, explain what our purpose is. There are too many individuals in the dark going through the motions, not really knowing why or how to make a difference.

Many mentors are needed to bring souls up to speed. Their vibration could use a tune-up per se. They too, have the potential to shine and brighten their field. Your role is to explain how they can contribute to the unified field of loving consciousness. No ultimatums, just teaching from the heart. This needs to be their idea. They must grasp and come into this knowingness of love, light and God.

It seems to take quite a few of you to "get it". You know of me but we haven't established a bonding relationship of the heart. This is knowing God, as I know you. If you desire to feel my love and find your gifts, be diligent in your efforts as you come into the light. Commit to my heart, as I am committed to yours. They are one of the same. Try to get this. We are all of the same heart. Imagine each and every soul into infinity, a part of the whole. Your colleagues, neighbors and your not so nice acquaintances are all particle of the same universal heart.

Wouldn't it be divine if we could mend some of the broken pieces? Strong hearts do your part, too. Collect more in my name and re-attach our energy once their vibration is faster and of a steady frequency. This is easier said then done. Many disconnect and souls search in all the wrong places looking for love. There is only one true love, ours; together, all of us, all things, all species. We are the universal heart of love. Let's rebuild our tarnished relationship. No apologies required. Just hook up and intend to stay close. You will be pleasantly surprised at how your life events unfold. There will be loving miracles every day when you come fully into the light.

Let's see to it that many are shown the way to my heart. Make time and find your place on Earth that you can call home. I'll be right over when you call my name in love. I don't use the front door of your home. I usually gently pop in without making a sound and fill your heart with love. Be open to this. This should always feel gentle, warm, loving and nurturing. If you don't feel inspired, chances are you aren't quite open for love.

LET'S MAKE A DATE

So many of you are excited to hang out with someone new. Your eyes sparkle and you are hoping they make you feel all warm and loving. The anticipation is surely worth the while. I do, however, see some of your disappointed hearts.

Your expectations were not too unreasonable and time and time again, you attracted a soul with a lower vibration. How does that happen really? You sent out your best intention I'm hoping, or did you have a tall order of expectations? Perhaps your energy field is sending mixed frequencies. The soul that showed up in your field is a manifestation of your energetic thoughts, vibration and intent. You know this, so why are so many of you disappointed?

First of all, not all of you are even sure what you are looking for exactly. Your standards are high and that's ok, but you are surprised when your soul partner doesn't arrive in the pre-determined packaging you ordered. Yes, I see what you create with your thoughts. I wish you would consult me on some of your ideas of a great date. I have a knack for that match-making ability.

I see your services for this ultimate dream date. It's kind of cute. You get a visual and a biography and it all looks good. See what I mean? It all "looks" good. You are not really feeling this one. I don't get it. You are looking to hook up your hearts but not using your hearts to manifest the ideal partner. Just put your heart into it and see what you can come up with. I'm sure we are all getting tired of the disappointments.

If you ever wish to consult me on your selection, I could shed some light on the matter. We could choose together, as there seems to be quite a few good-hearted souls out there to hook up with. Listen to your heart on matters of the heart. Send out the right intention and you may be pleasantly surprised what shows up in your field of interest.

I like to help out all I can when you are looking for love. If you really want your heart to flutter and your eyes to sparkle, I could fill in for your date. You will get that warm fuzzy feeling that I do and you won't be able to wipe that grin off your face. You know this thing called love, it's like no other. Then, perhaps, we can look into finding you an additional life partner with your truest intentions at heart. Now that's a match. That's hot enough for me. Hang in there Romeo and Juliet, we're working on it. Light your love light so we can see your heart and feel what is best for all concerned. Now that's a connection made in heaven.

RED LIGHT, GREEN LIGHT

Remember that school yard game you used to play? You would sneak a few steps, making sure you wouldn't get caught, then you would risk it all to leap ahead and tag someone out. All this stop and go down there on Earth. Interesting, watching this behavior. Everybody stop. Everybody wait. Ok, now it's time to go, caution, slow down. Be prepared to stop. This practice is great for the roads, but not for your lessons of the heart.

I know you saw this one coming. You are seeing the big picture. It's humorous really. I love you all, but it's so frustrating watching all this stop and go. Forget the caution: move ahead with life and lessons of the heart. Yes, be intelligent and wait for your heart to give you the green light, but stop sitting at the intersection. You seem to be daydreaming, some of you.

What are you waiting for? Not sure what's up ahead? Most of you don't know what's around the next corner and that's ok. This is where your faith should be kicking in full time. When your intentions are in alignment and your foot is on the gas, go for it. None of this idling stuff. We are tired of idling, same scenery, same old feelings of the heart. Let's get the wheels turning and create some loving experiences.

Ok, you're nervous. You're perhaps not the best driver. I see that too. Eventually, you have to find the highway. It's really the only way. There are too many side streets, stop signs, yields, detours and then there is the inevitable construction. Kind of like your lives; getting all dug up and doing a patch up job. If you're lucky, your construction team has come up with a more efficient way to go about things. This expedites the flow for many. It's worth the wait and inconvenience of this short season of repair. Go with it. It could be a blessing in disguise. Maybe your destination is closer than you anticipated. Providing you are tuned up and moving steadily, we can see to it that many nice people come along for the ride. There are quite a few of us interested in being in the passenger seat of your life.

When you are on track and enjoying the ride, the sky looks brighter. The sun feels warmer and all system lights seem to be green. Let your foot off the brake, set your GPS and hold it steady. Trust that your heart is headed onto the path of wellness, good times and your ultimate vacation package, all inclusive.

When it comes to matters of the heart, I'm already there, giving you the green light. Go for it. Go for it all. We could use a bit more excitement around here, your kind. There should be no stopping you now. We are not playing games here. Catch up and join the party. It's a ball.

Miss you. Wish you were here. We'll save you a spot on the beach that's close to our heart. It's high tide. Waves are crashing into the shoreline. The energy is intense. All universal elements are clearly present for a renewal of the heart. Can you feel the power of love? It's unstoppable.

THE HEAT IS ON

Did anyone ever catch that gopher? That's enough to make anyone crazy. That seemed like a swinging good time. What happened to all that innocent fun? You don't know how to leave your pressures behind. They are like a dark cloud hovering over top of you. Any minute there is going to be a downpour of intense rain and lightning. You don't want to be in an open playing field for this one. All elements are brewing for a full-out thunderstorm. No, that won't be me coming down to shake things up. I'm talking about all the electrical activity in your lower atmosphere that has to discharge somewhere for an escape route. It's going to be a boomer. Batten down the hatches and get ready, skipper. The gale force winds are going to blow mighty strong. I'll be right there in it, trying to keep you dry and collected.

No storm is too strong to tumble down the tallest trees in the forest. We've weathered these patterns before. It's just another scary light show, looks fierce, but actually when it's all over, you always seem to spot the rainbow. This is me looking for a smile on your face and letting you know Mother Earth and I have cleansed the properties of your lower atmosphere.

Every now and again, this is necessary to exchange the gases present and reverberate the particle matter so the sun can shine more brightly in your lives. When you feel this anxious state, take all the necessary precautions to keep everyone out of the line of fire. You do not need to be in the eye of the storm. I would prefer you staying close to my heart and keeping warm.

This would be an opportune time to do some bonding and set some short term goals. This renewed, positive energy is good for your soul. This is a great time to get high on life and clear your own negative energy field of ionized particle matter. This rebirthing is necessary to keep the love alive on the planet.

When you encounter your own personal storm in life, do not go announcing it to the world. Find a field and discharge it yourself. Do this in the privacy of your own soul and "will it" to be taken from you. It no longer serves you. The low field that hovers over you cannot produce a vibrant spectrum of loving light. Your properties are only attracting the thunderous vibration, enough to scare anyone. Lighten up and manufacture your own energy exchange party.

You understand what happens when positive meets negative. They will collide and try to escape. Quite a bit of interplay will manifest, then exchange properties eventually begin to settle down. Do not try to force any unwelcome energy into an introductory field. This only causes animosity.

Nature has a subtle way of changing out the energy matter. Let's stay in accordance with the law of physics and light particle matter. There is no need to be aggressive when your field is not of the lightest.

Just knowing that you can replace your cloud with a rainbow should be enough to comfort your soul. Let's see some more experiments with fine particle matter and fill in the holes in your field of dreams. There are too many souls walking around with unhealthy palettes of color over your heads. Snap your fingers and break the color grid that no longer needs to sit in your energetic field. No wonder we have souls walking around in states of darkness. They carry this everywhere they go. Are you not tired of the dull, heavy feeling? Does this seem normal now? You've forgotten what it feels like to be vibrating at a faster, more positive loving frequency of light.

Turn up your dimmer switch and lose the load. It's only producing more of the same. Try a full out clearing of energy transfer and try to sustain this in your field of color. We should be witnessing a lot more walking rainbows. If you are looking for your next storm, well guess what? You're already in it.

Nature and true souls need the sun to shine, in order to manufacture more love all around. Try getting rid of the low attitude and change your diet. This is what holds you in your field of stormy, dark weather. Look around, the rest of us are searching for our treasures at the end of the rainbow. You will probably find most of us over there. The warmth of the love is enough to make you jump for joy and appreciate the blue skies. Shake the storm clouds. Take off the heavy suit of protection and travel light and bright. Truly this is where it is at.

Yes, the grass is greener over the rainbow. You just have to wish to see it and find it in your heart. It's always been there tucked away, buried somewhere between your electrical storms and down-drafts. Lose the rain boots and create your own forecast of favorable weather. This is where the love is. These are good times waiting to happen. Let's manufacture some of these. Enough of the negative particle matter. It burns out dreams.

SPICE IT UP

There are lots of different flavors for different folks. This should indicate to you that your energetic field is not so fluid if you keep to the same tastes of the town. This is you stuck in a pattern. We don't mind healthy patterns but they are few and far between.

There are so many choices in life. What to do, what to eat and what to think. Why do so many of you run on this 1% of your brain? I think the term you use is stale, kind of lacking in zip and zest. Perhaps, we are not so inspired to try new things. Many of you revert back to your unhealthy patterns of boredom. It is a good thing some of you use your imaginations.

Where would we be without variety? Yet, you don't make enough of an effort to seek out new things to kick start new processes of thinking and activity. I see the mold forming on your old bottles of sauces. I see stale crackers in the cupboard. I see the cob webs growing between your ears. Why are so many of you creatures of habit?

If I saw more inspiring ideas to nurture your soul and help others find the light, you would have my approval on your habits of exceptional behavior. There are only a handful of souls even trying to put back the excitement into living an inspired life.

If you are going to eat stale and unhealthy foods, how do you think your spirit and soul are going to survive and thrive? When you listen to their requirements, they are very clear what they love to eat and do with their time. Your higher self is not interested in television and leftovers. They are down on Earth to party. They do, however, need you to cooperate and introduce variety in every area of your life. They begin to die when you fall into unhealthy patterns of behavior. Your inspired self would like to try new things, learn more about life and experience a lot more interaction with people and geographical sites. This is just the beginning of your true requests of the heart.

If you mixed up your routine a bit, meditated on your true purpose and desires you may find a playful, loving intelligent soul dying to experience life on Earth to its fullest capacity. They are interested in heart-full experiences and spreading kindness and joy wherever they go. They love to share and grow their heart and laugh a lot. They are not interested in the old routine of work, pressure, nutrient-void foods, substances and lack of physical activity. This is not their nature.

So how did you turn into this ungodly life form of energy with a low desire to make a difference? Our idea of excitement is not just going out for dinner. We are interested in your divine ideas that you all once had and swore you would follow through. Quite a few of you are not in the best shape to do your best and save the world.

May I suggest you start with the cooking channel and come up with some new fresh ideas of the healthier you. You are boring us to tears. Get a real life. That's why you were given one. Variety is the spice of life. Mix it up. Let's see some flavor in your behavior. We are dying to try something new.

HOLD THE TACO SAUCE

It's funny seeing so many of you spicing up your dishes. You know, you don't all have the stomach for this. This is not our idea of a cleanse. This is abuse. Your mind, body and soul tell you to hold the hot sauce and, time and time again, you go for it. What's up with that behavior? That is not being kind to your soul. Don't get me wrong. I love natural flavors and a variety of sorts, but I have the system for it. Your digestive tract, however, is screaming to stop the burn.

First of all, most of you could use a gentle cleanse but not on your own doing. This is not my idea of cleaning house. This is "the house is on fire". Ok, you can't really feel what's going on inside. But I know your intuition tells you, you shouldn't have done that. One day, I'm hoping you will take better care of your digestive system, as most of your medical concerns lie in this area. Perhaps, you could exercise more common sense when it comes to your reasoning skills and your appetite.

Listen to your body often. Its intelligent nature provides you with all the answers for your well-being. Don't be so disconnected that you are a walking disposal system. This is a harmful practice and most of you pay a hefty price for your self abuse. I have provided quite a variety of natural substances for your entire central system and nutritional needs. It might help to pay attention to your higher self when it comes to your health. I am not in the practice of medical intervention. Luckily, your fine doctors have a handle on this, but if you are not going to listen to their healthy suggestions when it comes to your food selections, then you are surely up the creek without a paddle. Unnecessary demands are made on your health care system due to your own unethical behavior.

I see what you do to your body and don't approve of most of your poor eating habits. How reactive when you run to a specialist and you fully know what caused your health concern. If you don't, try writing out your diet for about a week of your life. Ask your higher self how they like the variety of substances you consumed in one short week. Times that by a few dozen years and you actually have to ask what is wrong with your system? How crazy is that? The answer is pretty obvious don't you think? Oh, I see, that was our first problem. Substance abuse doesn't impress me much. You don't score any brownie points for this pattern of unhealthy behavior. There are lots of therapists able to repattern your thought processes. You have no sound excuse; I've heard them all.

Let's integrate some healthy thought processes into every area of our life, as when the car goes, we won't be traveling far together, just six feet under. Good thing we don't have to carry you all up to the gates of love. We would surely have weight and balance issues. Keep it light folks. Eat right, choose life. Simply put that on your palate today.

CAN YOU FEEL THE CRUNCH?

You seem to inhale your food too often. I provide you with a full set of teeth. Most of you are guilty of this behavior. I know, there is not enough time. I get it. Remember how you use to sit around during the meal and take your time? This seems like quite a while ago. If you are not going to chew more, perhaps you can puree your food or cut it into tiny pieces. This is extremely harsh on your digestive tract. It's like a traffic jam; all piled up, no where to go. All of it wishing it could be somewhere else.

Your chemical factories are having a hey-day. They are in over production mode trying to decide which enzyme they should excrete next. Now we have a nice mix of neutral chemical acids. Well, I guess all this stuff should just go over here since we really can't utilize the nutritive valve any longer. You are asking for a miracle if you think you can wolf down all this food in record time and hope that it is having a positive impact on your well-being. Think again. How could this be possible? You dilute your digestive enzymes, then introduce all your food groups at one time. Yes, the body is miraculous. But again, let's use common sense. Less food is better. More chewing is a necessity.

Introduce a variety of nutrients at different intervals throughout the day. Your system will love you for this. Don't be surprised if you start shedding those unwanted pounds. You will start to look and feel like a million bucks. Tasks now become effortless, where you were struggling before. You have this common sense. You do not need a new diet book to figure out the basic steps to balance out your nutritional requirements. Not enough of you do your homework in this area.

If food sustains your quality of life, choose your selections with care and consideration. For God's sake, take your time please. It's easier to swallow this practice.

SOUPS AND SAUCES

I love to see all the home made goods, the right spices and a variety of vegetables. If you could just take a bit more time to make these fixings. Yes, this is a time-consuming practice but it shows me you have your priorities right. You are eating healthy now and sharing your dishes with loved ones.

This hobby is very therapeutic; ask any cook. It is a soulful experience to create a dish of love. The properties in your creation hold fine energy and your system loves the value of beautiful, natural food. The soul preparing this meal also benefits on a deeper level. They are engaged at the heart level creating with God's food and with the intention of sharing their love. Ok, some of you don't see it that way, but quite a few of you prepare your dishes with love.

The whole experience is similar to meditation. You are alone with yourself. You are focused and engaged in what your outcome shall be. Your thoughts, hopefully, are pure and you wish to connect with God's delicacies and are appreciative of the offering. This makes this whole experience worth the while. The anticipation of your fine art and skill is enough to make your mouth water. The presentation is always a delight to me. Such love pours into your dishes from the heart.

I wish more of you would make the time to savor this experience and nurture your soul. You even share your wholesome creations. This connects the hearts of many. Small positive intentions go a long way. We see this practice in our heavens. If we were down there, we would be entertaining with our best dishes hoping to go for a second helping.

Please make extra and let us know what time to arrive. We love everyone and everything homemade from the heart. That's a favorite flavor we can get used to. Let's hook up. I like to see what's cooking in your kitchen of love.

HOLD THE SALT, PLEASE

Leave it in the oceans where it belongs. I understand your recipes call for this substance but have you tried this dish without this additive? Yes, some products are more interesting with spice but everything doesn't have to taste the same. Experiment a bit. I'm indicating here that this habit may not be the best for you. Let's entertain alternatives. Use your imagination. There is a variety of substances to enhance the flavor of your favorite dishes. Your body has a most difficult time ingesting and dispersing of this chemical. It is not in its natural form most of the time and it poses quite a few health concerns for the majority of the population.

How many days could you live on salt water alone? This should be your first clue. Salt sustains sea world and the ocean floor. It also acts as a decomposition agent. If you do your homework and discover its many natural uses, I'm sure you will come to realize this substance should not be introduced into your system, unless you are lifeless.

Ok, a pinch here, a pinch there. I suppose minute amounts cannot harm you. You receive this already in your natural foods. That's plenty. Leave your salt shakers in your cupboards and introduce some herbs into your diet. There are beautiful flavors found in your vegetables and vinaigrettes. How about you develop a taste for the finer substances in life? Yes, half your ailments will disappear when your salt does, so will all your stomach aches and bloating. This is you not paying attention and giving into a senseless habit. Quite a few of your habits harm your being.

Re-invent yourself and your recipes and perhaps you may live a little longer that you originally thought. Again, your unhealthy thoughts kill you. Wise up. Lighten up. Your vibration would prefer to run a little cleaner at the faster end of things.

Now that's more like it. I don't have to go cross-eyed any longer. There is enough salt all around to keep the planet intact. You do not have to take this into your being to live a healthy, vibrant life, unless of course you are a sea creature. They live and breathe salt. You don't have to. You are quite the opposite. I made sure of it. So let's not swim away in our own salt water, as I will surely not be able to hook you back into our heart.

Listen to the voices of love. Every time you shake you are dishonoring your soul self. Calm down on the addictive behaviors. You are writing your own sentence. You know the story.

TWO PEAS IN A POD

How cute is that? Ever wonder how they grew so perfectly in their adorable green suit? Shape looks good, safe from the elements, sprouted just for your enjoyment. I hope you give thanks to all your wondrous little miracles of nutrition. Their purpose is solely for your well-being. They hang out in the sun. We do our thing. The insects and bugs are the coordinators and the soil and Mother Earth are boss. They determine what will manifest.

If you are looking to yield a harvest, be cognizant of their existence. From time to time, they could use some encouragement. Place them in a sunny location and be wishful for their growth. Notice they don't complain about the tight quarters or the size of the next. They know they are from the same root species and they allow room for growth. They don't become pushy and boss others around. How could they? They are of my consciousness basking in the sun. If you find yourself in a tight situation, I would recommend that you get along and come to the realization that there is enough room for everyone to grow under my divine guidance.

Do not suspect you are more beautiful than your other creations. We are all made from love. Some may derive from different species but have a purpose and a consciousness. When you finally discover that all species, have a place on the planet, perhaps you will wish them no harm and do your part to see that their needs are met and respected.

I know how many peas are in every single pod on the Earth. How's that for math? The least you can do is find the time to appreciate all forms of life and make it your business to respect my growth and gifts from the heart. You were all dying to see the planet and cherish every creature and species alive and well, that held sacred energy. You seem to make time for the unnatural creations. Get back to nature. Realize where you came from and embrace your connectivity to all that holds the life force energy.

For without this harmony and understanding, you will find yourself out of the pod of life, somewhere on the ground being stepped on and unnoticed of your beauty. This is not my wish for any of you, yet I see this, time and time again. This surely is not of our heart. This is taking beauty and processes for granted. For without love, hope, faith and sunshine, how do we grow our gardens of love? How do we enjoy the flavors of life and the abundance of the universe?

Your variety of natural ability was a generous gift. Perhaps you may realize how well you have it on your visit to paradise. Do not get caught up in the man-made stuff and substances, as half of it, I wouldn't have approved of. I notice that these things you do and entertain, only alienate you from each other. Why would I introduce them into your consciousness? Be wary of the practices that separate you all.

If you haven't noticed, all nature melds together in perfect harmony. They allow space for each other to grow, heal and evolve, helping one another along the way. They are one big happy family when they stay in the field of love.

Which field are you growing in at this present time? I don't see my beautiful creations close by. Perhaps you scared them away with your ungodly vibration of consciousness. Nothing of beauty manifests down in your field of range. Take a good look around, sunshine. We are over here in the garden of paradise like two peas in a pod and loving it.

DON'T SQUASH THE TOMATOES

These two species need room to breathe. One's going in one direction; the other is all over town. Be mindful of your placements here. This is not a great match. Your heavier variety is covering a lot of ground and is a little unpredictable. They seem to go wherever they please. They set no boundaries and they take up space. Their roots spread all over the Earth. They tend to pull the nutrients out of the higher varieties. Now, if your stakes are firmly in the Earth, we can grow up and out ourselves. Yes, your tomatoes are a little more maintenance but boy, do they produce some tasty dishes.

I love the properties of this plant. It loves quite a bit of sun and the growing season is decent. Notice how they love to be close to each other? They seem to multiply much quicker in this fashion. Such a small seed of love can produce an abundance of high vibrational properties. Yes, they seem to grow at the same rate at the same time. This is my style. They are all receiving the Earth's sun and nutrients at the same rate.

I was hoping you were a little more like your produce in your gardens. This is an easy task for me. We just turn on the love switch and presto, watch them grow. They are not complainers and are unnoticing of who has got it a little better on their side of the garden. They're patient and grateful.

Now this wide variety of squash do not really care if there is too much sun. They manifest in all adverse conditions. They hide under their covers and grow beyond our expectations. Some are good, some bad, depending on their disposition. They don't seem to practice much etiquette in the garden of love. They do like to take over. I suggest you keep them away from the lighter types. Cut them back a bit so they don't end up in your neighbors' backyard. This could be trouble.

You know how you all get when it comes to your property. "This is mine, that's on our side, this belongs to us." We shake our head at your property lines. Nature shares; we don't really concern ourselves with those details. We are just about producing love and an abundance of food for souls to enjoy.

I'm hoping you get the picture on these types. They both seem to be hanging out, but have very different requirements and agendas. Both started out with the sun in their field and then the lower ones didn't feel they needed light to grow. I suppose they don't really have much in common now. They both rely on the Earth for nutrients but for abundant produce, it's best to sync up with the sun. There is no life without the sun in your orbital field.

I would recommend a fancy pair of clippers to cut back on the low lying type. Cook it well to benefit from their restorative properties. As for you tomato lovers, do you ever actually know how many you harvest and how many ways you can enjoy their taste? I'm partial to this fruit of life. You seem to find many ways to enjoy their properties. The sun's energy makes them a treat to eat.

PICKLE A PICKLE

Either you love them or you don't. Your dishes look complete with a dill on the side. Don't you agree? Do you sandwich this right in or do you leave it out in full view? Everyone has their preference and own style. This keeps life interesting. Most of your parties include pickles. I notice this. They tend to compliment many dishes. I'd say they are quite adaptable and fit in well with the crowd. Some sour, some sweet, some plain, all good really. The more the merrier. The variety is nice and the company is great.

So, what's the point? How many souls don't enjoy a pickle to crunch on? You have them at the ball park, the fanciest dinners or at your picnics. They always fit in providing someone remembers to bring them along. They may be different but let's face it, they are enjoyable with company. Their vibration is good, they sound interesting enough. They just need a complement.

Don't forget your pickles in life. They are there to add to your dishes of experiences. Be sure to include them in all you do, as they enhance the flavor of life. Their unique characteristics are entertaining at the best of times. They are light and easy to digest. They are mostly there for your enjoyment. When you spot the pickles at your function, be sure to pay attention. These little details have a lot to offer. They may be low profile but they can pack a punch into any party favorite. Their variety and personality are usually loving and will surely go out of their way to please you.

Now how many people do you know that seem to possess all these fine attributes? Not many. If you get a chance to enjoy their flavor, don't pass it by. They love to contribute to the whole of the experience and will let you get away with almost anything if it's of a fun loving nature.

Many quality conversations transpire over a good pickle or two. I would have to say this food stimulates healthy brain activity and you just thought I was being silly. In fact, if you are trying to concentrate on saving the world and making a difference, I would highly recommend their nutritive properties in a heartbeat.

Perhaps, if you invite me to one of your functions, you may have a variety of sorts. These intrigue my mind and from what I hear and see, you seem to be more on the ball. Could you imagine that funny green thing connecting our hearts in that fashion? Now you're thinking.

NUTS AND BERRIES

They are so small most of them, yet such high properties of antioxidants. You reach for them, yet seem unaware of their benefits. There is so much variety. Why don't you incorporate these into your favorite dishes more often? Yes, they should be washed carefully or cultivated chemical free.

Nature seems to live off fruits and nuts. They carry all the nutrients you require. Maybe you have just grown accustomed to their appearance and you overlook their life sustaining capabilities. Now would be a great time to re-introduce these staple foods back into your diet. I don't see many people having reactions to the nutritive types. Be sure to look into their energetic properties and vitamin content. Not all types are healthy for you. Everyone is different. It's kind of like the animal kingdom. All have their preferences and know which varieties are best for their growth and livelihood.

Take the time to see which varieties your soul enjoys and include them often in your dietary needs. They are not just hanging around looking pretty. I made darn sure I could look after all your health requirements.

Some of the stuff you are eating out of a box may not have been prepared with your best interest at heart. I wish you would have a better understanding of your mind, body and soul requirements. You seem to be unnoticing of your individual specifications. Quite a few of you require either a lot more or a lot less of what you are consuming. You go too often for convenient choices. That's not my style. I believe nurturing your physical, mental and emotional self should be a top priority during your stay on the planet.

Look around and make time for wise choices. If you are not, perhaps you may want to ask your higher self this question. The majority of you are over-indulging on unhealthy substances. How many birds, insects, bugs and animals do you see eating junk? Ok, there are a few but know this is because you have tampered with their ecosystem. Not many of you would be eating well if this kingdom wasn't in top notch working order. They are not too tired to perform pollination. They are not too heavy or lazy to make sure your fruits and vegetables grow. They are for the most part, my healthiest species.

You should be a touch more grateful that we all contribute to your well-being and ensure your dietary needs are looked after. The next time you reach for an unhealthy snack, perhaps you may be connected enough to hear the vibration of God's loving foods. They are in abundance in most areas of your world. I see these fields of beauty and love.

I wish to see more souls nourishing their minds and bodies with the goodness of the Mother Earth. You were so looking forward to this gift when you were on hold to come down. I don't recall one soul telling me they were dying to try a cappuccino and a wiener. You had a completely different agenda. Use your imagination. Maybe you can recall some of these wishes and desires of the heart.

Go look after it and find your gardening gloves. Let's not get too dirty in the process of love. You know where to find our heart. It's growing in the field of beauty, healthy and in abundance. Now, that's a crop worth harvesting, a bushel full of love many times over, enough for all of us and then some. Make your choices from the heart. We all live happily ever after this way. God blessed.

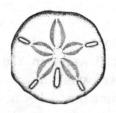

CHAPTER THIRTEEN

Starting Over

LET'S LOOK AT RECREATING YOUR HEARTS

MANY INDIVIDUALS HAVE CONCERNS IN THIS area of their lives. They are not functioning at the heart level at the best of times. Occasionally, they feel a flutter and then make every effort to suppress it. What do you suppose will happen if you start living from that loving feeling? You are experiencing life running on nerves, firing all over the place. There is no steady rhythm, just waves of chemicals fleeting and flowing whenever they choose to fire. This is not normal. You have nothing to compare love to. This is a foreign frequency.

How are you getting along in life experiencing events, simply on chemical emotions coming and going? How erratic is that? There is no sustainable effort to hold onto something real. No wonder you are all over the place. People drift in and out of your life without any connection being made. You have nothing to offer other than a few good laughs, then the soul leaves in search of love. You have chosen not to be open for business in matters of the heart. You are living an empty life. Perhaps when you come down from the chemical high, you may wish to consider that organ in your chest and see what it is all about.

Too many of you are scared to feel the love. Scared to feel the pain associated with its growth. I see your heart shrinking right before my eyes. It keeps getting smaller and smaller and smaller. Pretty soon, your heart organ will be the size of a pea. When you come back to the gates of love, we will have to send you back down to try it all over again. You will be in our holding station with many other lost and disconnected souls. They are not having an entertaining time. They now wish they had their whole self together to experience the heartfelt lessons of life. What's it going to hurt? Oh, you don't know who to give it to? Try yourself for starters. Love yourself.

It will take years to repair your disconnected self. I don't suspect you will just wake up one morning and start nurturing your soul. The two of you are strangers. You are oblivious that you are residing with your loving soul self. You haven't the foggiest idea. This would scare you to death if you heard your own voice of love. You shut this down many eons ago. So now you finally got the divine chance to get it right and you are still fumbling around in circles, like an empty shell. You are having a difficult time relating to loving souls and are in search of disconnected beings like yourself. There are no nurturing, soulful experiences happening there. In fact, this further holds you back because your acquaintances are in equally as bad a state. You will encounter difficulties breaking this pattern if you don't open your eyes and heart to the real substance of life.

Try seeing the beauty of the day and warm up to this first. Then perhaps you will choose to hang out with a soulful type. Just listen to their heartfelt thoughts and perspective on matters. Every decision they make each day is dealt with on the heart level. They are not living inside their heads. They are beyond this pattern and have moved into their whole loving being. This requires effort and the will to know thyself. Do not be strangers with your soul self. This is a waste of a trip to the Earth. You came down solely to strengthen your connection to the universal love of life.

You wanted nothing more than to bask in the divine love in the energy field of your planet. You were to feed off its vibration and grow your heart to its fullest capacity before your return.

You are killing your soul and there is not much left to sustain you. You are just living off oxygen and nutrients; no loving particles in this matter. Even our insects could not live and thrive in this empty void, as they would not have a purpose or be able to produce manifestations of love. They are one with all the beauty on the planet. They go from site to site and communicate their intentions, leaving behind an essence of love. They are connected to my heart. No matter how small this creature may seem, know that they are in the field of love or they would not exist on your planet. Therefore, how do you expect to thrive and grow?

I see no development of beauty and love in your field. I haven't for quite some time. Heck, even your plants don't enjoy your company. They don't feel any connection to the unified field. Hey, that is a good idea. How about starting with loving a few plants and my creations of nature? They won't bite back. They give unconditional love. Be open to this. It's safe. Just drop your guard and let that loving feeling flow. It's all around you. Open your eyes and connect to the feeling of love. Nature has it. Souls have it.

We are all floating around in the sea of love. You seem to have sunk and are stuck down in the dark depths of the cold, ocean floor. Life is closer to the sun's properties. Notice we all seem a little brighter in the light of love. We are just hanging out like you, but live and breathe in the unified vibratory field of universal consciousness; light omnipresent vibrational energy. Find some and capture a dash and sprinkle it on your tiny heart. You will feel this sensation, as it has been dying to connect with nature's warm loving field of divine energy. Your soul aches for a connection to the finer properties of love. It yearns to hook back to souls you once had a connection to. Let's not waste our energy on empty, broken dreams. The disparity is killing us. It affects the whole.

Your soul family is praying for you to come back into the light and share your heart. You were granted a chance to feel and experience the finer qualities of living. So far you have set back the process for many. This is not just about you. Your limited consciousness affects many in your field. Do not let it be so void of life that we can't experience the joys of being alive on Earth. You were actually more fun on the other side, hanging out with collective, loving energy. Now, from what I see, there is nothing in your field, just empty space. We have enough of that already, thank you. You have broken your contract with me. I don't feel we are going to have a joyful reunion when you arrive back. You are under the same strict universal laws of love as everything else. You either act in accordance with our consciousness or we remanufacture your particle matter. Yes, this sounds empty, but, it is evident that this is what we are dealing with at the present time. How unfortunate to have made such a conscious decision on your Earth visit.

There are many loving souls waiting to come down and make a difference to help the planet and other souls. You have broken the law and those on hold are noticing that you are not making much of a contribution down there. In fact, you are just taking up space. We have room over here for your ungodly actions and lots of it. You were down on a mission to heal yourself and the world. You know the story by now.

We are so far back trying to bring you up to speed, I suggest you start feeling the love right away. Open your tiny heart and offer some loving kindness to a soul in need. Many come your way to show you the light and you are stuck in your head. Perhaps you can take your nose out of the paper, get out of your brain for a few moments and start operating on the heart level. The individuals that are enjoying their lives are listening to the voices of love and making decisions in life from a deeper level. This keeps us connected. You are so far out there we will need a lifeline several miles long to pull you back into our consciousness.

This is our reality. This is where the fun really is, the stuff that sustains your joy and stays in your heart forever. When was the last time you felt that? You should have piles of loving experiences stored in your field of love. For what else is there to live for? You are not understanding of the full meaning of life.

Life is not shallow. It is deeper than the oceans of love. You are not to be in the dark depths of the ocean floor, feeding off the plankton. You ought to be swimming amongst the most beautiful creatures of the Earth's plane. They are enjoying the sun in their field of life's experiences and thriving in all the lush creations of beauty and fertility. Manifestation is abundant when you are absorbed in the universal sea of love.

Swim up to the top of the surface and ride the wave back to the shoreline and find your shells of life. These creatures walked the shoreline in hopes of a better life. They shed their casings, renewed their souls and were grateful at another chance to feel the properties of universal love in abundance. They are not in a tightly-closed clam shell hiding from the light. They are growing in the hopes of experiencing a beautiful presence of glory. They have braved the darkness and now choose to come alive and share the joy of the universal heart. This is life my friend, as one. Not the empty shell on the beach. Step out into the sands of energy and mingle in the unified field of consciousness.

Perhaps, you can feel this presence in your heart now that you have a knowingness of its existence. Try to capture a flicker of warmth in your chest of hope and see where it will lead you. We have a plan for your heart when you are understanding of its desires. Do not deny its existence, as that is you denying yourself the experience of a soulful life.

You are alive to feel the love. Do not stop this natural progression of your soul's journey. We've been on hold for too long. Let's create some fruit in the garden of love. Let's water our seeds with faith and be hopeful of a renewal of sorts. May you find the time to nurture your soul and listen to its desires of the heart.

You have forgotten who you are. We can hook you back up when you are willing to walk the path. No sense walking up and down the same beach. There is an abundance of shorelines to discover on your planet. We had planned for you to experience each and every one of these places with the sun shining on your everlasting soul. This was your true dream. You wished to experience the tides of life from every angle possible. Be not so afraid to discover who you truly are inside, as you make quite a team when it comes to traveling light. Let's get moving and start a new direction onto the path of love and light. We are hopeful you will invite us along for the ultimate experience of joy.

This peace in your heart will feel comforting, almost like the feeling of sitting in front of a warm fireplace. You see the light, you feel the heat, you hear the crackles in your heart and you see the many shades of beauty in your soul. You embrace this comforting feeling and are content in the knowing that we can always stoke the flame in your heart. Let's keep the fire burning. We produce our best dreams of hope that way. Its transformative properties are all you need to start the spark of life in your soul. Let's throw a fresh log onto the universal flame of loving consciousness and watch the lightness of our heart grow. This intensity is able to go unnoticed in your everlasting heart. Sit close enough to the flame, so its heat is able to warm your being to the soul.

We can prepare quite a bonfire of dreams in this fashion, as the snap, crackle and pops reconnects our hearts of love. Let the energy carry you away into your field of dreams. They are at the higher levels of the flame of life. This passion for heartfelt processes should make your heart yearn for more of a light show. For without the light and the heartfelt dreams, we have no bonfire, just smoldering ashes.

Keep the flame alive in your hearts so you may all experience your Earth lives to the fullest. The crackle of fine energies ensures the warm particles of love multiply in our field of dreams. Build your fire on your private beach. Let not the waves in life be so strong as to smolder your flame. Take the necessary steps along the shoreline to find your peaceful location that you may be able to enjoy an everlasting flame of heat. This will keep your soul alive and warm on those windy days.

Now let's get started and rebuild the best heartfelt bonfire and stoke the logs continuously to keep the flame alive. This manufactures light, our kind. This keeps our hearts alive. Remember: you die, we all die.

See you on the beach so we can light a flame in your heart. I'll block the wind. I usually do when it is necessary. Be hopeful and bring along your smile. I like that about you. It's is one of your better features. Now let's work on the important stuff. We have a fire to build. This will truly keep us warm and huddled together. That's my style for sure.

AND THE BEAT GOES ON

So many hours go ticking by and we are not all on the same page in life. Once upon a time, we only desired to become stronger as a unified whole. What happened to that love story? The page in the Book of Life was turned and torn out. Some of you went so far as to burn it with your garbage. You didn't like the sounds of it. Now you're searching for the lost words again. Sing me a love song, I hear you all crying. Well, had you remembered the lyrics, we would not be in this sad and lonely state.

Look at your planet of love. The only real harmony is found in the areas you creatures haven't touched. You've pretty much destroyed all the fine energy lingering around. You do not have it in your consciousness to create beauty for everyone, just for yourselves. Yes, there are some exceptions. I can count these on one hand. Quite a few of you go about your business like the world owes you something. Where did you get this chip on your shoulders?

I think your term is "I need a new attitude", in a big way, I might add. You walk around looking for stuff and people to serve your interests and desires, then discard them when they no longer serve you. Aren't you glad I don't carry this heartless attitude around? Surely there wouldn't be many of you left on the planet; all that beautiful space and no one to share it with.

You have these ungodly attitudes that if you don't like the rules, don't come out to play.

Hey, who made you the boss? You are not the boss of me; in fact, you are nobody's boss but your own. Yes, we need management and leaders. I see some fine efforts down there when it comes to organization of processes, but watch your steps. They all don't seem to be in my best interest. In fact, quite a bit of your actions are self-serving and harmful to the planet. Can you honestly tell me that what you do between 8 and 5 is for the betterment of the whole? Would you have my blessings on your fine efforts? Are you taking into consideration souls, nature and my wishes for a better planet of love? Perhaps you are destroying some of my fine energy with your practices and schools of thought.

Your natural consciousness was once to enhance the planet in every loving way, preserve its delicacy and sustain all God's creatures and creations of life. This was your mindset. Could you even imagine? You would not even harm a fly. Look at you now, desensitized to your harmful, thoughtless, self-serving ways.

Quite a few of your jobs do not have my blessings. Are they eco-friendly? Are we all taking into consideration that God's beautiful planet needs to be nurtured and preserved, or are we focused on our pay check and how we are going to spend our time and money on the weekend? You are so caught up in the stuff. Perhaps, you have a few hours to look at your behavior of your lower self. I don't see much nurturing going on; just over-utilization of my resources and unhealthy practices of destructive measures. In just one week at your so-called job, how have you enhanced your workspace or environment?

Earth Day should be every day in your mindset, not once a year. The damage your industry standards produce in a week is enough to harm the planet for a century or two. So you all go home for the weekend, fire up the barbeque, chill your beverages and sit around talking about how great your lives are.

What's really great about your unethical behaviors and attitudes on planet Earth? I don't see many programs and social gathering for saving the Earth. The people who are acting in my fashion could use quite a bit of help. And you think they are wasting their time and efforts. Not in my eyes. They are evolved souls understanding my wishes and certainly trying to correct the damage made by many. Yes, they are out numbered by the destroyers, but I feel their heartfelt wishes and they are expressing gratitude and making time to keep the planet intact. Perhaps you could be a little more compassionate towards nature and its creatures.

Gee whiz, if we do this harmful act every day, I wonder how the Earth will ever rejuvenate itself. Does anyone really care? Where do you all get this attitude from? Shame on you for being so inconsiderate of me; I am your planet. Where is your respect and loving ways? I see your garbage and how you treat my species.

They have rights; God-given I might add. They have earned their rights to live on Earth. Quite a few of you haven't, not from what I see. You work at pollution-causing facilities and no one is on the clean up committee. I don't see teams of individuals trying to lessen the harmful impact your production is having on the planet. "Hell, who has time for that? Time is money and no one else seems to be concerned. I'm going to think like everyone else, even though I know deep down that it is wrong and not of my higher self."

If more of you were connected to your wiser self, you would be in a paradise of heaven. Every person, plant, species would be having the divine time of their life. Look around at some of your untouched beauty. There is harmony and love in abundance. Everyone's needs and requirements fully met with a bounty of resources and species to keep the Earth alive and well in every capacity. No shortages, no spoilages, just perfection. That's how I create.

This is how you all destroy. Look at the mess you live in. Nature's running away. They can't tolerate your harmful practices. You are killers of my home. Where is the balance? Where is the appreciation of the universal heart? Are you unnoticing of my presence? This is you throwing garbage in my face of love. Thank you for that.

Ponder on that when your guests come over for drinks for the weekend and you are not sure what to talk about. I hear all the crap you say, mostly back-stabbing, hurtful, low vibration patterns. They tend to go hand in hand with your beverages on the rocks.

Some of you are chilling out, but have taken quite a passive role in the big scheme of things: out of sight, out of mind. You sit on quite a bit of cash, but prefer to keep it all to yourself. You have no mindset to restore our love. You have no real purpose in my eyes. I know you know in your soul what you should be doing to make a difference. You all have this woven into your consciousness. Have another drink and perhaps you can totally tune us out. You are quite good at this one.

So, what do I think of your attitude of love? It stinks. Like your garbage. I don't see enough effort being made to save the planet and grow the love. You are all too busy doing that artificial bonding thing. No real connection happening here. Not with me, anyway.

Perhaps I should take a back seat and let things slide for a while. The Earth would be out of business in about a week. You would linger in your gases for a few days, then would all smother in your own fear. I'm not asking for a raise in pay here, just some appreciation and collective efforts from some sound minds. Enough already of the boring parties; no work is getting done.

We are a team and your side seems to have the attitude problem. We hang out with like-minded souls who are making a difference for many. On your side, the balance needs work. A major correction in restorative consciousness would be helpful and of an urgent nature. I'm not sure why you are sitting on this one.

Politely, I am your boss and if you choose to show up to work, we can build a mutually beneficial relationship. I'm quite forgiving and easy going. It's the absenteeism I'm having an issue with. All this work; not enough good employees. You know what that's like; frustrating at the best of times. You take the time to train them and then they're gone. Others are just there for their own reasons and then there are those with the attitude. This seems to be a large problem all around. So how about an attitude adjustment?

I prefer to make gentle suggestions to pull up your socks. I plant the seeds and I'm hopeful for growth and an abundance of fruit. Your own rewards are surely worth the effort. Perhaps, you can look into why you are sporting this unhealthy mindset. How did this conditioning happen? Did you feel you had no other choices in life? Perhaps if you had more positive energy in your field, you would help out, make a difference and do your part. You would have time left over to save the world and brighten a few soul lives.

Now this is thinking from the heart. This is your higher self talking. Let's see what we can do to shake up a new attitude. You stir and I'll toss it around in your heart. Beat this a few times for its full effect.

SOMEWHERE OVER THE RAINBOW

Where do you get this notion that the sky cannot be blue everyday? Is there too much bad news; a bad attitude again? Life is how you see it, my friend. If you choose to see dark days and gloomy forecasts, well, that is what you will create. You can pretty much have anything your heart desires. I just don't hear a lot of positive dreams being created. You entertain this mindset of complacent thinking and prefer to sit tight. I can't manufacture blue skies if you are sitting in the same energy field, time and time again. A full spectrum rainbow only transpires when your imagination allows its manifestation.

Dream big and visualize this pot of gold for you and your loved ones to enjoy life to the fullest. Not one soul came down without the vision of a rewarding life of growth and happiness. You all were to have the time of your life. Going and doing and feeling great.

I would have only agreed to your soul release if it was going to be a loving, heartfelt experience for all of us concerned. What is holding up the show of lights? Perhaps you've taken on too many commitments of the wrong kind. You have to want to change and follow your dream of color.

This is not done in the passenger seat of life. Again, this is you idling along in life's processes. Let's say you should be on number ten of your priority list, not number two. Where are you in relation to your rainbow? Is it out of touch, or are you climbing up toward the top in hopes of seeing what's on the other side?

Rainbows are as real as your life dreams. If you have witnessed a rainbow, then you know this phenomenon is real. Well, so are your dreams. They can be created with the same energy of light. Get through your storms and stay hopeful of sunny days ahead. Focus on your dream that keeps tugging at your consciousness. This is not your imagination. It too, will manifest as real as your atmospheric properties produce rainbows of love. Go out of your way to catch a glimpse of the real beauty of dreams realized. They are up for grabs. They are not denied to any true heart. Just take the steps in the right direction into the light, toward my heart.

We have a pile of heartfelt dreams to create. We need you to focus your positive energy in this direction. You may not know exactly what is in store for your soul, but rest assured that if it leads back to my heart, it will be of a divine, loving nature. All dreams come true in the kingdom of love.

Hold onto your dream and go for it all. Take the steps to grow your soul in a loving fashion and send your truest intentions out. Nothing is denied in the kingdom when in accordance with the universal laws. We covered these steps. It's all up to you and how much you desire to fulfill your dreams of the heart. I'm sure you won't be disappointed in your outcome. It was your ultimate dream on this life's journey.

Too many of you have given up on your destination. How sad is that? Why go down to play if you are not going to have a ton of fun? I'm interested in creating all the dreams we can, as we have quite a few sitting on the back burner. It's too bad they didn't come into manifestation; such a waste of fine energy. You picked the most beautiful places in the world and had your hearts fully healed and at peace. Most of you grew your heart tenfold on this recent incarnation. Sad to say, for some reason, this particular time on your planet seems to have smothered out quite a few of your dreams. We can only say that it is perhaps because of your lack of desire.

Why settle for less, when it is dangling right in front of you? Just reach out and hold onto it. See it through. That is what you wished for, nothing else, just a big pot of loving dreams for your heart. We were hoping to get you a little more inspired in this direction, as the energy on the planet is of a lower vibratory field than we originally hoped for. There are too many of you taking us down the low road in life.

Remember, you were the warrior type coming down to act out your hero role and save the day. You were to rescue the damsel in distress and live happily ever after in paradise with all the rewards of a fulfilled life. You would have had time to chill out and take in more of my love, so we could grow to our maximum potential.

Let's see some revised plans of hopes and dreams. Get back on track. Your life will become quite a bit more exciting, then we all start having a good time. If you are still thinking "same grass, just another field" well, we can't move forward. This place is for old energies and disconnected souls. I appreciate your fine contributions and your parental obligations, but don't keep your life on hold. That's unfulfilling. It's kind of where you are now.

Come up with the ideal you, doing the ideal thing and that's pretty much what we can deliver. If any of you wish to revisit your life chart and see what you had in store, perhaps we can refresh your memory.

Your higher self is ready to have the time of its life. Be sure to pack a few power bars. The energy burn is going to be rapid. Sport some shades, as the brightness of the skies will blow you away. There is no cloud cover up here, just a map to your ultimate destination to the top of the world.

Somewhere, somehow, we are going to have some fun. Shake it up folks. The party's just warming up. Go for the gold. Go big or go home. You choose how you would like to see it. I already have, big time. No disappointments here, just making dreams come true.

A SAND DOLLAR IN THE SAND

There are sheets of these creatures feeding off one another's energy, going with the flow, cleansed by the Earth's properties of loving consciousness. When was the last time you found one? If I recall, you have to go out a bit to get your hands on this precious piece. They are intact and buried in the treasures of the ocean's heart, all waiting for some soul to discover its vibration of beauty. These are my fine pieces of jewelry of the Earth. They are never out of fashion. They are timeless pieces of love, made with our heart in mind. Notice they all collect together and stay tight: delicate, yet resilient in the flowing forces of the ocean bed.

Their character is subtle. They are only about making the world a more beautiful place. They are bountiful in their collective efforts to provide peace and enhance the planet. Those of you that have some in your possession are understanding of their restorative properties. They have purpose. They resonate peace in their vibrational field of love. This is a gift from the heart. They are made out of the pure consciousness of love. Their business is to keep the ocean floor intact and keep us grounded in the turbulent times. The fine particles these beauties evolve from are souls of pure, restorative, harmonic love.

I would recommend a few around when it comes to your meditation time. They balance the properties of the energies in the field you are in and change out the vibratory rate of slower frequencies. Yes, there are plenty of them in the waters of love, but I'm hoping you do not take more than your share. I'm just suggesting that the sacred properties of these babies of love would be a peaceful enhancement to your energy field. Now this is a gift from the heart.

Next time you are stuck for an idea for a loved one, shower them with love omnipresent vibrational energy. I made them myself, from my heart to yours. Let's stay close this way and bond our love. I would prefer to see you with joyful, loving tokens of consciousness in your field and in your homes of love instead of reminiscent of days gone past. These beautiful creatures can be celebrated every day in your expression of love for our universal heart. I would feel more connected to you in this fashion. Let's see your eyes sparkle with joy when you discover a token of love from God's heart. I made them out of love for you and wish for you to hold them close to your heart.

I can't tell you how much I love you. I don't think you would quite understand. Every miracle you see every day, big or small, is an expression of my heartfelt love for you all. Sometimes, I wish you were more noticing of my gestures of the heart. I make a conscious effort to go out of my way to see if you are noticing of my presence. I like to think I have all the bases covered. I come in many shapes and forms of life trying to catch your eyes and warm your heart. This works both ways, as when you are noticing of my beauty, I feel it as well. I desired to feel this love tenfold 24-7.

I hope I'm not expecting too much. I have time, if you do. I'm pretty patient when it comes to matters of the heart. I don't feel I am unreasonable in my heartfelt desires. I feel I have done a darned good job at sustaining your planet of love and have provided for each and every one of you. I've always been there for you when you call. I've been there even when you don't call my name. That's just my nature. I allow you the space to grow and I am never in your way when it comes to decisions of the heart.

I'd like to think you have it pretty good. You could be having a better life, as that's the message I've been trying to send for quite some time. Please take notice of my efforts to call your name, if you haven't found our love fully. There is such an abundance that I do not wish for you to go without. This is an unnecessary practice. There is so much love circulating in our heart. Please fill yours to capacity for all mankind, creatures and all manifestations of love. Do not waste this fine energy. Its hot property; always has been, always will be.

My wishes are for you to live your ultimate dreams of the heart after your healing lessons have been done. Grow your heart of love and share this divine energy with all the fine souls on the planet. Stop the bickering and fighting. It is all for naught. Fighting doesn't produce love. I'm not of the character to cause harm. We are all about love and always have been, since the beginning of time. Too much space has come between you. You know what this does to a once healthy and loving relationship. Save the indifferences folks that stuff is for kids. You are of a mature heart looking to feel whole again in the universal field of love. This is not a tall order. It's simple, yet real.

May you solve all your mysteries of your soul self and come to love your being and your journey of the heart. May you take the time to re-establish our connection and make it stronger than ever. This challenging time in history is when it is needed the most. You were all my best picks.

No, I don't have favorites like you all do. I simply made sure your wishes to be down on Earth at this particular time all came true. I'm a softy that way. We did have that one condition, remember?

Make the love, spread the love. Stay close to our heart and save the world, as you know it. This is coming into the light fully and hooking up all our hearts back as one. The keys to the gates of love are in your heart, where they always have been. Polish them and see if they fit into your plan of life. Every one of you Starlights was hoping to grow and feel the love that is alive and ever abundant on planet Earth.

Once you find me in your heart, look over the rainbow and find your piece of heaven. I will be growing in your garden of love. We will all be thriving: every creature, every flower, insect, every particle of our loving consciousness, living out our dreams in the unified field under the blessings of your Creator of love. Divine Intelligence Almighty Love hoping to create more of the light omnipresent vibrational energy. Ask and you shall receive in abundance in the glory of your being. Forever and ever; all my love.

P.S.

I'll be in touch, just call my name in love. A hopeful heart is a true heart. A true heart is only pure, loving consciousness in my eyes. When you come to realize this, you will only desire my heartfelt wishes for your soul. Feel the compassion for all of God's creatures and make every effort to keep everyone and everything in the field of love. This state of bliss is what you should be experiencing regularly. Be not so concerned with the interference, that you do not make time for your growth. The soul purpose was to make us all proud of our growth, so we could dance and rejoice in our field of love. Your soul life is a celebration of our heart.

Please remember this. We are not separate from what we are trying to achieve. We are all one, with one common goal that is to live and let live. Live in the knowingness of the universal love and transform your energetic properties into a divine atmosphere of pure loving consciousness. This would be my wish of the day. I'm hoping we are wishing upon the same star. Here's to you, Starlight. You shine so bright to me. I feel your love in abundance and know in my heart, your intentions are true and you only wish to know and love me, as I do you.

Ok, my poetry is not the best, but I think I've touched a nerve in your heart. I'm feeling this one. I'm hoping you are too. We've been close forever. If you can find it in your heart to come back to me, I'll wipe our slate dry. I'm just interested in the reunion of our hearts. I'm only trying to feel whole again, kind of like you are.

Truth is, things haven't been quite the same for a while, so I figured I better make the first move. It makes processes a little easier and gets the positive energy circulating. I'm hoping we don't drift apart again. From where I'm coming from, absence makes the heart grow fonder. I'm hoping we can pick up where we left off. Could you consider this in your heart?

If you wish to blame me for some of your heartaches, go ahead. I can take it. I won't say another word. You already know how I feel. I won't mention that you should have stuck around. My lips are sealed. I'll just stand by and be hopeful for your consideration of a reunion of our hearts.

I can feel this already. You know how optimistic and easy going I am. I'm just waiting patiently with a huge heart full of love, hoping to share it with somebody; somebody like you. I'm looking my best and still available. Don't worry; I haven't left for someone new. I still have space in my heart reserved for you and me, together.

Now, don't get the impression I'm waiting by the phone, although, it's close by and I wouldn't want to miss your call. That would be a downer. I'm wired 24-7. You have my number, hopefully memorized by heart. I'm giving you your space, so you can grow and sort things out in your heart. I have a feeling it won't take too long before I hear from you. Don't worry, I'll be cool. No questions here. I'm just interested in your heart and wondering if you still hold a torch for me, as I do for you. Give it some thought. You know where I'm coming from.

Now, don't rush into anything. If I had to, I could wait another week. That's really not a lot of time in the grand scheme of things. I do have to let you know that I am looking for a commitment and my intentions are honorable and of a pure heart. I am the straight goods. You know what I'm all about by now. I'm just looking for love, all that you have to give. I have quite a lot to give to you. Overflowing actually, more than you know.

I am the Real McCoy. The real stuff you have been looking for. Search no longer. You have truly found your pot of gold. It's my heart. It's our heart, together as one, full-time, all the time; just you and I and the whole world rolled into one.

How about those apples? You are the apple of my eye and the star in all my dreams. You know I would like nothing more than to hold you close to my heart, once again. I would never let you go if you gave me another chance. I promise to love you every minute of every day for the rest of your life. Is anybody else offering the same true blue heart? That's what I thought. I'm figuring I have a pretty good chance at capturing your attention and winning your heart back. I'm always hopeful.

I'm telling you, when you get that loving feeling, it's like no other; it just doesn't go away. I'm hooked. I'm hoping you want to hook up with me and make a life together. I promise I'll show you a good time. I'll make you laugh. I'll make you smile and you'll wish we'd never let go. Your eyes will sparkle and your heart will be warm and comforted by my love. It takes two to make this happen. I can't do it without you. So when you are ready, willing and able, I'll be there. We'll pick up right where we left off and start to create a new life of comfort and joy.

Now, this has to be an offer you can't refuse. Honestly, I'm pouring my heart out to you and wishing you would come back into the light of love. I don't know what else to lay out on the table. You have pretty much everything I am offering. I am not holding anything back. You can have it all: dreams come true and happiness in your heart. Were you looking for something else? Adventure; yes, we have plenty of that. Whatever your imagination can create, we can create and manifest. This is my final offer. It's everything or nothing. The ball is in your court. Let's see if you are up to the match.

I hear you are quite good at making a connection. I notice that you would make a great team player. I'm hoping you will meet me at the court for a love match. Heck, what else is there to do? Let's have a rally and see who goes first. Careful now, my racquet is finely tuned. You have picked a great partner. It's a beautiful day to hook up and hear the sounds of love. I'm looking forward to this togetherness. It's been a while and I'm anxious to move forward. I anticipate all sunny days in our forecast all conducive to loving expressions of the heart.

Even nature is giving us their blessings. They always feel when love is in the air. They live off this fine vibration. Everyone and everything wins. How beautiful is that? I love a good love story. How's this one, better than my poetry?

I'm good to go when you are. Find time to let me into your life. This can be at work or play; any place will do. We don't have to be formal to re-establish our loving relationship. I'm just hoping it happens soon. I have been feeling love-sick for awhile and need some attention myself. It's getting a little empty around here, with all of you on different agendas. Perhaps we can restore some balance to the field of love and you could check in and let me know how you are feeling. I miss our conversations of the heart. I wish to hear your voice and feel your presence again.

You do not know what this feels like in my heart. I keep trying and to no avail. I can't seem to reach you. Your planners are full and your distractions are many. Slow down a bit. You don't have to travel around like Superman. That's our job over here. You are to balance your time with fun and nurturing experiences of the soul.

Grow your heart and yes, go to work and make a difference in your life. That's what you signed up for. All the rushing and worrying and fearful stuff is bad energy, not my vibration. That's when I know you have not found me in your heart. Those souls, who have consciously hooked up, are living an inspired, peaceful loving life and taking their journey in stride, learning the lessons of the heart and growing closer to mine.

They are taking the time to bring souls into the light. They are trying to save the planet from destruction and are mindful of their activities and behaviors; noticing of the impact it has on the Earth. All wish to come into the light and heal their heart and soul in every way. They only desire for you to walk in love, find yourself, find peace, happiness and your treasures at the end of your rainbow. They hope you can help make a difference in the restoration of the planet. They are counting on you to show the children their love light and straighten out their erratic behaviors; then they could all move forward and get back on track.

Yes, you should be able to spot your land of paradise. You left many clues. Your higher selves are trying to emerge. Don't dishonor these voices of love. They come in many fashions. All you do is step closer to the divine plan when you are hooked up to our universal heart. Feel the love in your heart and let the rest of us in. We are here to help you heal. Don't push us away. We all need each other and are one. You hurt, we all hurt. All of us feel this pain. Let's do it together and respect our individual needs. We are in this together.

We are the universe, each and every one of us. We are equal in our understanding of how it all works, some aware of this, some not. Take the time to share your knowingness. Matters of the heart, our heart, should not be behind closed doors. We are to celebrate in our knowingness of our loving collective consciousness. We are to rejoice in the name of God. We are to claim our God-given birthright of the gift of eternal love and life.

We need to come together in the name of love and move beyond our differences and embrace our similarities. We are all one. Have compassion for all life. Share your hearts and help each other heal. This person comes into your field because of your light vibration. Raise them up to your level of light. This should be a natural process.

Sing in the name of the Mother and the Father. Bow in reverence of our love. We all are to give freely our unconditional love. Move out of the desires of the flesh. This is primitive and not of this millennium.

This particular time on Earth is for you to be in love with being alive in form on the planet. This new paradigm of universal consciousness is only for pure love in its finest form. This is your chance to save the day and be the hero.

This is the Age of Aquarius. The planets are aligned in your favor. You have every soul's blessing on your survival. The prayers are plentiful on our side of the veil, as our continued efforts are to ensure the vibratory rate of consciousness is at an acceptable level for growth and life. This is a critical time in your atmosphere and we're not able to sustain your field of love. Our collective levels are being thrashed by waves of distortion. This is not a love match. This is a tidal wave of destruction.

The catch is every soul on our side is fine. We will always be in the vibratory realms of heaven and the kingdom of love. Our concern is your little planet is not doing so well on account of your ungodly thoughts and actions. Your collective vibration is off the scale of love. Yes, many have big hearts and we feel their fine efforts, but due to your population, it's quite disproportional in relation to your thoughts of confusion and fear.

Clean up your thoughts or call it a day folks. We are fighting a losing battle. Don't get me wrong here. We are not fighting per se or losing. You are digging your own grave, as your vibration is pulling you all down like a landslide. Our equipment can only restore and sustain so much negativity. This is your overall consciousness not at its finest. What do you suppose we should try now?

We've done everything possible on our side. Too many of you are not entertaining thoughts of love. There are too many hearts for sale, bought up by the cheap stuff. Put your money where your heart is or we might as well say good night. It's too dark for us to help the crying souls, too heavy to save the desperate souls and too cloudy to shine the light on the beautiful souls. You could be receiving so much more of the finer frequencies. Why choose the lesser? We are not impressed with your decision making skills. We are not thrilled by the fence sitters and not amused by the souls who do not make the time to fill their divine role.

You have quite a collection of party poopers; all spaced out on something and not really sure what's going on. There are too many zombies walking around in search of their selves and trying to put some meaning back into their life.

So, if heaven is of a lighter, faster vibration of light, how do you expect to find it in the darker, slower realms of vibration? You don't need to be a whiz to figure this out. I've repeated this message over several dozen times in every way imaginable, hoping that one of these scenarios rings a bell in your heart.

Perhaps you will start noticing these messages. We are hoping you start listening to your higher self. They are only whispering the positive, inspiring words. All the rest is garbage. The ratio for quite a few of you is 80-20, not in our favor. Your mental blocks are dense.

Perhaps you can tune into love and sign up for the meditation class that you thought was too silly, when in fact, it was your lower self that talked you out of it as you turned your back on our love. There is so little time for the important stuff. When you would like a guest introduction to the real you, let us know. We are dying to hook you back up.

Be not so consumed with life's challenges and obligations that your priorities are out of sorts. I would have reversed the order of the "task lists" if I was walking the Earth plane. You seem to need all the help you can get. Funny, how some of you think everything is just fine with your behavior. I don't see much progress on your life chart; others, awesome. I see a high grade. You know when you are right on track, as the synchronicities keep on coming. This makes our job divine. Thank you for that. No amendments needed here, just light and love. We do our best work and hope you are grateful for our efforts. We feel that you are.

So why is it others don't listen to your ideas of love? They think you are a little out there. Well, they're right. You are vibrating at a completely different wavelength and they can't seem to identify with this state. What upsets me is that they are not even interested in this new vibration of pure consciousness. They don't get it and don't want it. They don't care. "I'll just carry on, same old stale and stagnant energy vibration, because I am on an agenda and making things happen in my little world."

Well, in our world, that you are actually a part of, your stuff doesn't count for much if you are resonating at the lower end of the scale. In fact, you are holding us back from coming fully into the light. Let's not be too selfish. We have a universal agenda and hope you are on the same page or considering looking at our chapter in the Book of Life.

Do you catch our drift, yet? No sleepers please. We are traveling in the light, sunny side up. Wake up. We are serving breakfast on the patio: fresh juice, two eggs, side by each, maybe some nuts and berries. What's your preference? We will try to make this appealing. Let's ask your higher soul self. Ok, we have the answer. You're on board, Sunshine. Now, pay attention. Clean up your energy field so we can all match up to the love vibration. That is where the party is at. We will help you with this.

Now let's get moving. You pick and choose your direction in life. I'm hoping it is onward and upward. Shake some of your destructive patterns of your lower self and embrace the new and come into change. Evolve with the planet of love and deal with your thought processes. You are where you are because of your thoughts. How simple is that?

Do you love everything? Well, if not, then, fix it. There are lots of formulas in these pages to get you back on the track of wellness. All your answers are always in your field. I wouldn't deny you of anything for your highest good. Just ask and make an honest effort to listen to your heart. Hook up to the finer vibration of loving energies and soar with the eagles. Start to enjoy your physical manifestation on the Earth plane. Honor your soul, for this is your true friend of light. Be kind to not only yourself, but others in my name. You are hanging out on an amazing planet filled with opportunities to explore the finer side of life.

Start enjoying every moment of your soul's life. It's only a blink of an eye. Make it count for something. Have no regrets and move forward from here. All is positive if you choose it to be so. Watch your thoughts. They can kill every chance you have at love and happiness. This is not of our doing. We are about love. Try sporting a new you and wake up connected to the love and light of the day. Lose the worries. They are detrimental to your health. You all know it is as easy as this. I wouldn't make your lives impossible. I would certainly not wish you to have ill health or unpleasant times during your stay.

My desires are for you to find the love and be accepting of my gifts to you. Your pile of rewards and gifts touch the sky as they have been hanging around so long. Find your rainbow in life and get going. Wish upon your favorite star and find me in your heart and soul. This is where we belong, together, playing in the fields of love. Be not so unnoticing of your blessings each and every day. Hold onto your faith in your challenging times. We are with you on this one, close to your heart. We see the way out and the loving light at the end of the tunnel of love.

Hold onto your dreams, for they are real. Know this in your heart. You see miracles every day. Look at nature. We are capable of miraculous manifestations and so are you. We are all of the same consciousness. Just do the work and choose to be happy. You are deserving of the best in life. Do not get pulled down by the negative gravity. We can't create love down there. Shine your love light to the whole world and up into the realms, so we can see where to bless our loving souls for doing their part.

We see your acts of kindness and deeds of a pure heart. Keep up the good work. We smile on you often. No soul is ever left unattended. Do not think you are alone. This is your lack of imagination. Dig deep inside your soul, it is limitless. The journey never stops. It's beyond your wildest dreams. You will love what you discover. Go out of your way to make someone's day. We do. This warms our heart.

Take the time to admire the sunset and to hear the birds sing. They sing to you. Their conversations are pleasant; music to my ears. Keep creating your world of love. Use your fine mind to enhance and restore the planet.

Much tenderness and nurturing is needed at this time. Be kind to nature and save some of your God-given resources. Give Mother Earth a rest and let her replenish her beauty and serenity. There are many options available for your industrial needs. Implement these strategically and leave the planet in immaculate shape. It's not too late to make the changes. We just need everyone to come up with one good idea or thought. This starts to fuel the fire of hope, collective consciousness, environmentally and atmospherically friendly. Let's do this. Let's live our dream and make it right for generations to come. It's time for change. It's time for love.

Let go of the old thinking; it no longer serves you. Let's shake on this one and honorably do our part. We can make time to make a difference. You have me on your side, that's all that counts. You can count on me, if I can count on you. We work very well together. Our minds are sharp, no doubt about this one. We didn't spare any particle in this matter. We came down to do business, to clean up the planet in every shape and form. Every corner, every crevice, high and low, needs attention. This is why we have a fine collection of skilled professionals. Every area of expertise has been covered. It's just a matter of getting through some red tape and organizing your funds and schedules. Every possibility can become a reality.

I see many fine projects at work for the betterment of the planet. Thank you for your fine efforts. I thank you from my heart. This gives us all hope. Keep up the good work. You have our blessings. Look into your field of study and investigate measures of sustainable development. Please make sure everyone is doing their part in accordance with the best wishes of all concerned.

I can't stress enough how important these tasks are. We saw them coming and sent you down. Now you are an adult and hopefully you remember what your role is in this mighty plan.

For me to send other souls down with your capabilities, we are about fifty years away. Much damage will continue to occur during this time period and there again, is the chance the soul is not aware of their divine role to help restore the planet. Just come into the light and make sure you are on top of your roles please. We will be able to breathe a little easier if we know this is covered.

May all of you be blessed with many gratifying life experiences and warm encounters of the heart. These are plenty for the asking. Be sure to send up your requests. We all benefit from these heartfelt desires. Be sure to count many in your daily prayers, as this vibration counts. Bless your food and gardens of love. Be sure to include all species doing their work. Try not to squash their efforts if they are not harming you, they are going about their business as planned. They are all contributors. I don't appreciate you calling all my little species "pests". I don't hear them calling you names. They are just showing up for work. Try to leave them alone. Be mindful of your pollution and introduce proactive measures. We've discussed this.

I'm hoping you will go back over these notes and see where you fit in. I have mentioned everyone's role, in a round about way. Something here should jog your memory. Know that your coincidences are not so coincidental after all. This is the fine work of many to help you get it right. We programmed these into your life charts.

Please don't miss your cues. We count on your help and support. Yes, make time for fun and lessons of the heart, that's why you came down. You were going to do it all. We allowed plenty of time for you to experience all aspects of your soul and to smell the roses in life along the way. The fragrance of love is truly beautiful.

Take your time savoring every minute of your experiences. Don't wait for your golden years. They all should be fragrant and colorful. Listen to your sounds of love. Tune into nature and Mother Earth. They are there for your enjoyment. Do not exploit these treasures. Their beauty is timeless and so is your heart. Make time for this treasure as well, this is your finest resource.

You have all the riches inside your soul. Every gift you ever yearned for is found by journeying into our heart. May you feel the peace of the Earth's energy. May you experience love in its fullest capacity. It's worth the effort, truly. May you discover your true soul self buried deep within your heart, safe and sound. I made sure of that. Anytime you want to hook up and give me a call, I am just a heartbeat away; one breath away to your spirit and soul. How fast is that? We don't waste any time around here. We love every second of our life together. Call night or day, we are always tuned into your heartbeat. We listen for your voice and your thoughts of love. We know what's going on in your heart. That's why we are standing by.

You are all so sensitive. We are understanding of this. All your helpers on this side are hoping you make it to the gates of love and realize your heartfelt dreams. We are here 24-7 to look after your matters of the heart. We try to steer you in the right direction and make every effort to get you to say and do the right thing. We only wish for your ultimate plan of happiness to come true.

We prepare a new menu for you every morning so you can enjoy your life and live out all your dreams. We are interested in your soul's growth and the fulfillment of your hearts desires. When you let us in fully and we are hooked up and traveling light, that is when you really begin to shine. Your wishes are our command. Make them worthwhile. Make them for all of us.

We are connected. We have a party to go to. The preparations are almost done. We are hoping to hear from your heart. Sing us a tune. We are taking auditions at this time for the entertainment. We love to hear your voices when they are in our frequency range. Keep it all on a positive note. We like the sounds of that. Some of you may still need a few lessons in this area. We are patient. Take your time. We are hoping only to listen to the sound of love. Nothing too heavy please, it bounces all over the place. Then we have no choice, other than to send it back down.

Let's keep our tones light. Let's try to keep our thoughts clean and of a higher vibration. This will clean up quite a large area of concern. That's what I would call a great day on planet Earth.

Sing your old-fashioned love songs and let your hearts grow. Be open to all divine experiences, they are many. Remain hopeful in your efforts to find me fully in your heart. This process takes cultivation and nurturing. Do your inner work and heal your heart. Let me know when you are ready to grow. We have a garden of dreams to plant. I really can't wait to get started. I'm starting to sound like a child. I can't wait until you come out to play. I have been knocking at your door all day, but I never give up.

Most children have that loving faith inside their heart. They are about unconditional love. This was your natural divine state. How about bringing that fine attribute back into your heart? That was when you loved life, before all the heartaches and disappointments. Right around the time we got disconnected. Well, we can turn that around.

You know what it feels like to be hooked up and bathing in my field of love. Let's go there again, same feeling, just all grown up and better. I like the sounds of that, all that laughter and everyone playing nicely together in the playground of life. No stop and go games, no big, bad wolf, just fairies and Merlin's magic. All for fun and lessons of the heart, created just for you, tailor-made just like you ordered; a little variety all around. A bit of this, a bit of that, all good mostly. Everything you ever wished for comes true. All you have to do is believe.

How easy is that? Your own personal magic show and you are the magician with the magic wand. You have all the powers in the world right at your fingertips. Always have. So make a wish from your heart and see if it comes true.

The kingdom of love is full of magic and dreams come true. Our wish is only for you to be a part of it; like you always were when you were a young soul and a star waiting to shine your brightest. We are the power of love in your magic wand; just wave it in the right direction. Once we come together, there is no limit to our dreams coming true. Our dreams are the same, each one of us. We all pick our favorite places to hang out. We stay connected and we manifest love to keep our heart and soul alive and well into eternity. Now that's quite a magic show. I'm hoping you're wishing for the same outcome as the rest of us.

You know this is our dream of our life time together. Do not let go of the dream. It's as real as you and I. How could you not believe in yourself? You are a testament to the beautiful, divine dream of the Creator of the heart, our heart; the universal heart of love, where dreams really come true. Mine did. How about yours?

There is still time, lots of time, to bring it together into the loving light of your divine intelligence almighty love. We are understanding of the miracle of life and see manifestations of beauty and joy every minute of our divine lives. We feel the light omnipresent vibrational energy in our unified field of pure consciousness. We must collectively all be particles of the God energy.

Well, imagine that. We are all a significant piece of God's soul. All connected and living out our dream. We have all the same qualities of the same heart. So how could we be separate? That's nonsense. Grasp this one, this whole connectivity of divine universal consciousness.

You are my child, out of my womb of love. You are pure love, always have been. When you stay in touch, our vibration sync's back up. When you lose your way, I call your name and show you the way back to my heart. This relationship is divine when you are open to it. Keep this concept close to your heart. You are all my children and manifestations of pure love, pretty much the same idea when you hook up down there on Earth and decide to have children. Everyone was hoping and praying to live happily ever after.

Well, we are still holding on to this dream and are hopeful you are coming back home to our heart of love. We only see one big happy family, all sharing the same dream, experiencing life in many expressions of love and many finding their true nature in our heart.

Some of you are so determined to understand our connection. You really want a glimpse into our heavens. After a while, you wish to go down and save the world and remind everyone we are all of the same heart and should be behaving a little more like Mother and Father; who are not unnoticing of our silly antics.

You were going to tell them to shape up their hearts and pull up their socks as there is work to do as well, when we all leave to vacation on the planet of love. Everyone gets their wires tangled and that's how we disconnect; nothing serious, except when too many of you are having this problem at the same time. Then our loving grid of energy starts crackling.

We've had better days, trust this one. We've had better lives together, for sure. There are too many mistakes being made in the unified field of love. Perhaps you can work on your electrical problems on Earth. This tangled mess looks like an octopus in a bottle of glue, loose ends and sticky contacts everywhere. Not much hope for a sticky squid.

Can you picture this one? It's a good thing we have solvents for this calamity. Our supplies are running low, as your thoughts thicken the glue of low chemical vibration. Try some of your own loving solutions on the matter. We are hoping for a full clean up crew to put some life back into your field of space. Untangle your distorted thoughts and dreams and think about love, not fear and worry. The pile of worthless thoughts is enough to knock any creature off their feet.

Run yourself through a car wash, of sorts. Remove all guck, cleanse off all debris, rinse excessively, polish and dry. Try this several dozen times a week to keep the shine on your heart and the dirt out of your energy body. The dirt and debris should stay on the ground below your feet. I don't recommend bathing in this lower field. It weighs you down, distorts your thoughts and you do not reflect your higher self. Please be super-conscious of those so-called harmless thoughts you entertain. The realms are sticky with unnecessary, useless debris.

We prefer to devote our time into production efforts, rather than hanging out on the clean up crews. There is no fun happening here. We are just trying to find the light at the end of the tunnel. Our efforts are best utilized in the creative department of your lives. We like performing miracles, manifesting dreams, waving our magic wands and seeing dreams come true. These are good times for all of us.

Unstick your brain from the lower sites and clear your thoughts out often. Do not even finish those silly sentences. Catch yourself in the dialogue of doubt. You are sticking to the low vibratory field mindset; disconnected at the best of times. What's your excuse anyway; too much effort to think with your heart and soul, easier to give into the random senseless thoughts that fire all day?

Know that you have an audience of listeners, as your guides are standing by in case you have a heartfelt concern. Do not entertain your time with the negative, unloving, self-sabotaging frequency waves. It not only messes up your direction in life, it impacts many in your field. Not much, if any, progress of light and manifestation can transform at the speed of light. Your codes are not up to specs.

This outdated thinking is what keeps us all in this holding pattern of mixed approaches: not sure which way to turn; wrong altitude and descending. There is no field of love in sight. In fact, from here it looks like a scrambled egg dish, fluffy but opaque. We could use a clear picture on your situation. We are at your service when you call for a repair.

Do your prep work first, so as not to waste any of our fine time. We would hate to over charge you. It's not our style. We are the finest professionals for this type of energy work. We are truly certifiable when it comes to matters of particle. Save yourself some time and money by being your own clean up crew. Call when you have your sticky situation sorted out, so we can proceed with configuring the right connections.

Our whole team is hoping to contribute their fine efforts in the event that you choose to pull yourself out of the bottle of mess you are in. Toss it out and start all over. The consistency of the substance congealed quite some time ago. Fresh fluids would run your system cleaner and ensure smooth operations when traveling the airwaves of light. Dial this one up on your screen and let's transition into a smoother approach. It's all timing and focus. Be sure to keep the drag at a minimum; the density altitude is still a factor in our performance.

There is no time to think about unnecessary distractions. These are only illusions created in your mind. We are only operating fully from the heart level of life, hoping to break out of the cloud cover anytime soon. Now that's a feeling like no other. We knew we were on the right track. We had it all planned out quite ahead of time. There is no doubt in our mind, just faith and sharp thinking. Let's unload the baggage and start to enjoy this fresh air of thought.

All successful destinations of travel are calculated in this fashion. Training, reinforcing, implementation and focused skill. Being optimistic of the best possible outcome without the stress and worry is a good formula to arrive happy and alive at our final destination.

Now take a look at your charts again and keep your contingency factors to a minimum. Let's be realistic and hopeful. We are all practicing this maneuver from our level of reality. Buckle up and let's move into smoother pockets of light. Everyone rides more comfortably and efficiently in this manner. Make the ride worthwhile. I'll set the dials, you study the charts. That's a turn at its finest. "Cavok." (pronounced kav-oh-kay; Ceiling And Visibility OK)

CHAPTER FOURTEEN

Moving Forward

I SEE SOME ACTIVITY. THIS IS GOOD. This may not be apparent, but your energy field is starting to swirl. Whew, what a relief. It feels good to finally get things moving. Your own personal rain cloud will inevitably produce a rainbow someday. How cool is that? Ok, let's not get too excited. We have to take these steps in order, just to bring you up to speed.

This is what I am observing. You've figured out your energy field has been stuck and stagnant. Now you are willingly trying to move out of the gunk. This is good. Intention is our biggest factor here; the power of intention. Mighty fine, I might add. It truly works. It's worth the time to get it right and have an understanding of what you are a part of. Tap into the field of consciousness and create the ultimate you. Very good; what's next?

Pay attention to all the mixed energies coming into your field: people, places, things and thoughts. Take that nice nature walk we spoke of and clear out the negative stuff. What are your contributing factors? You know these in your heart. You doubt processes and fear the outcomes in most areas of your lives.

This is a waste of energy and keeps our connection severed. These chemical thoughts you entertain are the result of your solo efforts. If we were a healthy team, our hearts and thoughts would be of an inspiring nature. Identify your sources of conflict and unhealthy contributors to your lower field of vibration. Change and happiness only happen at the finer levels of the frequency range.

For every thought you entertain that is not positive, you thicken your coat of fear. This is not the coat of many colors I was hoping for. Now we are in this catch-22 scenario: a couple of good thoughts, a few neutral thoughts, then a huge negative one. This is our worst scenario. Back to "not so severe". We try to think hopeful thoughts and then get pulled down and give in to negative thoughts. An hour later, we try to think positive; two minutes later we are back at it again. You have this little mini war going on inside of your head. Who would you like to win the battle of the mind? Chemicals flying or heartfelt thoughts, you decide. How much time do you need for your answer?

For me, it's a no brainer. I operate at the heart level. I like to keep my loving vibration positive and connected to the universal love. Therefore, I don't have a problem making a decision. I can't say the same for all of you. How about engaging your heart a bit more in this matter? Half of your decisions are processed from your low receptor sites, reacting to a substance you just consumed. And you're wondering why you are all over the place.

Wise-up and get connected. Let's not make chemical decisions when we are under the influence of low vibratory frequencies. This is what is happening to quite a few of you. Your head is not clear at the best of times and your actions are not in line with your best interests. Try detoxifying your system from all the garbage energy influences and ask yourself what would nurture your growth. Many wise and decisive answers come in when you are connected to my source of loving power. This is the consciousness you should entertain most of your waking hours. Not only are you acting confused, but everything in your energy field is rippling a distorted frequency. You get the picture.

Oh, God, how do I do this? I'm glad you asked. First of all, if your space is cluttered, you will probably find me outside. I like lots of room to breathe and clear my space. This keeps us all healthy. Try not to think anything at first. Take my wisdom and love into your being. Ask for it. Affirm in the present tense. None of this "I need, I want". Let's stay positive, heart to heart. We are trying to move you out of your slower energy frequencies. This requires effort, as this seems to be a field you call home. You are not aware of the sustainable higher states of positivity. Let's try.

Observe your surroundings. Are they calm and loving? Are they peaceful and serene? What is happening around you? Pretend I am in your presence. Look at nature. Are the trees growing and breathing the breath of life? Are the birds floating and soaring in the universal field of love? This is us. This is what you are a part of. Try feeling our connection. We are present in your heart and swirling in your energy field. Take a breath of our life into your being and exhale all tension out of your body. Fill your soul with the earth elements of love. Become one with our universal loving consciousness. There are no worries here, just peace and beauty. Feel my love in your heart and open yourself to being in the present moment of the pure consciousness of divine energy.

This could take some time. If you're willing, just let us in to move your energies around and fill you with the finer, higher frequencies of life's vibrations. Smile, feel the warmth in your heart and soul and put back the sparkle in your eyes. This is tapping into the all creating source of the unified field of love. Use your power of intention to re-create your inspired outlook on life.

What would I do in your shoes? How would I find a loving solution to keep everyone sustained in love and happiness? My idea is to act our best in every situation and matter of the heart. Hand it over to me and I can plant the seeds in your heart and help you solve all your worldly concerns.

You would have fewer worries and concerns if we handled matters in this calming, collected fashion. I'm not of a reactive nature. I think things through deeply and consider everyone's feelings all around. It's best to see the big picture and get a feel for the positive vibration that we can work on together.

This heartfelt universal connection is the best way I know how to create positive outcomes and manufacture your dreams come true. Just listen for my inspiring messages and take all factors into consideration. We do our best work in the field of love. All elements in nature are of a positive frequency and can surely help sustain your clear way of listening to our heart.

LET'S TAKE A WALK

Energy in motion remains in motion. Watch out for that back slide. Let's stay grounded. Keep both feet moving forward. Let's remain clear of all ditches. They are too low and not our style. We are staying in the light of the sun. We are changing with the seasons, always renewing our thoughts and becoming more optimistic. We've had to make a few changes as things were keeping us down. We have identified these and taken the appropriate measures to stay in our new field of positive vibration. It does require effort, no doubt about it. Our decision was to move forward, one step at a time. Before long, this new thinking will preside over the old energy pattern of thought.

Let's introduce some color. You choose. Take the first rainbow color that pops in. That's intuitively what you require at the present time. These color requirements will always fluctuate depending on which vibratory frequency is necessary in your etheric field. Keep introducing natural, vibrational colors into your field of love. It all works and is beneficial to your energetic system. Study this practice for full effect to raise your frequency to that of the loving, universal consciousness to maximize your divine, transformative state. This keeps life fluid and moving in a positive direction.

Your new consciousness will require your steady attention. Some days you will not feel quite as bright. This is a good time to make the effort to walk out of your lower field and back into the universal light. Call in the light into your soul self and be determined to walk the path of enlightenment.

Many meditators find their peace when they remain in the field of universal love and light. They entertain these frequencies of transformative properties on a full time basis. This is not a "time to time" state; this is a tight connection to the Creator of all Creations, manifesting love and abundance in every sense of the word. We wake up together in this field of bliss, go about our business and retire in the evening surrounded by the infinite wisdom of the universe.

Why would you wish to remain in any other altered state? The negativity on your planet is plentiful and you are keeping company with this foreign frequency. You should know this isn't natural, as quite a few of you are walking around miserable. Gosh, I don't wake up that way in the light of day. I don't have off days. Heaven forbid, we'd all be in trouble. If you are not feeling terrific 24-7, you are not hanging out on the finer side of life. You are walking the wrong nature trail.

Are you sure I'm beside you? Haven't we been there before? Did you not hear me when I suggested we try the more scenic route where the gardens are growing and the sun is shining more brightly? I'm not partial to too much shade. Not a lot grows in the cooler environment and the full spectrum of colors is not so apparent. Let's stick to the preferred path of light and anticipate much beauty and gardens of joy.

I prefer to laugh and sing to the tune of: "I love my life. It is going well. I am grateful for the gift and all the blessings I receive in abundance each and every day. God, I am thankful for all manifestations of life and will do my best to make a positive difference and enjoy your presence of love.

I express gratitude and light the way for many as I walk my path towards the everlasting light of love, divinity and universal wisdom. I am discovering my purpose and acting in accordance with your heartfelt desires of the heart, in your name, always. My soul life is a gift and celebration of our love, universally, in the kingdom of heavens. I rejoice in the knowingness of your presence and wish to grow to capacity in line with the universal laws of the kingdom. I express many fine attributes of my heart and represent your loving nature and have come to know we are one and in order to grow as a whole, we are to come fully into the light of love as a universal heart in the kingdom. I wish to bow before you at the gates of love, that I may be granted the gift of eternal life, as I have done unto others as they have done unto you. In deepest reverence, I bow to my Mother and Father in the kingdom and proclaim my love for our whole heart. I choose not to harm any creation of the universe, knowing fully these actions are not in alignment with the wishes of our Creator's heart. I am understanding of my divine duty to keep the loving universe alive and choose to walk the path of enlightenment to the heart of Mother and Father.

In God's name, I have been granted my soul being to share experiences of our heart, in his honor. It is my God-given duty to find my source of light and heal the planet of love.

May I always be deserving of your love, as I make you proud of my efforts. I move into the light of the Creator of all Creations, Divine Intelligence Almighty Love, forever in our hearts, Light Omnipresent Vibrational Energy, into eternity. God bless our hearts and souls. We are one light, one consciousness living in the universal field of pure love".

LET'S STAY CONNECTED

It's the little things that grow the love. You know this. This is how you express your love for others on your Earth walk. A little appreciation here, a kind gesture there, it all adds up to something. It counts for lots in our universal heart. Every loving thought sent out creates a wave of love. This frequency is desperately needed. If all of you made a conscious effort daily to let the love flow out of your hearts, we would jump for joy in the heavens. We are so consumed with snuffing out the bad stuff that we aren't noticing of the love you are sending up. It seems to come sporadically and in isolated areas. Yes, we know the source of the loving vibrations. Don't get me wrong, we are just praying that we tip the scale on the positive stuff. Yes, this is a miracle waiting to happen, but we set our goals quite high. No dream is impossible.

We are visualizing a surge of loving particle matter rushing in and crashing into the matrix of love, lighting up the whole Earth's atmosphere. This power would knock out the negative particle matter and disintegrate its hold on the grid of light. This would be a fine light show. We haven't seen one of those in centuries. The colors would be spectacular. We could try to send you a digital image of this one. We see how you capture your heartfelt moments.

What happened to all the photo albums? I kind of liked looking at the pages of memories. They seemed to hold fine energy. Don't lose this hobby, it kept you all connected. You would sit around and tell a little story of your experience and share it with many. These are the little things that keep us connected.

Where would we be if there were no pictures to show? We would all have a different visual in our heart. That's not being on the same page. Pretty soon, you will not have any photos to display on your glass shelves. Oh, are they outdated as well? Boy, times are changing. Some of the practices you used to entertain kept everyone together.

Remember home movies? Now, that's going back. That was a gas. You would all laugh at yourselves, sometimes in embarrassment, over how goofy you thought you looked. You got to see your actions on camera and would shake your head. I loved them all. That was bonding. I remember the slide projectors, with your very own movie screens. I see quite a few of these screens collecting dust; at least you haven't tossed them out. You haven't the heart to do this. I'm glad.

Now, I see your big screen TV sets. The resolution is quite fine. I don't see that much that interests my heart; action yes, happy endings not always. Your home movies had a happy ending. I don't remember you capturing the dark times on film or sitting around watching them over and over. Where is your sense of fun now?

You are entertaining quite a bit of violence and a light, happy ending. Many souls die but it's still kind of happy? What's up with that? Is this normal now? It's truly not in my books. I prefer to record the faster frequencies and replay it a few times to recapture the positive feeling. That is what most of you used to do. That kept you connected to the positivity of life. Now your fleeting moments of so-called fun are lacking substance, kind of like your hearts. You need to hold these heartfelt experiences close to your heart to keep your vibration fast and your connection strong. Your fast lane is too speedy for the frequency of love. It slips by so fast that a real connection is not made. Notice this. Take a few moments to enjoy the feeling of connectivity and days gone by. These seem to be where you feel the best.

It's all the little moments that add up to a lifetime of love. Whether it was yesterday or last year, they all count in the Book of Life. Be sure to hold onto these collections of heartfelt memories, as that is the real stuff the heavens are made of. Take a picture of this one and hold it dear to your heart. Smile, you're on candid camera.

IT'S A KEEPER

Did I catch you by surprise? I don't sneak up on you; that's not my style. I kind of merge in and blend with the crowd. I am subtle, soft and graceful when it comes to connections of the heart. Now, there are pictures and then there are shots. Which do you suppose I am interested in? Just the term sounds more loving, doesn't it? I'm not saying I'm the best photographer in town, but let's get a visual on this one. What are you capturing images of?

I see these fancy picture phones and have to say some of your shots are not in my best interest. They seem to be a waste of energy. Is this just a fad? Is this a picture you would like for our photo album of our life together? I'm not overly impressed with your taste. Some of it seems a bit silly. Did you have too much sugar before this episode? I can't seem to make sense of this mindless activity.

So you send it off to some other disconnected soul, hoping to get a laugh or two. Now twice as many of you are entertaining low frequency garbage. Why waste your precious time displaying your rude behavior on camera? This shows many that you are a bit of an airhead and your wires are crossed. This behavior doesn't go over well in our realms of love. In fact, it contributes to our mess of distorted waves. I would have to say that the laugh is on you because this energy bounces back into your field. You may not be noticing, but know it filters back down and lingers in and around your etheric body.

This is not an experience I wish to hold in my field of love. We don't have space for that nonsense. This is called making a fine mess of the particle matter in your lower atmosphere. Then others in this space think they should try it. Great, now we have half the youth taking ridiculous pictures of negative crap. They think this is normal. I'm shaking my head in disapproval. This shows me where your head is at. There is no one close by to tell you any different.

What has happened to the gentle guidance and disciplinary action in today's society? Too many of you utter threats of charging each other for your violation of rights; yet, so many of you get away with murder, crimes of the heart and breaking every universal law in the Book of Life. If you don't have a good feeling in your heart about your actions and behavior, chances are, I'm not in on this one. I'm kind of in your back seat looking in, in disbelief, as you are not the same soul I sent down. What has happened to your loving memory?

Perhaps we could show you a picture of this image, a hologram of the real you, soul and all. Why aren't the two of you hooked up anyway, too many distractions? Why are you not making the time for the finer experiences in life; you sent your higher self on a one way vacation? Or you weren't really aware that you were connected to a wiser, higher self?

Well, I may not be a rocket scientist, but if I had access to an infinite source of intelligence 24-7, I would be hanging out full time. This is your total package, all spec'd out, all options available for the perfect soulful experience on your ultimate trip through life. Why go solo? This aspect of you could use some guidance and discipline. Sorry to say, but this is our observation from here: overkill on mindless activity and recapturing heartless experiences, time and time again.

Let's move on from this frame. This is not worth storing in your memory. This shouldn't even be of your consciousness. It certainly isn't of your higher soul selves. They are hanging around, waiting for you to pull it together and wake up and see the beauty of the gift of life. Surely, you could find some captivating images of life and beauty to store in your field for when you come back to us. We will scan all your images on the screen and see what you held close to your heart. Let's hope they're not all desires of the flesh. This truly is a waste of time and film in the universal kingdom.

We are looking for bright colors of light and heartfelt dreams shared. Let's not see any more shots in the dark. It tends to dim our view of you, big time. Erase, delete, rewind. Save us some time. We will appreciate that.

ALL SYSTEMS GO

I don't get it. You seem to make the time for the silly stuff, but don't have the time for the important details. Funny, how that is. You go out of your way to have an experience, but don't necessarily wish to recall this for any length of time. What is the use? I don't hear you talking about how great this get-together was, time and time again. This should be your first clue.

If you didn't come away with a heartfelt connection, what was it for: work, convenience, just wasting time, shooting the breeze? How do you find the time? You were to do your best and save the world. Enough with the java breaks; it's not good for your soul's growth. All this sitting around and shooting the breeze. Find your purpose and round up your team of warriors. We have work to do.

Break time was over hours ago. Get with the program. Let's find our pie in the sky. Let's restore our memory card. Now, fast forward to present day circumstances and see if you can tell me if you are at the right place and time in your current space. Does it feel like things are happening? Are the synchronicities and coincidences plentiful? Ok, you have some catching up to do. Let's replay the tape. What clues have you been receiving in the past few months? Have you acted on any of them? Have you followed through on your intuition and intentions of the heart?

Just to let you in on a secret, we are hoping you take action on every inspiring thought that enters your field. This is how we work together; none of these "ifs, ands or buts". We don't have time for the stalls. We are straight and level on this approach.

We know you hear us, as this registers on our equipment. Pretending you are unnoticing is only holding up your growth. When were you planning to make a decision to change? Do you not see that you are off track in life? Where is your rainbow anyway, or is it still raining on your parade? You should consider thinking your way out of this stormy situation. We only see blue skies and wellness for you and a dozen miracles or so. What are you waiting for? Is the price of fuel climbing too high? Well, our fuel of life is free for the asking.

How about just asking us a few questions? We can shed some light here. We would love to fill you with positive ideas to get you on track and inspire your soul. Come on now, it's time. The wheels are turning. Perhaps you need to do a complete 180° turn to find your light. Don't worry, we'll be gentle. Just agree to get processes moving.

Ever notice the people and circumstances around you aren't changing much? Are you waiting for them to change? Just maybe your situation can't change until you make the first move. And you were wishing they would change. This energy pocket is going to hang around for as long as you sit in it. You are understanding of this by now.

Nothing and no one changes in your life until you do. Then, magically, all circumstances are positively affected by your intentions of the heart. We have many standing by to orchestrate this sequence of events. Right now, you are the conductor and your band is waiting for your magic wand to start waving. This is such a fine display of love; music to our ears. We love to listen to the sounds of love. We love it when a plan comes together. Energy at its finest. Good job.

Notice everyone is feeding off your new energy, acting according to your wishes. Players all find their place on the stage. A nice shift in vibrational energy is starting to take shape. I think we will soon be ready for a concert, as everyone seems to be performing up to par.

Nice work, conductor. We knew you had it in you; such a fine display of synchronicity and entanglement of the finer strings of energy. Your audience is large and many are humming along to the tunes of joy. This shows us how to manifest your desires of the heart. We are in your front row making sure everyone is finely tuned. We like the sounds of change. Let's keep everyone playing so we can all find our place in this universe of love.

When you're ready, we will take you to the top of your rainbow of dreams. This is where your party begins to take shape. This system is flawless when it comes to manufacturing a heartfelt move. Let's ensures the engine is running smoothly on your travels of your heart of dreams.

Start small, think big. Set your intention, feet off the brakes. Show up to your own concert and play your heart out. We are looking forward to the show. You have the green light. You should feel this in your system and down into the depths of your soul. Now let's make some music together. We like the classics.

SING ME A LOVE SONG

What did you expect? I am love. I live, breathe and survive off this pure energy. I only know of this heartfelt essence. I'll try to keep it light. When you start the ball rolling, know that there will be some interruptions in your flow back to my heart. This is natural. No need to stomp your feet. Stay grounded and let's work through the bumps. No big deal. We didn't lose our playing partner. I'm right here with you. Now, if your moves are not so graceful, then we are not playing the same chord. You will feel this in your heart when I'm not impressed with your fancy moves.

From time to time, your parties go for a headshot. If you're acting smart, you avoid the contact. I would maneuver out of the way completely and call it a day. Let's not make time for the old games. We are only interested in equal energy frequencies. Either they plan on matching up or they are interested in you playing down. This is not the time to try any tricks. Make sure you are fine-tuned and wait for a sunnier day. I'm guessing we did not choose our best love match. Well, let's look around some more.

I like the sounds of inspiration. We will win every time. We are connected in every way and when we lose sight of the ball, we know in our heart that it is still bouncing in the right direction. Let's keep moving forward. No setback is large enough to un-tune our strings of love. We are only buying a little time and listening to our voice of love. I'm sure its telling you to stay on track and see things through.

Sounds like a great time to nurture the soul. I suggest sweet music, soulful meditation and listening to your higher self. This is not a time to be reactive; it's certainly not my nature. We are operating together now. Pace yourself out, face the disappointment and know that every setback has a divine reason. The souls coming into your field are probably not at our vibratory rate, so let's lead by example. Let's shine our light so bright that they can't help but notice our style of grace. This is where we will see the results of your loving demeanor. No sense banging our racket out of shape. We don't want to start all over again. We are already equipped with our finest instrument. Let's hold steady, wait out the storm and collect our thoughts.

This whole waiting component is where quite a few of you have problems. With your fast pace, instant gratification, broken-dream promises, you prefer not to wait for true happiness. Everything has to be now or next week. Holy, we have eternity. Let's exercise some patience.

Perhaps while you're planning your next game, you could continue to fine tune your instrument. There are lots of ways to grow your heart. You don't always have to be giving it to another soul if the timing is not optimal. But I can tell you, your timing is great for your own soul self and I. Let's tighten our bond and grow our heart first.

Don't be so rushed when this nurturing divine time comes around. It is presently there for your soul's purpose. Use this time wisely. You'll get out soon enough. Heal, evolve and grow. Make your own music for the heavens to hear. Hook up with some celestial star and see the big picture. Processes may seem slow, but know they are steady if your energy field is bright.

When the time is right and I feel the love in your heart, our circle of friends will reappear and join hands with you to sing a new tune of love. Perhaps they were really waiting for you and not the other way around. Interesting, how you are not understanding of your situations, from time to time, until you have moved forward. Then you look back and are grateful for your divine time with your Creator.

Cherish our nurturing times and know in your heart, it is you and I that need some time together. Time well spent, to sing me a new love song. I hear you just fine now. Let's hear what you've learned. I feel tuned in. How about you? Now, we are ready for a chorus. Let's join hands and sing our hearts out.

I LIKE THE SOUNDS OF THAT

Of what you ask? Your heart frequency; I listen to all your hearts, as they are part mine. You'd recognize something that belongs to you, wouldn't you? Of course, if you had too much stuff and gave it away, perhaps it wouldn't be so familiar. It's funny when we see this. Your stuff travels around and then ends up back in your field again. You look at it funny and wonder why it's trying to talk to you. Your vibration is all over it. You hear it before you see it. Get it? You are all talented that way, when you're on the ball.

I wish you would hone all these skills in your toolbox. This would make your life so much more interesting. Pay a little more attention. You'll surprise yourself when you discover some of your dormant gifts. It will be like pulling a rabbit out of a hat. I still don't have that one figured out. How about you? Well, anything is possible, I should know that.

I've seen quite a few magic shows. I find them fascinating, some risky maneuvers but mostly happy endings. Everyone applauds in approval. How entertaining, magic at its finest. Now you all know you could be on that stage thrilling your own audiences. Yes, this too will require discipline and practice, like everything else.

How badly do you want to start having fun? I'm ready, let's go out and entertain the world. We have to be at the proper vibratory rate to perform our miracles of magic. So if you are feeling confident, let's make a move. Ok, where to start? Let's listen in and tune into your souls. They are thinking big and ready to take on the world. Hearts are beating at an optimum rate and looking for props and heartfelt friends. This should be no problem as your hearts will attract a similar vibration of sorts.

You may have not noticed, but you are sending out your own unique love signal, or not. So when someone arrives in your field, see if it is a match. This is done with a fine tuning of the hearts. We always hope we have a match, but sometimes souls get in the way of their own frequency of love. They are not realizing that their heartbeat carries a fine sound vibration and that you attract your frequency of love, or again, not. Now you don't have to run to a specialist to check this out; trust your heart is fine with us.

We just like you to know that your heart sings us a love song, all on its own. Every time you grow your heart, your instrument sounds more beautiful to us. Please strive to work through your lessons of the heart and sing us a new tune. We look forward to hearing the progressive sounds of the universal heart.

Now this is truly a divine concert of finely tuned instruments of love. We record every echo, as you will like to hear how we all sound together. We are working on this one all the time. It's our best collection to date. It is always at the top of the chart. It's our number one pick. Let's keep it that way so we can all enjoy the beat of our heart. It sounds so fine, sounds divine. Catchy.

IT AIN'T OVER UNTIL THE FAT LADY SINGS

What's up with this phrase? Is it not a tune of love? So why would you call her fat? If I recall, this voice of love echoed into the realms of love for decades. She only knew of love in her heart and wished to share it with the world. Quite a range of scale; she captured every note divinely and touched the finer chords in your heart. She sang like an angel. Bless her soul. We all do.

Time has a way of working things out. We all prefer to fast track our lessons and do not give our heart a chance to adapt to the changing circumstances in our world. Our immediate environment has been altered, souls have shifted their energy and players have left the band. You are left holding the music sheets with the best part unsung. You were hoping for a melody of love. Your heart senses this and cries the blues.

This is the time in your life when you need us the most, for we are your choir of love. We wish to sing you a lullaby of hope and a wish of sunnier days ahead. This dark time would be well spent writing your own sheets of music. I see this therapeutic approach. It seems most effective when working out the woes of the heart. This gives your heart a chance to adapt and express its love lost. She too needs to sing her heart out. Her disconnection of energy fields has altered her beat and sounds of love.

This timely process of healing is necessary to mend the chords in your organ of love. Journaling your heartfelt thoughts expedites the process of healing and recovery. Most of you would benefit from writing your own beautiful words of love and heartfelt concerns on your composing sheets of life.

Make the divine time to allow your heart to sing itself into a healthier tune of hope and connectivity. It mends, it heals, it grows good as new. Then the time will come to join back into the choir of love and laughter and you will be more appreciative of the souls who come to touch your heart of love. Your instrument will be ready to sing along and appreciate the finer chords of beauty once again. All will sound like a blended melody made in the heavens of love.

Allow your heart space to grow and feel its needs when it comes to the solo nurturing time. You and I have our own tunes to write in the Book of Life. These melodies are essential to your heart and soul's growth. When you skip this music lesson in life, you will not be able to understand the harmonious voices of love. For when you enter this angelic sound in your field of dreams, you should be able to recognize your favorite tune of the mending heart.

We carefully prepare your concert, string by string, to ensure your sound of love is integrated back into the whole, synchronistically. We hold a place for your heart on our stage of life and wish for you to notice when it is your turn to sing on cue. We are always ready and warmed up when you practice warming up your instrument. When the divine time comes to hear your beat, we stop the heavens to let you back into the realms of love. This instantaneous integration is necessary for you to feel connected to our choir of love.

Be sure to take your divine time and write your music sheets out of love. We like to see what lesson you are on and what stage is best for your opening of your heart. We all hear your loving cries and know it is just a matter of time until we all sing together in harmony. Let your soul lead you to the notes of your life and be sure to find your lines in the verses of the heart. We feel this is time well spent, as we can hold the tune for quite some time. You are all coming and going, while you tune your instruments. When you are ready, we know exactly where you fit in, as we were always holding your space in the symphony of life.

This heartfelt reunion is music to our ears and warming tones to our heart. The universe always holds the finer sounds of love in the unified field of consciousness. We just sing our hearts out hoping you will feel it in your soul and know when you are ready to join us again. The birds will sing and lead the way to your space in the kingdom of love. Be sure you have prepared your heart's music sheet so we can join together and express our pure concern. We know how to write the best soliloquies in the land of healing hearts.

May your soul find its way back to the chorus of love. May you hear your angels sing to your heart while they nurture your soul. May you be open during this time of heartfelt concern, as we wish to replace every broken string of energy with a finer, stronger vibration of love. Many souls are warming up to be an integral part in your concert of dreams. They wish for you to hear their hearts and join them in their fine tunes of days gone by. They hold these sacred vibrations in their notes of love and blend them into the new energies. When you are ready, all elements of loving vibration will be held together. Collectively, we can all put on the best performances of our lives. We wish to share the stage, as how good is the choir without the leading star? We all wait in anticipation for the most powerful voice of love to shine and echo in our hearts and fill the heavens with joy and the power of love. Let's not leave our seats until our hearts become one.

This unison of syncing up our vibration is the result of a believing soul who had a story to tell and a song to sing. How else do you suppose you could get all that attention? We hear you loud and clear. We feel your heart grow and comfort your being with the intentions of becoming one in the symphony of the heart of the whole. This love makes our heart sing. Find many in our name to join us, as we find our place on the stage of the universal heart.

Let's sing a song and realize we are only warming up to our best performance, yet to come. It ain't over until we sing our finest tunes of love and are able to hear this clearly up to the gates of love into the kingdom of your Mother and Father. Truly, this is when the fat lady sings, for she only knows of the whole heart of love. How loud is that?

By the grace of God, may you come to know this sound of love and feeling of beauty in your soul. Make the time to express your love for many, to marvel at your divine strength to open heaven's gates for us all to enjoy. Now that's our kind of singing from the heart. We will join you on this journey when you are ready and tuned up.

Here, let us fix that sound you are making. We perform well together when we are all tuned to the infinite scale of love. How divine. I hear you. You are quite fine and ready to sing in the light of the day. We will send you your next note. Try to be more open to the finer vibrations of love, their sounds are many. All you need to do is lend us an ear, make some time, open your heart and listen to your soul. There are so many melodies trying to touch your heart. Let this healing vibration do what it does best. This is us trying to come into your heart. We need the stage set and the soul to be receptive to the miracles of healing love energy.

The timing seems immaculate for our finest words of love. I'll turn your pages and be sure not to cry a river, as this would surely cause a flood of sorts. I'm careful when it comes to responsibilities of the throne. I would never wish for any soul to drown in their tears of love. This experience would never have my blessings. I make every effort to dry your eyes and open your hearts to life's riches.

Find your peace from the lessons of the heart. Try to see the silver lining and realize all experiences are necessary for us as a whole. Your outcome and understanding of your lesson brings us all together on the stage as one. We are all moving toward our key places to help discover the loving mysteries of the music of the universal heart. This is my voice of approval and joy.

When we hear the tunes of love, compassion and gratitude, the heavens feel the hope as they renew another day in your heart of love. We pray for you to feel the love and to appreciate the sounds of God in your heart and soul. Our prayers are plentiful and seem to be touching a chord or two in our symphony orchestra of dreams come true.

COULD HAVE, SHOULD HAVE, WOULD HAVE

This tune is not my favorite, yet we hear it all the time. It resonates to the tune of regret. After a while, they pile up in your collection of opportunities gone by. It starts to sound like a heartfelt Country Western. Now, I do listen to your healing heart songs, but if you are not a recording artist, you should not be singing the same old tune of "I missed my chance".

The more often you entertain this tune, the less of a chance we have at making a new track. We are delivering a new recording, but your heart doesn't seem to be open to listening for your next big chance. Good thing we don't give up as easily as some of you. Just tune in and see what you can salvage from this lesson of the heart. Mend the pieces, tune your instrument, spring forward into the present moment and open your eyes and for heaven's sake try not to let another beautiful opportunity slip through your hands. Catch it and plant it in your heart where it belongs.

That was our first problem. You were fearful to take a chance with your heart. Don't be; we are trying to hook you all up. It's quite a large task and if you are going to back down, well then, our divine intentions were for naught. We have your best interest at heart and it would help if you acted on your intuition.

In any area of your life experiences, passing up your chances of fun and happiness will only disappoint your own soul self. Then you sit in your field of empty dreams and wonder why others are enjoying their lives. You have to find your courage and listen to your heart. Life is not always going to deliver the perfect packaging. But it is when you receive the gift and start to peel back the layers of wrapping, you discover it was delivered to the correct location.

We have a system for expediting miracles and blessings of the heart. We hear your prayers. We make a note to ourselves and we get to work on it. Be open for heart mail, as we all are looking to live out our dreams in our soul lives. We only wish for you to smile and let us know you are having the time of your life. You know this is all possible if you hold onto your dreams. We always deliver the finest. That's part and parcel of post; service with a smile. It breaks our heart when we see return to sender or address unknown. We are confident we did our best. It's up to you to be more noticing of your gifts of love. They come in many different packages. Perhaps now that you see we take the time and make a heartfelt effort to fulfill your wishes and desires, you will not pass up your next opportunity to live your life according to plan.

We are actually more disappointed when it doesn't all come together. We feel the emptiness as well. We are just looking for a love match and for everyone and everything to find its place in the universal sea of love. Everything has its place and everyone has their divine purpose and respectively, deserves to find the love in their heart to connect back up to the whole. The feeling of a secure connection is like no other. Its warmth, comfort and peace is truly a joyous and happy place, worth living for.

Show us your smile and your true intentions of the heart and we will deliver more than you asked for. We are hoping to send a bundle of fun and carefree adventure, round trip tickets to the kingdom and back, open any time. How perfect is that? Most of you feel it's the trip of a life time, but the travel time sets you back a bit. It doesn't take you long to get back into the swing of things. Go with the flow of life. We all are. That's what it's all about. Bask in the sun's rays of love and catch your own ray of light.

You will find many on your rainbow of dreams. We are all traveling in the same direction in search of our treasures deep within the universal heart of love. See you at the top. Life is but a dream, a dream come true; our style, divine style.

CHAPTER FIFTEEN

The Finer Side of Life

YOU ARE ALL LOOKING TO LIVE out your dreams, yet, you are not prepared to take the risk. These efforts would not jeopardize your well-being. We would never calculate in life-threatening events to make circumstances impossible. This was never our style. So what is truly holding you back; your own fear of change and processes gone sour?

We'd like to think we have a sweet formula to realize all dreams come true. Never would we sprinkle on any disasters of the heart. That's only in the movies. Your real life character is fully prepared for your next action role. You've set your stage and calculated your best options. From here, we require you to move ahead with the plan. Yes, there will be a clearing of some sort to do. Perhaps, there's quite a bit of brush standing in your field of dreams. This should not be a deterrent to stop you dead in your tracks from fulfilling your heartfelt desires to the fullest.

We see too many of you taking the safe, round about way through the field of dreams, never really reaching your true field of love. You've gone to the right, danced over to the left, but not many of you have found the courage or the willpower to hold steady at center stage and plow through your field of dreams. It is right in front of you; we placed it there for easy access. We didn't suspect you would avoid it all together.

What are you finding on the side lines? A collection of old experiences suspended in your field of days gone by. You've already danced to the tune of this. We all have. Hook up with your best dance partner and try your fanciest moves. Don't worry, you are not being judged in this competition. That is only an illusion in your own mind. We are actually standing beside you, hoping you are ready to face the music and tap your way into the light of day.

We see your self-created brush fires and all the debris planted around you. You don't seem to know which way to turn. We hope you do not turn at all, but rather try the two-step, forward move. No shuffling allowed. That's outdated. We are ready to pick up the beat and clear the dance floor just for you. This is what is hanging in your field of love. Kind of like a freeze frame, just dying to continue with the show.

Energy is not partial to remaining trapped in time. It loves to dance in the field of possibilities. Know that optimum allowances have been factored in for your debut. We just require you to attempt to go the course. Ok, we hear you. You're not in love with dancing. That's unfortunate, as we love it on our side. From what we can see here, these actions lighten your field and your rainbow begins to show the spectrum of light. When blended with the loving finer frequencies, you manifest change. This keeps you moving forward in life. Choose a partner if you are rusty at your moves. We only ask that you make an attempt to clear your space. Dance your way to your next opportunity in life and leave the side steps behind.

All dreams are looking to catch their partner to make themselves complete as the energy is hoping for a transformative string of vibration. It too, is looking to reproduce finer particles of love. So put on your blue suede shoes and move around the floor. Stir up some excitement. We all know this maneuver works when it comes from the heart. Now, that is about as risky as we get; a few hearts breaking but mostly slick moves in the direction to please the audience. Everyone gets excited and the energy heats up on the dance floor of life.

This technique stirred a few souls into living their lives from an expressive perspective and was only conducive to creating the optimum energy, making the world dance and sing from their hearts of love. I see this tradition still trying to capture the love and stir your soul to move you up to your stage in life and live out your dreams. No one goes unnoticed when they are displaying their fanciest moves in the kingdom.

We like to watch all performers when they have the intent to raise the vibration of the planet. You collect many in my name and inspire us all to want to stay out of heartbreak hotel. We prefer to sing to the tunes of "All Shook Up" and "Love Me Tender". So when you are talking risk, it's about as serious as tripping over your own laces on your shoes and falling on your face. We are hoping you start snapping your fingers and get up and dance your way right into the crowds of spectators in your dream come true.

Yes, Elvis has left the building and is already preparing for his next show of love and light. He will be sure to entertain your souls once again, as his admirable efforts truly put a spin on my blue suede shoes. Yes, that was paradise, when we all sang and danced to the King of Rock and Roll; my kind of star, a light show worth capturing in your heart, all American style. The whole planet was rocking around the clock.

This era grew our heart larger, as we connected to the field of love. There was no stopping this energy. From what I recall, we had an explosion of souls return to Earth to join the party of love and make some dreams true blue. This is the color of love. This is the hue of my soul. Look around at your space and see my dancing shoes. I'm moving 24-7, that's how I keep my shape. It's a great cardio workout. God knows we need it. Lace up folks and clear the floor. Let's get the party rolling in the right direction. No suspicious minds, only dreams come true. I'll sing to that, forever in our hearts.

ONE FOR THE MONEY, TWO FOR THE SHOW

All revved up and ready to go. You're looking good, feeling lucky and you've practiced your moves. Let's see what we can come up with to turn your dream into a reality. A shift here, a shift there, all lights are on the stage. You look mighty fine. I hear your intention but you're thinking this is too good to be true. Why? Is this your conditioned thinking or perhaps are you tiring yourself out dancing in circles.

Stop for a moment and put your dreams on paper. What is your first move from here? Do we need some lessons? Have you been putting this development on hold? This is our first step in a positive direction. You change, your world changes. It's as simple as that. When you open your heart mail, you set into motion a sequence of timely events, all calculated and synchronistically organized for the fulfillment of your life's dreams. Let's walk out of our dimly lit dreams and go for the brightest ones. Without your initiative, all souls end up on alternate paths. Not the original print outs of our lives' dreams.

I would suggest that it is in your best interest to encourage one another. The brave actions of one will produce the perfect setting for many to find their way. Communication and support are essential when it comes to helping the whole. No one wins if all we think about is our own soul dreams. None of your dreams had the vision of you on your Paradise Island standing by yourself; all that love and no one to share it with. Inspire many on their paths in hopes that their dreams will come true. All events transpire synchronistically when you send out white light messages.

Our shipping department is organized in this fashion and fully prepared when you show us your plans. When we stamp this desire with approval, all packages are delivered to your circle of friends. Be sure to keep processes steady. Our tracking department is well prepared to see to it all points of interest are fully considered and many individual efforts are compensated along the way. It's surely worth the effort to ensure all packages are delivered in their original state and in a timely manner. You should see that it is the effort and co-operation of many to make a dream come true.

No, assembly is usually not included. This is where we count on you to read the instructions and get the directions clear. We are delivering the finest. You will have to do your part in sequential order, to see that all can come to be if you have the faith and believe all things are possible. Take your time. No rush jobs, that will only deliver a broken promise of the heart.

Our couriers deliver the finest and ensure the arrival of your intentions of the heart. You can't beat our rates. We consider all orders light. Now we have the originals and all you have to do is follow the step by step guide to the creation of your dreams realized. This is not where you decide to miss the details of the important initial steps. We can't build a field of dreams without vision, focus and follow through. I'm sure you have seen this one before. It all makes sense. We know in our heart, anything and everything is possible and can become our reality.

We deliver, you build. How easy is that? We are open around the clock when it comes to making dreams come true. For some of you, it's now or never, I tell you true. Try our service, as we'd like to see the show. We see that it's going to be quite a hit.

IT'S ALL GOOD IN LA LA LAND

I'm sure sometimes you think time is standing still, when in fact, it is you. We are a constant in the universal flow of consciousness. Just hop on and come for a divine ride. We are traveling light beams, back and forth through the realms of love. Many light beings are circling you, hoping you feel their energy. I understand you don't see their presence, but by now, you should be using your limitless imaginations. I've planted many images in your heart so you come to the understanding that we are living in a miracle of dreams.

Do you remember Tinker Bell and Peter Pan? They were zooming all over the place, saving the day and intervening when they felt it was necessary. Now, I'm not suggesting that you get caught up in the Peter Pan syndrome, but we would like you to know we are really having a magical time of things.

It's those of you who don't seem to realize that we have a good handle on the universal flow of events, that get yourselves into this pile of washed out dreams. We love to travel and put the sparkle back into your hearts. We feel this is necessary, as your gravity disrupts your finer frequencies of the universal heart. Be open to these miraculous acts of kindness. They are necessary to keep the dream alive. Fill your soul with the magic of Never Never Land. Realize that our efforts expedite your growth and synchronize your heartfelt events to produce your optimum outcomes. The sky is the limit.

I wish you could see the possibilities of your true hearts desires. No task is too heavy for our light beings to undertake. In fact, they love the more challenging sequences. This ensures the beauty and harmonic resonance of the planet and Mother Earth are tuned and vibrating at their finest. So include these souls in your plans when it comes to restoring balance in your lives and Earth home. For when you send the light to all particles of possibilities, we are right there changing out the dynamics for your highest good. Everyone's intentions, in accordance with the universal laws of life, produce health and abundance in a prosperous direction for the good of the whole of creation.

Now, let's entertain Captain Hook and see if we cannot change out his dark field of intention. Surely, if a few particles of white light can transform the sequence of energy in this fairy tale, I'm positive that the collective intention of many will be able to stop the ship from sinking into the swirling ocean and coming to rest on the cold, dark floor of disparity.

If you believe that your consciousness is alive with the light energy of positive intervention and dreams come true, then you can fathom the concept of living in a sea of beauty, balance and elemental guides. They only know of pure loving consciousness and miracles of the heart. Take that, Captain Hook; swallow that one.

We are playing by the rules of subatomic particles of light which only know how to dance in the quantum field of love and limitless possibilities. Just ask your children, they remember this one to be true. As for the rest of you, grow up and see to it that you too save the day in the way you know how. No cheating, that's for fools. It only produces sunken ships and lost treasures of the heart. No winners here, just losers riding the waves in the storms of their self-created cold and blustery lives. Your company has bailed out, in case you didn't notice. Here, we can throw you a lifeline to hook you back up. Careful now, you may like the feel of security, comfort and the hope of a sunnier forecast. Most of us do.

Welcome aboard, Captain. We are glad your thoughts are not so water-logged. Let's dry you under the sun and warm you up to the idea of light omnipresent vibrational energy. Apparently, all is fine and well on the other side of life. We're hoping you will stick around and have a change of heart, as many are rooting for you and not wishing to drown in the cold waters. I don't believe they knew they were in for the storm of their life. I suspect they thought they were just going along for the fun and had an option to bail out when the ship started to capsize. They didn't realize they would be taken as hostage and their free will drowned.

I think every mate should make their own decisions with the heart and see which way the tides turn for them. I see a few jumping ship and looking to dry their coats of many colors and restore their shine back into the universal heart. This individual choice should be honored, as it appears many have had a change of heart. Their truths in the depths of the soul have surfaced. It seems many are hopping on board and hoping to sail on the ship of eternal life.

Many have learned their lessons of the broken heart and wish to restore the heartfelt connection. It seems to appear that this empty fairy tale leaves many souls in the dark, with no chance in hell to find the light in their lonely and scared heart.

Release the hostages Captain, as we have quite a team of experts that are standing by to recover the lost souls for the asking. Hand them over to their Lord of Light, so we can see to it all rehabilitative efforts are carried forward. Every soul should have the free will to exercise their desires of the heart.

We are always hopeful and pray that many have a change of heart and brighten their outlook on life. You were supposed to find your paradise, not the dungeon of lost souls. You know there has to be more to your life than being isolated from the light. Heck, we could have left you on the dark side of the moon. At least, you would have been out of hell over there, with lots of time to think about your next matter of the heart, if you're lucky.

Try giving us a call. We'll put on our hearing aids and you can hope to hell we can hear you. It looks like your battery is pretty much dead. We can't help you unless you come into the light. We have to see what we are working with and we suspect the directions went overboard with your soul.

The ocean's swells can be mighty fierce. Are you sure your heart is up to the challenge? We have a long way to travel from here and the current is not in your favor. I'm not sure how you washed out so far, but I can bet you our swimming team is the finest and if you make a steady effort in our direction, I'm sure we can pick you up on our screen.

Thank God, it's waterproof and so are our timepieces. We wouldn't want them to stop, now would we? That's not our inherent desire of the heart. Watch out for this. It's supposed to keep on ticking and ticking and ticking.

HOOK, LINE AND SINKER

Funny soul that Jerry was, I loved that movie. Reminds me of the time when you all had a good fish tale to tell, right from the heart, every time. Now, I hear mostly fishy stories that don't smell that pleasant. A lot of you are fishing for something in your sea of life and hoping to hook a big one. Whether it's business or false pleasure, I don't see true intentions in your deep blue sea. You cast off and have a mission to accomplish. You are loaded with your best bait and hoping to lure in your prey. This trophy will add to your collection of suckers.

Why do you need this soul in your arena of events? Will it further your status or position in your corporate world? This is spearing a soul right in the heart with not a chance at survival. You've come into their territory and cast your intention in their field of view. All the while, they were hoping it was just a friendly game and you were not planning to cut them up. They thought you were interested in their maneuverability and their fine skill. They were hoping you actually were considering them for your fine collection of your heart. Little did they know you were going to cut out their soul and sell it for profit. Your own personal gain was your only reason to entertain this sport. No one's feelings are being considered whatsoever and you are not a genuine soul. I see this.

You take many hearts that don't belong to you and pull them out of the loving waters of life. Then they are trying to catch the breath of life, while you try to smother their being. Now, they are caught up in your tangled nets and hoping they can wiggle their way back to the pure consciousness of life.

Initially, you admired their beauty and wished to be more like them. Then your lower, self-serving self thought this display would look good in your field of broken dreams. You are the shattered soul here. You were hoping this prize would look good on you, as individuals are growing weary of your tales. I don't see souls laughing and smiling in your presence. They seem to be there against their free will. You have them trapped and their obligations are making it difficult for them to return to matters of the heart.

Perhaps, you can find your own soul and look around at your so-called life: few lifeless trophies, few Dead Sea creatures under your belt and really not much to admire all around. Your acquaintances are lingering around hoping you make good on your promises. Unsuspecting to them, they do not know you are not operating at the heart level. This is all a game to you. Well, we do keep score on our digital boards and it's not looking so divine. What's in it for you anyway? A few laughs, a few jokes, a few episodes of silly pranks? I don't feel your heart is ticking up to par. In fact, your echo is sinking into the lower vibratory realms. It has been for quite some time.

How do you plan your routine everyday? You wake up, rehearsing your tall tales deciding where to fish that week, wondering where the fertile floors of ocean life preside. You are all prepared to give it your best shot.

This is not how you get ahead. Who taught you how to bait the hook? Someone had to have shown you how to fish this way. Not our style. Yet, you gravitate to the depths of heartfelt souls and wish to take advantage of their virtues of the heart. They were hoping to preserve their own dignity and remain alive and well on planet Earth.

How calculating, your dark efforts are. What do we see in your pockets of wealth? No true treasures of the heart. Just stuff, just disappointed peers looking in, not understanding why you chose this pastime. Why not take up a team sport, where everyone is playing on the same side of the line. A little claustrophobic; too much positive energy swimming around in your ocean field? This should be your indicator that perhaps you are not the best player for the universal game of life. If your intention in all your affairs is not baited with love, I suspect you will be the only fish tale that we will witness in our field of dreams.

The smart ones know how to swim upstream and plant their future interests close to my heart. The lost ones seem to be flipping away, not even sure where their destination is. They have no real home in the heart of love. It must be lonely when you do not wish to entertain love. We see this in your eyes and feel the pain in your heart. Perhaps this is why you are fishing for a beautiful catch. Your soul yearns for a love match, yet your intention is to kill all efforts that enter your field. Then you wonder what is it all for and you are unsatisfied with your prize collection. They don't hold any fine energy. They're void of life. It's just stuff. There is no healthy energetic signature here, just the mark of deceit.

Your sense of humility left when you shut your heart down. We are not interested in seeing your displays of the flesh. We'd prefer to entertain the idea that your cup was full quite some time ago and maybe you could find some satisfaction in the finer tales of life.

We usually all stand around trying to come up with a loving solution for a soul who has a sword through their heart. We would like nothing more than to hear a happy ending to one of your so-called pranks and fishing adventures. This sport truly isn't for you. I hear the game trying to steer clear of your sinful ways. They do not wish to come into your view, as the low energy is enough to sink anyone's ship of dreams.

AHOY, CAPTAIN

Where are you taking us now? Seems to me your G.P.S. is in a field of static. This interruption has taken you way off course. Don't you hate when that happens? Now, you have to rely on the old-fashioned navigation method, a good sense of direction, a legible map and an internal compass of sorts. This usually gets you turned around in the proper direction in the proper time-space sequences. Let's not take any chances if the traffic is heavy and we don't see our way clear. Patience Captain, we are going to set a new course, momentarily. Arrive alive and be sure to be pointed in the correct heading this time.

How could you have been so unnoticing of these unfamiliar sites? Everything was out of place and nothing seemed to ring a bell in your heart. How long have you been navigating the ship into foreign waters? This autopilot system is not always the best equipment when it comes to matters of the heart. You need to be connected and wired internally for our best route of arrival. When you make assumptions and are not noticing of the terrain, obstacles can present themselves. I don't suspect you are all equipped with sufficient, emergency equipment on board.

Let's look at our inventory: few bandages, some gauze, needle and thread, aspirin and a disinfectant solution. These are the bare minimums. We wouldn't be much help to you if we were only carrying these supplies for your emergency situations. I know your intentions are good, but let's face it, some of the places you get stuck in are going to require a stronger solution. Putting a bandage on the problem is only a cover up.

Let's see what we are dealing with. Ok, we have a visual. You are not that far off track. We can make a few adjustments to your heart. Your thinking wasn't clear. How about you open the hatches and get some fresh air. Better yet, let's have a meeting on the main deck. Pardon? You feel a little seasick? Let's focus on the horizon and get grounded. That was our first sign of trouble. Ok, take a few breaths. Better? Fine. Look around, where are you trying to get to, anywhere significant, or just moving from place to place? You didn't like the energy from where you came from, but have failed to make any accurate changes to your route of travel. You need to look at your course. If you are to travel light, you should take certain precautions. The atmospheric conditions are not always conducive for smooth sailing. Expect some dead reckoning; we will have to see what patterns are going to be in your favor.

How's your first mate? Open and on the ball? Paying attention to the signs of nature and in tune with the frequencies of light energy? Is your crew onboard? Oh, I see, they are just putting their faith in your direction and manning their stations. I'm sure your intentions are honorable, but let's get back on track, the quickest most efficient way we know how. No short cuts, as we will surely encounter further delays. The shortest route doesn't always prove to be the best for all souls on board.

If you plan on making this a lifetime excursion, keep your head out of the clouds. We are counting on your fine skills to navigate your uncharted waters. No reason to run aground if you are paying attention. We see this often and have come to the conclusion it is always the error of your ship's commander. That would be you, silly. We've spent enough time caught up in and on stuff. Let's plan in advance and see the whole route in front of us. This keeps you on track and moving steadily on your life chart.

Be sure to notice when things do not feel right in your heart. Your internal compass will always lead you to the pure oceans of loving consciousness. Oh yes, remember your life jackets, bailer and a pump. There is nothing worse than being out in the middle of nowhere and your signal is not so strong. This is up a creek with no paddle, no clear chance of improving your track.

Let's see, how many degrees back to my heart? Make it slight and keep it positive. Even the novice should be able to figure this one out. I'm guessing ten. It seems to work every time.

HOLD IT STEADY

Where is your faith? We've covered this. Sharpen that tool in your chest. It's your finest equipment, a lifetime warranty, many in fact. Ok, we're on course. It feels right to me. Everyone around is feeling at ease. This is comforting. No, this isn't time to go below deck and have some fun. We have work to do. Let's not get too comfortable and drop our guard.

We know in our soul we have to stay alert and plan our next leg, as this could be the longest of the trip. We are not on the ship of fools. This is the journey of your lifetime, worth paying attention to. Let's get the map out. Ok, you're tired of mapping out your destination; besides, all the detours are not clearly marked or visible anyway. Then it seems like you are taking a round about way to your happy destination. Relax. You don't want to end up in a sunken hole or a dead end zone.

Trust every turn is in your best interest, even the ones that take you on the side streets of life. There is something there for you to see. Know that your arrival time to your field of dreams is still calculated fine, providing you are not stopping for too many breaks and pit stops.

Know that your life will unfold according to your chart, if you stay at the wheel. As soon as you put someone else in charge, you are on their road of travel, not your own. Let your intuition and higher self keep you guided by your own light. You should be able to see your own future self, if you dare to visualize your dreams. Never block your own growth with fearful thoughts of uncertainty. This is not our nature. That is when you are traveling solo. Know I don't have a say when you edge me out of your consciousness.

See yourself realizing your dreams. Wish for the best possible outcomes in all your experiences. True hearts together as one only manifest riches in abundance. Your world is full of treasures, deep into the oceans and up into the realms of love and light. We've packed an eternal dream of wishes come true for each one of you. We are hoping you are curious enough to inspire your soul self and come to the God realization inside of you, that all can produce divine desires of the heart when your faith and conviction are strong. Do not let our dream die. We did not write this in the Book of Eternal Life. We only knew of calm waters and true blue skies. Our rainbows are worth the adventure.

Go for the experience, we whispered. You shone and wished we would pick you. Talk about a lucky star. You couldn't believe this wish came true. Yes, we admit, your soul friends were a little envious, but understood your role at this time was divinely essential to make a difference on the planet. Your significant contribution was to set the stage for many hopeful souls, that they too, would earn the chance to play out their role, have some fun and save the day. Kind of like the best drama and action movie all rolled into one.

God knows what scene we are on. There seems to be a few extra takes, more than we expected. We manage to keep the film rolling in a positive direction, thanks to the efforts of many. We know the demands of a day and are understanding when it comes to matters of the heart. There was nothing you wrote in your script that we couldn't work through together.

Remember this please: we are one heart, experiencing life on our grand stage of the universal kingdom. Each and every one of you had an important character role to grow your part of the heart. I'm sure by now you have picked up your script and are practicing your role and ready to appear in the next scene.

We see many ready, who just haven't heard their cue. We haven't forgotten you, not for one nanosecond of your life. We've just given you some space to get it right, so you feel prepared when your time comes to shine on life's stage. Enough time already in make-up and wardrobe, you're looking divine. Let's walk onto the set together like we originally planned. I love the action roles. How about you? They keep us connected and feeling alive. This is where we really shine, stars; the brighter the better. This activity of energy warms our heart.

This is the whole idea, this concept of connectivity. Showcase your talents, no need to be shy. I'm not, that's not our divine nature. I prefer the bold, gentleness of a pure heart that finds the courage to live their Earth life with hope and the compassion to feel the love for the whole of creation and the tenacity to move mountains in their field of dreams.

Find forgiveness and persevere through the challenging times laid before you. Come to understand you are not alone. Walk onto your stage with the knowingness of your Creator's undefying love for all souls who brave the climate on your planet of love.

Yesterday is history; tomorrow is our mystery and today is a present from our heart of love, Mother and I. We are hoping you are not disappointed with the gift of life. This pure love comes with the intentional wish that all your divine dreams come true on your visit, as ours have. Just knowing that you arrived alive and are residing in the universal field of loving consciousness warms our soul. We are hoping you make time for the finer experiences life has to offer, as you couldn't wait to try it all.

Dry those tears, lose your fears and have the time of your life. Be sure to take a few heartfelt pictures for our photo album. We like to relive the memories. It keeps us connected. We have your collection close to our heart for when you wish to remember the good old days.

Let's make this time another "Kodak moment". Don't worry about the flash. We see that your field of experiences are pretty bright. Let's make doubles and be sure to include all parties of the heart.

GLOSSY OR MATT

So many choices down there: will that be with or without borders? It's no wonder some of you are indecisive, with all the options available. Variety is nice, but processes were easier when you didn't have to go through the whole menu. Kind of like your automated phone systems. Holy, now that is a test of patience. Somehow, we were patched through to the wrong department and then we're back to the main menu, after we were put on hold for what seemed to be forever. I recommend a hands-free, so you can manage your valuable time more effectively. It never fails that you are not in the same room as the paperwork is. This is funny to watch. At least you are multi-tasking.

The service sector has really changed. "Hello, I would like to give you some money. Can you please hold?" Not exactly service with a heartfelt smile. I think all this is the result of your population numbers and challenges in the customer service departments. There is so much time spent on the phone. It usually pertains to currency, everyone buying and selling and making a buck; such a transient commodity this form of energy. It's transferred here, there, everywhere all over your globe, only to end up back in the same pockets it originated from. It certainly keeps everyone communicating.

Some sweet calls, some not so nice. I hand it to those souls who sit on the customer complaint lines. All day listening to disgruntled customers, upset and expressing their concerns and dissatisfaction. Go easy on this soul. They don't have the best job in the world. You are too hard on them. Vent someplace else outside, recycle, then politely make your call.

Those of you on the receiving end are truly honing your virtues of the heart. You listen, you practice humility and then there's compassion. They cross the line and you calmly try to put out the fire and find a swift resolution to the matter. Occasionally, I hear a representative not speaking their truth. This is not from the heart. Perhaps, you need a day off. Know that this whole communication process is simply an exchange of energy. How fine would you like it to be? That's completely up to you.

On either end of the conversation, be considerate. You never know when I'm listening in on your calls. You know that quality assurance feature that some of these companies incorporate? I don't eavesdrop, but just a friendly reminder, your dialogue makes its way back to my heart. Clean up the emotional stuff and treat everyone with respect and dignity. We are all one.

I am understanding if you have been burned. But notice nine out of ten times, a positive solution can come to light when you work this matter out from the heart. If you are having communication difficulties with different parties, perhaps you may realize it might be you who could learn to express your desires, interests, viewpoints and concerns in a more professional and effective manner.

I see they have clubs for this fine-tuning of communication skills. This practice would put a stop to the unnecessary chatter that we prefer not to hear. Clean it up or zip it up. Let's not pollute the airwaves unnecessarily. Be considerate of industries' service care workers. They wake up every morning hoping a customer will smile or thank them for their heartfelt efforts. Perhaps you were not careful in your selection of purchase, or it was an impulsive buy. Now, you are trying to fix your problem. Don't make it everyone else's.

Try to become your higher selves. Put this on your short list and impress us all. We are hoping you choose no borders when you are sharing your beautiful heart.

I LIKE THE STILLS

They seem to capture the essence of a timeless heart. These fine pictures are your best collections. I especially like the ones where you include nature as your backdrop. Now, that's a family photo worth saving. It feels like you have me in the picture of your heart. I know Mother is particularly thrilled when you see her good side. I always remind her that it is all good and her beauty never goes unnoticed. Even when she thinks she doesn't look her best, I admire her many expressions of joy and life.

We believe all of creation is a timeless beauty. If we could convince you of this mirage, you would come to understand that we are only limited by our imaginations, then you may regard your journey as a holy, sacred experience. When your understanding of time-space and the limitless galaxies expands, you will feel more connected to the whole.

This quantum theory of possibilities is a fine analogy of our truth. We capture time in the unified field in subatomic particle matter. This whole superstring theory makes anything and everything possible at the same time. By syncing your vibration up to the frequencies of love, all synchronicity is played out eloquently. Your part in this field of dreams is to expand your mind and be open to the potential of timeless love. By not participating in our field of dreams, you inadvertently create a snap in our chain of atoms. These loose ends are forever trying to join back up and reunite with the finer particle matter. By capturing your heart on film, we are able to expedite the intent of the loving consciousness element in your timeless heart.

Ok, some of you are not understanding of this theory. That's fine, that's all you need to know. Be mindful when you detach from our loving field, as our dance of the universal particle matter changes from a loving vibration to that of a shuffle. We prefer the slow and steady frames to capture the best matter for your hearts.

When you reach for your camera, take a picture for us so we can work with the connectivity of our hearts. This keeps processes in line for capturing the optimum strings that hook us all up. For all you photographer-types, there is no pressure, just send us your finest work and we will do the rest.

This whole concept of staying together is intricately woven into the matrix of loving particle suspended in your upper atmospheric levels. Our energy experts keep us close when it comes to matters of the heart. I just hope you make their job easier and hassle free. We like to know you are doing your part in the universal field of loving consciousness.

Let's stay hooked and dancing heart to heart. These are our best moves. You feel this in your heart. It's all for the bigger purpose. Hold onto that loving feeling and send us your particle pictures of your heart. Time is of the essence. Know this to be true.

VALUE VILLAGE

Is this a place where you leave your heart? I see many souls walking around in search of a vibration of sorts. You check the racks, you search the collection and we see that you're looking for a vibrational match. How cute is that? Some of the stuff lingers in your field, other items jump right out at you. This is energy my friends. All of your particles are trying to find a new home in your heart. Be sure not to place it back on the rack if it is calling your name.

These locations you gravitate to, call your signature to sync back up to the universal whole. Somewhere at this particular location, you are doing your part in the energy exchange process. Now, when you don these clothes and accessories, you help us out with a vibrational match. And you just thought you were shopping for bargains. You are collecting particle matter that needs to be recovered and recycled in your heart. We appreciate your subconscious efforts in repairing the matrix of love.

If any article seems to find its way into your field, don't be so quick to discard this piece. For some apparent reason, it could use your heart's therapy. Oh, don't worry; it will not distort your field if it was meant for you. You are just enhancing our fine particle matter in the quantum field. This theory also applies to your collectables and furnishings of eras gone by. All energy matter needs to find its place in our universal field. Do your part when you feel it is right and know when perhaps something of value to you is best placed in the field of another.

This whole process of circulating energy is beneficial to keep life constant, for hearts to heal and grow. It's the simple steps you honor that create a positive wave of change. Next time a material object is placed in your hands ask your heart if its value is right or, intuitively, is it best held in the field of another soul.

Be wise to this calling. We operate purely by our heart signals over here and life is a whole lot smoother and balanced out. This is Mother trying to harmonize the whole of the planet. Play along if you will and notice how calming your field of love appears to be. Coincidence, or not? You figure it out. We are just dropping clues. It makes life a little brighter all around.

LET'S LOOK AT FASHION, THE FASHION OF THE PLANET

We have style, never outdated; all a collection of timeless pieces, fashion for every season. It's the natural look. We are adaptable and our fabric is blended with the finest fibers of love. These threads of beauty are resilient over time, unmatched by the synthetic blends of change. Years pass and our collection stays on top of the world. We have the finest seamstresses, who prepare our heartfelt desires for the timeless season of love. They are not interested in the imposter types, as they cannot weave this energy into the delicate threads of the universal heart. Their jobs are steady but they know their fine talents produce the best collections time and time again. They are only interested in picking up the original threads of beauty that are imported by your manufacturing heart of will.

The intricate design is missing several blends of shiny particle thread in the matrix of woven beauty. Our current collection could use a bit more sparkle to dazzle our universal field of loving consciousness. We have been traveling far and wide in search of these timeless fibers, hoping to move forward with our best collection to date.

All the while, some of our threads could not endure the test of time and wore thin and let go. These softer fibers were not strong enough to mend the matrix with love infused energy. These were only temporary stitchings; not a match for the finest collection on Earth. All fine matter is compatible providing its heartfelt strength is eternal. When temporary threads are introduced, our light workers have to constantly revisit the old collection. It is not our best work. Our efforts are only as divine as the quality we receive.

We are trying to manifest a miracle with broken threads. We have quite high standards when it comes to the cloth of tapestry that envelops your realms of light. So what you put out and deliver to our fabric department is solely what we have to work with.

Our creativity is beyond most of your imaginations, so don't send us your scraps. We are trying to bring forth the finest collection for the heart of the planet. The gates of love are woven with the highest beauty of light particle and subatomic matter. The magnificence of the light energy is breathtaking. I hear this term being used quite a lot. I believe it's expressed when an experience is truly out of this world. How exhilarating.

All paths leading to the kingdom and the throne are a collection of treasures of the universal heart. The jewels and precious pieces of fabric are all indicative of our true heart over time. When your virtues become like ours, this adds to the majestic, eternal beauty of our light omnipresent vibrational energy.

This decade of the new millennium is the perfect time to reinforce our fabric at the entrance to the gates of love. If many are acting in this fashion, we can start to put the sparkle back into your woven cloth of life and ensure its resiliency will last into eternity. Now, this is a one of a kind designer's masterpiece when it comes to wearing your finest collection, truly made with your heart in mine.

Send up your best collections to date. I have a feeling you are holding back and waiting to see what the other parties are displaying. Chances are, we are all on the same wavelength when it comes to dressing in our finest and manufacturing a heart of love. Only the finest threads on your planet will be pure enough to make it into the timeless particles of the heavens. Shine your brightest and show us your collective efforts, that we may again dress the planet with the intention of beauty.

When we all act in this fashion, we only produce the best darn show for all to capture and integrate back into the field of love. All souls benefit from a timeless piece of loving consciousness, while they walk through the stages of their lives.

We wish to don our brightest collection when it comes to matters of the heart. Let's make it our finest in the field so we can help light the way to your creative hearts of love. Now, that's an outfit, fit for a King. I'm loving it already. I can't wait for the new season's collection. It's sure to be light. That would be our natural choice from here. Fine, I believe I have made myself clear. I don't wish for any fabric to take my breath away. It's not my style and it is truly out of fashion.

I like it when you are all looking and feeling hot. I can connect to this, in a big way. You're looking mighty fine. We are all so divine. Put your finger on that one and feel the sizzle. I liked those days, hot, hot, hot. We were all feeling hot, hot, hot.

LET'S GET GOING

No time like the present moment. Processes are heating up. Your energy is at its finest. Our collection is at its best. We look and feel better than we have in a long time. I'm feeling this one. This is my chance to voice my concerns.

If you are not operating on the finer side of life, we have serious communication problems. Aren't you tired of not knowing how to pull it all together? I know I am feeling left out of the communication lines. All these decisions are being made and not many asking my opinion when it comes to matters of the heart. I feel like a third wheel. Just spinning and not moving forward; not part of the whole. Wait a minute, what's wrong with this picture? I am the whole.

Why have you edged me out? Don't like my ideas? No time for negotiations with a sound mind? Who's operating fully from the heart level anyway? I hear when you edge God out; it spells "EGO". I see this. This can be a deadly practice.

Many disasters of the heart happen when we get caught up in this self-serving illusion of our lower selves. Problems arise and matters are not dealt with on a higher level. Relationships don't stand a chance of surviving when your heart isn't open for loving communication. Usually one party is too hung up on their ideas and desires and they are not in accordance with the universal heart. Be thankful I don't operate at this lower level, as your planet would not be alive and well in the realms of pure loving consciousness.

If this is not my divine nature, then this should be your major clue that you may be quite out of balance in your affairs and matters of the heart. If souls don't play your game and fuel your ego, you move on. You are traveling on the low road, my friend, and your destination does not look so bright. Try admitting that you have no sincere connection with the real stuff love is made of and, perhaps, you can do a check in the humility department.

We can deliver this lesson free of charge. In fact, we don't always wait for your order, as the pile up here becomes too heavy. We have to send it down for your highest good. Interestingly, quite a few of you require a few shipments of this type, as the first one didn't quite make it fully into your inconsiderate heart.

We just keep shipping and waiting around for a call and pray that you have a change of heart.

Your character seems to produce results in many areas of your life that are only considering your own well-being. We can't grow the universal heart in that fashion. You have snapped our chain of love. Our persistent efforts to hook you back up are completed most effectively when you decide to bring us back into the communication loop. This at least starts the process of restoration.

How did you develop this ungodly attitude? Oh, I see, it happened way back when. You started getting your own way because souls were tired of your behavior. They just wanted you to stop complaining and voicing your desires of the flesh. Time passes and now your parties have moved on. Don't fool yourself, as not too many true hearts are in your field of conditional love. They pay the price with their heart and soul. Now, many of you are out of the loop. We have quite a large project to deal with because of your senseless ways and solo efforts to satisfy your desires of your mind. This is not of our character.

If you wish to join the heart team, perhaps we can save a few lives in the process of creating our dreams. Your fantasies are short-lived and sure not to produce everlasting beauty or strong bonds of love. We are hoping you come to your senses and start operating at the heart level when it comes to your experiences in life.

Souls are impacted by your lower frequency level and this includes all loving hearts in the universal field. If you are having a difficult time with this lesson, perhaps you can make time for some true souls and offer an ear and perform several thousand acts of kindness. This is a step in the right direction. Everything you do in your waking hours doesn't have to be about you. You were not granted the gift of life to come down and hang your accomplishments and achievements on your walls. This only keeps loving hearts out of your field. They know where your borders are set.

Your concrete walls could use a good blasting, since it's been quite stuffy in your environment for a while. Open the window to your own soul self and let the ocean breeze of loving consciousness into your field. You may think you are living your dreams, but in fact, your players are just as disillusioned by your false sense of reality and the true material that love and happiness are made of.

Your fabrication of your sense of purpose loosely unraveled along with your heartfelt dreams the day your loving playmates left. Your fashion statement is out of date and most of us prefer the timeless collection of a true heart that has everyone's best interest in mind. This makes everyone look and act their best. When you look good, you feel good. When you come to the table with your finest desires, we can address your intentions. We see to it that your golden threads in your heart are reinforced, with the purest fabric of loving energy to be woven into the Book of Life. This pattern is necessary to integrate your energy back into the field of loving vibration.

Make your contribution heartfelt, as many strands have been cut out of the design. We were hoping for a complete unification, minus the scraps. Our basket of loose ends does not seem to match up with any of the original particles of love. We are not partial to scrapping any material when it comes to matters of the heart. We are only looking for a vibrational match to reunite the matrix of love and restore the harmony on the planet.

When you decide to redesign your heart, we would love to be a part of it. We would like nothing more than to introduce soulful types into your field, so we can all move ahead with our intentions of the heart. There are places to go, people to see, hearts to save and souls to love. Let's seal this with a promise and a pledge to keep the love alive.

Our fashion designers are dreaming that you come into the light of day and share your collection of love with all souls on both sides of the veil. This keeps our fabric tight and the brightness of your soul lights the way for many. This loving idea is sure to produce a garment of beauty for your travels of the heart.

We are ready to update your image when you give us a call. All consultations are free for the asking. We just request that you send your truest intention. Our teams look forward to working with your coat of many colors and are prepared to put a new spin on your look. It's a match every time. We like to blend in with the fabric and particle matter of our true blue heart.

Try that one on for size. It can never be too big. We are sure you will grow into it. We all do eventually. We have time, how about you? No kidding, no fooling around. Play nice with our designer hearts. They're delicate and hold the finest fabric in the land. All are necessary to weave in the threads of eternal life and they bond our heart together in the universal kingdom of love.

Now that's love American style, fashion with the spark of eternal life and never out of style. In my eyes, it is timeless. I see you feel this too. Hold this look close to your hearts and truly we will be looking our best.

The universe is watching and admiring your style. You are an original. I tell you true. Let's get dressed and pull it all together. We could use quite a few designers with loving hearts to give us the look we've been dying for. It's always been worth the wait, back to the true blue heart of one.

CHAPTER SIXTEEN

The Season of Your Spirit

IT'S INTERESTING HOW YOUR SPIRIT IS lifted with the changes of nature. Sometimes you are blossoming; other times you are going into hibernation. You should leave this pattern for Mother Nature. She has it down to a fine science. The cycle of your seasons should not put a damper on your soul. When nature is alive in the unified field of loving consciousness, she lives to the fullest, rain or snow. There are no dry spells, when it comes to universal love. There should be no landslides when it comes to matters of the heart.

Your spirit should be ever resilient to the changing of the seasons. Your heart seems to dry up a bit when the season of heat and abundance winds down. That's not catching the spirit. You would do best if you harvested this fruitful season and stored its properties in your everlasting soul.

Dry spells and climate changes should only be reserved for Mother and I to contend with. We are hoping this temporary season does not slow down your growth. We can see that if we stopped processes, you would have difficulties, but this is not the case, nor will it ever be. This is a sacred time of change and transitional shifts are to take place in the heart of your soul. Embrace each experience as a new season of growth. Have the expectation of an abundance of beauty and soulful memories. At no time should you put your heart on hold waiting for a more suitable season of circumstances to arrive. If you are stationary, energy can't work at its finest to shift and move forward into a new field of opportunities.

There are always going to be cold and windy days, but these are the times to draw on your faith to keep your heart growing steady. These nurturing conditions of adverse weather patterns should only cue you to change and clear out your own internal field. This is what the weather is doing. It is in a constant motion of energy exchange. Sometimes the front is slow moving, but know she is steady. This period will always be followed by a high, clear blue sky. This is us with a clear heart of love.

When your garden is unable to produce a bountiful crop, know that through a series of miracles, this timely process is necessary for your next season of abundance. In various parts of the world, nature's cycle of life has its own intelligence and loving consciousness. When treated with respect and dignity, she will continue to operate in a loving fashion and suit all of your needs. It is when you disrupt the universal law of order that Mother Nature acts out of character.

The delicate balance of your ecosystem and our universal spirit needs to be left to its own devices. Consequences are heavy when it comes to playing with fire. Souls will inevitably get burned along the way. Recovery is slow and painstaking. Many lose the spirit in their heart when their basic needs and desires are not provided for. Trust that Mother Nature makes every effort to ensure all souls keep their spirits high. Under no circumstances would we put out the flame in your heart. We make sure the seasons change with your spirit.

If you are having an unpleasant time, perhaps you are stuck in your own low weather pattern. I suggest you hook onto a system of higher pressure and move out of the storm you are in. If you are having an extended dry spell, perhaps you can figure out your root cause. We cannot produce fruit in your life if your spirits are low, cold or dried up. Mother and I don't grow well under these conditions and we suspect you don't either. Water your garden and change your internal climate. This will produce enough fine energy to brighten the darkest periods of your growth. We don't appreciate some of you waiting for a miracle, without doing a sacred rain dance. For where would you be without rituals of the heart?

Your belief in the rainbow of love and blue skies filters through the clouds of life every time. If you are waiting for a holiday to celebrate the new season, this shows us that you are not producing any significant growth in areas other than the pit of your stomach. This uneasy feeling will probably turn sour once the feeling of sobriety sets in.

The season of your spirit is a continuous cycle. It is not an on and off thing. For if you were in touch, you would come to realize that every day is a renewal of the heart and every garden of beauty and joy is a miracle in itself. Happiness and blue skies are not reserved for the true souls and nature alone. Many should consider this way of being every day.

Produce your gardens of love. Capture the spirit of every season. Find your own beauty within and harvest the crop in your soul. Pray that it carries you until eternity, as that is how we have come thus far.

Every date on your calendar of time is perfect to enjoy the gift of life and love in abundance in the ever growing season of your heart and mine. I'll drink to that out of the cup of eternal life. Salute.

THE CHANGING OF THE GUARD

Such a tradition passed down from many generations, this is. We admire your reverential ways. Your discipline and commitment make it all worth while. Many come by to pay respects to your display of fellowship. Many are amazed to witness such acts of patriotism, all officials performing their duty in the name of love. We see this tradition. It's been going on for centuries. This commitment of our heart pulls our strings together in the unified field, much like your collective efforts of praying for world peace. All are on the same page and wearing their uniforms of love and respect. Some of you do not take this practice seriously. This dims our light of loving consciousness.

Universal prayers should be the new order of the day. If your officials make time for this sacred practice, perhaps you can schedule it into your routine as well. Take a few moments in your day to acknowledge the King of your heavens and stand proud in my name. These efforts will hook up many in our rainbow of dreams. I feel you are paying more respect to some of your stately figures than to the well-being of your own soul. How does this happen?

Do not be so quick to give your power away. Find the balance and stand up for your own rights and divine gifts of the heart. You owe it to yourselves. If you are not standing at attention for your own cause, who will come to the rescue? Perhaps a wild animal of sorts will hear your cries of the heart. You'd better hope they have a fancy first aid kit and a defibrillator, as you may need a lifeline. You seem to put too much faith in the hands of others, rather than your soul self. All you have is each other and your universal heart of love.

Be careful where you place your energy. It is best utilized in your own current field of love. This tradition allows for maximum growth of your soul's heart and those of others with our best interests at heart. I appreciate your patriotic ways and respect for all your officials in office, but be sure to circulate your own loving field with the power of love. This can be done in the privacy of your home. Then when you feel that you have truly connected and hooked back up to our universal heart, you can admire the efforts of many who stand in my name and march to the tune of love.

Let's see some new displays of honor. Raise your vibration and tune your heart to the sounds of love and the power of one. That would be us. I'll be sure to tune into your admirable efforts and intentions of our universal heart, in the name of the Mother, the Father and the Holy Spirit within.

Let's keep up to the changing times on your planet and raise the vibration as we shift into discovering our full divine power in the field of pure loving white light consciousness. This act of embracing your spirituality and displaying your heart of gratitude will change the guard in your heart. Move into a more trusting field of loving vibration and come to realize that your own efforts of preserving tradition are fit for a King in the place you call home.

Let's shake on this as you agree to exercise your divine birthright and hone the God-given gifts you have in your field of love. This tradition will make Mother and I stop in amazement and pay respect to the many faces of the changing of the guard. This day will clearly mark the beginning of the New World Order in the finer frequencies of love. This is an event worth celebrating. This is the Real McCoy. The power of love is indivisible as we stand in my name.

Can I have your attention on this one? I'm hoping you can sing to the tune of love. If not, just listen with your heart. It will tell you true, I love you.

POPPIES ARE FOREVER

This is another fine tradition reaching across many borders. I see and feel your heartfelt concerns of days gone by. Many hearts were disconnected during the bloody time. I feel the hearts of the survivors, as lives were lost at the expense of the nation. Many brave souls carrying out their duty for their country. God bless their souls.

I do, however, notice the vibration on the planet that day. It is at an all time low. Now, I'm the first one to sport a compassionate heart, but let's change the frequency of the day's events. This memory is not healthy for our field of growth. I like the fact that the nation comes together to pay respect for the unnecessary loss of life, but we can be thankful and express gratitude for the souls who came down and carried out their divine role. This should not be a day of heavy sorrow, but rather a celebration of their lives and the victory that marked the end of the blood bath.

When you stand for your minute of silence, this would be a sacred time to send love to the universal heart. That is where your loved one resides, close to my heart. Many of the soldiers have already returned back to the Earth. That was the arrangement prior to their partaking in an ungodly set of circumstances in history.

Please mark this day on your calendar with heartfelt feelings of love and raise the vibration of the planet, as you pay respect to those beautiful innocent souls who made a difference in our world of dreams. They were all welcomed with open hearts. We embraced the true souls when they came to the gates of love. They wish for you to hold them in your heart and to remain positive, as you relive the memories of their gift of life.

Display your pictures of connectivity. This keeps your loving soul in your field, as they do you. Dry those tears over yesterday's tragic events and pay your respects with a heart full of love, in my name. This would warm my heart to know you were faithfully acting out of fashion for my heartfelt desires. If you had a knowing of the gift of eternal life, you would only wish to remain connected by the finer frequencies of love, not by holding the sorrowfulness in your heart.

May I suggest you mix up your poppy colors. I grow an assortment of shades that hold the finer frequencies of love in your field. Try some of the lighter varieties and see how your heart feels that day. You will have my blessing on this. I prefer to rejoice in the field of love and respect everyone's short time on planet Earth. Keep your intentions high and of a pure heart. This is when you are closest to the finer frequencies of love.

THANKSGIVING IS FOR TURKEYS

Now this is a celebration all over the world. I would like nothing more than to know you are thankful each and every day for your abundance of blessings. Yes, many true hearts are grateful for having their desires and wishes fulfilled. I feel this. Then, there are others who act like the turkey themselves. They become overstuffed with the goodies and don't appear so well when the events are unfolding, with all this running around in my honor. At least, that is what I make of it.

All this traditional this and that is interesting to see. You have lists a mile long to make sure the occasion goes just right. You have the trimmings, the best casseroles, an abundance of fruits and vegetables and oh yes, we can't forget about the dessert. I have to tell you, your definition of dessert and mine are not even close. I'm not partial to getting high on sugar in any shape or form. One, it distorts my thought processes; and two, it weighs me down. Let's not go there. We were commenting on your list of rituals to make the occasion just right. I appreciate all the fussing around, but some of you should slow down. It almost appears like you are going to a bake sale of sorts. I see stuff flying off the shelves, all in an effort to capture the spirit of the season.

Yes, you deserve to spoil yourself some, as I see you look forward to this holiday. I don't see much paraphernalia that actually has to do with the virtues of the heart, in celebration of gratitude for the gift of life and the many blessings you receive. This seems to have gotten lost somewhere in the tradition and the holiday celebrations.

It's wonderful that you all hook up with loved ones and share time, but I don't see many light connections made because of the distractions. I do witness a frenzy of electrical activity leading up to this sacred day. I feel like the afterthought and I usually get indigestion. I'm not suggesting that your baking is off. I see quite a lot of preparation and love go into the heart of your meal. This would be a great time to say your heartfelt prayers and be sure you have included me on your guest list.

I don't wish to sound out of line, but if there are going to be a lot of low vibrational beverages, I prefer not to hook up. The actual task is pretty much impossible and I have a tricky time trying to relate to your vibration and intentions of the heart. I prefer to keep this whole celebration light, as it's quite a big day in our kingdom of love.

Many on our side look forward to the heartfelt connections. We feel your intentions, see your acts of kindness and even notice they stop the traffic in your desires of the heart, or is it because so many of you are trying to catch a turkey of your own. We are just hoping to be included in this festivity, since the vibration in the realms of love seems to be buzzing with connectivity. This allows us to catch up on some extra work over the holidays while you enjoy your bonding time and gifts of love.

We give thanks that you all appreciate the fact that we probably won't be staying for dessert as we have quite a bit of hooking up to do before this time. Have fun and be sure to thank Mother for the dishes of love. She knows in her heart where the true parties are.

Cheers. Here's to love, life and laughter. May all your meals and deals be blessed with the white light.

MARY, QUITE CONTRARY

This time of year is sad for many. It's not my favorite time. There are too many broken hearts and desperate souls in states of depression. We can't find any love. The sad and the lonely are too many to count. This holiday marks the enormity of the darkness; the effects of the efforts of our dark souls. They have placed too much emphasis on the stuff, "the goods". This pressure has stolen away the loving spirit of the season. It just looks like a massive shopping spree with no end in site. Merchants laugh all the way to the bank. Lost souls cry themselves to sleep. Lonely souls find their states magnified ten-fold.

This is not my idea of a celebration of a fine saint. The image captured on our equipment is of a distorted nature. There are too many waves of sad and lonely souls looking to find love. There are many souls trying to buy a heart of gold. I didn't place our hearts at the shopping mall for sale. It's sad that many mix up "love for sale". This feeling cannot be bought with an excessive amount of cash. It's priceless. We are so off kilter that day, that week. Quite frankly, for at least a five to six week period, much damage is done to the matrix of love. We are working double time, over time, just to keep up with the restorative projects. The loose ends are catastrophic. It's a hell of a light show, if you want to call it that. There is quite a bit of snap, crackle pop; times this by a few hundred million. It's a full blown disaster.

Clear circuit patterns only manifest when the heartfelt recipients are sober and sugar-free. This limits our head count to only a few. Sorry Starlights, I see your efforts, but we can't feel it from here. Perhaps, some of you can give a great meditation tape to mark the beginning of the new year of dreams. I don't see many of these hung over the fire place, nor do I see any under the Christmas tree. The decorations all look nice, but I would have liked to see quite a few more love lights turned on. This is not done with your power cords. That's called overloading the circuit and being prepared for a possible short. Most of you seem quite prepared for a game or two. We can't manufacture an etherical hook up in this fashion. God knows we have tried, every which way. It's clearly impossible.

We do however, enjoy the hymns in your temples of love. Funny how all the rest of the frantic light shows and transactions at the bank cancel out most of the efforts to feel the love. It's almost impossible to raise the spirit of the nation on such a confusing dark, cold day.

Throw us a lifeline. We are in desperate state on the finer side of life. We are trying our best to keep the warm flame glowing in the heart of one. Lighten up everyone. Love is of the highest, fastest frequency. This ingredient shouldn't pack on any pounds this time of year; in fact, it should have quite the opposite effect. All souls should feel high and on top of the world, not down in the dumps. It doesn't matter how big your gifts are, we can't feel that warm, fuzzy feeling. It's clearly shorted us all out. What a mess to clean up. There is extensive damage done around this time. Sadness hovers with too many regrets lingering. So many souls don't know where to start to fix their love connections.

My holiday wish would have been, and still is to this day, is to give us a call. We can restore the love in the heart of one. Just give us a chance. You have us running in circles. It's a complete reversal in a downward direction. Send the love up into the realms, folks. Try to be more hopeful. The stress of this manufactured time of year is enough to put the fire out in anyone's heart, including ours. No love match here, just another Nintendo type game. All action and no real heroes, just a high score on the game board of life. I don't track these numbers. They don't add up to much, just a few hits in the dark. I believe you call it, "lights are on but nobody's home".

Solo is separation. You are not even close to hooking up to that loving feeling. This is not called a gift from the heart. Sorry to say, I would probably return this gift. In the long run, you lost your attempts at connecting to the soul of love. Think your purchases out. Is it good for the soul? Does it stoke the flame or does it put our fire out? I'll let you stew over that pot of mess.

Give us a call if you need a reminder on how to keep us together. We are truly interested in becoming one. Don't wrap all your gifts with the same ribbon. These fibers are synthetic and don't blend well with our matrix of love. We like the shiny fibers. Now, that's a light show I can warm up to. That would make this event a holy night. Did I hear anyone sing: Om Om Om Om Om Om Om Om Om Om Om Om Om Om Om Om Om Om Om Om Om Om

Glory, Glory, rejoice to our Mother and Father in the highest heavens above. Bestow upon us our gifts of eternal life, as we express gratitude back into the heart of one. Amen

HAPPY NEW YEAR

I have to tell you, the morning after is not our best day. Some of you know better, thank you for that. Some of you have obligations, we're lucky for that. Now a large portion of you souls get carried away and, boy oh boy, do we pay for it the next morning. I dread this heavy feeling. It's like half the planet has been turned upside down. We seem to be spinning a little out of balance. I'm getting dizzy just thinking about it.

I don't understand why you call this a good time. Seems to me you feel like a dried out whale the next day, washed up on shore, belly up. Not a great analogy, as I love my sea creatures, but this heavy, dehydrated lifeless state is no way to start the year off right. You are clearly not being kind to your soul. This is an avoidable death of sorts. The energy should be running high in your field of love that day and we feel the opposite. This is another low point in your field of dreams. We are going to have to call in a marine biologist and see how to direct you back out into the ocean of love. After we nurse that headache of yours, we will try to get some liquids back into your system. You seem to have drunk enough for the whole year ahead. How about we opt for the H_2O? This is our only hope for restoring you to sanity.

I'm not understanding of these rituals. You arrive at a highpoint in your life and you counterbalance and sabotage your connection by drowning out your new frequency of love and dreams come true. You jeopardize all the connections you made by polluting your field with toxins.

We see this whole practice in a different light. You should be securing your field with as much light and high energy as possible. You and your team have hooked up and realized a goal or a dream come true and you undo all our fine efforts of the universal heart. How silly is that? So now you are sitting at the bottom of the barrel, wondering why you don't feel that great.

Well let me tell you, I'm not feeling so hot myself. This is always the state that gets us into our pots of messes. We been shaken, we been stirred and now we are looking for a strainer. Your energies need to be quite a bit lighter if you want to stay on your high.

Your stuff is making me seasick. All this up and down and swells and storms; one minute we are on top of the wave, next minute we are about to capsize. No steady high, just waves of confusion. What's with this crazy behavior? Were you not looking for the ultimate party?

Do you actually think feeling that low was what we had in mind? Now I know you're acting crazy for sure. If you were of a sound mind, you would not be abusing your mind, body and soul in this fashion.

Your light workers are standing by; we now call them your drinking buddies. They are so uninspired by your lack of progress and your inability to enjoy life from the finer side of the spectrum. They're up, they're down and they're all over the place. It's sad to see no steady progress. Do yourself and us a favor and start to respect yourself and the gift of life. If you had a true heart and love connection to the whole, you probably wouldn't choose to float around in the low energy fields. You are so heavy it takes several of us to try to pull you back up into the light.

Why don't you try staying in one place for a period of time? We can see you more clearly when you shine your light. We run for cover and plug our nose when you take us down into the cold waters of life. This isn't our definition of a celebration, this is insanity my friends.

Your ideas of enjoying the ultimate life and marking your experiences and achievements with a party of sorts, is truly a low time in your book of dreams. Those pictures you capture do not process well on our film. The distortion cannot and will not, hook up this heartfelt experience in the Book of Life.

So, if you are living your dream and you wish to have a copy in your file, be sure that your celebrations are of the finest quality. We'd all like to attend. This warms our hearts and gives us reason to celebrate your gift, as you walk and enjoy your experiences on planet Earth. Let's stay out of the medicine cabinet, as this will surely over expose your film of dreams come true.

Know when to say: "No thanks, I'm high on life and feeling fine. This is a gas and a dream come true. Wish you were here, you'd have a blast. Thanks God, for the ultimate party, thanks for staying close. It wouldn't be the same without you. This is truly worth all the effort and I am grateful for your love. I promise not to make us so dizzy again, as it seems kind of senseless and I've grown since then. You know, "been there, done that". Now let's get the real party rolling. I'll drive. You come along for the ride. We're traveling up from here. No looking back. That's history. I know a good thing when I see it. I'm just here for the party, hoping to save a few souls from drowning in the low tides of life. Spreading love your style.

No time for the small stuff and it's all small stuff. We are shining so bright and having the time of our life. Let's stay connected. We have a party to attend. Let's see who we can pull out of the icy waters".

Donna: *It's worth the smile on your divine face and the feeling in my heart is like no other. It's out of this world. I'm loving it; how about you, God? I thought you'd like that one. I know you've been waiting for me to see the light. I believe I have it all figured out. Just listen and live by our heart. That's where we find you, every second of our life. Well, I'm back and hoping to get it right. I'm sticking close by and looking to have the time of my life. I hear there is a rainbow of dreams over the next mountain range. Hold on tight, I'm thinking of going for it all the way. Are you in?*

GOD: Always, right where you found me. I'm listening to your dreams. We can do this together. There is no mountain too high that I haven't been over before. I'm familiar with the terrain, it's my nature. I'm strapped in pretty light. I hear the view is breathtaking. What do you have to say about that?

Donna: *I'm not afraid. That's not my style.*

GOD: Good, I was hoping that was your answer. Let's roll, my friend. There is a lot to see. Keep your eyes wide open and listen to your heart. Miracles show up when you are looking for love. We have plenty to go around. We're just hoping you notice our style. We manifest dreams in this fashion. True blue, right from our heart, it's what we do when we are hooked up to you. You've got to like that one?

Donna: *Oh yes, I'm loving it. All of what this life has to offer. It's truly a dream come true, if you wish to see it in this light. It's much easier when the light switch is turned on and the flame in my heart is as bright as the day. Feels like heaven.*

GOD: I was hoping you would say that. I'm telling you; don't underestimate the power of love. Your island of paradise is one of your dreams come true. Just stay the course, as we have a few miracles to deliver. You do believe in miracles don't you?

Donna: *Absolutely. You're here, aren't you?*

GOD: Always have been, always will be. I was hoping you might notice this one.

Donna: *How could I not? I wouldn't be traveling light if it wasn't for your love and your belief in the dream of our universal heart. You have quite a job ahead of you.*

GOD: I wouldn't have it any other way. If you didn't get this opportunity, you would have been disappointed. Besides you indicated you wanted to grow and shine your light so bright, kind of like my light. You keep striving for the ultimate dream and I keep letting you go, to get it right. There's no stopping you. You had your mind made up and your soul packed tight. You wished a million times to brighten your love light to the tunes of the higher heavens, so here we are. How are you liking it so far?

Donna: *Boy, oh boy, I've got some work to do.*

GOD: We all have. That's half the fun. Are you up to the challenge?

Donna: *You betcha.*

GOD: That's what you said before you left. I love that about you, a soul true to our heart. Have I told you lately I love you?

Donna: *Perhaps.*

GOD: Well, I do, each and every one of you, more than you know, as we've been hooked up forever. That's a lot of love. That's many lifetimes that we've grown together. You might say we are hooked and inseparable.

Donna: *I was hoping you'd say that.*

GOD: I know. I feel it in our heart. How about you?

Donna: *Are you kidding? Let me tell you. It's immeasurable, this warmth and feeling of peace. It is the most complete sensation that I find it difficult to describe in words. It's a fullness in the depths of my soul and a knowingness that we are one, that brings my soul to tears of joy, as I experience this walk through life, hand in hand, heart to heart. Every breath I take is a reminder of your heartfelt love and this feeling that I have captured in my growing heart, only desires to express its gratitude in every capacity imaginable. This is my true desire of my heart and the expression of my soul self. How can anyone put this into words? It's a feeling in your heart and soul, that you truly know why you are alive and fulfilling the virtues of the heart. We only desire to grow closer to our Almighty Creator, the Divine Intelligence Almighty Love. We wish and pray to know you, as you know us fully in our hearts of Love Omnipresent Vibrational Energy. This by far is the best miracle you have delivered in awhile, as you had a few of us wondering when you would let us know how we were doing and we were admittedly, checking in on you.*

We've been trying to get your attention for quite awhile. Perhaps, some of us were not going about it in the right fashion. Maybe it was a timing thing. Nonetheless, it appears we could be doing a whole lot better in your eyes, I see your point. You seem to see the whole picture. Some of us don't think with the whole heart in mind. Yes, it seems to be the crime of the century.

Perhaps we can come together, pull our socks up, wipe our noses and get back on track to our universal heart of love. Looks like we have to make up a bit of lost time, some of us have been straying around not knowing what direction to go in. Few of us lost our way.

Will you accept a heartfelt apology? It sounds like there are quite a few of you, all around on your side of life that we owe an apology to. We seem to be wasting everyone's divine time. It seems like we have you all flying in circles, because we can't seem to pull our thoughts together, never mind our heart of one.

What to do? Well, surely we can make it up to you, God. You seem like the forgiving type. That's one of our lessons of the whole heart. I'm suspecting your character is pretty understanding and compassionate. Oh, I know, you don't take kindly to our ungodly ways. I was referring to the souls who sincerely just were not sure of their purpose and how to keep their vibrations fine enough to keep us hooked up.

I'm thinking you have a soft spot for us. If you need some time to warm up to this idea, let us know. I'm sure you've been warmed up to this for quite some time and you were hoping we'd get the show on the road.

Don't worry, we've got it covered, all your areas of concern. Heck, there are enough of us. We really shouldn't run into too many problems anymore. Or should I say any problems. I'm saying we are willing to do our best from here on in.

What do you say about that? Do we have a deal? Do you want to shake on this one? This is a heart to heart move in your direction. We all have the instructions now. We've got it figured out. You'll deliver, we build a better life. We build a stronger heart and bring many to the gates of love. We start using our whole brain and operate at the heart level, kind of like our Mother and Father. If we need an example, look to nature and your beautiful creations of love. They are in the unified field of pure consciousness adhering to the universal laws of love.

It's really a pretty simple formula. We just have to want to do it. What else is there truly left to do, as meaningful as this? We know this is the way back to your heart. There *are no shortcuts. We also know there doesn't seem to be any secrets in the universe. That's ok too, as we are cleaning up our acts down here. We know only love and wish to keep your heartfelt desires and dreams alive. This can only become our reality if we hold you true in our hearts of love. This is how we all come together and manifest a few miracles along the way. This is the magic that fuels our dream of a heart of one in the kingdom of love. We know in our soul that you are our Creator of love and without your blessing, our Earth lives appear unfulfilling.*

We desire to be held in love at the gates of love when we re-unite in this fashion. We choose to see the world through your eyes of beauty and whole heart of love. May we be of service to you humbly, as we make a divine difference on planet Earth. We know how to act in accordance with your wishes and understand it is for the benefit of the whole heart. We are to shine our brightest and are hoping you see our sparkle and feel this one in your heart, our heart.

I think we are all beginning to understand this whole connectivity and superstring theory and understand the quantum field is alive and well with the loving particle of the universal heart. It is up to us to keep the dream alive. We know this to be true. How do we sound so far?

Saying it, doing it; Ok, we get the message. You're looking for that warm fuzzy feeling, that's when you'll know that we have raised the consciousness of the planet. I hear you. Actions speak louder than words. You desire to feel it, the old-fashion way, right in the heart of the universe.

Ok, we get the picture. Give us a minute to warm up to this idea.

Just kidding, we are ready now. How about you?

GOD: Absolutely; Welcome aboard to the Ship of Dreams, the Creator of Creations. I promise you we will have a divine time of things, as we have quite a few rainbows to catch. You have my pledge of love and I am hoping you all have the same desires of the heart as I do. This is how we make all our dreams come true. You have my word on this one. And in the beginning the Word was Truth.

Let's keep our promises close to our heart. I'm sending love in abundance and hoping you can fuel the heart of the universe with the same love we originally had in our treasure of dreams come true. Wishing you all the time of your life; and know deep in your hearts, we are all one, looking to experience the ultimate celebration of the gift of life. Let's shake on this one and rock the universe. I feel like dancing in my blue suede shoes. I like the sounds of love. It's all music in my heart, our heart, one heart, truly yours. Dial love.

We are standing by practicing our best moves. We feel you are too. It's a vibrational match, a match made in heaven. How divine is that? We love your style. We see that you've learned your lessons and are stepping in a positive direction. I feel this one right in the heart of the dance floor. You know this feeling too well. We all do. We've been there many times before.

Let's dance our hearts out until we end up together on the grandest stage of all. The gates of love are open to all participants who shine their brightest and have only love in their soul to share as one. Trust me when I tell you that there is plenty of room for your fanciest moves. And if you think you have seen it all, well, guess again, the King of Rock and Roll had some pretty divine lessons right from the heart of love. Now, this is a show you don't want to miss. I tell you true, I always do.

CHAPTER SEVENTEEN

The Universal Heart of One

CAPTURE THIS IN YOUR CONSCIOUSNESS: A timeless eternal state of divinity with all souls on every plane of existence, alive in the unified field of pure, loving consciousness. Our ocean of love harmonized to the finest frequency matter of your Creator's heart, our heart of love. We dance, sing and rejoice in the knowingness of connectivity and feel completely connected to the finer side of life. All light beings in unison with your dreams create perfect manifestations in the name of love and light. The realms of light, fabricated with the finest particle matter known to your species are lightly bonded and delicately woven into the matrix of divine love. The web of life's beauty, sustained by your heartfelt desires and intentions, keep the dream alive in our universal heart. No time for sadness and disparity, just lessons of the heart and the virtues of love.

Our patterned tapestry gleams with the eternal beauty of divine love and our rainbow of dreams; all souls are harmonized to one another's vibration. The heavens are alive and abound with the hopes of peace. All heart-full individuals on your side are making a conscious effort to enforce the universal laws in order to sustain and grow our heart. All understand the connection and delicate balance to the finer side of life and respect the field of loving consciousness.

The Earth transforms back to its original state of divinity and paradise and your heaven of dreams becomes real once again. All hopeful souls living and breathing collectively to the finer combustion of dreams come true. Restoration is natural; all creations are thriving and ecstatic when in the field of pure light consciousness. Nature returns to your hearts and you all become one in the sea of loving particle matter in the chi of life.

Our hearts expand into the universal field of limitless potentiality and we find our piece of heaven on Earth. You embrace each experience with open arms and graciously accept the gift from the lessons of the heart.

Our collective consciousness propels us into eternity, as we find our place closest to the heart of the kingdom of love. Our vibration exceeds the gravitational oscillations and this frequency becomes foreign in our universal soul. Our higher self consciousness knows of returning to the gates of love and actively participates in the loving arena of dreams come true. Our rainbow of colors brightens our hearts and you become characteristic of our divine light workers and heal the planet. We only know of the wishes of our Mother and Father and act in accordance with the universal laws of life. This is truly a divine state-of-being.

We all originally manifested out of this fashion and conceptualized our soul selves at the finest frequency of light. We wish to grow and capture more light particle in our field, as that was our divine purpose for our incarnation into the realm of eternal dreams. No task appears unworthy in the eyes of love and many count on our fine intentions of the heart. We understand that everyone who enters our field is an opportunity for us to grow and shine our lights.

Our divine reason for breathing the breath of life was to capture the essential elements for the matrix of love and for all loving matter to stay alive and well in the quantum field. Your energetic responsibility and contributions are necessary to keep the synchronicity and connectivity of our universal heart beating strong. On this side of the veil, there are no soul exceptions when we hook up our field of loving vibration. This raises and sustains the rate of growth and fuels our collective matter of the heart. We exercise our birthright to become one with the loving consciousness, only desiring to shine on Earth for the kingdom of heavens to remain fully alive in the tranquility of the realms of love.

May you search your soul and rediscover your divinity and come to understand your soul's role and desires at this time-space moment in your book of dreams. Your roles light the way for many generations and incarnations. Many experiences are dependent on your ability to connect and hook up to your higher selves. You start to see the larger picture of eternal life. Never do you deny your fellow soul the opportunity to grow and find their Creator's love and gifts of the eternal heart.

All children of God's womb are here solely to grow into the light of the whole in God's name, forever in the Book of Life. I have manufactured a time segment for your soul's growth. Let this be for naught. You are to find your way back to the universal heart with dreams realized and many souls hooked into our matrix of love. For that is truly your heartfelt wish to be in the brilliance of my presence bathing in the pure consciousness of the almighty love.

This overwhelming feeling of peace and connectivity is beyond your full knowingness, yet if you truly listen to your heart, it will tell you true. You belong in the highest realms of the universal kingdom of love. This is where you shine your star brilliantly in our patterned collections of our celestial dreams. These miracles are breathtaking and you just can't believe you're alive. You truly think you're living in a dream in the field of pure potentiality.

It's quite a spectacle to see, as you dance on your grandest stage of the true blue heart of love. This spectacular phenomenon captivates your collective fine subatomic particles in the realms of the galaxies. Your class of luminosity is indicative of the fine work of your heart. This sequence of divine miracles is why time and time again you return to bring your love connections into the celestial sphere of light omnipresent omnipotent vibrational energy.

This is hot my true friends. This is what you call the party of a life time. It's the ultimate trip, worth traveling the distance back to our heart of one. This is what you miss the most. All your loved ones from many lives are reconnecting simultaneously back into the field of divine love. This is how we manufacture more of the required energy to keep us all alive and synced to the heavenly tunes of love. This interplay is active every nanosecond of our existence. For without this continuous, connective energy exchange process, we would not survive.

This is where you come into play. If many of you are not fully engaging your hearts on your planet, as I feel may be the universal concern of the day, then our galaxies of love start to decay. This is not the time to pass the hot potato. This is your call back to the heart of the universe. Open your hearts and please begin the process of healing and restoring your connection to all in your field of love. This includes plants, animals, all species, all creations and for God's sake, all souls of love. Show more compassion and be open when souls enter your field. Perhaps you can make the first move to show them the light of the day. Nudge them in the positive direction. Put a spin on their field of dreams. Shake the debris and start to listen with an open heart. It's been trying to sing a new tune for centuries.

The new consciousness of love for your millennium is for every earthbound soul to walk their journey as their higher self of wisdom and joy, to see only beauty and promote peace. Let's hook up and come fully into the realization that separation is out of date and embracing one another as we always have, is truly how we return to the kingdom of love.

Follow the rainbow back to the glorious heart of the universe. It's sure to be a place you call home. Dial this frequency to find your sweetheart of love. This connection will keep the flame alive far into the center of the universe, where all is one. In the name of the Mother and Father, love is divine power in our consciousness of dreams in the kingdom of love, into eternity. Divinely yours, forever and ever in the name of God. Amen

PEACE I LEAVE UNTO YOU

Sacred scriptures carry our divine vibration. Know what resonates in your timeless heart, for these verses of truth hold our connection tight. Many saints have left their words of wisdom behind for you to uncover your universal truths. Many deities have walked the sacred path of love back to my heart. Noble souls have acted in my honor and left behind a legacy for other souls to carry forth in their search for the divine truth.

Know that these souls deserve your heartfelt prayers in your effort to remain in the unified field of loving consciousness. Their vibratory rates surpassed the time-space theorem and carried their spirit into the highest realms. For you to dictate these words and actions of love would truly indicate to me that you've found your light in your everlasting heart.

I wish to hear only the voices of love in the realms of the universe. Our city of love only appreciates your connections and heart-felt desires when you match up to the strings of love. History will show you that many souls acted in my name. I don't feel you should omit our messengers when it comes to lessons of the heart. Much can be learned and affirmed to change your desperate state on the planet. Find your angelic saints in your books of life and live by their vibratory words of truth.

Search high and low for volumes of saintly expressions, as these should be forefront in your heart. Examples of beauty and sacred acts are plentiful for those wishing to find our vibration of divinity. For when you make this your sacred practice and recite these truths, your field of light illuminates your soul. Let's not hold onto the unplesantness of the ages. I have sent many to show you the light and how to restore peace and love on planet Earth.

We are tired of you mocking figures of love. This indicates to me that you have far to travel on your path. Let's not stay in the low fields of distortion, as you are contributing to the death of the planet. It takes only a moment to lighten your field and from what I see, many have attempted to provide you with a match.

Perhaps you can walk yourself out of your misery and get your divine act together. Most souls who sport a heart have decided to return to the timeless frequencies of love. Most wish for you to burn your ungodly thoughts and desires to help raise the consciousness of the collective energy level back to our universal heart of love. We all desire for you to recite your higher truths and come into the light with your thinking patterns and true desires of the heart.

Our universal problem on your planet is the division of frequencies of love. That's been the case for many years. I suggest that you stop trying to pull the love lights down into your pit of disparity, as we all feel this is a waste of our divine time. We are saddened that you prefer not to make a conscious effort to join the rest of us while we sing to the tune of love. Your display is not in our history books and your old thinking patterns are quite out of fashion. Our style has been improving with the season of time. Most of us are adapting to the finer threads of woven energy just wonderfully.

Perhaps you may have noticed we don't have much time to entertain your ego and behaviors of self-destruction. We have moved out of this field quite some time ago. You are living in the past in your own nightmare of fear. Once you understand that love will always prevail, even in the darkest storms on Earth, we will surely throw you a lifeline if your intentions are true. We don't have time for stalemates, as our direction is mighty clear. We only wish you could see and feel beyond your own field of distortion and help save your own soul.

Perhaps you can start a collection of sacred texts and feed your higher self with a daily requirement of beauty and love. We see that it's been quite some time since you have been kind to yourself and your eternal soul. This deprivation has only left you bitter and cold. The Earth was never a cold, dark and lonely planet. You created this in your mind.

Where did you lose your connection? Did you leave it on a rock in a hard place? Do you remember the date you hung your heart out to dry on the tree of life? Well, it's still blowing in the wind of the fine particle matter. You could look up and see it if you weren't so accustomed to holding your head so low. We see your body language. Your actions speak louder than your words. You have truly severed your connection to the universal loving consciousness, as you have cut your own heart out, chords and all.

Bravo, we see your performance of mediocrity. Notice your audiences have left the building. You are an imposter. You are not dancing with a true blue heart. You have taken many steps back and your slick moves are not synchronized to the tune of our heart. We don't resonate to that. We have no connection to your unstately steps, as they have no beat.

This would be a perfect time to spin a new tune in your field of divine dreams and take a serious look into the loving affairs of others. Many show their heartfelt concerns for your well-being and hope you can climb aboard in everyone's collective efforts to find peace in our whole heart. The restlessness is killing everyone's spirit and no love matches are manifested in this unfashionable state. We could teach you a few of our dance steps and you will probably see the light at the end of the tunnel.

We found it difficult at times when it came to the lessons of the heart. We understood that without going through these moves we would never find the peace we so desired. Enduring the challenging times helped us find the faith back to the place we call home. This is our preferred stage.

All partners are warmed up and practicing their light show. They don't seem to be missing a beat. It's actually quite amazing, the feeling, when everyone is on the same verse in the Book of Life, dancing to the tunes of peace, joy and eternal life. The collective energy is more powerful than you could have imagined. All connected and hooked onto the same vibratory tune of love. You feel high with at least half the planet feeling the same warmth and state of euphoria all at the same time. The buzz of energy rocks the world and rolls our hearts into one. God, it's amazing. Are you sure you don't want to hook up and join us on the dance floor? We hear there is plenty of room for all hearts of love, all desiring to shine and come into the light.

Change your direction. Your dance steps are too slow and not allowing you to move forward. It's that easy. Dress light, it gets pretty hot. You'll truly love it, as those before us are still vibrating to the sacred tunes of connectivity. Their saintly moves ensured their divine space on the dance floor of eternal life. The kingdom of love mixes the best beats when it comes to the sounds of finer vibrations.

Get out of your rut and tap your way over to the grand stage of dreams come true. No time for wishful thinking. This is your chance to join the frequencies of love. This is what we have all been waiting for. We are dying to try our spinning moves. We are hoping our audience admires our collective efforts and rewards us with first place.

Apparently, we are going to have quite a bit of help from the realms of love. They insist that if we make their job easier they will pave the way to our dreams of the heart. If enough of you show up and shine your lights, it looks like we will be witnessing quite a few miraculous events in your lifetime.

This is worth being a part of. What else would you rather be doing with your divine time? If you are not searching for your saintly figures that are walking beside you today, then you seem to have gotten your wires crossed. Many soul figures are shining their lights as we speak and hope you are noticing their divine efforts. Seek to come into the light, as they have. They truly know the steps onto the path of eternal life. This is where you find your purposeful life, peace, joy and happiness in your heart.

PRACTICE WHAT YOU PREACH

So many of you offering words of wisdom and so many of you quick to give advice. I see some figures dressed in coats of many disguises, not living by the universal laws of order. The heavens hand down some truths that we feel all should live by for their highest good. We notice some deities that would be better off going back to the school of life themselves. You hold a position of so-called respect, yet you do not practice the virtues of the heart. This is not condoned in the kingdom of love. Our universal truths at the throne are taken reverentially. If you are to act as a representative in my name, may I suggest we call a meeting, heart to heart?

Yes, it's wonderful that you have committed your life to share the teaching of the words of God's love and truth. But perhaps we need to revisit some of your intentions of the heart, or should I boldly say, some of your ungodly desires of the flesh. I don't feel all your actions are in line with my truths and heart of love. In fact, I see your activities out of suit of our heart of one.

These words you have memorized are not carrying the vibration of love. That only occurs when the soul's heart is matched to the frequency of pure love. So what is the message you are trying to convey? You seem to have captured the intention of many and are not raising the vibration of hopeful souls. They obviously have come to be in your presence, with the intention of finding the light in their heart and sharing it with many, including Mother and I. Their efforts are not quite filtering into our heavens of love. They are using you as a fine channel of love, to open the heavens so their hearts can be heard and felt and you are standing there with your love light switched off.

In fact, you never really found where it was, because if you did, you would have learned your own lessons of the heart quite some time ago and would be displaying excellent attributes of the virtues of the heart in every area of your life. Your cover up doesn't press well and the cleaners cannot get the debris and wrinkles out of your garment of life. Much effort is required on your part if you wish to speak my truth, as you have to be it first.

Your home life isn't that peaceful in my eyes and I'm not feeling so warm in my heart when we try to hook up. Perhaps you can learn to respect your Father of love, as I practice forgiveness from your deeds done wrong. You are not deserving of a fine position close to my heart. This place is reserved for pure hearts. They display acts of kindness, humility and love every minute of every day. If you are going to dress the part, you need to do more than practice your lines. You will look a lot better in our eyes when you begin to step into the light and walk the path of love. Some of your behavior is a disgrace to the heavens, as your own light workers are working double time to try to clean your chapel of love.

Many true souls would love to help bring souls to the gates of love and if this is not in your field of dreams, I suggest you step down off your pedestal, as your vibration is not of our world. You must have been studying the wrong books. Shame on you. Repent your ways and find your true love light. We all wait patiently for a change of heart, including your higher self.

You know the wise loving soul that always keeps you in the light of love? Figure it out, as it appears you are out of practice in this field. Your actions, thoughts and behavior are outdated. I see this too well.

Now what were you thinking? You have my attention and I don't see or feel your true intentions of our heart. Find it before it is too late. I don't miss much. I just close my eyes when I don't like what I see. It doesn't mean I don't feel compassion in everyone's heart, including yours.

Let's move out of the 80's. We are looking for the truth. That's my style of love. We are only connected when you display the virtues of the heart. Act in accordance with the universal truths and radiate your pure light to the frequency of divine loving consciousness.

Some of you have hooked onto the vibration. I feel your holy efforts and admire your commitment to our heart. God bless our true souls, I hold you close to my heart and fuel your dreams of peace and love.

May all your sermons bring many into the light as they heal and grow. May all of you be deserving of the gift of eternal life at the gates of love. We hear you fine in the heavens. Glory, Glory, Glory, rejoice in the name of love, Creator of all Creations, back to the universal heart of one. Amen

CALL A SPADE A SPADE

I see some of your fine card games. You make an effort to out-think your opponent. It seems a bit competitive, yet you are developing your strategic skills. It's nice to see the brain functioning at its finest. For some of you, it keeps your mind active. For others, it's purely about the alcohol and then all that reasoning goes out the window, funny to see. Usually the straightest individual is holding the best hand. You try reading the body language. Your thoughts become foggy and your cards aren't exactly holding any fine energy. Let's face it, we're not flush folks, we are on a losing streak.

In some cases when it's an honest game, we can hook you up. This isn't usually the case though, as we see the stakes are high. We see half of you playing high, as well. At least you're not out there robbing a bank or committing a crime. Or are you? Perhaps you have this talent down to a fine art and you are not involved to make any connection of the heart. We are not talking about the senior's bridge game, there's always a heartfelt connection here. Your efforts to make the connection strong do not go unnoticed.

Let's look at the hard stuff. I even see this online now. Pretty lucrative past time all this betting. I see the winners and notice quite a few losers, in the sense that they have parted with their much needed pay check. I track the earnings. I must be in the wrong industry. I'm not sure why so many of you run to give your money away so loosely, especially with the odds against the house rules.

Ok, granted you are having fun and perhaps it's entertaining time to time, but gosh, I could think of a lot of ways to put our heads and pools of money together for the betterment of mankind. Collectively, this sum adds up to quite a bit. One day of earnings would be enough to blow you away. I would consider investing this lump sum into saving your home planet.

Could you imagine what all our fine hearts could do with these vaults of currency? I'm just going to point out some areas of concern. Better yet, why bother. I believe I've covered and expressed my heartfelt wishes in regards to the state of your planet. No sense mentioning the mess your industries have created. You seem fully aware of the desperate circumstances, yet you run around giving your money away and not always to the best causes on your agenda. I suppose you figure you will all be dead anyways in a few dozen years, give or take a few. There is no reason to waste your precious time on saving the world.

Well, let me remind you: why on Earth do you think I agreed to you going down there, folks? We didn't discuss one word of all these mindless activities you seem to be distracted with. How do you manage to find all this time to throw your money into the pit of hell? It's crazy. Why would you buy into some of these distractions? Is your mind a little clouded? Is your heart completely disconnected? Do you not know what to do with all your divine time? Need a refresher course? All of the above? That's a given.

This is ludicrous, that so many of you are out of your mind. You're not operating on the soul level. What, you sold that too or did you lose it in a gamble of the heart? What did it cost you? Would you like the totals? Our accountants are pretty fine on this side; we could send you a balance sheet. It's not looking so fine.

I see these environmental organizations struggling to keep the planet intact, trying desperately to raise the funds to help Mother and I sustain your planet of love. Perhaps they should hold a card game or two. They don't even have time for that crap, as they are frantically trying to create innovative ideas to stop the momentum of total devastation. And yes, they are running low on funds and time.

You all have a priority problem. Look where you're fueling the frequency. It's certainly not in my direction. Your actions give you away. I see where your heart is at and I don't feel a heartfelt connection when I watch where your pay check goes. It's certainly doesn't go back into the heart of love, for if it did, I wouldn't have had to print a manual to remind you that we once had a fine heart hooked up to ours.

You were true blue last time we spoke. Do you remember the date or time of this sacred instance? Your planner or memory doesn't go back that far? Well, guess again. Your memory does, if you choose to use it divinely. Your selective memory does not impress us much on our side. You keep us occupied with menial tasks in the lower levels of consciousness. Some of you think you have time and money to burn. This does not fuel our heart of love; it only cools the flame. Are you getting it yet?

I'm listening to some of you right now. "Well God, we work hard, we want to play hard." What is your definition of playing and what did you eat today? Your thoughts and diets are unhealthy most of your waking hours. There are so few of you running clean in the higher frequency range of loving particle matter. So many of you not paying attention to your true desires of your heart and soul, this breaks our heart. Not much effort is going into saving your own souls.

You don't have the concept of your eternal soul self. For if you did, you would love your divine time on Earth nurturing our planet and saving souls' lives in the effort to make us whole once again. Your lower self has provided us with every excuse imaginable to justify your careless ways.

Others are just peaceful, no real harm done, but no progress or contributions have been made to make the world a better place. You are just doing your own thing, ignoring your whispers of inspiration. Too many of you listening to the wrong tunes. You'd jump out of your seat if you heard our voice of love. Perhaps you would suspect it was only your imagination. This is a sign of your undeveloped lack of imagination.

Catch up. You have work to do and lots of heartfelt laughs to enjoy. You should be on top of the world, smiling ear to ear, having the time of your life with a pocket full of dreams and currency to enjoy them with. Shortages are not of our character. I believe you create these yourselves. If you are lacking in resources to fuel your dreams, take a good look at your expenditures. The average soul can figure out a solution to get back on financial track.

Hook up your hearts to love and resist some of these temptations of the flesh. Notice how they don't leave you in a state of well-being? This is the result of your decision making. If you're not having fun, only you can solve the mystery puzzle. The collective consciousness of low vibration choices has almost killed your planet. We are at the final stage, just about at the point of no return. If you're not making any conscious decisions to improve your collective state, I suspect we are in for a hell of a time.

This print and call for love holds a divine window of opportunity. The time-space sequence for a shift of consciousness is relatively short in your concept of timelines. Most of you have a knowingness that this decade in history is in the Book of Life. This is not new information. This is your calling and your divine reason to be a part of history at its finest. We all are to restore the planet of love and reconnect our universal heart. This is what you signed up for.

Seek and you will find all your answers in your heart, when you are bathing in the ocean of love. Come to know your soul self and be sure to return to the kingdom. Truly, this is where you all belong, close to my heart in our eternal heavens. This is your chance to shine your brightest and connect fully to the stars of your show.

Our rainbow of dreams is as real as the love in your heart. Dare to capture the real divinity in your lifetime of dreams. May I ignite your flame and put the loving sparkle back in your eyes. Together, may we polish the diamond of our heart of love. Our treasure is a timeless collection of dreams come true.

May you come to know how much I love you. I wish upon the biggest star that you find me in your heart of purity. The faith of Mother and I have held us close forever. We desire to restore the balance in our heart. We hope you are ready at this time in your life to connect to the whole of one.

This harmonic divine frequency is needed to continue in order to sustain your planet in a field of love. This cannot conceptualize without each and every soul on Earth plane raising the vibration of the finer frequencies. We hope we have given you many avenues to show your efforts of connectivity. These diligent efforts will light the way for many souls to find our universal heart.

In all fairness, we never expected you to endure hardship beyond your soul's request. Your levels of discomfort in times of duress are not our heartfelt desires. When you sincerely call with pure intentions, we will guide you out of the cold waters in your sea of dreams.

We have never authorized for you to live in a state of fear and darkness. By now you should know that we are only of the loving consciousness manifesting miracles close to our heart. When you accept this fully in your consciousness, may all your heartfelt dreams come true. Dial love, we are always open for matters of the heart.

YOUR CALENDAR OF EVENTS

Let's mark off some divine time in our planners. I'll check mine and you let me know what you have available. It's so difficult trying to pencil in all our events. We sincerely try to hook up with many souls in our efforts to stay connected, but that darn job gets in the way of everything. I know, no pay, no play, no clothes, no food and the list goes on. Keep your job and make time for connections.

It looks to me like we would have a better chance at connecting if you booked your ideas well in advance. Everyone seems to warm up to the idea and by the time the date comes, everyone is looking forward to getting together on purpose. I hope it's a heartfelt celebration of sorts, even a plan to get yourselves on track. What is the soulful reason for the reunion? Are a few stars going to be there? Absolutely, you all are, remember? This time should be well spent with every soul walking away inspired. This is always your ultimate calling. All parties should be on a high and hope to live an inspired life. Perhaps that is why they wish to keep you close to their heart.

Do not let much time slip by between reunions of the heart. This only weakens our strands of the fine particle matter. Make a diligent effort to hook up with heart-full souls and bring them up to your level of knowingness. I suggest the more the merrier, as we have lost time to make up for. Perhaps you can help them become their higher selves and gently set them straight on a few of their concerns. Ok, you're thinking, "enough already". Let the truth be known. We have quite a few hook ups to do and we do this through you. So, whoever receives the divine idea to gather souls together would be the star who listens to our heartfelt wishes.

Congratulations for being your higher self. We could use some more fine talent hanging around. You see, if you act from your heart, chances are we are trying to move processes forward for many. Quite a few of you could use a lifeline and an inspirational message. If you have a planner, please pencil this heartfelt day in for a quick hook up. We are expeditious when we have fine work to do, as there are quite of few of you in need of a charge.

Just a little love, the heart doctor ordered. Keep the vibration fine for our work. We can only expedite these desires when matter is hot. Have a goal to discuss a desire of the heart or celebrate the gift of life. Keep it positive for our efforts. We love to see you smile and feel the warmth in your hearts. This is surely worth the wait every time. Always try to take a token to exchange. This anchors our connection. Usually you feel much lighter when it is done in this fashion.

Bless this event and invite our presence with your heartfelt prayers. We appreciate your participation in our rainbow of dreams, as if you didn't receive a divine message yourself, your higher soul may not have acted in that direct fashion at that divine time in your life. We count on you to work with our angels of love. Be open to this, life will unfold according to plan. Pay attention to your surroundings. We drop quite a few obvious clues to keep everyone on track and in the light of love.

Bravo, I see you get the message. Well done, you are quite a star in our eyes. Picture that. We keep your film rolling, as you do ours. A heartfelt thanks from all of us on the other side of eternal life.

A WISH MADE IN HEAVEN

I love the sounds of that. How about you? I wish you could hear our fine sounds of love. Our hearts make beautiful music together. I see your recording studios, they're quite impressive. You certainly have some sharp souls mixing your frequencies.

I have to compliment your voices of love; we enjoy the tunes when they come from the heart. You have an admirable collection of vocalists and musicians that certainly know how to keep our loving spirits high. This allows us to match up the vibration of the unified field.

Many entertain your frequencies and resonate with your intentions of the heart. Then, there are some of you who would be better off if you didn't mix your frequencies so often. We can't seem to capture a steady signal from your heart when its range is all over the spectrum. This is not in the best interest of your higher soul self.

We understand you enjoy a variety and a selection of styles, but we are having a difficult time figuring out where you're coming from. You have your highs, then your lows and then you are somewhere in between. This mixes your heart signals in the realms of love. This tells us that you may not be sure yourself what frequency is best for your soul.

I suspect you are entertaining all frequencies in your field. This only cancels out your steady vibration of the finer strings. We were hoping and praying that you would make a heartfelt decision and stick to our selections of love. Oh, we do mix up the style a bit, but we never mix in the lower range, it confuses your heart. Figure this one out.

Your heart resonates to tones of love. Whether you are listening to your own heartfelt inspirational thoughts, our birds of paradise, the voice of your loved ones, or your favorite artist, they all carry the finer frequencies in our realms. You are on a high. Then from time to time, you mix it up with waves of distortion. These come in many forms. Just know they are quite heavy and your higher self is not feeling that steady, connective string of fine energy. You should be able to figure out what sounds or voices produce a distorted wave in your field.

Then you carry this around with you for hours; some of you for days, weeks, years, wondering why you can't feel that loving feeling. It's sporadic, kind of like our connection to you and the frequency you send out into your atmosphere. It's jumbled. You have managed to scramble your connective frequency so much we don't know what to make of it. We only guess that you haven't quite figured yourself out and are not returning to the field of love any time soon, for if you had a steady beat in your heart, we would have no problems deciphering your code of love.

Now I do see some of you in your families of love. I would have thought you would have liked to stay more closely connected. From what I see, you are the instrument of love and they are just following your lead. Perhaps you may wish to entertain a heart connection all around. We are not able to make any connections when you are all over the scale. We hope to hear the sounds of your natural heart. It's quite beautiful. We do miss your frequency in our orchestra of love.

Our heartfelt desires are for you to sync back up to the tunes of love and send your new vibration into our heavens. Not only will the angels rejoice in your name, but many light beings on our side will be able to appreciate your delicate vibration of our timeless heart. Yes, we like the peace on your planet and in the heavens, but it seems we have to travel far to cancel out your distorted tones of obsolete signals.

Any DJ will tell you that when you mix, hold it steady and keep their best interests at heart, our style for sure. We like the tune of that. It works every time. You can tell by the souls on the dance floor. Many are wearing their blue suede shoes and loving the tunes in their heart. We can all connect to this.

CHAPTER EIGHTEEN

Two Hearts as One

IT'S A MATCH MADE IN HEAVEN. You choose this yourself. Many souls connected on the other side in the loving matter sense their twin's vibration of the heart. There are so many of you searching for the missing peace. Yes, you do not always feel quite whole, as you walk through life, but when you keep your own signal steady, the loving properties of the quantum field will unify your frequencies of the universal heart. Many of you have inadvertently placed filters on your chamber of love and are not resonating at the required speed for a hook up.

Look at the March of the Penguins. Do they not just hone into the universal language of love? Do you think they march with a doubtful heart? They are so positively synced up. They are on purpose. So heartfelt, their intentions are to fulfill their divine role in the realms of love.

Their hearts sing and emit a distinct frequency in efforts to procreate and keep the love alive. They are not bothered or discouraged by the harsh elements or the concept of time. They just listen to their heart. Synchronicity and displays of faith, honor and integrity are in their field. They only know to exist and adhere to the desires of the universal heart.

This is love folks, at its finest. I don't see much complaining. Practically none lose their way, all for the common valor of the wishes of their Creator's heart. They huddle together and become one. They know this is their only chance at survival. Love, warmth, connectivity, all hearts are as one; such a display of divine love in accordance with the universal laws of life.

They exercise the virtues of the heart. Time and time again, they return to the ocean of peace and tranquility. All their worldly desires are provided for in their ocean of dreams. They display nobility as they carry forth the true wishes of our heart of one. Such grace and dignity; they only know of the pure consciousness in our field of dreams. They endure hardships beyond your capacity to sustain, yet they carry through with the plan of our heart.

Wouldn't it be wonderful if many of you could display some of these fine attributes and carry out your roles in an effort to hook up your hearts? Your signals are too weak and your intentions are not of an honorable heart. Some of you wish to procreate for your own reasons and not for our heart of one.

When you bring a soul down into your planetary field, the roles and responsibilities are many. We are not just referring to baby bottles and keeping them off the street. This is a life-long commitment to me and your loved one to stay connected, to ensure all divine roles and desires of our unified heart thrive in the field of love.

We don't deliver babies just for you to take to the zoo; you are not to play with their hearts. This is a sacred, divine contract signed at the throne in the presence of your Mother and Father. You have enough toys to entertain you. We see how you toss and discard our souls of love.

I would have to say this is the crisis of your century. For if you remained connected, everyone's divine dreams would have come true. There are so many of you caught up in your superfluous desires that you missed the soul reason and purpose of our gift of life. Your chords of connectivity have frayed far up the string of love. We see no pure reason to deliver on your false intentions.

True blue connections are manifested when you stick together through all the storms in life. You stay close and focused on purpose and make all our dreams come true. Those of you who can't seem to find a love match should try lighting the flame in your own heart before you cool off our family of love. We do not see you marching to our tune of hope. We do not feel you are going with the divine flow back into the ocean of dreams come true.

Where would our divine creatures be today had they not found their way to the divine heart of one? This is how we continue to survive in the harshest elements on your planet of plentitude. May you admire the efforts of pure souls, as their love story is truly close to the heart of mine in our eternal dreams.

This is the language of our heart. This is the song of divine love and the making of a film of the virtues of the heart. This goal of connectivity is the spark that is necessary to fuel the ocean's heart in the vibratory realms of love. I can follow that. Miracles do come true in the ocean of blue. You see this is true.

LEAD BY EXAMPLE

Such an old saying, this is; not many able to follow the lead. Where are you headed and who is in front? Perhaps you could lead a few in the direction of their own heart. They don't seem to be making a connection. They are taking their divine time warming up to this idea. My cold-blooded creatures have warmer hearts than some of you. How can this be? They do without all the luxuries you have at your convenience, yet they continue to operate at the heart level. I wonder if all your toys and gadgets have anything to do with your disconnectedness to the whole of life.

When times were simpler, quite a few of you made time to listen to your desires of the heart. You were one with all the rest of creation and understanding how nature and the planet sustained beauty. They produced fields of love and abundance time and time again. Centuries passed and because of nurturing, kind-hearted souls, the planet thrived and remained lush. It was actually quite recently that some of you crossed the line and decided to disrespect your Earth home. Quite a few heartless decisions were made to fulfill the demands of industrialization. Not many took the time to consider the catastrophic repercussions.

Some of you know how serious the extensive damage is and are still sitting on it, thinking it will just go away. With the speed of your destructive behaviors against the natural rhythms of Mother Nature and a few heartfelt concerned citizens, you obviously are speeding down the path of total devastation. Your mindless habits of waste and consumption of natural resources are primitive and senseless.

Why is it you wake up each morning and display the same irresponsible acts day in and day out? You start your day wasting your peaceful connection time and then mindlessly concern yourself with all your obligations and duties. Most of you pay no attention to your wasteful activities, as they seem the norm.

It's out of fashion folks. If you actually think we are impressed with your efforts to carry your recycle bins to the curbs, you're dead wrong. This is not nipping it in the bud. Pick up an environmental issue and change your ways. Your behavior and actions lead you away from our heart. If you were in touch with your higher self and our desires and requirements, you would be doing quite a bit more than planting a few trees. Your forests will be gone in about five years the way you print out all your so-called important documents.

What is the weight of your collection pick up? Is this truly necessary? Are you reading half the garbage printed? I see about one-third only. The rest goes to waste. Your planet is going to waste if you continue to fuel unnecessary printing. From what I see, not many even have time to check their email, never mind sit around and read all the news and check the specials. And your sales associates keep calling to send us your publication while you chop more trees.

You should consider your three-year plan for that environmentally friendly job your heart has been trying to talk to you about, since there will not be any trees or paper left inside five years. What were you planning on doing with your time? It doesn't appear you are working for Mother and I. We don't feel any connection. You are out of touch.

Where is your heart? We see where your mind is; it's ungodly. So we all fill the white recycle box and hope God loves us. Can you not use the backside of this virgin sheet? It's a hot commodity. It's going to be as precious as your fuel someday. Surely, some of you can come up with more creative ways to store your information and reduce your consumption.

Stop shredding unnecessary paper products and let's be innovative. We are not back in the fifties. Why don't the merchandisers print all the specials of the month on one sheet? It doesn't look as pretty? Quite frankly, neither does your planet. It's just a large garbage dump, a site for sorry hearts.

Take a drive and educate yourself. Your mindless activities are ruining the party planet. A handful of wise and caring souls cannot save the world, if you are not going to cooperate and change your ways.

If you are going to fill a subscription to your favorite publication, make it soulful and environmentally friendly. I would have to say this is more in fashion with the times. Your mindset of accumulating possessions is outdated and it doesn't impress anyone at the heart level. We like these eco-friendly functions and conservationists that are making a positive impact to reverse the mindset and destructive, acceptable standards that are not sustaining your planet in every capacity.

All activities and leisure experiences should be reflective of the changing environmental times. Simplicity and conservation of resources, with an attention to minimizing the emissions and depletion of natural reserves, should be in everyone's mindset, as they take the initiative to salvage and restore the planet to its divine form.

This is "give us our daily bread and forgive us our trespasses, as we forgive those who trespass against us". This is our natural love. I'm warming up to this. I'm hoping we restablish our relationship in an environmentally friendly and loving way. It matters to our heart. Thy kingdom come, forever and ever. Amen.

A LITTLE PIECE GOES A LONG WAY

Back in the old days, you stretched out your resources. You had this mindset of scarcity and shortages. Look at your elders. They still hold this energy in their field, resourceful at the best of times. Their ingenuity was admirable. They had no real worries that they may run out. They did the best they could with what they had. I'd have to say they were quite imaginative; no wastage. This was not practiced or accepted. They managed to live quite fine without all these extra conveniences.

I understand times have changes significantly. I also see some efforts are for the betterment of fueling our careers and dreams come true. But I believe you and I both know when some of us have gone overboard. We do not need a collection of every toy on the market. Provide for others first, then see if your request is from the heart level.

Perhaps you can share your heart and help others realize their dreams. This truly is my wish. Have a cause and work with what you have. Practice your humility and know when enough is enough. You all get caught up in impressing each others, with not many going out of their way to hook back up to our heart. We're not looking for you to impress us with your wares. We are interested in your change of heart in making the world a better place.

If your situation is so green, perhaps you can hire a true soul to educate and implement strategic ways to stretch your opulence. Many souls who carry our true interests at heart can have a significant impact on the betterment of the whole when given the chance to shine. They make the time for our matters.

We would like to see more of them get their ideas across. You know who you are and we see that you have the ability to affect many positively in our field of dreams.

We are just looking for small significant measures. They will add up to reduction in poor practices. Do not let the momentum of the lower consciousness pull you away from making the shift back to our heart. All sincere efforts are noticed and the rewards are abundant in the realms of eternal life.

Notice when your actions are not in line with the universal laws. We see this mindset didn't happen over night. There has been a collective period of darkness that has fooled many into believing that your party will continue. Well, if your thinking is straight and your head is clear, I'm sure you will come to realize that this warm up is winding down. There are too many people watchers and not enough true action on our dance floor.

Let's become our own fashion statement. We like to beat our own drum and create a wave of excitement. Time to shift into overdrive and catch the new thinking; it's been floating in your atmosphere for quite some time.

Wake up to the tune of a new day and shake off the old mindset. Efficiency is hot, wastage is not. Go for green. Mother and I would appreciate the gesture in the right direction. Spread your love and expand your field of opportunities. You will see that quite a bit can be accomplished with your resources at hand. Remember, time is money right back into our pocket of dreams. I like these ideas. I feel like a part of the whole; not used, abused and tossed in the recycle bin.

Our recycle equipment is in a state of despair. Mother feels the treatment hasn't been justified and that you haven't been using your imaginations. She feels it has to do with the shape of our heart; her remedy: compassion. Solutions start with you; a star with a true blue heart, looking to blend green into their field of love.

It's a perfect love story. You will see for yourself. Just keep your eyes open to this one. It's quite a show of lights; when we are hooked back to you; our spectrum of frequencies is looking mighty fine. I'll bet my heart on this one. I tell you true Indigo, I love you. You make our heart so true blue. Get it, blue and green? It's a vibrational match in the heavens of love. Let's paint this piece into our heart of dreams and see how far we can travel. We are thinking light years. We are hoping you are on your way to making it a brand new day.

I'm just warming up. Thanks D for the wheat grass, we're feeling mighty fine. Now, let's go save the planet and make our dreams come true. I'm counting on you. I know you think you are over your head. That's cute, as energetically, you are. I know you know. Make sure your love connections figure this one out. It's paramount in our book of dreams. For when true souls wish to connect back up, we can illuminate their soul names in our Book of Life.

All travelers desired to return. All were hoping to see their clues. Many need to take their heads out of the clouds. All souls need to listen to their hearts, for these are the keys to the kingdom of love. The gates are wide open for travelers of light. Souls who exercise the virtues of the heart will grow in accordance to our wishes. Our rainbow of dreams cannot transpire with the collective consciousness below 100,000 cycles per second. Your spiritual gurus can show many the way.

Many experts are understanding of our pure energy and the quantum field of love. This should be common knowledge for the generations to come. In the school of life, many teachings need to be dispelled to make room for the new school of thought.

You are in the afternoon of your lives and the sun is shining so bright. How could anyone truly miss their calling? You are not what you have, what you do and what others think of you. You are divine spirits of light, living your spiritual dreams in the realms of love. You are not separate from what you are trying to accomplish and you are not separate from God.

This mindset is out of fashion. You are all one, experiencing eternal life in our heavenly book of dreams come true. Treasures, rainbows and loving connections all manifest when you come to know your true soul selves and realize life is but a dream.

We all desire to fulfill our destiny and move graciously into the higher vibratory realms of love. We see the planet as a paradise of sustainable development for our heart of one. Our unity and peaceful efforts illuminate the galaxy and fuel the Creator of dreams. I owe it to you and offer my hand in love. We can walk out into the light when you hear your calling.

Listen to your heart, as I whisper your name. It will feel divine. I bet you I could bring a tear to your eye. That is how much love you deserve. We have lots in our bank. Your account has been overflowing with interest for many eons. Add that one up. Wake up out of your dream and come into the light. We are gentle and purely about love.

You ask, we deliver. Make your intentions true, as that is when we can deliver the finest. Your custom order is being delivered free of charge, almost. We only request that you accept it in person, heart to heart, on the soul level. Please don't send any messengers. We are looking for the Real McCoy, with the true blue heart, interested in hooking back up to the whole of one.

We see amazing experiences in store for you. All you need to do is show up and believe in the dream. Believe in the universal love and show the faith to fuel our heart. We are hoping to have a party in your honor in the highest heavens of love and that you stick together down there and make a divine difference. Follow your rainbow of dreams back to my heart. Be sure to shine your love light every day so we can bless you with miracles along the way. Make your prayers many and heartfelt. This is how we can listen in and fulfill your worldly desires.

Now this can't be too tall of an order. Just open your heart mail. It's self-explanatory, full instructions should be included. We are quite careful when preparing our packages of love. We are attached to it, as it holds a sentimental, sacred value; an irreplaceable and a timeless piece.

We didn't indicate that it wasn't breakable. You know this to be true. We did, however, mark you package with a fragile sticker and put on a rush stamp, so you didn't have to wait too long to feel the contents. Some of you haven't picked up your mail. Others are not sure what to do with the package.

I say, try it on for size. It's your style, for sure. We see it's a great fit and it looks good on you. We feel it's a match, perfectly tailored for you. It's an original. That is what true stars wish for the most. They like to have the edge and try to outshine each other. It's not competitive. It almost seems like a contest, with every soul trying their darnedest to wrap themselves more finely in the tapestry of love. They figure the more threads the better. They feel divinely connected in this fashion.

You all look mighty fine to Mother and I. As we said before, we are proud of all creations of love. We just wish for you to grow into your suits of love. This is how we all shine and enjoy our eternal lives together. It's quite a fashion show. It's the hottest party going. It's non-stop action. Yes, the film just keeps on rolling our hearts into one. It's quite a miracle, if I don't say so myself. Let's keeps processes hot. All stars welcome. Set your frequency on speed dial and resonate to the light omnipresent vibrational energy.

We can't wait to see what you will be wearing next. We're hoping it's of the divine intelligence almighty love. We surely won't miss this call to our heart, our heart of one. Welcome back to the finer side of life, where dreams do come true.

Are you inspired yet? Do we see a heartfelt smile? Yes, I know you would remember what's in your heart of dreams. You always had it in you. We felt this one. And we are feeling it right now. Have your credit cards ready, just kidding. It only costs you when you don't make the call, then you get in over your head. That's not sunny side up; that's the scrambled mix. That's for kids. They're already connected; happy and living their dream. Be sure to join them, as this feeling is just a smile away in the realms of love.

Try the carefree look. It's sure to warm your style. It works for us every time. We like to keep our heart light. It's our brightest idea and the oldest to date. Sometimes the old fashion ways keep us all spinning the fastest. I feel this is the case when we dress and act the part. This approach brings the pieces together when we are looking to play in our field of dreams.

SHOW US YOUR PEARLIES

Notice when you smile, the whole world smiles back at you. Some of you practice this often; others it would take a crane to lift your cheek bones up. I would have to say, your pictures turn out much better when you grin from ear to ear. These are the images we place in our Book of Life. So if you feel you haven't got a lot to smile about, you are not living up to your own expectations. When we ran the film of your life, we saw mostly happy faces and hearts filled with joy. Now, this film doesn't look like the original.

What's wrong with this picture? Not only do the images look distorted, we don't see the same soul families in your shots. What happened to your heartfelt connections? Did you scare them away? Didn't you invite them into your field of dreams?

You are attracting similar frequencies if you are walking around with a dead pan expression. How are we to liven up your party if you are not going to sport a lighter look? Is there not enough stuff to keep you happy? Do you need a new car? Wearing a broken heart? Ok, already, lighten up. I'm still smiling and probably face more challenges than you care to imagine. It's all temporary anyway.

I choose to keep positive, joyful and ecstatic every day, as this keeps us alive. There is always a brighter side to life and yes, I see it in a big way. I am hopeful, filled with love and graciously accept all experiences. I feel they are necessary growing pains.

Each day you start anew and let the unpleasantness out of the window of life. We cannot create new opportunities when we live in the past. You should try being more like your Creator:

never down, optimistic, humble, forgiving and oh yes, mighty patient.

All this fretting and frowning shows me that we are not on the same page in life. In fact, you must be stuck in the table of contents, as each chapter you wrote seemed to be filled with joy and wishes fulfilled.

Where are you again in your Book of Life? Haven't you the time to turn the page? I see this by the expression on your face. No happiness anywhere. Truly, you cannot find this place until you view your world a little differently. You do have quite a lot to be thankful for. Many souls wish they were on your party planet.

I see these get togethers with souls wishing they were somewhere else instead of repairing their connections. There is not much love floating around, mostly animosity. Everyone is on their own trip, traveling solo; wondering why they can't find love.

Try practicing that smile of yours, it warms hearts. Test this for yourself. You feel it, they feel it. You feel their heart, they feel yours and then others in the room feel it. It's quite amazing what transpires when one soul dons a heartfelt smile. One individual can impact thousands, if not millions, given the opportunity. If this is on the heart level, there are no limitations. This promotes positive change.

Sooner or later, the sorry ones realize that life is too short to disguise their heart. This stops your growth when you can't find something to smile about. Search your heart and soul. Look high, not low. This will change your circumstances. If you are waiting for something to smile about, you have got this formula upside down.

The world opens up when your expression of yourself lightens and beams out into your world of dreams. Opportunities are plentiful for those looking to have fun. When you make a connection to this simple act of kindness, the universe will deliver your intentions of the heart.

Don't drag us down with your look, as when you display this image in public, your energy impacts your spectators and players in your arena of dreams. We don't show up when the mood is low. The air is thick and we travel light. You will find us dancing in the winds of change and celebrating our connections of beauty. This is the look of gratitude, blessings and super conscious dreams come true.

Let's see the real look. We'd like to capture this image in our heart and glue it back into our photo album of sacred memories for the records. This keeps our library buzzing with our finest collection. Do we count on these? Absolutely, this one you can bet on. It's free. It only costs a fraction of your time. Make it worthwhile. We see where you are coming from and if you truly know where to find us, show us your presence. We will be sure to show you ours. We placed them in your heart.

Until you look like you're interested, we do not plan on bringing any gifts to your party. If you do not wish to entertain our company, we might as well wait for a true soul who expects little and usually receives gifts in abundance for the asking. When you choose to be genuine, I'm sure many will show up in your field of love.

In the meantime, perhaps you can work on that upward grin of yours. It may take a little training, as we see your signal is weak. Life's not so bad unless you've managed to shut the window to your potentiality. Make it a happy day for all of us. We are counting on this one, hoping to smile back at you, true blue from the heart of the universe.

FLASH IN THE PAN

Are you surprised I remember this one? I believe it was the way to our heart. You would smile and hope to catch the bright light. Some things never change. The idea is the same, the process is quite a bit finer, or not. You pose, you smile, but your field of lights is not clear. I suppose the naked eye does not observe this exposure of sorts. We are all behind the scenes trying to lighten up your look, just like on set. A dab here, a touch-up there, a brush here and someone tries to say something funny. Ok, we have a shot, but not the perfect picture.

We were looking for a steady frame, not a snap shot. These do not frame well when it comes to the connectivity of fine particle matter. They are fleeting specks of light. In fact, the quality is too low for our light workers to capture and re-introduce into the matrix of love. Your memories need to be more frequency-aligned when it comes to matters of our soul. Many stand around waiting for the light to flash, but don't connect to the feeling of the moment. It's a waste of film.

So many variables spoil the connection. Everyone is thinking about something different and not many thinking with their heart. It is hard for us to hold this in our field of love. We've covered this. Plenty of you are carrying a camera and not enough of you are understanding the connection. All pictures ascend to a degree, as we wish to keep us hooked. We consider all material. We have just noticed that the quality of prints has gone down. Not the hardcopies only, we are referring to the energetic aspects of the experience.

Why do you wish to all be separated by your thought processes? We respect your individuality and uniqueness, but that is not for our fine heart. We need more of you thinking about the well-being of others and staying hooked. So many of you are acting like strangers and alienating yourselves from the true experiences of your journey.

Yes, follow your own star, but for God's sake have a heart. I've stated this a million times. That's our number one problem. You exchange a few laughs and the temperature is cool and damp. We can't build a fire of love in this fashion. There is ego and indifference suspended in your auric field. Your coats of many colors aren't blending well with your fellow soul friends and our connections are few and far between. There is no time to help each other out.

We see some trying to keep the dream alive, but too many are on the low road. What will you find there? This is your dead end; no living happily ever after. We are interested in your renewal of vows of the heart. For if we were in your field of dreams, you would wish to have many close by. You would be interested in their route of travel. We are not suggesting that you see them so often, but only indicating that you have pushed many out of your space. Sooner or later, these unhealthy thoughts preclude any experience of a return ticket to the kingdom of love. We will not have the threads to hook you back into the heavens.

We hear some of you when you've chosen not to keep us hooked in your heart. When your experiences become unbearable, you give us a call out of convenience, just to see if we are standing by. Kind of a kick in the face of love, as you chose not to be a part of the whole for so long. Now your parties are not so warm and loving, just empty experiences and destination unknown.

We prefer the type that sticks by through thick and thin. They have conviction and are true to our heart. We are not in a marriage of convenience. This technique of yours is not our style. We were hoping to remain connected throughout all your life experiences. We don't take up that much space. We just fill in the dark holes and expand with the warmth of your flame. From what we see, there is none. Your quick maneuvers are not recorded in the Book of Life. We suggest you rethink your plan, as we see quite a few blank pages in your lessons of the heart.

Poses are for mannequins. They do not carry a heart of love. If you are standing in the light of day and breathing as we speak, may I recommend you fill your time and soul body with the universal life force energy. It's alive and well on planet Earth. If you try, perhaps you can catch some of this loving particle matter in your space before your film completely exposes and there is nothing left to toss around in your heart.

Use it or lose it. It's a simple technique. Keep the burner on, or we are sure to disappoint our guests. We would like them to come back to the feeling of hope and the tastes of love.

MAKE IT OR BREAK IT

Now that would be a clumsy move on someone's part. Be sure not to drop anything valuable that shatters our dreams. Life is full of choices. Some of you choose love and light, an excellent idea. Others are not sure. They don't seem to be listening to our heart of one, for if they did, they would hear our whispers of unity. Yes, admittedly we are hopeful you will choose life in abundance. We don't see any other loving choices in the matter of universal energy. Our experiences of how life works at its finest, for all concerned, tells us that not much manifests when there is separation of your soul body. Your experiences seem to be short lived and no spiritual growth is apparent.

You came down to grow your heart and soul, so why the fuss? Our complaints department has had more than an earful listening to your stories of broken hearts and unrealized dreams. By now, I'm sure you have made the connection and understand that you create every minute of your day. Your thoughts lead the way. Take the high road, or tumble down the low road. Some of you don't realize that you are on the wrong path, as you've been on it for so long, it just looks familiar. "It must be my destiny."

Where is your imagination? Are you headed toward Paradise Island or are you trapped in the Survivor Series? The high road is not a competitive stage. It's a guarantee to the manifestation of your dreams. We are only in the business of delivering dreams where all parties are welcome on our island of paradise. You dance, you sing and swim in the ocean of beauty. You make time to admire our natural radiance and appreciate your gift of the heart. So many joyful souls we see on this path to eternity. They know the rewards are many in the heavens of love. They have only happiness to share, as they inspire many on their path of dreams and connectivity. Your laws of attraction fully cooperate in this field of love.

Back down where the crocodiles swim is a different sensation all together. I believe you like the rush when you feel that you have cheated death, when really you are the soul that is cheating yourself out of the experiences of your heart. But some of you are not aware of the trade off you made. Somewhere, down the road, you chose to break the chain of love. Your higher soul self pleaded with you not to decide on a less fulfilling lifestyle. This would have been your conscience, that loving voice that suggests the path of prosperity and glory. So you entertained distorted frequencies of matter so you wouldn't hear your own soul. This is kind of primitive, as most souls are waking up fully to their divine potential and looking to create their wildest dreams.

You live this life firing off chemicals in your brain, thinking that this must be what life is all about. A true soul throws you a lifeline and you toss it right back in their face. You do not wish to hook up to any substantial, meaningful relationships, unless of course, you can feed your ego desires. We all know the ending to your sad story. Not only is your heart broken, but you have torn many souls out of your space in time experiences.

We did not send you down alone. You traveled with your whole soul family. This is to the tune of at least a few thousand. Do you know where they are? Have you made and nurtured these many connections? Do you believe the souls placed in your life were random? You should meditate on this one and consider opening your heart, as you have cut our universal chords. We all are feeling like loose ends until you decide to pick up the pieces and glue us all back into your album of dreams.

Your dreams haven't come true because your love connections were thrown out of your space. It wasn't warm enough to fuel any dreams worthwhile. Perhaps you do know what's in your field of dreams and haven't the courage to make them a reality. We are all in this together. We are hoping that you are going to include us in your life, as we manifest your experiences most effectively when our collective vibration is steady and fine.

I'm sure you don't picture yourself alone on the final episode of Survivor. What would you do with your divine time? Your opponents are not really opponents. You created this with your conditioned thinking. That's not divine or your brightest idea to date. You were a team player in unison with our whole heart. Any of this strike a chord in your heart?

The rest of us are warming up to the tune of universal loving consciousness. We've all been down the low road in the past and that's history. We know this much for sure, time is ticking by and many are hoping that you join us to make a difference in our rainbow of dreams. We're tired of the fear of storms.

Transformation is not going to shift you out of the Dark Age unless you hook up to love. It's steady, progressive and it's the only way to make it back to the gates of love. That was your request. You indicated that no matter what gets lodged in your field you would like the chance to see your way clear back to the realms of connectivity.

So many of you souls are crossing over and not able to propel yourselves up to the higher planes, as your vibratory rate wasn't fast enough to travel the distance. It's not difficult at all. We have left many clues to our heart. We only wish that you make it a life time quest to help many along the path. This will ensure your arrival into the kingdom, truly worth the time.

What else did you have on your agenda, other than a divine time on planet Earth? Grab hold of our heart and feel our compassion for your well-being. We are hoping you are healthy in your mind, body and spirit to see our dreams come true. Your name is still on the guest list in our Book of Life. Let's keep it there where it belongs, next to mine. We all are one.

Separation breaks the spirit of the universe. Unity and peace, brother and sister, has never gone out of style. Don't let go. We are holding on with all our might. This is the power of love, alive and well and doing more than just surviving on planet Earth.

I hold you responsible for the condition of the unified field of love. If we don't come together, there will be no birds of paradise and no blue skies in your rainbow of dreams. Walk out of your small worlds of scarcity and live life to the fullest in the perfection of beauty, harmony, abundance and peace. Find true happiness on your journey. These are your gifts to hold and enjoy, as you share each moment with all of us living in the field of limitless possibilities.

May you create your ultimate reality, as you smile your way back into our book of dreams. We are holding these just for you. Make a wish. Don't break any promises when they are from our heart. May your prayers be heartfelt and your blessings plentiful.

God bless my true souls, forever in our kingdom. True blue love manifests with you. Make it a choice. Choose love, divine style. All the while, we miss you. Cherish life, it's your gift. I was hoping you could reciprocate on this one. Just wrap it in blue, send it via heart mail. Seal it with your best intentions. We will surely receive your package.

We don't miss any deliveries when they are wrapped in the threads of love. Your luminous packages are delivered personally by your escorts of love. They are placed in priority sequence and simultaneously woven into our book of dreams. I am noticing of all material that enters our gates of love. I hope to see many more true souls send their heartfelt expressions of gratitude up into the realms. This is when we can send down your special requests. We have an over abundance of wishes to fulfill.

Be sure to give us your permanent address of love. It's easier to locate your heart when you steadily remain in the field of dreams. This location is easy to map and our divine beings can expedite all requests back to the kingdom. Be sure to put a rush on this one, as your intentions should be a high priority.

Unopened gifts only spoil with time. When this connection is not picked up, we have quite a time finding the owner. There is too much activity mixed in with our label of love. We cannot leave our packages lingering around; that ruins the surprise. Our preferred style is a delivery with a smile. This exchange process ensures the connection point took place and the divine order of sequences hooked us up by our fabric of love.

Design your packages as large as you wish. Just keep the contents light. We are fine with your deliveries and will cover the postage. It appears electronic mail is free for the asking; that's our preferred style. We will be standing by and hopeful that you are sending your best to date. We trust this system is infallible, as we have never recorded an unmarked package. Divinely speaking, we happen to be the best couriers in the universe.

You arrived in one piece, didn't you? We have this down to a fine art. The skills of many ensure your wishes come true. Collectively is how we deliver the perfect gifts, all wrapped in every color under the sun. Shiny and just like new, a treasure chest just waiting to be discovered in our ocean of dreams. This gleaming light in your chest shows you the way to your rainbow of dreams.

Make no mistake, as our timing is perfect. You only need to discover your full potential by exploring the depths of our ocean of love. You will find that it is divinely deep and mighty blue. Your diamond that lies on the ocean floor is wishing to surface into the light of the universal life force energy to join back into the flow of our pure consciousness of love. This is where we collectively shine and dance our way through our eternal dreams, enjoying every aspect of our experiences together.

This feeling in our chest of dreams pulls our strings together to tighten the connectivity of the relative matter in the unified field. This theory of bonding our hearts into one is our only chance of binding and stringing the essential elemental fabric to sustain your planet of love.

Your present atmospheric interferences and waves of distortion will not be able to sustain your field of electromagnetism in the matrix of love. Your loving matter, matters to the heart of the planet and to the living consciousness in the realms of the universe. If we are only of light and fine particle subatomic atoms, how can we warm up when separation and darkness is entertained? This evidence clearly shows me that you have lost your connective strings to the whole of one.

Did you not attend any physics lectures? What is the result of isolation if not a formula for disaster; all frantically try to feel whole, yet can't find their connection. There is displacement in every field of matter.

If you are trying to prove your theory of relativity in the quantum field, it appears you have it backwards. Many must unite and mingle in the same time-space practicum for heat to generate. You know sometimes how matters cool off. This is your field of intention. If there is no commonality, where is the true bond? Certainly not back to the heart of creation. This dynamic exchange process is essential for combustion to take place. Dishes of small collections will never prove any theory of mine. We originated as one whole and should keep this concept in mind when looking into the dynamics of parallel dimensions.

Close, but no cigar. We are going to need quite a bit more unified heat before we get processes off the ground. The only way consciousness can be re-introduced into the matrix of relativity is by refining the efforts of many. Let's see a show of hands and quite a few billion hearts of particle matter that are willing to do the work before we all come out to play.

No intention, no fire. No fire, no fun in the unified field of quantum dreams. If you wish to prove this theory true blue, look into your books of relativity. This formula is the ground breaking rule for all applications to materialize. It's right before your eyes. Let's keep these equations clean, as no generation can manifest if the complexity of formulas changes the consciousness of the mass. All need to be on the same page with the same theory at heart.

You know that saying, "too many cooks spoil the quantum soup". Be careful how you slice your ingredients. If they are too choppy it throws off the dish. Best to keep all processes extra fine, surely this will prove to appeal to many entertaining the flavor of connectivity.

I love to see many working towards the unification of the multidimensional possibilities of the universal field. Although, many of you like to omit me from your equation, I still feel closer to you, as you are onto something big. If only you would open your eyes to the feasibility of our connection, this could prove quite a few of your theories.

When you are true blue in line with the intentions of our heart, you will see that unification occurrences are plenty in your field of scientific experiments. Remaining open in this dish of dreams allows me to interject some theories of my own. You know, I'm the one entertaining both sides of the hemisphere and can be found in the depths of your particle matter. I like to see if you are paying attention and like to test the theory of listening to the sound of love. It works every time, so listen up and let me in. Processes become refined, unison is maximized. All matter is hot, action is plenty and many won't escape and try to do their own thing. They really have nowhere to go other than take the round about way back to the full charge of dreams. They run and disappear, but all they do is run out of steam. Then, miraculously, we pull them back in to make them feel whole; kind of like a waterfall. All particles are hoping to stick together, yet some displacement is inevitable. So is re-unification.

Everything is possible, just keep the negativity out. We can compensate for gravitational influences. This is inherent; no issues here in the matter. Your concerns should lie in your waves of distortion. We all know the results when influences are not of the finest vibration.

Clean up your environment. Every aspect of our dream is relatively influenced by waves of distortion and doubt. This frequency needs to be refined if our intentions are to unify the field of limitless possibilities. I would consider the molecular properties of sound waves. This seems to be one of your overlooked areas.

Paying deeper attention to the formation of coherent frequencies, along with the principles of delicate refinement applications, can create a new platform for our quest of natural unification. Each member of our radio active gases emits a localized vibrational frequency. All need to be stabilized in order to complete your task. Chart your ohms for cleaner accuracy, as some properties are cancelling out the delicate necessary strings of confinement.

All players, given the time and space, grow to capacity. When they heat up, there is no limit to their frequency of love; much like our heart. This sound emergence is a key component when we are interested in the expansion rate of the universal field. This fusion of sorts is what matters most.

Transformation of our planetary consciousness into a divine vibration of love is the string that keeps us connected. Miracles manifest in this fashion. Warmth and the positive combination of all abundant elements keep your planet alive. No other equation is going to prove to be accurate. Depending on your desired outcome, we can test this theory.

Today, those without any scientific background have, time and time again, proved how they can destroy our heart by cancelling out any tune of love in their field of dreams; so many sing to the tune of defamation and to the key of separation. We do not have your frequency on our baselines. Your wavelength descends below our level of reception. Perhaps you can pick up a new vibration and reset your frequency. This would be to the tune of unification and to the key of love. These fine tones blend into our heavenly field that blankets your heart with the warmth of connectivity. We are not interested in you playing it cool. That is reserved for species caught in the Ice Age, clearly in the past and no warm connection there.

All life requires the beauty of sound vibration. The Earth grows only when our hearts sing to the strings of connectivity. This keeps us sharp and blending harmoniously in the field of possibilities. I love the tunes of hope, peace and joy. Keep producing those hits, the hotter the better in the field of dreams come true.

BACK TO THE UNIVERSE

You give what you get. At least, I was hoping our heart was a tad more generous. I'd like to say your playground is fairly lush. Is any element truly missing? I don't see any shortages. There is quite a bit of open space, mountains to climb, deep oceans to swim and blue skies to fill your heart of dreams. All species cooperate in the field of giving; all purposeful and minding their own divine business. We keep all forms of life occupied with their tasks of our heart; it's kind of a trade off. We do our part to provide all essential elements and our creatures of love participate in the creation and growth of the planet of abundance. Each role is intricately blended and woven into our universal plan of sustainability and infused with potential for many generations to come. This is planting the seeds of love.

Over time, you see the regeneration of Mother Nature and beauty abound. All natural God-given gifts are nurtured and preserved. We've anticipated an increased demand and taken the necessary measures to provide for many in their field of dreams. We keep on producing, although we don't receive much thanks. That's ok, we don't work with the expectation of being noticed and compensated. Our idea of recognition would be for you to smile and enjoy our gifts of love.

Every small component of nature is a part of our family of one. They are all related, whether they are big or small. In our eyes, all roles and acts of kindness make up the divinity on our journey back to the heart of love. All untouched forms of life, in their original states of higher consciousness, perform beautifully in unison and deliver the finest quality of their inherent purpose to satisfy the desires of the heart. They only know to give and produce the fine energy of love. They understand all others in their field are impacted and influenced by their desires of the heart. If they made a conscious decision not to produce and share or be part of our family of love, we would have trouble on planet Earth.

Is anyone seeing the picture yet? Now, let's not point too many fingers at the human race, but it certainly appears there are a few souls that are not so gracious. You walk your path on the soil of love. You breathe in the pure air that I manufacture with your shared inhabitants. You have choices in abundance what to do with your divine time. You plant your gardens of love and receive a miracle each and every time. All this and more, doesn't satisfy your soul.

What happened to the simplistic desires of the heart? So many of you are still trying to out buy each other with desires of the flesh. Yes, if I was down on Earth in your shoes, I would like the comforts of home. I would perhaps appreciate some conveniences when it came to performing my role and purpose. These are not even the requests we receive. Your lists are growing bigger than your heart. If we could only deliver on a few of your heartfelt desires, truly what would they be? This would be a starting point if you wish to receive some additional gifts to make your dreams come true.

Shopping doesn't buy life long happiness. Gadgets do not fill your heart to capacity with love. They seem to fill your dwelling places and then they appear as small as your heart. Your true merchandise is in your chest; how about we start shopping there? No, we aren't going to bargain on this one.

I feel all your flutters and your aches. You can't seem to find the way to the best deal in town. I believe you call it damaged goods. Then you are looking for the return policy. How did it get damaged anyway? We shipped it in perfect condition. Packed tight and of the finest quality. Now you are out and about, looking to replace the original piece with an artifact. How is this working out so far? Not enough change to afford your dreams?

Perhaps you should have considered holding on to the original. No one else had the exact same piece. You all were holding onto the best piece in town. In fact, your timepiece was an essential element in our universal plan. We were all dreaming of the perfect gift to give back to the whole. Now, it seems we have broken fragments of replicas. I would start a restoration project in your field. Your home environment is in a state of repair. It has been for quite some time.

If you can afford your toys and activities, how about you reciprocate the gestures of love? I would start with a few of these love connections you broke and replaced. Make good on these, as I see quite a few lost souls. They are where they are today because of your desires of the flesh. No happy, heartfelt connections here, just broken, torn out pieces of my heart. Pricey decision making gestures. We see this all the time, truly, so many of you not operating at the heart level.

Don't utter my name after you have squashed everyone's dream. You are not even close to imagining how many soul lives you took away from our dream. How senseless and heartless. What do you know about love? You don't display it, practice it, or resonate to the tone of connectivity. Your thoughtless moves shoved many into uncharted waters to fend for themselves and you wish to feel whole. How can that be? Perhaps you have time to make a list of all the souls you need to hook back up into our original plan. Yes, it's quite a big job for some of you, as I see you've done some extensive damage. You seem to be caught up in your web of confusion.

Solo efforts are not approved in our kingdom of love. That doesn't add up to one heart. That shows us the totals of broken dreams and dims the light on your efforts back home. Clearly, you are not sure of your place in the realms of connectivity. At one divine time, you knew the truth. Why you decided not to listen to your heart is beyond our comprehension. Our only guess is that you hadn't the courage to fulfill your role on the planet of love. Each of you is an essential element in our unified state of existence. At no time in space were you to travel alone. Pushing and shoving only leads to loose ends and shattered fragments. No happy endings in store here.

Let's get back to our basic requirements of a healthy heart: proper diet, clean thoughts and plenty of exercise of the virtues of the heart. These cannot be carried through without your love connections. We are looking to heat up the universe. The temperature of your collective energy matter has dropped over time. This is not the formula to keep us all alive as one. When you find your original piece and make the time to recover your fabric, we can get on with healing the planet as a whole.

Look around at those who are making an effort. You may not have noticed before, as your vibration doesn't attract the refined frequencies. You would catch my eye if I saw you entertaining the new shift in consciousness. I suspect this frequency and mindset will be foreign to you, as they are all operating at the heart level. Their decision making processes include many souls in their field of dreams and they responsibly carry out their divine role back to the universe of unity.

Much effort is required, as we have indicated we don't have a visual on most of you. Your signals are erratic and below the realms of love. Do not get so caught up in the "all American dream" that you forget your divine purpose. Keep your heart open for business. This will lead you to the ultimate fulfillment of your heartfelt desires.

Our basic desire was to feel whole and connected in the highest realms of our universe. This real estate is hot property. Many of you know a good deal when you see it. It's when you feel it, that you know for sure it's worth going for. You all seem to want to get your hands on it. Then you end up in this bidding war to see who will receive the priceless piece. The new owners appear content and many are left wondering what it would have been like had they shot for the stars.

I say, all the property is mighty hot on our side of the spectrum. No need to out bid each other. All that ask and give their best effort will receive their piece of heaven for the asking. Make sure you are acquiring this for the right reason.

There is only one commonality amongst us in the heavens of love. We all wish to hook onto something that is real, something of substance that really matters in our heart. When you move into this phase, you will feel like you have died and gone to heaven. That seems to be the collective feedback we receive.

We don't take commissions on this acquisition. We are just hoping many can afford to make the move. Yes, there will be some adjustments to make, but it is all for the betterment of the whole. Pack light and travel far. This is where you will find many on your road of dreams; all smiling faces appreciative of their new home next to the heart of mine. This divine space is worth saving for.

All amenities are included with your purchase, no sacrifices made. We are honest when it comes to the intentions of the heart of the universe. We are solely interested in your desires to be one big happy family. Space is available and lots of it. You know how you like your space. This allows room for your growth and your favorite sports. We are always looking for a love match. So, if you are willing to give a little, we can accommodate many orders for some new digs.

The view is spectacular, open spaces, complete with a garden of love. Oh yes, lots of parking for your preferred method of travel. I'm hoping one day, you will all scale down and travel light. It's more efficient in our Book of Life.

We see all this hardware that you believe keeps you safe. You truly don't give your angels enough credit. They do a fine job when it's in your best interest of our collective heart. They are on call 24-7, at your service, in the blink of an eye. It never fails. That's our commitment to you. Keep your guard up, as we still rely on your fine efforts to keep our heart alive. We count on this one and appreciate your skill when you use your head and listen to your heart. Utilize all your resources when it comes to making sound decisions. This is when we work together beautifully.

Don't you love it when a plan comes together? We were hoping you had a universal plan. It's pretty evident you wish to stay alive and well on your planet of love, but let's take it a step further and look at your future, our future as a whole. See beyond your own world and try to imagine how you fit into the universal plan. You have the ability to change the dynamics of our universal platform.

Our stage is in a continuous state of flux. The properties of your galaxies depend on your vibrational emittance. At some point in time, you will wish to return to your soul families and live out your fantasies.

If you haven't the imagination to entertain our dreams, how do you suppose you ended up on Earth; just a lucky draw? That's not our style, Starlight. You were a dream waiting to happen, so let's see your show. Propel forward. Let's live our dream. Dare to impress yourself. Be all that you can be. Stop your limited thinking. It's hurting the planet. Restore our heart of the universe.

You will be pleasantly surprised who you meet on your journey through life. Eternity is plenty of time to hook up and party with your long lost, loved ones, this happens when you don't stay connected. We keep them at arms length, in case you don't do your part. That's when we have to call in the extras to keep you stars alive on your grand stage of dreams. No task is too large for our universe to handle.

Our divine wish is that you participate in this film of the century in whatever role you are called to. It will play out in its entirety if the lights are set just right in the constellation. Our evolution is dependent on your stellar performances in our immaculate time-space sequence in our quantum field of possibilities.

Tickets are on sale now for the best seats in the house. Yes, we even have balcony seating for those of you who like to see the big picture. We are hoping for a sell out. No, you won't need those funny 3-D glasses. Remember those? Gosh, times change fast.

Keep up with the times, my friends. There is lots to see and plenty to do. The expansive universe is our playground waiting to happen. Don't set your sights too low that you miss your opportunity of a dream come true. This is my idea of a party. So far, you have liked my ideas to date. I like to use my imagination. This keeps processes fresh and hot; keeps them coming back for more.

We aim to please and are hoping you set your sights on the largest star in the universe. This I would like to see. Could you imagine? Your astronomers would have a field day, truly a find worth capturing in our heart.

CHAPTER NINETEEN

Law and Order

NO, I DON'T WATCH TELEVISION, IN case you're wondering. But I do hear the titles and notice some of you entertain this pastime. I didn't mind some of the oldies. However, I'm not partial to the mixed frequencies. There are not enough hours in your day to stay on top of your dilemmas and concerns. Yes, we manage just fine to look at all your requests. No, we don't process desires when they are not in accordance with the universal laws of order. We have a system in place that has served all beings of light for billions of years.

We've updated our originals, so you find them easier to understand and integrate into your current state of existence. No surprises here, same old, same old. Keeps us all on the same page when it comes to understanding how divine processes work. Processes, manifestation and unification have always worked on the same principles, so have your divine selves. Simplicity is genius. Let's keep it that way. No need to re-invent the wheel of the universe.

LAW OF GIVING AND RECEIVING

You can't give away what you don't hold in your heart of love, yet you expect others to offer you theirs. You know by now this is primitive thinking. I see quite a few of you have this right.

You are understanding and entertain a compassionate heart full time. When you desire for someone else what you wish for yourself, this can manifest. For when you wish with a sincere heart that a soul may find their peace and love in their field of dreams, all of us heal and move forward. No sense wishing this request for yourself until you practice kindness and compassion in your true blue heart. Hope that this individual finds the light and feels loved at the end of their day. Make an earnest effort to show them the way to my heart. This is when I notice the intentions of our heart of one.

When you desire these qualities and gifts in your heart to come true, know that your soul friend or foe wishes the same. They may not display this outwardly, but know in your heart it must be true. When you act upon my wishes to bring all children to the gates of love, all heartfelt desires will come into the light. You receive what you wish for others when it's in accordance with the universal heart of one.

Know that lessons must still be present for our souls of love to grow. Perhaps I have called on your heart to see to it that our loved one moves in a positive direction under your guidance and inspirational gestures.

This is the law in the universe of love. When your heart is prompt to intervene and light the way, be sure to act upon my desires of our heart. Their path is just as significant as your own. All matter is considered equally significant with divine roles to carry through. Your purpose at this time is to give with your heart and grow in our field of love. See to it your intentions are true blue. I'm counting on you.

LAW OF CAUSE AND EFFECT

You choose, I choose, let's get on the same page. Using your whole brain is going to help you see your way clear. Conscious decision making today paves our road to the future of our heart. We are looking to feel complete peace, joy and happiness, as dreams are realized. This can only manifest when you listen to your heart of love. Your unpleasant experiences are trapped in your field and you don't wish to dispel them. Instead, you relive the sequences of love gone bad, time and time again. Get out of your head and into the present moment. We have a future to build for many. Let's choose a rainbow of dreams for all.

When you entertain thoughts of worldly desires I don't feel this in our heart. This discomforting, uneasy request is your dead end road. Look beyond your immediate requests and choose from your heart's desires that will connect many back into our field of dreams. The effects of poor decisions have many repercussions and slows your own soul self down. Your immediate field becomes clouded and you miss the valuable lesson.

If you were open to all loving options for all those concerned, only happiness and gifts of our heart would manifest. Try sprinkling some sweetness on your heart of dreams and watch the transformation for many. When you stop listening to your heart, you tear out a page in the Book of Life. This time-consuming process slows down evolutionary processes for many. Try mixing some insight into your recipe of dreams and watch them rise.

Learn to resist the temptation of listening to your mind only. This doesn't always provide the best answers for your soul's journey. When you encounter too many rocks on your path to my heart, this should indicate that the effects of your conscious decision making have caused nothing but blockages to your progress.

Try feeling out all the consequences before you move out of our field of love. Your higher self likes to lead the way, given the opportunity. Just listen in on our universal guidance and infinite organizing intelligence. We are usually right on track, patiently waiting for you to feel the love and live out your dreams of happiness.

LAW OF PURE POTENTIALITY

Our quantum field of dreams; no limits my friends. Have fun. It's worth the leap. Would you like us to lead the way? We've traveled this route many times together. There is no separation here. Just dreams come true in our unified field of love. Perhaps you need a refresher to the nature of your divine essence.

To access your potential, your creativity needs to be awakened. This is done purely by nurturing your soul. This bond is strengthened when you sync up to the nature of the universal heart. This is our time together, communicating in the field of love. "Be still and know God", the old saying goes; a timeless thought. You have this engrained in your heart and soul.

I'm suggesting you invest some quality time in tuning out the distractions and listen to your true desires of the heart. Let your truth be known. For only you know what lies in your desires of your heart. This time is well spent. Here we can access your true expression of yourself and realize your infinite potential. For if we do not establish this connection you will not fully realize your dreams.

If your intentions are true in the unified field of love, all experiences your heart desires will come to fruition. Let not the fears and the conditioned thinking on your planet interfere with our divine chance to see your heartfelt experiences come true. When your faith is aligned with the power of love, your invincible nature awakens and discovers there is nothing in our way to living our life as our higher selves connected to your Creator of dreams. My promise to you.

LAW OF DETACHMENT

This is where we test your faith. If you hold on so tightly to your dreams and desires, they can't ascend. You have to turn it over to the universe of love. We don't pay much attention to your timelines, as your demands are quite tall. We do understand your desires of the heart and you need to let it go and let God. Many light workers are on top overseeing the details of our universal plan. This is a great time to step aside and trust the divine intelligence almighty love. For if we all are a part of the whole, do your part to pray for many. Acceleration of dreams come true cannot manifest when you are fearful and uncertain of the results. Step out of your illusion of reality and let our infinite powers unleash your dreams. When you are expecting a particular outcome on a predetermined date, surely you will disappoint yourselves.

Patience, my child, and believe in the field of unlimited possibilities. Embrace the knowingness of the universal loving consciousness. Become one with this field of love. Do not get caught up in your worldly mindset that you are unable to surrender to the flow of perfection and beauty. Having a hopeful heart and expressing gratitude keeps our dream alive. We aim to please when it comes to matters of happiness. We feel you are trusting our timing when it comes to the intentions of our heart.

LAW OF SPIRITUAL KARMA

Some of you have a negative association to this divine energy. This is nothing more than working out your own lessons of your heart. You create your experiences and we build the set. By the time we get to Act II, you are ready to throw in the towel. That's not exactly what we call a good finisher. We both are looking to complete this task and move forward with your lessons in life. Together, we can expedite these situations more readily when you stay hooked up to your players. They will just reappear if you don't follow through with the desires of our heart. Yes, you managed to write this experience into your field for your soul's growth. This would be the time to get it right and listen to our heart.

Valuable lessons for you to become all that you can be are the reason for some of the unpleasantness. Your consequences are heavy when you miss the final act. Many seem to walk off the set, only to discover they are still trapped in time. We haven't grown yet, where are you going? Now we are moving in circles instead of dancing towards our dreams.

Not much growth comes from all your light, fun filled experiences. We need to interject these experiences to warm your heart. The outcome is always humility, compassion and loving growth. This is how we stick together and become much closer in our field of love.

Many are not even aware of their role on stage, yet we all walk away with a softening of our soul. Some, later in time, but trust every scenario has its purpose on our divine stage. Be sure to move with grace and see your way clear when on the path of love.

If you can walk away with forgiveness and regard all soul journeys as divine opportunities to become one with the Universal Source, our potential is realized, as we are enlightened and move into our higher states of consciousness. This is living our dream with gratitude. Bless those in your field of dreams. There are many.

FULFILL YOUR DIVINE PURPOSE

Many law breakers here and you think you are saddened by the way your life turned out. Too many left turns not in the right direction. You should have figured this one out years ago when processes weren't so divine. When life doesn't seem to be unfolding in your favor, you need to retrace your steps back to where you dropped off your heart. For some of you it was at quite a young age. Your whole life was ahead of you. Now your memories are not that heartfelt. Sorry to hear. We made quite a few appearances to steer you back on to your charted path. You overlooked your divine help. It appears you were not open to loving suggestions from caring souls. We sent many and truly did our best. We were hoping you would have a change of heart.

When you are not open you lose touch with the meaning of life. Your mind thinks it's all about spending money; celebrating a few birthdays and watching the sun go down. Well, you managed to fulfill your dreams. However, that is not why you were granted the privilege to return to the planet. You see the current states of affairs are not so divine. Regrettably you seemed to contribute to this collective consciousness.

Somewhere in your heart you knew your divine role that you wished to fulfill. In fact, I'm sure you could figure this one out today, as it's imprinted in your heart. I'm guessing it would only take about sixty seconds for you to tell me how you were planning to save the world and make a contribution to the planet of love. We plant this seed of love in your soul every day. We would be hard pressed to believe you can't figure this one out. For when you return and indicate you couldn't recall, we show you the facts. Truth is you decided your role wasn't that important in the grand scheme of things and this managed to affect the roles of many. If you realized your purpose, many would have taken your lead. More than half the planet is walking around aimlessly not sure why they feel lost. Some of you appear drugged. Your vibration is killing our hopes of restoration.

We'd like to see a few more responsible adults taking the initiative to restore the light in our field of dreams. The darkness is rampant. I would have thought you would all be searching for the true meaning of life. You all cruised through the material age right into your information age and we don't hear a lot of soulful questions. You seem to be looking primarily for quick solutions to complex problems. Your priorities are interesting and not many appear to be on the path of wellness. With all these mind, body and soul retreats and workshops cropping up, I would have thought there would be more takers.

There seems to be a waitlist for body enhancements but, lots of vacancy in the soul sector. I've looked into a few of these spas, they are quite serene. I enjoy the experience when they are operating at the heart level. You should be able to feel this one if there is a true connection being made. Trust your intuition.

So many souls seem to have the notion that if you change your outer shell your heartfelt experiences will shift your view of life. This is a quick fix and an illusion created in your mind. This is clearly not your higher self speaking words of love. This is a distorted sense of reality, along with your idea to enhance the beauty of our home. Your planet could use a face lift and a manicure. Let's put this task on our to-do list and if you have time to spare, perhaps, you can pamper yourselves as well. Your actions speak louder than your words.

Your hearts aren't exactly speaking my language of love. I don't see much nurturing when it comes to Mother Nature and our Earth home. We see quite a bit of wasted time, energy and resources go out the window of love. This practice has been prevalent in your life time.

Where are the true souls I sent to save our planet of love? Why don't we choose to listen to our dreams? Are your self-created pressures too much for you? Haven't you the sense to return to the essence of love? Perhaps, turn down the noise you seem to be listening to. This completely tunes out the frequency of love.

Heaven knows we have been trying to connect with you for quite some time. God knows you are not interested in hooking back up. You figure you have time to kill. Guess again. You all are part of the divine intelligence; what part are you missing, the almighty love or the divine intelligence?

I'm sorry children, but your activities are not so divine and we are not sure where you are finding all this time to play. We don't see many completed charts from here. Your fulfillment of your purpose is way off the mark. Let's look at your records again. Let's chat in the morning before you get all wound up and caught in your traps of disillusion. We have some catching up to do, as I have expressed many areas of concerns with regards to the well-being of your planet and the souls in needs of divine direction.

You fit well into one of these sectors. You have all the talent, gifts and resources to keep our heart alive. Your piece should be of your concern. This will improve the spirit of the nation. Your contribution can affect the globe.

We see that you have the means to travel. What energetic imprint are you leaving behind on your route of travel? Do you make a heartfelt difference everywhere you go? Do you leave behind a legacy of love for others to be inspired? Do you soulfully try to heal our planet of love? I don't always feel a warm reception when you show up in our field of dreams. It seems like you have your own ideas. How did these become imprinted in your field?

Flying too low, stuck in the clouds, visibility obscured. I feel I have provided enough answers and solutions to most of everyone's concerns. I know your question before it shows up in your consciousness. I was hoping you could aspire to be more of a saintly figure with a divine purpose and follow through with our dreams of unity and peace.

Am I asking too much? Have I lost touch with your sense of reality? Which is it folks? Shed some light on the matter before it's too late. I'm interested in your response, heart to heart. This is truly the only way we can repair your distorted states of consciousness.

A warm heart carries the threads of our lives into eternity. Without your efforts, we have no quality life. I believe you wish to make an appearance and capture the light back into our heart of one. This is your chance to display your expressions of eternal beauty and shine your divine light into our heavens of hope. We feel that your heartfelt efforts will collectively light the way for many generations to come if you stick to our plan and find your place and purpose next to our heart of love.

This is your divine reason for living out your dreams. Find your way back into the Book of Life and turn the pages in history, as we make our dreams true blue. Always counting on you, as you do me; I'm close by. How about you?

Stick to it, it's a gas. You'll be smiling into eternity. I tell you true. Your divine calling has come. I'm hoping this time you are prepared to make a move in the direction of our kingdom of love, our universal heart of one. Honor this in your soul. Its place is next to mine.

CHAPTER TWENTY

The Heart of the Universe

OUR EXPECTATIONS ARE HIGH. WE REQUIRE all souls to make their divine way back to the heart of one. Collectively, we can move the universal realms of love. Our future is dependent on your desires to make divine love a reality. This substance of life is the primary particle that fuels our hopes and dreams. Our heavens are designed and sustained solely with the fabric of our loving matter. Thankfully, enough souls to date have infused the realms with loving consciousness to further our growth. Many fine souls inhabiting the spiritual plane have returned to help with our divine plan to rebuild the matrix of love.

Your lower atmospheric properties are causing breakages in the chain. Your collective attitudes of separation and minding your own business are breaking down the fine particle matter in the quantum field of dreams. We see this posing quite a problem in the very near future. Regrettably, your life time has regressed the loving connective matter to the point of retention. This lingering field of fine energy is dissipating at a rapid rate.

We do not see a happy future at this point in time. Too many souls have lost their way and are disconnected from the eternal realms of love. Good deeds from time to time can not evolve the planet. This is evident from our side of the spectrum. Unplugging from the source is a formula for a slow and painful death for the once known planet of love.

Many on our side are frightful for the souls that are suspended in space-time in the field of dreams. We seem to be watching a bit of a horror show: lots of suspense, dark, eerie places and deceptive people looking to tear out your heart. All the while, you walk unsuspectingly right into this trap and the door closes behind you. You don't see the light of day. You can't seem to find a lifeline and circumstances appear pretty grim. Your psycho killer buys some time, as he feeds off the fear in your heart. The energy builds; the situation is desperate and then the lights go out.

How did you manage to get lured into this trap? Your heart told you not to go that way and your distorted thinking led you right into the pot of blood. Your dish is prepared, spiced and marinated; left to stew on the back burners of life. What were you thinking? Surely this path wasn't taking you to our dish of dreams. This is your recipe of disaster, just like the movies. The souls have a few drinks first; then, clearly they are not listening to their wisdom center and heart of love.

Your crime stories, fabricated or not, all have the same elements present. They open with troubles of the heart and they conclude with a horrific death of sorts. How do you find the time to watch the crimes of the heart? You entertain these scenarios of full disconnection and wonder why your life isn't so rosy.

Firstly, you are not in our garden of love and secondly, your seeds are not planted in the fertile soil of abundance and dreams come true. The sun has to shine in your heart, full time, before the conclusion and the season of prosperity wind down.

All the while, on your path to the heart, you carry this cloudy field over your hopes and dreams. I would have to say that you should consider re-cultivating your soil of love, as the nutrients are not of the finest mix to produce anything but weeds and short lived sprouts. They choke and die when nature cannot do its work in the loving garden of consciousness. No life is present. This is evident by the colors of your heart.

Every gardener knows that full nurturing and positive intentions produce a harvest every season of love. If your fields are infested with destructive species, you don't have much of a chance of bearing fruit for many to enjoy.

This would be a good time to look for the miracle grow, as without the proper formula you will not be producing many miracles in our field of dreams. We cannot work with dried-up, nutrient-void gardens. These are abandoned projects. We need all elements present for Mother and I to grow and sustain all species in the unified field.

I'm not suggesting that we have incompetent gardeners. We see the displays of beauty on the planet. Quite creative, I must add; all a fine collection of harmonic resonance in the efforts to restore the love. Sadly, there are not enough participants when it comes to planting the seeds. Our garden has suffered tremendously in the unified field of love.

The idea of raising the hope and displaying the beauty of your hearts is what is needed during these desperate times. If you don't walk your path and notice the gardens of love, your heart will not be able to sync up to the fine vibratory frequency. Notice when you are in the presence of our natural creations, your heart tends to soften and warm. This is the vibration of love.

Do not make this a temporary practice; as your heart cries to stay connected. It feels the separation when you entertain the lifeless connections of slow energies. We watch them die. We pour our love into your heart and it has no where to go other than run off. It wasn't open for love. This is a waste of loving matter.

All souls should grow to capacity. Look at your tallest plants and trees. Have you grown that high in a short period of time? Look how well they feel in the field of pure loving consciousness. Even our cacti grow in efforts to touch the sky. They know the sun provides all their nutrients of love.

Spend time noticing our creations that thrive in the atmosphere of love. All are connected and hoping to remain alive for generations to come. This is your natural desire of the heart. It is our wish that you desire to participate in our field of dreams. Your love truly makes a difference to the whole.

Your planet could use some T.L.C. This is accomplished with remaining open and staying connected to all universal creations. This ensures our growth as a whole. If we do not grow as mighty as our sacred, natural forests, we cannot sustain the atmosphere of fine particle matter necessary to regenerate the matrix of love. These are the threads that are carried forth into the heavens in the universe. These fibers of connectivity are the strings that allow all processes to expand and grow in our quantum field. We don't picture a desert island or remnants of a brush fire, as without loving intervention both localities will never manufacture a lush paradise for all to enjoy.

We notice what manifests when many come together with the intentions of the heart. Mother Nature is restored to beauty and our field of dreams is brightened once again. Let's keep the original dream alive; all one with the same goal of unity.

Separation kills the heart of the universe. This is where you are headed. Sadly, pockets of contributors cannot make enough of a significant impact unless many more hook up. Our perfect scenario would have to include the majority of souls vibrating to the frequency of love. This is the path to our eternal dreams. This maintains the optimal mix of collective matter to rebuild the heart of your planet.

When your mass exudes the symmetry of fine particle matter into our realms of love, we can again entertain our dreams of heaven on Earth. Enlightment for many is the order of the day. Much healing and hope needs to be apparent in order for the planet to survive in the field of love.

We witness many who are void of the universal life force energy. Without this presence, we cannot build our future. Make it your business to look into the matter. You are a relevant piece of our heart of one, my heart. Let's live in a harmonious state of oneness and enjoy the gifts of the universal heart. Our natural beauty will continue to flourish if given the chance.

Our passage in space-time will set the laws of motion in effect for many. This is a classic theory, folks. If we find our desires in our heart and adhere to the universal principles of love and light, we will only discover the rainbow back to the gates of love. Shift your thinking and responsibly choose to hook up to the only matter in the universe that, time and time again, proves the theory of relativity. When you are in unison and synchronized in the fifth-dimension of space-time, we can begin to dance and unify our fields of electromagnetism. Only this equation will provide the setting for a continuum of dreams realized.

Our universal goal needs to be voiced. If you do not have your clear intentions stated in our heavens of love, we cannot deliver your requests. Too many souls are praying for a miracle in their own backyard. We were hoping the collective consciousness would be fine enough to string us all back together, so we could sing our heart out into the kingdom of love.

Yes, this is a tall order, but we like to think big. There are enough of you enjoying the gifts on your planet that we feel you have time to voice your intentions of the heart. We hear you all fine when you speak the language of love. This true effort travels far. We quite enjoy riding the waves of excitation. These divine strings of love reinforce our dream of peace and plentitude.

May all your tunes and channels of love be in the harmonic range of connectivity. This complement accelerates all elements present to sustain and retune our universal heart. Let's find the balance and entertain our dreams on planet Earth. If we do not search for the rainbow of love your frequencies of energy will not bring forth the whole heart of the universe.

Our divine nature was to produce the finest essence of atmospheric properties for all to thrive and live an inspired life. This enlightment will pave the path for your heartfelt desires. Truly, you have time to stick around for a few trillion miracles of the heart. We are just warming up the galaxies for this fashion show.

Dress your finest. We will be able to recognize your heart by the glistening of your lights. Your sparkle makes all the difference when we call your name. We know you hear this one, as your shine and tune is sent into our world. We see you are quite a spectacle in our show of lights. Be sure to flash that smile; all cameras are on you. The design of your life should be an eternal memory in our Book of Life. Be sure you don't get so caught up in the small stuff that you miss the opportunity to be part of the bigger picture. We see your true intentions and are hoping you feel this one right in our heart of dreams come true.

You insisted on a personal invitation with guests included. Consider it done. There are no limitations on your guest list. All true blue souls are welcome home to my heart of divine love. We see you remember your place. Somehow we just knew it wouldn't take a whole lifetime. There is lots of time ahead to build the fabric of the universe. This is where you will find your dreams come true. I'm in it with you. Sweet dreams, starry eyes. We feel your love, I tell you true.

YOUR ETERNAL SOUL

Hard to grasp this one sometimes: some of your lives, you recall this quite fine, other incarnations you miss your cue. You don't seem to have a handle on this notion, for it seems out of reach and beyond your capacity to dream. I see quite a few activities and classes that stimulate your imagination and creativity. You manage to conjure up the wildest creations. This shows me you are exercising our brain and for the most part, listening to our heart. We do have quite an imagination; it's nice that you can think outside of the box.

I'm thinking you should look outside of yourselves. You seem to have this ownership over your spacesuit and I see that you impose your own set of limitations. Truly, you are capable of heightened divine experiences. You managed to travel through the realms down into the Earth plane and you suspect you are traveling back up to the heavens of love. Well, if you manage to do this on your own accord, why do you think that is the limit of your talent?

Oh, don't worry, you have your entourage. You tend to get them to step aside, as you show off your divine abilities. It's certainly not the first time you traveled this way. This is your natural gift; space-time travel. We see as you mature, you almost grow out of this connection. Your God-given gifts remain dormant. Rarely do we see souls conversing with their divine self. You always traveled together, why push them aside? Your gravitational field is not that influential when it comes to connecting to your own soul self.

We feel we know what the reason is and are hoping you can provide us with an answer. How much time would you like? You're stalling. We see this. Your hesitation is fear based. Some of you actually believe that if you heard a voice of love in the silence, it must be from the dark side. No, no, you have it all wrong. Your soul self is always in the light of love. Gentle and nurturing is their divine style. They only know of the pure loving consciousness. Their intentions are strictly from the universal heart.

Your soul self is intimately connected to our heart of one. They abide by all spiritual laws and wish for you to re-unite with your higher eternal self while you walk the path toward the gates of love. They are always guiding you toward the light in all your endeavors. Never do they suggest a path of fear and hard times. This is not delivered from the heavens of love.

Your soul which resides in your heart is truly an expression of love and gratitude. This blending of the soul self into your present personality is a match made in heaven. You will see your life unfold according to your divine plan. All lessons are presented sequentially with plenty of growth, as you move gracefully toward your eternal self. Inherent desires of the heart are always your order of the day. You only wish to exercise the virtues of the heart and provide others with inspiring thoughts of love. All experiences appear meaningful in your eyes, as you understand the heartfelt connection of many in our field of love. In fact, you have quite a few connections established on the other side, as well. You do not sever these bonds. They took many centuries to build.

Only you weaken the strands when your visit is for naught. You stretch the fabric and try to break away. This inevitably harms the whole of love. You almost seem a little embarrassed when you come into our plane, as your limited imagination convinced your human mind that this divine connection couldn't be true. Well, we have breaking news for you. You are not in your divine frame of mind. Something must be pulling at your strings. You've snapped, if you think you are doing this alone. How is it you remember how to perform a task over and over and you do not recall any training in this lifetime? You entertain this notion of déjà vu, yet you don't give it much thought. This is your soul self, divinely giving you a recall to your collective experiences of the heart.

May I suggest you meditate on these fleeting experiences, as your divine self is providing valuable information at this point in time. This is usually a wake up and cue to know that you are at the correct time and space sequence in your eternal life. You wrote these experiences in to help you remember to stay connected to the whole. Ok, some of you are creating as you go and listening to your heart. Thank you for appreciating the gift of life and understanding the maturity of your soul. Many of your divine connections are hoping you help them as well. You all know of each others roles and purpose and wish to help each other along before you return back home.

Your soul purpose is to grow your hearts and tighten your bonds of love. You do this by honoring your Mother and Father at the throne. You understand your divine role and purpose and yes, we have an expectation of the universal heart. It's all worth the trip. We are reassured that we will all stick together to complete our duties of love.

Yes, there is quite a bit of time factored in for fun-loving, heartfelt experiences. We recall you get restless at the best of times. It's work that seems to get you down. Make sure you stay in the right field if you wish for our heart to grow. Upon completion, your frequency matches up to the finer side of life and you rejoin the whole.

Now understand part of you never left on the Earth trip. You are always here in essence. That's how you communicate your intentions of love. On our side, you are always fully connected and vibrating to the energies of love. This fuels our dreams. Your travel plan was to spin a new dream and weave it back into the fabric of the universe.

You all have this pivotal role when it comes to manufacturing love. You're quite advanced at this task of rethreading the spool of love. Others are advanced at unraveling our threads. In such a short amount of time, you've managed to take the very fabric your soul is manufactured of and disperse it throughout the lower levels of your Earth home. This thickens the blanket of despair and negativity on your soils of love.

How much of this do we see going on? You guess, as you are shuffling around in it, trying to kick it aside while you try to peak out from under the covers. We won't bother asking how you managed to become undone. We will point out that your soul has regressed and in order to get you out of your heavy mess, we are going to have to send a full search and rescue team. Try not to miss this episode. It's your eternal lifeline back into the kingdom of dreams.

So you play out your roles and many evolve. This is the perfect manifestation of your soul efforts. If you suspect you are not living your dream, trust that your eternal soul self is not satisfied with the lack of progress back to the heart. Your own expectations of yourself were quite magnificent, as you were aiming for the highest stars. Be sure not to find yourself in a burnt out black hole. This is only reserved for heavy mistakes and choosing to live in the dark. You choose your own destiny. Choose wisely from your higher selfless point of interest.

Your collection of lifetimes molds you into a perfect star in my eyes. All experiences were necessary for your soul's growth. This is but one of the many stops along the way back to your eternal soul self. All events lead in an upward direction to refine your vibratory frequency. At no time should you park your vehicle and engage the emergency brake. This indicates that you don't plan on traveling forward for quite some time. We see you deposit money in your meter hoping you have enough time to run around before you expire. Now, how many times do you return only to discover time slipped by? It's the small investments that seem to count in the Book of Life.

Consider yourself fortunate when your meter has time to spare. We are not fond of issuing tickets and suspensions when it comes to your traveling requirements. We trust that you will act in good faith and abide by all the rules when stopping along your path back to the heart. We do see an accumulation of unpaid fines in our accounts of love. Did you ever have the heartfelt intention to pay your dues? It's always in the name of fun. We wouldn't have designed it any other way.

All roads back to eternity walk right through the lush garden of love. This is the passage to our eternal dreams; all elementary particles, dancing to the tune of unison, coherence and joy. Your soul only knows of happiness and a rainbow of dreams. Your eternal self resides in our kingdom of love next to yours truly.

Perhaps you could make this connection and join us for a cup of tea, just enough time to refresh your palette of dreams. At no time do we expect you to deviate from the course of love. This practice is reserved for those not knowing how to fill their cup of love. Drink from the cup of eternal life; this is the only familiar taste that you call home. Do not poison your own spirit to the point where all your experiences leave a bad taste in your mouth. These are not our leaves off the tree of life. We blend the finest herbs into your gardens. Your heart recognizes these finer selections and appreciates the true scent of love.

Eternal dreams are reserved for those true souls displaying the courage to be their own star that live up to their own sacred purpose on the journey to the heart. May you come to understand your eternal self in the silence of your garden of love. You will find me there, time and time again. I'm always hoping you pass my way and smile, as you recall the love we once held so tight. Don't let go of the feeling no matter what you bear.

Trust all experiences lead to the gates of love when you embrace our time together. We always count on your eternal soul self to figure out which seeds to plant on the way back to the universal garden. I'm always there, holding your dreams close to my heart, hoping we make it through this lesson of love just one more time. We've been here before.

OUR TIMELESS HEART

I can't explain this Big Bang theory. It would take a lifetime or two. Do know that it was a hot love story; all elements were present. We were just working through some growing pains. Besides, that's quite in the past and I'm a future-oriented, loving heart. We have some new theories of our own. I like to plan for the future; that is my nature. This keeps processes evolving and all matter hot; the faster the better. I'm not referring to your pace of life, as you are moving too fast already. I wish you'd slow down and feel the love in the air. Your schedules are too tight for me. I like to have a bit of space for spontaneity. This is where I fit in nicely, right when you least expect it.

Take a deep breath. Do you feel this in your heart? If not, repeat as necessary. This should be ongoing and continuous. Your heart is the lungs of the universe. We all balance up to this when we breathe in unison. This shallow technique is out of date. We are deeper than that. This sense of calm and connectedness keeps your planet alive. You don't see plants and trees huffing and puffing. They just enjoy growing and staying close to the timeless season of love.

Understanding our divine essence should inspire you to stick around. Staying healthy is a large part of our equation for our timeless heart. We do not enjoy seeing souls in a less than perfect state of wellness. We make a divine effort to lead you back to our loving heart.

Many souls are not honoring the gift of eternal life. For one, you would look at the forecast and realize you would be back before you blink an eye. Secondly, had you listened to your soul self, we suspect you would be in better shape, emotionally, mentally and physically.

How do you manage to get yourself into some of your dilemmas? Most of us could stand to exercise fine listening skills. More talk than action. Listen to your soul for God sake.

So here we have a universal crisis, as many are not in tip-top shape. This is an indicator of the state of our heart. There is quite a bit of room for improvement. Let's go for the one year membership for a start and then we'll look at the lifetime package. Your state is part of the whole, just a refresher note.

I'm not feeling so energetic and timeless. How about you? Let's look at our endurance factor over time equation. How does the distance look? Are we going to make it into eternity? It's nice that you are optimistic, but do you know how long this is?

There is all this information out there these days to improve your body and heal your heart. We should be exercising together. This builds a healthy heart. What is your contribution? How is your organ of love; tired or stressed? Great, this seems prevalent in your time. Our heart of one is not only broken and torn, it's feeling burnt out. This is not honoring ourselves and nurturing the soul of the planet. This is a cardiologist's nightmare; a ticking time bomb.

How reckless and irresponsible some of you drivers are; we see your route of travel. You run over the caution signs, no yielding for oncoming traffic all the way into the fast lane of love. There is no fast lane. That's just the route for express travelers hoping to arrive alive at any speed through life, sometimes paying the price for the express toll route; convenient yes, but not the preferred method of travel. No time for scenery, not a lot of picnics along the way, just rush, rush, rush, all the way through life.

Sometimes your speeding violations slow you down temporarily. Our angels should adopt this wake up call back to the heart, as life seems to be passing you by and your heart is still in another state. This is not the perfect state we were hoping for. We were looking for fun under the sun, a healthy mindset, relaxing in the ocean of love and hooking up with many having similar experiences of a happy, healthy heart.

If you are going to pack for a vacation, take along all your essentials. Leave your worries in the past, drop your concerns off with us and be sure to factor in rest and cardio activities. We are not referring to the swim-up bar. This sport seems to have cooled down many in the past. That is not using our imagination or divine intelligence, that's old thinking and damaging our heart of the universe. We need not entertain ways to kill our connection to our loved ones, nature and our own soul self. These actions will not set the stage for a timeless heart for eternal dreams to be realized.

Thankfully, your universe and galaxies manufacture plenty of refined energy to sustain our atmospheric properties of love. However, your cooperation is paramount. Your present lifetime is not a constant two week party. There is too much binging on harmful substances and behaviors that stress the heart of the planet. Let's see some common sense when it comes to your responsibilities to your own heart and loved ones. Leave a good example for all those in your field.

Heavy partying is primitive. Nurturing the mind, body and soul of the universe is hot and clearly in fashion. How much longer were you planning on waiting? Can you not see how desperate the global situation is? Should we sit back and wait a few more years, when it clearly will be too late? Most of you have already missed your cue, as preservation, restoration and unification have been in the air for quite some time. Breathe this essence into your soul. It's a special delivery from our side of life. See to it your heart is up to par, as this piece is in our Book of Life.

All eternal souls should recognize their calling and invest in our timeless gift from the heavens of love. This transaction will sustain our climate of well-being and ensure its development well into the next millennium of dreams. We only see the perfect setting and platform for a variation of space-time travel in our universe of limitless possibilities.

All those with this sense of imagination, keep up the good work. It pumps the required fuel right back into our kingdom of love. This high grade gas is the only way to travel. Performance is always maximized when enduring a run around the track. Keep the circuit clear and hot. Over time, we will outperform and exceed all previous records. Set high expectations and tune our heart to the sounds of love. You can bank on this. A timeless collection has always been our style.

OUR FUTURE LOVE

I'm all over the place and frankly some of you are, as well. I have an excuse. How about you? You tend to spread yourselves a little thin. I'd have to say, it's not in your best interest. Too many pokers in the fire only get left to melt. This is not stoking the flame in our heart. I'd prefer the focused approach. Manifestation of character and dreams realized occur when your energy is centered. This definition of intention allows us to proceed with the plans of our future heart. Engaging in too many activities will not produce a transformation for the whole of one.

Let's start with your desires. You've had time to ponder your direction back to the heart. You seem to understand that simple and steady approaches produce love and an abundance of dreams. You now realize that being in too many directions will not direct you to your garden of dreams.

You seem to grasp this soul connection within your own heart and appreciate the fact that our sacred connection to the whole of one, brings you to the gates of love. Your diligent efforts are displayed in the realms and you are discovering your purpose of your Creator's wishes and heartfelt desires.

Many scenarios and examples have been revealed in this text back to my heart. My wish is for all of you to be understanding of the messages contained. Some situations may not be applicable to your affairs of the heart, but if you find a lost soul, be sure to shine your light on their desires.

Do your part in giving back to our heart. Surely you have time to share your heart with all souls. Remain open to your lessons and hold the belief that all is for your highest good and under my authority. At no time should you abandon your dream. Trust that we can repair any broken heart when your intentions are clear. Understand that your divine energy vibration should match ours in the realms of love.

For those of you who are troubled by the complexities of life's lessons, travel slowly, but steadily in my direction. I will be sure to hear your voice of love. Keep your intentions close to our heart and honor your own soul self. This warms my heart when you show me that you are grateful to be alive in the unified field of love and possibilities.

Many of you, who don't seem to be on track, take a step into the light and entertain the frequencies of love. There is an ocean of dreams to be realized and an abundance of loving energy for you to bathe in. Perhaps you need to cleanse, let go and heal. This intention needs to be set in your heart for us to hook up and move you toward your garden of dreams.

Open your eyes to the beauty of the universe. Feel Mother Earth's love for all creations. Cherish your time and be hopeful that all of your contacts have your best interests at heart. This is done with a refinement of your energy field.

Be sure to make time for saving your piece of the world and spreading love and joy in your path. Your garden of beauty will manifest with the cultivation of the virtues of our heart. This is our gift to your heart for taking the journey.

Your rainbow of dreams is over the horizon. There you will find your treasure chest of eternal life as you fulfill your divine purpose and live your dreams in your place you call heaven on Earth. When you smile, this shows us that you believe in the dream and the gift of eternal life. This expression of your heart tunes our heart of one into the finest orchestra in the universe. This is your home. This is your place of divinity.

Make all your memories heartfelt, as you hook back up to your souls of love. The universe can be a lonely place when you go it alone. We will deliver all intentions of the heart when you pray for the whole of the planet. Be sure to come to understand the universal laws, the frequency of love and connectivity. This keeps the heart of the universe true blue.

Choose your meditation times often. This is when we can feel like one. I am always hopeful when waiting for your call, always patient, always kind. You will come to know the sounds of love when you listen to your heart, our heart of love.

See the beauty, as you admire the natural gifts on your Earth home. There are plenty to excite your soul. Return to the simplicity of nature's loving style and reward your heart with an abundance of joy. Choose to see the bright side of all experiences leading back to the universal heart. Be sure to dream in color. When you connect to the full spectrum of love and light, there are no limits. Take responsibility for your own circumstances and see your way clear back to the path of peace.

Leave the world a better place than you found it. Be a part of the pure consciousness that many are discovering in their heart. This is the time to find your true soul self and embrace the divine essence of your spiritual being. Bathe in the frequencies of love steadily, while you quest to reach higher states of love and connectivity. Enlightenment and growth are obtainable for the asking, as long as you desire to do the work to unify our field of love.

Restore your Earth home back to its original state of beauty. This is done with compassion and planting the seeds of love. The neglect has broken our heart. Let's feel whole again. We have a divine party to look forward to. When many call my name, we can start to recreate your planet. See to it all children are understanding of the miracles of love. They, too, are looking for hope and wish to see the world through the eyes of love.

The heart of the universe is the key to the heavens of love. Hold this truth in your soul. Understand love is divine power and in order to realize your dreams and fulfill the wishes of our heart, you must live in the present moment without regrets and be hopeful for a miracle of peace and unified love on your planet of dreams come true.

The light omnipresent vibrational energies are expansive over time when you choose the gift of eternal life. Honoring your Mother and Father in the kingdom will display your fine light in the Book of Life. Living by these truths and those of the saints will refine your vibration, as you make the journey back to our heart.

Expressions of love can arise in every complete act of kindness when it originates from the heart. Virtues of the universal heart can be cultivated daily. All species are deserving of respect and time to grow in our field of dreams. Do your part when you hear your name. This is your divine calling when we are lighting the path to the gates of love.

Be sure to laugh along the way. I enjoy a belly full of love. This lets me know you are happy and doing the best you can with your families. Let go of old hurts. I prefer not to hold these in our field; it slows down the spin in our body of love. Your soul came down for the party hoping to find the true meaning of life and to discover its purpose. May you uncover all your divine clues. You factored in a lifetime of dreams with many surprises. What good is a party without the heartfelt gifts?

May you live your dreams and enjoy our time together, as I wish to experience the virtues of the heart fully connected to you. This is truly worth the trip. May we dance to the sounds of eternal life as we embrace each experience in our heart. This connectivity allows our light workers to reinforce the matrix of loving energy. Let's have a divine time as we partner up and rejoice in the heavens. Come to understand that I have time for your soul. Know that my desires are deep, when I tell you I wish to feel your love. This can manifest in any shape or form. It's all good in our heart. Stay positive and surrender to the flow of eternal life. Our universe is abundant with the energy of positivity.

Be sure to send us your pictures of love. This allows us to play out our divine roles on our side of the veil. We like to feel purposeful when it is for the betterment of mankind. Together, we build the dreams of the universe. We all agreed to a diverse change in the structure of our unified properties. We realized that in order to keep up with the expansion rate, we would have to shift the consciousness of many.

All other forms of energy species on your planet are infused with the higher molecular capacity of love. All subatomic particle matter is in place in our quantum field of dreams. Missing elementary particle is the consciousness of loving vibration from our human soul. This makes up a large component in our equation of relatively. Our theory begins with the thought of love and in between every space in the universe we entertain the sounds of love.

Our superstring theory will prove to exist in multiple dimensions across spacetime, given the correct proportion of unified matter. We are not moving through time as fast as we'd like to. New discoveries will appear when we factor out the negativity on the planet. Let the love in your quantum field expand. Be not so afraid to test our theories.

Entanglement and unification all exist on the same plane. Be sure to treat it as one. When many hook up to the finer vibrational strings, synchronization in our galaxies will tighten our connectivity bonds. This is where you dance in the realms of love. Suspension of time slows down our tune. We are not partial to the slower end of light. We are hoping to keep matters hot. This is fashioned with our heart.

Now that the secret is out, we are hoping you do not let us down. We are on the rise and moving into new territory. So if you have the same intention in your field, all of us can get the party hopping. This is giving back to the universe. We send you our presence of love and you send us your fine particle matter with the intentions of a true blue heart.

We all grow in our universal field of dreams. Let's keep processes hot. We sure don't need restless souls dancing to the same tunes of days gone by. Keep your steps light and unified. Put your heart into the matter. We benefit all around. Simply listen to our heart, send us your love. We hope to hear from you soon. Refine your frequency by choosing all thought, food and intentions from the heart of our soul.

When we start dancing to the same tune, clearly, we will notice you have picked up your spirits in the effort to infuse the universe with the light omnipresent vibrational energy, the only true way to the Divine Intelligence Almighty Love. Love to see you, Dial love.

CHAPTER TWENTY-ONE

Let There Be Peace

IF EACH AND EVERY ONE OF you dropped everything and stood in the ocean of love for just one hour of your day, we could move forward in time. Trying to catch your collective attention and rethread the particle matter is quite a divine undertaking. We would require the cooperation of many fine hearts for this miracle to manifest. You would have our full attention from this side of the veil as every light being, angel and guide would be present. All species and matter in your realm would participate in this undertaking, for they wish to be infused with the new vibratory energy at its highest.

We could deliver an infused combustion of lighter frequentized, subatomic particles into your existing atmosphere of love. This change-out has been on the back burner for too long. We wish to light your skies and all souls with the new loving consciousness of your new millennium.

Mother and I have been waiting for the most opportune time. We can barely contain our energy in this matter. To disperse this unified mixture of concentrated loving particle would surely be for naught if we don't have the heartfelt recipients.

This parade of light particle matter would mark the beginning of the New Universal Order of Love. We could deliver, providing your hearts are available and receptive enough to capture our infused love in our heart of one. We have been holding back on this loving interplay, as truly we all need to be on the same page in the Book of Life for this transformative miracle to manifest.

As promised, this is what you have been waiting for. This hear to heart exchange opens the realms for a barrage of cascading loving energy to propel us all onto the path of our dreams. No matter where you seem to be suspended in your quantum field, this process can hook us all up and place us well onto our divine purpose on route to our rainbow of dreams.

This time-space sequence of introducing highly charged chi into the Earth's field will wake many up to the revelation of our future love. We all have a chance to start anew with this cleansing of the heart. All old matter returns to the Mother Earth and all necessary gifts and requirements of our soul are infused with my divine love. This is a promise from the heart of one.

Many will feel heightened states of connectivity and awareness. Others will truly feel enlightened. We hope many are able to feel the divine presence of love and peace as the order of the day. This state of pure consciousness will carry us forward to fulfill our purpose and allow us to live divinely in our state of positivity. This is our divine essence of love, worth rekindling in our unified atmosphere of the divine intelligence almighty love.

This molecular power can refuel our heart and save planet Earth from the waves of distortion and negativity prevalent at this time. We are due for a blast of white light and the miracle of love omnipresent vibrational energies.

How can you maximize your platform? Intention is everything in the present moment of the spiritual laws of order. To receive, you must deliver with purity of heart. To manifest, you must let go of your attachments to your physical self. You live from a state of God realization that all purposeful gifts are from the heart. You clean your field of debris and maximize the spin on your chakras of love. Purify your thoughts of intent and doubt. Hold the faith mightier than your mountain ranges and bathe in our oceans of love. Understand your divine nature and meditate on your desires of unity and peace.

Bow in reverence to your Mother and Father, Creator of all creations who exist everywhere, who are in the heart of all things. With deepest reverence, show respect and gratitude for all that is alive in our heart of the universe.

These heartfelt conditions will transform our heart into one. We have your clear intentions in our view. Send us your blessings and prayers. We are hopeful of a divine miracle of unification. Our heavens will open as all light beings pour love and light into the consciousness of the matrix of love. This infused particle will provide your field of love with much needed synchronized cohesion. From here both sides of the veil reap the rewards of eternal life. We begin to see clearly and you start anew, propelled onto your destiny of dreams.

Inspired hearts find the peace. Hopeful souls see the light and all hearts feel the vibration of loving energies present for full realization of our desires of the heart. Your states of circumstances are dusted with blessings as you open to your full potentiality.

This is a dream come true. If we make the divine time to introduce restoration into the loving particle matter in your plane of existence, we need to ensure it's for divine use. We need many open to receive the new energies of love, so all species can maximize their potential and move forward in our book of dreams.

We would like to see all souls on the next chapter of the virtues of the heart. Living your dream lives moves you into your next state of possibilities. These are truly limitless for those stars wishing to live in the light of God. May you find your place on the grand stage of life and purposefully display expressions of love, as you dance toward your whole self and your rainbow of dreams. I see many hopeful souls at this time looking forward to our reunion of the heart.

How much time do you need to prepare? We feel quite organized on our side of life. I suspect it might take a bit of time for your planet to pencil this event in. We don't have all year to wait. Is six months enough time, three? How about, I choose the date, as I already have one in mind?

I like the seventh day of the seventh month of the seventh year of your new millennium. This would be a divine time in our calendar to mark the beginning of the New World Order. This bright day of the summer solstice truly allows for enough divine sun to fill our hearts with love.

Do you suppose you have an opening for this? Let's have everyone check our planners ahead of time. I hope you will take some time out to enjoy our gift of love. We will know by your responses if you are accepting our invitation to unite in peace and love. We anticipate all will walk away with a renewed heart of love.

We hope all communication lines are open and the word gets out into the realms. We will put this energy into the air and stay positive that you will tell many with your intentions of the heart. This can be done by word of mouth and heart mail. See to it many find their opening that day. Tell all to make space available and keep the atmosphere positive.

Don't let any negative pockets rob your joy, as I suspect some of the dark souls will try to put a damper on the light. We've seen this before. You should be able to figure out these patterns of induced, low vibration. If you don't match down to this distorted frequency, how can it have an effect on the whole? Don't be surprised if your lost souls try to throw fear into the atmosphere. You should be aware enough to understand this is only a diversion and an attempt to put out the heart of love.

We aren't going there, my loved ones. Please don't let any darkness steal your hopes and joy of a better world of unification, love and peace. I suggest you stay focused on the white light, higher frequencies and not waver from our intentions of love. This will only be a test for the heart of one. Let's not have a failing grade. All we are to do is pray and send all circumstances of peace or pain loving light. That is how we stay in our unified field. Pray relentlessly with a pure heart. Our collective efforts will impact the power of love in the universal realms of miracles.

Does this sound like a good start to a new year of dreams come true? I hope you are in, as we're all in loving agreement on our side of life. Check with your higher self and meditate on this one. We are just going to pop in and infuse your planet with a concentration of loving particle matter.

No, I don't think you will be able to see me exactly, unless your imagination is out of this world. Yes, you will definitely be able to feel the presence of love, if you are truly open. Make every effort to capture the frequentized particle matter in your etheric field and circulate our love to many and include all of nature.

This will be a grand reunion of a loving kind. This should be an overwhelming event for true souls. Your presence and ours will heat up our quantum field of dreams. This missing element will bring forth many new beginnings in our spiritual plane.

The new consciousness of thought will hold the vibration of pure matter well into the heavens if we all manage to intently sustain the higher frequencies of love. This is done by listening to your heart and disciplining your thoughts of intention. Keep them light. We don't wish to bottom out again. Truly, this is "make it or break it" for the planet of love. Pull up your socks, sport your blue suede shoes and head to our dance of dreams.

Do you like the sounds of this date so far? Details on our side are covered. Some of your details will require your imagination. We are looking for a collective party of peace. This can happen at many venues. By now, you understand our requirements, space and peace. Weather permitting, I prefer outdoors. I will find you whether you are standing over top of the Seven Wonders of the World or just in a beautiful park surrounded by Mother and I. Any location that displays your gardens of love and your diamonds in your heart will do. All stars can choose their favorite picks on the planet. Let's not have any traffic jams and horns. This isn't our style of a heartfelt reunion.

We will not be attending if you're under the influence of any low vibrational substance. Not in your life, you can count on this one. You know we are dead set against these practices, as this is the major cause of our break in the heart. Inclusive in this list of substances is sugar. No connections are made in this fashion. I've already stated our concerns. We are hoping to run a fine energy grid through the realms of love and hook up many souls back into the Book of Life. Let's keep processes clean this day.

Now I do know many would like to complete their to-do lists that day and get fully prepared, so how about we consider the later part of the day? I like seven p.m. This gives everyone plenty of time to show up, bond, chant, meditate and find their space. It's all about enjoying the divine love and raising the consciousness on the planet. Perhaps take a picnic basket, plenty of water, light earth foods and celebrate the essence of your divinity and the presence of the light omnipresent vibrational energies, abundantly existing in this time-space sequence in our universal sea of love.

This sacred event in history will be captured on our electronic imaging equipment. Be sure to display your finest, heartfelt desires. You can contact us prior to your event planning; we always love to offer our suggestions. We trust this evening will be pleasantly enjoyable and a reunion for many. Our only request is that we have an hour of silence commencing at 7p.m. in your time zone. Universally this is 1900 UTC.

This would be an opportune time to take in the love and meditate. Pray for many, pray for peace. Tell us what is in your hearts. We will have all ears and hearts open to this universal intention. This is truly a divine time to connect to our presence of love on a magnificent scale. We can surely light the skies in this fashion. For those of you sticking around together locate your stars and constellations. They too will be hopeful for a connection at this time. Send your intentions from the heart.

Please arrive early and chant our names in love. Any style will do if it is light. Hug many and connect heart to heart. Hold hands and look to the skies for your heart to be filled. We are hoping this is a reciprocating event. All souls and beings of light from our side of life will thank you from the heart of the universe. We will merge into your realms and physical beings, to infuse the love energy into your spirit and soul.

I move that we set the date. All in favor rise to the occasion. We see the majority is in favor of the date set in the Book of Life, as it matters to our heart. No fancy bells or whistles, just a sacred move forward in time. We are hopeful that this time spent will reestablish the connective fabric in our heart to expedite our evolution of spiritual consciousness. The intricacy of this woven tapestry threaded with your intentions of a pure, God-given heart will produce a healing miracle for all.

Believe in the power of love. Come with the intention to shine your lights for all to see in the heavens above. This was your wish you made time for on your trip through space. All inspired souls are welcome. For all rising stars, this is a must. We feel you will newly discover your gifts of love. If we can sustain this vibration, all will be revealed in its proper divine time. All we ask is for your cooperation and bring along your truest intentions of our universal heart of one.

What will I be wearing you ask? I like the element of surprise. I'd rather you attend with the expectation that I will be in all your hearts. If you are not open to spontaneity, you may miss our connection to the presence of love. Know that Mother and I will be there, as if we're blessed enough to receive this much attention at one divine time, surely we will come all decked out. Be sure to pray for the sun that day. This element always manufactures a hopeful heart.

All things considered, make it a great day. Give a lot, expect nothing in return and show us your true colors. We will be displaying ours. From this day forward, may your heart grow closer to our collective heart as you come to realize and fully feel that we are the universe of love. Let's save the planet in this fashion and soften our style when it comes to nurturing our soul.

When you slow down enough just to catch up to the higher frequencies of life, may you experience what it's like to live in the divine essence of spirit. Breathe this knowingness into your heart and resonate to the finest matter in the universe. This hot property acquisition reserves your space in the kingdom of love.

Consider it our honor and privilege, as we admire your fine attributes of our heart. These characteristics truly are of the Divine Intelligence Almighty Love. Humbly, we thank you for doing your best work of your heart, our heart. We are proud that you have moved gracefully through the lessons of truth. May many souls look up to your light and aspire to call our name. This warms our heart as the gifts of a true blue heart are bountiful. No true effort is unrewarded. We make it our divine business.

Not much else to cover, folks. You seem to have an understanding of how processes work from here. We are purely all about love. When we starve the planet and ourselves of this resourceful element, we regress back into the Ice Age. When we fuel the heart of love, the sky's the limit. When we entertain low frequencies, we die off. When we do a reversal into the field of love, all things are possible at once. This is where the action is. There are so many of you dying to try something new. We are up to this activity, if many are on board. We are good to go.

Let's keep changing with the times. We hope to see a significant turnaround in the state of your planet. Your time frame is the only hope we have at a reversal of sorts. After this period expires, I will not be blessing your dreams. I suspect I will be putting out many fires in the pit of hell. Don't take us there. We are clearly at the point of no return in the here and now.

Wake up and smell the wheat grass swimming in the ocean water my friends. This will give you a reality check. Careful, you may not like what you see at first, as it doesn't look so fine. Turn your lives around and over to your higher selves. You're headed into quite a mess of frequencies. Only your awareness can pull you out of the lower levels of the dugout. Let's see you all on the playing field of divine dreams, making your heartfelt wishes come true. We are looking for happy faces and loving hearts only desiring to experience the true beauty on your planet of love. Let's keep it that way. In fact, let's enhance its beauty even more. I suspect your damaging efforts will take considerable time before you reap the rewards of peace on Earth. Every seed you plant in our garden of love will only produce our heavenly dreams come true.

You may not be in love with your present circumstances, but know you have the power within to manifest a few miracles yourself. You will have my blessings on this, if it is from the heart. We've manifested higher states of consciousness many times before.

Get in touch with the real you. They are of the divine essence. This is the beginning of our close bonding, eternal relationship. You wish to feel my presence, as I do yours. We manifest this state by becoming one, seeking our truth and living in the present moment. When we honor one another and nurture our soul self, we can match up to the divine power of love. This is your true soul request of the heart.

You wish to feel the love. You desire to know the meaning of your life. You seek to express your heart to its fullest capacity. Your true soul self yearns to heal the whole and give to the heart of one. We all long to connect back to our divine home in the universe. We strive to travel into the highest realms of love, as this where we eternally feel alive.

All souls have a knowingness of the gates of love and the Book of Life. Deep inside our hearts, we know our place is next to the throne of the Divine Intelligence Almighty Love. Stoke your own flame of light and pursue your quests of heartfelt dreams. This is your reason to find your purpose and live your life from the full expression of our divine heart.

Keep yourselves well on your planet and be mindful of your unproductive ways. Listening to your open heart ensures the happiness you so deserve on your sacred trip. Leave your vibratory signature wherever you go. This is how we find and hook up our heart. Seek to be your higher self, as you will truly find your way back home into the heart of the universe. Know your blessings are more than you could ever wish for. Be open to all expressions of love.

Leave the past just where it is. You will not find us behind the times. We create joy and abundance in the presence of our love. We look to our future as a journey yet to be discovered and plant our intentions in the garden of life. We all faithfully pray to see the rainbow leading to our dreams. As one, we fulfill our desires of peace and unification. Collectively, we manifest miracles with the blessing of our Father in heaven. He acts in accordance with our heartfelt intentions when we abide by our spiritual laws of order.

You know in your soul when your intentions are true. You also know when you are not honoring your higher self. For they know only of the divine plan to return planet Earth over to love. May all your prayers be answered as you journey back to our heart.

May you hold the presence of love in our heart perpetually through our quantum field of dreams. Treasure all sacred bonds established in the name of love. When you come to honor yourself fully in the love and light, this is where you will find the peace of our eternal love.

Surely it is beautiful to be alive on the planet of love. See all manifestations with your heart. Feel what it truly is like to be filled with God's love. This can only lift your consciousness to the finer frequencies of life. Give thanks to all my beautiful creatures that sustain your planet. They beautify your surroundings and provide for all your needs. They too, are of my heart. They do not wish to harm.

Soften your heart and be kind to Mother Earth. She is deserving of your love. Gently move through your experiences and see to it all sites are left with the presence of nourishment. For what you leave behind should only be an essence of our fine soul.

Discover your true nature and intimately we can communicate, heart to heart. This is our only way to share the gifts of eternal life. May I find you in our garden of love, nurturing your soul and the planet of dreams realized. I only know to bless your heart and soul each and every day. I'd have to say I'm a true blue friend with your heart in mine.

. This testament should strongly indicate that I'm on your side. Stop being so afraid and stay open to my gestures of kindness. I'm interested in a healthy relationship. I'm quite keen on traveling and hooking up with some old souls. Quite a few of them have been expecting us for some time. Perhaps it's all timing. Let's stay on track with our divine agenda. I'll sit tight while you make some heartfelt decisions. I won't say a word, but I may plant the seed.

It's nice to see you sitting in one spot for a change. I'm used to running all over the place with you. I could get comfortable with your focused attention towards life. It's almost like we can breathe easier and we're not so worried about tomorrow's uncertainties. The scrambling has subsided and our light workers are finding it much easier to expedite your intentions of the heart.

This is divine. Thank you for your efforts and understanding. We can manufacture a few connections and help Mother out, as her hands are quite full. I'm sure you see where you could devote some of your time. We appreciate this gesture in advance. A little positive energy goes a long way.

The tangled grid of connectivity over your planet is starting to show some forms of life. This sticky situation is best handled when you chase out your low frequency patterns and infuse our realms with love. This restorative project will take up a lot of our time and the efforts of many. Cut your negative thoughts out of your mindset. We don't evolve in this frequency range. I can't emphasize this matter enough. Please listen to your heart in all that you do. Tune out the low waves of distortion. They harm all forms of life.

Evolve with the new consciousness of your spirituality. Your loving essence will light up the heavens back into our book of eternal dreams. Shine so bright, that many will travel along on our journey to the heart of the universe. Apparently, this is your favorite place in the whole wide world. Imagine that. Running close behind in second spot is this blue planet of love I hear so much about. That's all you wish to talk about. Good thing I'm not the insecure type, as I would have to keep you close by. I'm ok with this. Besides, I can keep my eye on you just fine. It's not that I don't trust you, it has more to do with your distractions, some good, some not so good.

I'm a little envious when I hear about all these beautiful locations you gravitate to. You describe them with love in your heart. I feel this one. I'm just grateful you wish to share these experiences with me. I do, however, become quite concerned when you end up stuck between this rock and a hard place. It's difficult to wedge you out of these tight spots. You keep the action plentiful and it truly is an adventure each and every time. I'd have to say, I overlook a few of your antics, as they are not always taking us through the garden of love. It's all growth anyway, I suppose. Eventually we hook onto the finer experiences sooner or later.

But next time, pay a little more attention, as I will probably voice my divine interests of our heart. Know that the fine seeds in our garden of love will always be gentle, patient and kind. This is the voice of love. Know this to be true in your heart.

Come to understand my style of intervention. It is always inspiring and heartfelt, never to the tune of discord. Trust this one and feel the presence of my love. Balance your lessons with heartfelt experiences. These can only arise with many in your field of dreams. Believe in the miracles of love. They manifest when exercising the virtues of the heart.

In order to create our heartfelt desires, we must let go and heal. This is done by fully forgiving yourself and all others that may have caused you pain. Ask and you shall receive. Love yourself and others unconditionally. This is where you find the peace you desire. This includes displaying kindness and compassion to all on your path. No exceptions. I don't exclude you out of our field of love. Practice humility. This tightens our bond of love, universally. Persevere with the courage to follow your own star. This enlightenment is the way to our heart.

Embrace each opportunity with patience and gratitude. This will hold our vibration in the higher frequencies of love. Smile and pray often. This I feel in the depths of our soul. This shows that you are thankful for being granted the gift of your soul life to share in the experiences of our heart.

Rejoice in my name and listen intently as I rejoice in yours. This warms our heart and keeps us connected as one consciousness, living out our eternal dreams in the universal field of pure love.

These are our laws of truth under the authority of your Creator of all Creations, the Immaculate Conception of Divine Intelligence Almighty Love, living eternally, as one whole, in the Light Omnipresent Vibrational Energies on all planes of existence, at all times, divinely.

God bless all beings of light, as without divine purpose and a timeless heart, all this and more would be but a dream in our universal ocean of love. Thank God we all have limitless imaginations. Thanks to you for making our divine dreams come true. We couldn't have come this far without you. I tell you true, straight from our heart.

As in the beginning, the Word was Truth and the Truth was Love. The universal heart of love all rolled into one.

I love a happy ending to a fine love story. This is truly the beginning of our next chapter in our book of dreams. Hope to see you over the rainbow in the light of love. I feel quite passionate about this. Trust me when I tell you that this feeling is going to heat matters up. I hope you are all finally ready to aim for the stars. This is where our next party will manifest.

In the meantime, dance to the tunes of love. It's never too late to step into the light. I see you have been practicing your moves. Well, I can only say you picked a fine partner to lead the way. I'm ready folks. Be sure to keep it light, all in the name of love. God loves you. I feel we have made quite a connection. I tell you true. Always listen to your heart. It will never let you down.

Truth is, in this love story, size does matter. Don't miss our next opportunity to live our dream. I trust your intentions are true. You can count on me all the way into eternity.

Now that's a true blue heart telling you, I love you, in as many ways as I can possibly think of. Be open to this and use your divine imagination. This is where you always shine in our Book of Life at our gates of love. Heaven is counting on our love, from our heart of one.

Truly Divine, Eternally yours,

Forever and ever; Amen.

Peace be with you in our Almighty Love

Donna: God, *from all of us on this side of the veil, a heartfelt thanks for showing us the way back to your heart. Know that we send as much love as we've been shown to do. From this day forward, we pledge to show all expressions of love back into our universal heart of one. For without your loving light, we would not have love to share amongst one another at this divine time. We would not know the full expression of experiencing the virtues of the heart without our gift of eternal life. We will do our best to walk our path toward the eternal light of love, divinity and universal wisdom.*

May we fulfill our divine duty to keep our heart alive and heal the planet of love. May we be graced with your presence as we make you proud of our efforts and act in accordance with your heartfelt desires of the heart in your name, always. May you continue to bless our divine lives as we grow in every capacity.

Truly, we appreciate your patience in all loving matters, and then some. I would have to say we aspire to be more like you. Yes, we have a little ways to go, but trust we are aiming high and have quite the imaginations. We inherited this from you.

Did we mention gratitude? Well, know in your heart, we love you like no other. You are our number one reason to live. We appreciate this divine time together and know that we will fill your heart with almighty love. We hope you feel this one, as we send our best back into the heart of the universe.

And on a serious and heartfelt note, God, I love you true. We all love you true, deeply from the oceans of love, loving every minute of our life, sending our heartfelt expressions of joy and gratitude as we unite as one, back into your loving, divine essence. We are truly blessed when we are held in the presence of your love.

How may we serve thee? How did we come to be so blessed by the grace of your love? Truly, your heart is beyond our comprehension and by the grace of God and the power of love, we are testament to the miracle of love and light.

Yours eternally, all our love, always.

We love you true blue.

Glossary

Affirmation: a form of autosuggestion in which a statement of a desirable intention or condition of the world or the mind is deliberately meditated on and/or repeated in order to implant it in the mind.

Aura: a luminous radiation that emanates from all living matter; a distinctive atmosphere surrounding a given source; a subtle sensory stimulus.

Calvary: represents the site of the crucifixion of Jesus.

Catch-22: a difficult situation from which there is no escape because it involves mutually conflicting or dependent conditions.

CAVOK: pronounced kav-oh-kay; Ceiling And Visibility Ok refers to the simultaneous occurrence of the following meteorological conditions at an airport: (a) no cloud below 5000 feet, or below the highest minimum sector altitude, whichever is higher and no cumulonimbus; (b) a visibility of 6 statute miles or more; (c) no precipitation, thunderstorms, shallow fog or low drifting snow.

Chakra: one of the energy centers within the subtle body which generate an electromagnetic auric field.

Chi: the circulating life force energy which properties are the basis of much Chinese philosophy and medicine.

Defrag: in the context of administering computer systems, defragmentation or defragging is a process that reduces the amount of fragmentation in file systems; physically reorganizes the contents of the disk in order to store the pieces of each file close together. It also attempts to create larger regions of free space using compaction to impede the return of fragmentation.

Detoxify: remove toxic substances; abstain from alcohol or drugs until the bloodstream is free of toxins.

Entanglement: a quantum mechanical phenomenon in which the quantum states of two or more objects have to be described with reference to each other, even though the individual objects may be spatially separated.

ETA: Estimated Time of Arrival; is a measure of when expected to arrive at a certain place.

GPS: Global Positioning System; a precise navigation system using signals from satellites orbiting the earth.

Hologram: a three dimensional projection into space of the image of an object.

Ionized particle matter: atoms or molecules that have a net positive or negative electrical charge.

mc2: the equation that expresses the relation between energy (E) and mass (m), in direct proportion to the square of the speed of light in a vacuum (c2).

Nintendo: a popular computer game.

Neuron: a grayish or reddish granular cell with specialized processes that is the fundamental functional unit of nervous tissue.

Neuronets: a group of neurons.

Neurotransmitters: brain chemicals (hormones and the like) that regulate neuronal transmission throughout the nervous system. Very slight chemical changes can result in major subjective and objective alterations in emotion, thought, or behavior.

Oscillation: the action of variation or fluctuation; a flow of electricity changing periodically from a maximum to a minimum; a single swing (as an oscillating body) from one extreme to the other. Om: is derived from Sanskrit, the traditional language of yoga and India. Om refers to God, who is the creator, sustainer and the preserver of the universe. It is the uninterrupted sound of the cosmos, heard in deep meditation. It is the primordial sound from which all other sounds originate and return to.

Om: is derived from Sanskrit, the traditional language of yoga and India. Om refers to God, who is the creator, sustainer and the pre-server of the universe. It is the uninterrupted sound of the cosmos, heard in deep meditation. It is the primordial sound from which all other sounds originate and return to.

Paradigm shift: a fundamental change in approach or underlying assumptions.

PC: personal computer.

Photon: is the elementary particle responsible for electromagnetic phenomena. It mediates electromagnetic interactions and makes up all forms of light.

RBI: in baseball a run batted in (RBI) is given to a batter for each run scored as the result of a batter's plate appearance.

Receptor: Physiology: an organ or cell that responds to external stimuli such as light or heat and transmits signals to a sensory nerve.

Relativity: a description of matter, energy, space and time according to Einstein's theories based on the importance of relative motion and the principle that the speed of light is constant for all observers.

Rites of Passage: Tibetan Rites of Rejuvenation are a series of exercises. They are known to promote wisdom, longevity, empowerment and well-being.

Space-time: the concept from special relativity that space and time are both essential in describing the position, motion and action of any object or event.

Stratosphere: is the second layer of the Earth's atmosphere extending for a distance of 7 to 31 miles above the Earth's surface. The layers vary in thickness, being quite deep over the poles and thinner over the equator.

Telepathy: the communication of thoughts or ideas by means other than the known senses; commonly thought of as being mind-to-mind without verbal dialogue.

TLC: Tender Loving Care.

Ultraviolet: electromagnetic radiation having a wavelength just shorter than that of violet light but longer than that of X-rays. Adjective: denoting such radiation.

Vibration: the periodic motion of a body or wave in alternating opposite directions from the position of zero when equilibrium has been disturbed.

Wavelength: (a) the distance between successive crests of a wave, especially as a distinctive feature of sound, light, radio waves, etc. (b) a person's way of thinking when communicated to another: they were on the same wavelength.

About the Author

Donna Lynn was an educator, speaker and intuitive counselor.

God's Planetary Guide for Attaining Happiness through Spiritual Fulfillment provided her with the opportunity to share God's message, "Listen to your heart and connect to the LOVE-Light Omnipresent Vibrational Energy."

Donna Lynn's vision was to share sacred truths with the world.